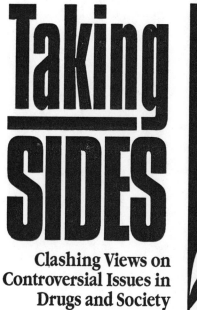

Taking SIDES

Clashing Views on
Controversial Issues in
Drugs and Society

Third Edition

Taking SIDES

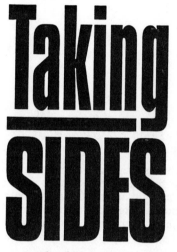

Clashing Views on Controversial Issues in Drugs and Society

Third Edition

Edited, Selected, and with Introductions by

Raymond Goldberg

State University of New York College at Cortland

Dushkin/McGraw-Hill
A Division of The McGraw-Hill Companies

To Norma, Tara, and Greta

Cover Art Acknowledgment

Charles Vitelli

Library of Congress Cataloging-in-Publication Data

Main entry under title:
  Taking sides: clashing views on controversial issues in drugs and society/edited, selected, and with introductions by Raymond Goldberg.—3rd ed.
    Includes bibliographical references and index.
    1. Drug abuse—Social aspects. I. Goldberg, Raymond, *comp.*

362.29

0-697-39110-8

1094-7566

 Printed on Recycled Paper

PREFACE

One of the hallmarks of a democratic society is the freedom of its citizens to disagree. This is no more evident than on the topic of drugs. The purpose of this book is to introduce drug-related issues that (1) are pertinent to the reader and (2) have no clear resolution. In the area of drug abuse, there is much difference of opinion regarding drug prevention, causation, and treatment. For example, should drug abuse be prevented by increasing enforcement of drug laws or by making young people more aware of the potential dangers of drugs? Is drug abuse caused by heredity, personality characteristics, or environment? Is drug abuse a public health, medical, legal, or social problem? Are individuals who inject drugs best served by the provision of clean needles or treatment? Are self-help groups the most effective treatment for drug abusers?

There are many implications to how the preceding questions are answered. If addiction to drugs is viewed as hereditary rather than as the result of flaws in one's character or personality, then a biological rather than a psychosocial approach to treatment may be pursued. If the consensus is that the prevention of drug abuse can be achieved by eliminating the availability of drugs, then more money and effort will be allocated for interdiction and law enforcement than education. If drug abuse is viewed as a legal problem, then prosecution and incarceration will be the goal. If drug abuse is identified as a medical problem, then abusers will be given treatment. However, if drug abuse is considered to be a social problem, then energy will be directed at underlying social factors, such as poverty, unemployment, health care, and education. Not all of the issues have clear answers. One may favor increasing penalties for drug violations *and* treatment services. And it is possible to view drug abuse as a medical *and* public health *and* social *and* legal problem.

Many issues debated in this volume deal with both legal and illegal drugs. Although society seems most interested in illegal drugs, it is quite pertinent to address issues related to legal drugs, which cause more deaths and disabilities. No one is untouched by drugs and everybody is affected by drug use and abuse. Billions of tax dollars are channeled into the war on drugs. Thousands of people are treated for drug abuse, often at public expense. The drug trade spawns crime and violence. Medical treatment for illnesses and injuries resulting from drug use and abuse creates additional burdens to an already extended health care system. Babies born to mothers who used drugs while pregnant are entering schools, and teachers are expected to meet the educational needs of these children. Drunk drivers represent a serious threat to our health and safety while raising the cost of everyone's auto insurance. Drug use on the job means that productivity and quality of products are diminished. The issues being debated are not whether drug abuse is a problem but what should be done to rectify this problem.

Many of these issues have an immediate impact on the reader. For example, Issue 3, *Should All Employers Be Allowed to Drug Test Their Employees?* is fitting because the majority of large corporations in the United States now test job applicants for drugs. Issue 7, *Should Tobacco Products Be More Closely Regulated?* is relevant to smokers and nonsmokers when restrictions on smoking are discussed. Issues 12 and 13, *Are Too Many Children Receiving Ritalin?* and *Is Prozac Overprescribed?* are important since many children are diagnosed with attention deficit disorder and adults with clinical depression. And the question *Should Marijuana Be Legalized as a Medication?* (Issue 8) may become relevant for many readers or their loved ones someday.

Plan of the book   In this third edition of *Taking Sides: Clashing Views on Controversial Issues in Drugs and Society*, there are 36 selections dealing with 18 issues. Each issue is preceded by an *introduction* and followed by a *postscript*. The purpose of the introduction is to provide some background information and to set the stage for the debate as it is argued in the "yes" and "no" selections. The postscript summarizes the debate and challenges some of the ideas brought out in the two readings, which can enable the reader to see the issue in other ways. Included in the postscript are additional suggested readings on the issue. Also, I have provided Internet site addresses (URLs) for each part, which should prove useful as starting points for further research. The issues, introductions, and postscripts are designed to stimulate readers to think about and achieve an informed view of some of the critical issues facing society today. At the back of the book is a listing of all the *contributors to this volume*, which gives information on the physicians, professors, and policymakers whose views are debated here.

Taking Sides: Clashing Views on Controversial Issues in Drugs and Society is a tool to encourage critical thinking. In reading an issue and forming your own opinion you should not feel confined to adopt one or the other of the positions presented. Some readers may see important points on both sides of an issue and may construct for themselves a new and creative approach. Such an approach might incorporate the best of both sides, or it might provide an entirely new vantage point for understanding.

Changes to this edition   This third edition represents a significant revision. Nine of the 18 issues are completely new: *Should the United States Put More Emphasis on Stopping the Importation of Drugs?* (Issue 2); *Should All Employers Be Allowed to Drug Test Their Employees?* (Issue 3); *Is Harm Reduction a Desirable National Drug Control Policy?* (Issue 6); *Should Doctors Promote Alcohol for Their Patients?* (Issue 9); *Is Nicotine Physically Addictive?* (Issue 10); *Are Too Many Children Receiving Ritalin?* (Issue 12); *Is Prozac Overprescribed?* (Issue 13); *Should the FDA Prohibit Tobacco Advertising?* (Issue 14); and *Is Total Abstinence the Only Choice for Alcoholics?* (Issue 15). For five of the issues retained from the previous edition, I have replaced either one or both selections to reflect more current points of view: Issue 1 on the legalization of drugs; Issue 5 on prosecuting pregnant drug users; Issue 16 on the effectiveness of the DARE program; and Issue 18 on drug treatment services.

A word to the instructor   To facilitate the use of *Taking Sides,* an *Instructor's Manual With Test Questions* (multiple-choice and essay) and a general guidebook called *Using Taking Sides in the Classroom,* which discusses methods and techniques for implementing the pro-con approach into any classroom setting, can be obtained through the publisher.

An online version of *Using Taking Sides in the Classroom* and a correspondence service for Taking Sides adopters can be found at www.dushkin.com/takingsides/. For students, we offer a field guide to analyzing argumentative essays called *Analyzing Controversy: An Introductory Guide,* with exercises and techniques to help them to decipher genuine controversies.

Taking Sides: Clashing Views on Controversial Issues in Drugs and Society is only one title in the Taking Sides series. If you are interested in seeing the table of contents for any of the other titles, please visit the Taking Sides Web site at http://www.dushkin.com/takingsides/.

Acknowledgments   A number of people have been most helpful in putting together this third edition. I would like to thank those professors who adopted the second edition of this book and took the time to make suggestions for this subsequent edition:

Donald Brodeur
Sacred Heart University

David E. Corbin
University of
    Nebraska–Omaha

Nancy Fiorentino
Rutgers University

Randee Gallo
Cabrini College

James R. Little
University of Hawaii–Manoa

Donna M. Videto
SUNY College at Cortland

Charles Zola
University of Scranton

I am also grateful to my students, who did not hesitate to share their perceptions and to let me know what they liked and disliked about the second edition. Without the editorial staff at McGraw-Hill/Dushkin Publishing Group, this book would not exist. The insightful and professional contributions of David Dean, list manager of the Taking Sides program, cannot be overstated. His thoughtful perceptions and encouragement were most appreciated. In no small way can my family be thanked. I am grateful for their patience and support.

Raymond Goldberg
State University of New York College at Cortland

CONTENTS IN BRIEF

CONTENTS

Princeton University professor Ethan Nadelmann and Jann S. Wenner, editor
and publisher for *Rolling Stone*, maintain that the war on drugs has been futile
and counterproductive. They feel that drug abstinence cannot be achieved
through legal mandates. Tremendous sums of money are allocated to stop
the use of drugs, they argue, yet the availability of drugs and drug usage are
as great as ever. University of Delaware professor James A. Inciardi and his
associate Christine A. Saum contend that the war on drugs is not a failure
and that legalizing drugs would worsen drug-related problems. Legalization,
they maintain, would increase the numbers of people using drugs, which
ultimately would escalate criminal activity. Also, they question which drugs
would be legalized and the kinds of restrictions that would be placed on
them.

Barry McCaffrey, director of the Office of National Drug Control Policy, argues that the importation of drugs must be stopped to reduce drug use and
abuse. If the supply of drugs being trafficked across American borders was
reduced, then there would be fewer drug-related problems. He maintains
that a coordinated international effort is needed to combat the increased production of heroin, cocaine, and marijuana. Mathea Falco, president of Drug
Strategies, a nonprofit policy institute, asserts that the emphasis should not be
on curtailing the availability of drugs but on factors that contribute to Americans' use of drugs. She notes that blaming other countries for drug-related

problems in the United States is one way for politicians to deflect criticism from themselves. Moreover, she argues, people involved in the drug trade in other countries have little incentive to end their involvement.

Attorney William J. Judge asserts that companies should have the right to test their employees for drugs because of the high costs of drug use for American businesses. If there is "reasonable suspicion," Judge believes, drug testing is warranted. He maintains that companies that have implemented drug testing programs have seen a marked decline in on-the-job accidents. Philosophy professor Judith Wagner DeCew questions the accuracy and effectiveness of drug testing and is concerned that the practice is intrusive and violates individuals' right to privacy. She also contends that a link between drug use and unsafe job performance has not been clearly established.

The editors of *Consumer Reports* assert that needle exchange programs not only reduce the spread of AIDS among adults but also curtail the risk of children developing the disease. The Office of National Drug Control Policy, an executive agency that determines policies and objectives for the U.S. drug control program, sees needle exchange programs as an admission of defeat and a retreat from the ongoing battle against drug use.

Paul A. Logli, an Illinois prosecuting attorney, argues that it is the government's duty to enforce every child's right to begin life with a healthy, drug-free mind and body. Logli maintains that pregnant women who use drugs should be prosecuted because they may harm the life of their unborn children. Writer Sue Mahan asserts that the prosecution of pregnant drug users is unfair because poor women are more likely to be the targets of such prosecution. Instead of treating these women as criminals, Mahan believes that both society and these women would be better served by providing them adequate prenatal care and treatment. Fear of prosecution may dissuade them from seeking prenatal care.

Peter Reuter of the University of Maryland and Jonathan P. Caulkins of Carnegie-Mellon University support efforts to reduce the violence and disease associated with drugs and the drug trade by minimizing the harm caused by drugs. Professor Robert L. DuPont of Georgetown University and Professor Eric A. Voth of the University of Kansas argue that there is insufficient evidence that a policy of harm reduction is beneficial and that the notion of harm reduction is just another way for some people to rationalize legalizing drugs.

Writer Margaret Kriz maintains that current restrictions on tobacco products are minimal compared to restrictions of other products and that public concern over the health effects of smoking justify sensible regulation of tobacco products. John Hood, vice president of the John Locke Foundation in Raleigh, North Carolina, argues that the tobacco industry is already heavily regulated and that the Food and Drug Administration is attempting to intrude too much into the lives of individuals.

Professor of psychiatry Lester Grinspoon argues that marijuana has been proven beneficial to patients suffering from chemotherapy nausea, glaucoma, chronic pain, epilepsy, migraine headaches, and AIDS, and he feels that the federal government is unjustifiably prohibiting its use. Eric A. Voth, medical director of Chemical Dependency Services at St. Francis Hospital in Topeka, Kansas, contends that reports of marijuana's medical benefits are invalid.

Psychologist Stanton Peele, an expert on alcoholism and addiction, feels that physicians should recommend that their patients drink alcohol in moderate amounts. He maintains that numerous studies demonstrate the benefits of moderate alcohol use in reducing the risk of coronary heart disease, the leading cause of death in the United States. Albert B. Lowenfels, professor at New York Medical College, feels that recommending moderate alcohol consumption is not prudent, especially since many people come from families with histories of alcohol abuse. Lowenfels believes that it is inappropriate to extol the merits of moderate alcohol use to people who have abstained throughout their lives.

Carl Sherman, who writes on health issues, maintains that nicotine is a powerfully addictive drug. Overcoming addiction to tobacco is as difficult as overcoming addiction to alcohol and hard drugs. Most nicotine addicts are incapable of quitting their nicotine use despite the adverse health effects that are known by most smokers. The problem for many people is that cigarettes satisfy emotional needs that are rooted in physiology. Professor Richard J. DeGrandpre of St. Michael's College contends that cigarette addiction is due to social, cultural, and economic factors and not because of physical dependence on nicotine. DeGrandpre points out that nicotine replacement to help people stop smoking is not especially effective and that it is not just the nicotine that smokers desire when they light up a cigarette. Psychosocial factors are instead responsible for cigarette addiction.

David A. Kessler, the commissioner of the Food and Drug Administration, and his associates contend that tighter restrictions should be placed on advertising by pharmaceutical companies. Paul H. Rubin, a former senior advertising economist with the Federal Trade Commission, argues that restrictions on drug advertisements are already excessive and inefficient.

Harvard Medical School professor Richard Bromfield contends that physicians are often too eager to prescribe Ritalin for children with attention deficit/hyperactivity disorder (ADHD). Bromfield is concerned that Ritalin's long-term effects have not been adequately researched and that its overuse may be masking other childhood disorders. George Washington Medical School professor Jerry Wiener maintains that Ritalin has been proven to be safe and effective. Wiener argues that attention deficit/hyperactivity disorder is underdiagnosed in many instances and that children who could benefit from the use of Ritalin do not receive it.

Writer Mark Nichols states that many physicians prescribe Prozac too read-ily. Nichols believes that Prozac is used too often for ordinary problems of daily living such as discontent and irritability. He contends, moreover, that its long-term effects are not known and that some people experience nega-tive psychological reactions while on Prozac. Health and psychology writer Nancy Wartik notes that Prozac is helpful for treating chronic depression, especially among women. She asserts that with less adverse publicity sur-rounding Prozac, more people could benefit from its use. Wartik believes that Prozac's purported dangers are overexaggerated.

Richard W. Pollay, a professor of business, argues for greater regulation of the tobacco industry because it has a history of presenting misleading and inaccurate information. Pollay also maintains that cigarette advertising in-fluences the perceptions, attitudes, and smoking behavior of young people. Barbara Dority, president of Humanists of Washington, supports free speech even if that means protecting the rights of the tobacco industry to advertise. Dority feels that the government should be less intrusive. If it wants to re-duce youth smoking, then the government should place more emphasis on education.

Professor Thomas Byrd maintains that Alcoholics Anonymous (AA) provides more effective treatment for alcoholics than psychiatrists, members of the clergy, or hospital treatment centers. Byrd contends that AA is the most powerful and scientific program, in contrast to all other therapies. Author

Audrey Kishline supports principles based on moderation and behavioral principles for treating alcoholism. For some alcoholics, Kishline feels that the concept of a lifetime of abstinence may be counterproductive and that many are capable of controlling their own behavior.

Michele Alicia Harmon, a doctoral student at the University of Maryland, reports that Drug Abuse Resistance Education (DARE) had a positive impact on fifth-grade students in terms of attitudes against substance abuse, assertiveness, positive peer association, association with drug-using peers, alcohol use within the previous year, and prosocial norms. Author Stephen Glass, challenging the benefits of DARE, reports that DARE has not been shown to affect drug-taking behavior. His special concern involves youngsters mistakenly reporting their parents to police officers for drug use, and he questions the circumstances under which children make these reports.

Sociology professor Ellis Cashmore argues that the notion that anabolic steroid use violates the rules of fair play is illogical because competition has never been predicated on fair play. Joannie M. Schrof, an associate editor of *U.S. News and World Report,* asserts that athletes who take anabolic steroids are not fully aware of the drugs' potential adverse effects.

Professors Charles P. O'Brien and A. Thomas McLellan contend that treatment for drug addiction is vital even though many types of treatments appear inadequate. They feel that successful treatment should focus on patient improvement rather than cure. Assistant professor of psychology Robert Apsler questions the effectiveness of drug abuse treatment and whether or not drug addicts would go for treatment if services were expanded. Apsler argues that many of the drug abusers who cease drug use do it on their own without undergoing treatment.

INTRODUCTION

Drugs: Divergent Views

Raymond Goldberg

AN OVERVIEW OF THE PROBLEM

In schools, coffee shops, and Congress, very few topics generate as much debate and concern as drugs. Drugs are evident in every aspect of life. There is much dismay that drug use and abuse cause many of the problems that plague society. Many are concerned that individuals, families, and communities are being destroyed by drug use and that drugs will continue to fester moral decay. The news media are replete with horrible stories of people under the influence of drugs committing crimes against others, of senseless drug-related deaths, of men and women who compromise themselves for drugs, and of women who deliver babies that are addicted to or impaired by drugs.

From the fetus to the elderly, no one is untouched by drugs. In some cases, stimulants are prescribed for children so that they may learn or behave better in school. Sometimes students take stimulants so that they can stay up late to study for a test or lose a few pounds. Many teenagers take drugs because they want to be accepted by their friends who do the same or to deal with daily stress. For many people, young and old, the elixir for relaxation may be sipped, smoked, swallowed, or sniffed. Some people who live in poverty-stricken conditions use drugs to anesthetize themselves from their environment. On the other hand, some individuals who seem to have everything also immerse themselves in drugs, possibly out of boredom. To cope with the ailments that come with age, the elderly often rely on drugs. Many people use drugs to confront their pains, problems, frustrations, and disappointments. Others take them simply because they like the effects or out of curiosity.

BACKGROUND ON DRUGS

Despite one's feelings about drug use, drugs are an integral part of society. The popularity of various drugs seems to rise and fall with the times. A recent survey of eighth-, tenth-, and twelfth-grade students, for example, found an increase in the use of LSD and marijuana among teenagers despite a steady decline in use throughout the 1980s (Johnston, O'Malley, and Bachman, 1995). Especially alarming is the fact that the largest increase has occurred among eighth-grade students.

Understanding the role of drugs in society is critical to our being able to address the problems they generate. It is also helpful to place drugs in a historical context. Drugs have been used extensively throughout history. Alcohol's role in the early history of the United States was significant. According to Lee (1963), the Pilgrims landed at Plymouth Rock because they ran out of beer. Marijuana use dates back nearly 5,000 years, when the Chinese emperor Shen Nung prescribed it for medical ailments like malaria, gout, rheumatism, and gas pains. Hallucinogens have existed since the beginning of humankind. About 150 of the estimated 500,000 different plant species have been used for hallucinogenic purposes (Schultes and Hofmann, 1979).

Opium, from which narcotics are derived, was alluded to often by the ancient Greeks and Romans; opium is referred to in Homer's *Odyssey* (circa 1000 B.C.). In the Arab world, opium and hashish were widely used (primarily because alcohol was forbidden). The Arabs were introduced to opium through their trading in India and China. Arab physician Avicenna (A.D. 1000) wrote an extremely complete medical textbook in which he describes the benefits of opium. Ironically, Avicenna died from an overdose of opium and wine. Eventually, opium played a central role in a war between China and the British government.

Caffeine is believed to be the most commonly consumed drug throughout the world. More than 9 out of every 10 Americans consume caffeine. Coffee dates back to A.D. 900 in Arabia, where, to stay awake during lengthy religious vigils, Muslims drank coffee. However, coffee was later condemned because the Koran, the holy book of Islam, described coffee as an intoxicant (Brecher, 1972). Drinking coffee became a popular activity in Europe, although it was banned for a short time. In the mid-1600s, coffeehouses were prime locations for men to converse, relax, and do business. Medical benefits were associated with coffee, although England's King Charles II and English physicians tried to prohibit its use.

One function of coffeehouses was that they served as places of learning: For a one-cent cup of coffee, one could listen to well-known literary and political leaders (Meyer, 1954). Lloyd's of London, the famous insurance company, started around 1700 from Edward Lloyd's coffeehouse. However, not everyone was pleased with these "penny universities," as they were called. In 1674, in response to the countless hours men were spending at the coffeehouses, a group of women published a pamphlet titled *The Women's Petition Against Coffee*, which criticized coffee use. Despite the protestations against coffee, its use has proliferated. Today, over 300 years later, coffeehouses are still flourishing as centers for relaxation and conversation. There is much debate, however, on the potential harm of caffeine (*Consumer Reports*, 1994).

Coca leaves, from which cocaine is derived, have been chewed since before recorded history. Drawings found on South American pottery showed that coca chewing was practiced before the rise of the Incan Empire. The coca plant was held in high regard: it was considered to be a present from the gods, and it was used in religious rituals and burials. When the Spaniards arrived in South America, they tried to regulate coca chewing by the natives but were unsuccessful. Later cocaine was an ingredient in the popular soft drink Coca-Cola. Another stimulant, amphetamine, was developed in the 1920s. Amphetamines were originally used to treat narcolepsy, and they were later prescribed for treating asthma and for weight loss.

Minor tranquilizers, also called "antianxiety agents," were first marketed in the early 1950s. The sales of these drugs were astronomical. Drugs to reduce anxiety were in great demand, principally because people felt they were under much stress. One group of antianxiety agents are benzodiazepines. Two well-known benzodiazepines are Librium and Valium. Valium ranks as the most widely prescribed drug in the history of American medicine. Xanax, which recently replaced Valium as the tranquilizer of choice, is one of the five most widely prescribed drugs in the United States today. Minor tranquilizers are noteworthy because they are legally prescribed to alter one's consciousness. There were mind-altering drugs prior to minor tranquilizers, but they were not prescribed for that purpose.

COMBATING DRUG PROBLEMS

The debates in *Taking Sides: Clashing Views on Controversial Issues in Drugs and Society* confront many important drug-related issues. For example, what is the most effective way to reduce drug abuse? Should laws preventing drug use and abuse be more strongly enforced, or should drug laws be less punitive? How can the needs of individuals be met while serving the greater good of society? Should drug use be seen as a public health problem or a legal problem? The debate regarding whether the drug problem should be fought nationally or internationally is addressed in Issue 2. One could argue that America is best served by focusing its attention on the proliferation of drugs in other countries.

One of the oldest debates concerns whether or not drug use should be legal. Issue 1 deals with this question. In recent years this debate has become more intense because well-known individuals such as political analyst William F. Buckley Jr. and economist Milton Friedman have come out in support of legalization. The issue is not whether drug use is good or bad but whether or not people should be punished for taking drugs. One question that is basic to this debate is whether drug legalization causes more or less harm than drug criminalization. A related issue, Issue 6, discusses whether the United States should adopt a drug policy that results in the least harm. Another pertinent issue concerns needle exchange programs, in which clean needles are provided to individuals who inject themselves with drugs (Issue 4). There are obvious inherent dangers to injecting drugs. Does the provision of sterile needles help these people? Should people be given equipment that is used for an illegal act? What has been the effect of needle exchange programs in cities in which they have been instituted?

In a related matter, if drugs have the potential for abuse, should they be restricted even if they could be of medical benefit? There is concern that drugs that are used for medical reasons may be illegally diverted. Yet, most people agree that patients should have access to the best medicine available. In referenda in the states of California and Arizona, voters approved the medical use of marijuana. Is the federal government consistent in allowing drugs to be used that are potentially harmful? For example, narcotics are often prescribed for pain relief. Is there a chance that patients who are given narcotics will become addicted? Whether or not marijuana has a legitimate medical use is the focus of Issue 8.

Many of the issues discussed in this book deal with drug prevention. As with most controversial issues, there is a lack of consensus regarding how to prevent drug-related problems. For example, Issue 5 debates whether or not prosecuting women who use drugs during pregnancy will affect drug use by other women who become pregnant. Many drugs damage the fetus; will prosecuting pregnant women who use drugs help prevent others from using drugs during pregnancy? Will pregnant women who use drugs avoid prenatal care because they fear prosecution? Will newborns be better served if pregnant women who use drugs are charged with child abuse? Are these laws discriminatory, since most cases that are prosecuted involve poor women?

Some contend that drug laws not only discriminate according to social class but also according to age and ethnicity. Many drug laws in the United States were initiated because of the drug's association with an ethnic group: Opium was made illegal after it was associated with Chinese immigrants (Musto, 1991); cocaine became illegal after it was linked with blacks; and marijuana was outlawed after it was linked with Hispanics.

Drug-related issues are not limited to illegal drugs. Tobacco and alcohol are two pervasive legal drugs that generate much debate. For example, should there be stricter regulations on tobacco use (Issue 7)? The answer to this question depends heavily on whether or not nicotine is viewed as an addictive drug (Issue 10). With regard to alcohol, Issue 9 looks at whether or not physicians should promote moderate alcohol use, and Issue 15 examines whether alcoholics should totally abstain or whether they can learn to drink moderately. Other issues related to legal drugs deal with whether or not prescription drugs should be advertised to the general public (Issue 11) and whether or not the children's stimulant Ritalin and the antidepressant drug Prozac are being overprescribed (Issues 12 and 13).

GATEWAY DRUGS

An inhalant is a type of drug that is popular with many young people. Like tobacco and alcohol, inhalants are considered to be "gateway drugs," which are often used as a prelude to other, usually illegal, drugs. Inhalants are comprised of numerous products, ranging from paints and solvents to aerosol sprays, glues, petroleum products, cleaning supplies, and nitrous oxide (laughing gas). Inhalant abuse in the United States is a relatively new phenomenon. It seems that until the media started reporting on the dangers of inhalant abuse, its use was not particularly common (Brecher, 1972). This raises a question regarding the impact of the media on drug use.

Advertisements are an integral part of the media, and their influence can be seen in the growing popularity of cigarette smoking among adolescents. In the 1880s cigarette use began to escalate in the United States. One of the most important factors contributing to this was the development of the cigarette-making machine (previously, cigarettes could be rolled at a rate of only four per minute). Also, cigarette smoking, which was considered an activity reserved for men, began to be advertised as an option for women. By marketing cigarettes for women, cigarette smoking became more widespread. Issue 14 deals with whether or not the Food and Drug Administration should prohibit tobacco advertising. As one can see from this introduction, numerous factors affect drug use. One argument is that if young people were better educated about the hazards of drugs and were taught how to understand the role of the media, then limits on tobacco advertising would not be necessary.

DRUG TREATMENT AND PREVENTION

Some maintain that educating young people about drugs is one way to prevent drug use and abuse. Studies show that by delaying the onset of drug use, the likelihood of drug abuse is reduced. In the past, however, drug education had little impact on drug-taking behavior (Goldberg, 1994). Some programs actually resulted in an increase in drug use because they stimulated curiosity. Does this suggest that drug education is worse than no education or that more effective programs need to be developed? One nationwide program that deals with drug use is the Drug Abuse Resistance Education (DARE) program. Issue 16 examines whether or not DARE is an effective program for reducing the incidence of drug use and abuse.

Besides addressing the legal aspects of drug use and the effectiveness of drug prevention efforts, this book looks at the efficacy of drug treatment. Despite a sagging economy, drug treatment is a growing industry. Drug treatment is expensive, and consumers need to be aware of the different modalities. However, a more basic concern is whether or not drug treatment is effective. A study by Glass (1995) shows that methadone maintenance, a treatment for heroin addiction, may have some benefits. But do those benefits outweigh the costs of the treatment? If society feels that treatment is a better alternative to incarceration, then it is imperative to know if treatment works. Issue 18 deals with whether or not drug treatment services are effective and whether or not they should be expanded.

DISTINGUISHING BETWEEN DRUG USE, MISUSE, AND ABUSE

Although the terms *drug, drug misuse,* and *drug abuse* are commonly used, they may have different meanings to different people. Defining these terms may seem simple at first, but many factors affect how they are defined. Should the definition of a drug be based on its behavioral effects, its effects on society, its pharmacological properties, or its chemical composition? One simple, concise definition is that a drug is any substance that produces an effect on the mind, body, or both. One could also define a drug by how it is used. For example, if watching television or listening to music are forms of escape from daily problems, then they may be considered drugs.

Legal drugs cause far more death and disability than illegal drugs, but society appears to be most concerned with the use of illegal drugs. The potential harms of legal drugs tend to be minimized. By viewing drugs as illicit substances only, we may fail to recognize that commonly used substances such as caffeine, tobacco, alcohol, and over-the-counter preparations are drugs. If these substances are not perceived as drugs, then we may not acknowledge that they can be misused or abused. Definitions for misuse and abuse are not affected by a drug's legal status. Drug misuse refers to the inappropriate or unintentional use of drugs. Someone who smokes marijuana to improve his or her study skills is misusing marijuana because it impairs short-term memory. Drug abuse alludes to negative physical, emotional, financial, intellectual, or social consequences arising from chronic drug use. Using this definition, can a person abuse food, aspirin, soft drinks, or chocolate? Also, should a person be free to make unhealthy choices?

THE COST OF THE WAR ON DRUGS

The U.S. government spends more than $10 billion each year to curb the rise in drug use (Herman, 1991). The major portion of that money goes toward law enforcement. Vast sums of money are used by the military to intercept drug shipments, and foreign governments are given money to help them with their own wars on drugs. A smaller portion of the funds is used for treating and preventing drug abuse. One strategy being implemented to eliminate drug use is drug testing. Currently, men and women in the military, athletes, industry employees, and others are subject to random drug testing.

The expense of drug abuse to industries is staggering: Experts estimate that almost 20 percent of workers in the United States are under the influence of dangerous drugs while at work; the cost of drug abuse to employers is approximately $120 billion each year (Brookler, 1992); as compared to non-addicted employees, drug-dependent employees are absent from their jobs 16 times as often (Wrich, 1986); and drugs users are less likely to maintain stable job histories than nonusers (Kandel, Murphy, and Kraus, 1985). In its report *America's Habit: Drug Abuse, Drug Trafficking and Organized Crime*, the President's Commission on Organized Crime supported drug testing for all federal workers. It further recommended that federal contracts be withheld from private employers who do not implement drug-testing procedures (Brinkley, 1986).

A prerequisite to being hired by many companies is passing a drug test. Drug testing may have a positive effect. From 1987 to 1994, workers testing positive declined 57 percent (Center for Substance Abuse Prevention, 1995). Many companies reported a decrease in accidents and injuries after the initiation of drug testing (Angarola, 1991). However, most Americans consider drug testing to be degrading and dehumanizing (Walsh and Trumble, 1991). One important question is, What is the purpose of drug testing? Drug testing also raises three other important questions: (1) Does drug testing prevent drug use? (2) Is the point of drug testing to help employees with drug problems or to get rid of employees who use drugs? and (3) How can the civil rights of employees be balanced with the rights of companies? These and other questions are addressed in Issue 3.

Athletes are periodically screened for anabolic steroids. Issue 17 discusses this practice and raises the question of whether or not an athlete's use of steroids is a matter of concern to anybody other than the individual him- or herself.

How serious is the drug problem? Is it real, or is there simply an increasing hysteria about drugs? There has been a growing intolerance toward drug use in the United States during the last 20 years (Musto, 1991). Drugs are a problem for many people. Drugs can adversely affect one's physical, social, intellectual, and emotional health. Ironically, some people take drugs *because* they produce these effects. Individuals who take drugs receive some kind of reward from the drug; the reward may come from being associated with others who use drugs or from the feelings derived from the drug. If these rewards were not present, people would likely cease using drugs.

The disadvantages of drugs are numerous: they interfere with career aspirations and individual maturation; they have been associated with violent behavior and addiction; discord among siblings, children, parents, spouses, and friends; work-related problems; financial troubles; problems in school; legal predicaments; accidents; injuries; and death. Yet, are drugs the cause or the symptom of the problems people have? Perhaps drugs are one aspect of a larger scenario in which society is experiencing much change and in which drug use is merely another thread in the social fabric.

REFERENCES

R. T. Angarola, "Substance-Abuse Testing in the Workplace: Legal Issues and Corporate Responses," in R. H. Coombs and L. J. West, eds., *Drug Testing: Issues and Options* (Oxford University Press, 1991).

E. M. Brecher, *Licit and Illicit Drugs* (Little, Brown, 1972).

J. Brinkley, "Drug Use Held Mostly Stable or Better," *The New York Times* (October 10, 1986).

R. Brookler, "Industry Standards in Workplace Drug Testing," *Personnel Journal* (April 1992), pp. 128–132.

"Coffee and Health," *Consumer Reports* (October 1994).

Drug-Free for a New Century, Center for Substance Abuse Prevention, Substance Abuse and Mental Health Services Administration (1995).

R. M. Glass, "Methadone Maintenance: New Research on a Controversial Treatment," *Journal of the American Medical Association* (vol. 269, no. 15, 1995), pp. 1995–1996.

R. Goldberg, *Drugs Across the Spectrum* (West, 1994).

E. S. Herman, "Drug 'Wars': Appearance and Reality," *Social Justice* (vol. 18, no. 4, 1991), pp. 76–84.

L. D. Johnston, P. O. O'Malley, and J. G. Bachman, *Monitoring the Future* (National Institute on Drug Abuse, 1995).

D. B. Kandel, D. Murphy, and D. Kraus, "Cocaine Use in Young Adulthood: Patterns of Use and Psychosocial Correlates," in N. J. Kozel and E. H. Adams, eds., *Cocaine Use in America: Epidemiologic and Clinical Perspectives* (National Institute on Drug Abuse, 1985).

H. Lee, *How Dry We Were: Prohibition Revisited* (Prentice Hall, 1963).

H. Meyer, *Old English Coffee Houses* (Rodale Press, 1954).

D. F. Musto, "Opium, Cocaine and Marijuana in American History," *Scientific American* (July 1991), pp. 40–47.

R. E. Schultes and A. Hofmann, *Plants of the Gods: Origins of Hallucinogenic Use* (McGraw-Hill, 1979).

J. M. Walsh and J. G. Trumble, "The Politics of Drug Testing," in R. H. Coombs and L. J. West, eds., *Drug Testing: Issues and Options* (Oxford University Press, 1991).

J. T. Wrich, "Some National Statistics: The Impact of Substance Abuse at the Workplace," in H. Axel, ed., *Corporate Strategies for Controlling Substance Abuse* (Conference Board, 1986).

On the Internet ...

http://www.dushkin.com

National Institute on Drug Abuse (NIDA)
The National Institute on Drug Abuse is an agency of
the federal government that publishes reports on topics
ranging from drug use trends to the effects of various
drugs. In addition, NIDA conducts workshops dealing
with drug prevention. *http://www.nida.nih.gov/nidatoc.html*

The UCLA Drug Abuse Research Center (DARC)
The UCLA Drug Abuse Research Center investigates psychosocial and epidemiological issues pertaining to drug use
and abuse. The DARC also conducts evaluations of interventions regarding drug dependence.
http://www.mednet.ucla.edu/som/ddo/npi/DARC

The American Council for Drug Education (ACDE)
The American Council for Drug Education is a nonprofit
organization that gathers, analyzes, monitors, and dis-
seminates information pertaining to substance abuse as
well as develops programs to reduce substance abuse.
http://www.acde.org/

The Office of National Drug Control Policy (ONDCP)
The Office of National Drug Control Policy develops
and coordinates the policies, goals, and objectives of the
nation's drug control program for reducing the use of
illicit drugs. *http://www.whitehouse.gov/WH/EOP/
ondcp/html/ondcp-plain.html*

PART 1

Drugs and Public Policy

Most people recognize that drugs are a problem in society: The psychological and physical effects of drug use can be devastating; drugs can be addictive, and they can disrupt families; disability and death are caused by drug overdoses; and drugs are often implicated in crimes, especially violent crimes. Identifying drug-related problems is not difficult. What is unclear is the best course of action to take in dealing with these problems.

Three scenarios exist for dealing with drugs: policies can be made more restrictive, less restrictive, or remain the same. The position taken depends on whether drug use is seen as a legal, social, or medical problem. The issues in this section do not debate whether drugs are good or bad, but how to minimize the harm of drugs. The following debates discuss these issues.

■ Should Drugs Be Legalized?

■ Should the United States Put More Emphasis on Stopping the Importation of Drugs?

■ Should All Employers Be Allowed to Drug Test Their Employees?

■ Do Needle Exchange Programs Reduce the Spread of AIDS?

■ Should Pregnant Drug Users Be Prosecuted?

■ Is Harm Reduction a Desirable National Drug Policy Goal?

■ Should Tobacco Products Be More Closely Regulated?

1

ISSUE 1

Should Drugs Be Legalized?

YES: Ethan Nadelmann and Jann S. Wenner, from "Toward a Sane National Drug Policy," *Rolling Stone* (May 5, 1994)

NO: James A. Inciardi and Christine A. Saum, from "Legalization Madness," *The Public Interest* (Spring 1996)

ISSUE SUMMARY

YES: Princeton University professor Ethan Nadelmann and Jann S. Wenner, editor and publisher for *Rolling Stone*, maintain that the war on drugs has been futile and counterproductive. They feel that drug abstinence cannot be achieved through legal mandates. Tremendous sums of money are allocated to stop the use of drugs, they argue, yet the availability of drugs and drug usage are as great as ever.

NO: University of Delaware professor James A. Inciardi and his associate Christine A. Saum contend that the war on drugs is not a failure and that legalizing drugs would worsen drug-related problems. Legalization, they maintain, would increase the numbers of people using drugs, which ultimately would escalate criminal activity. Also, they question which drugs would be legalized and the kinds of restrictions that would be placed on them.

Every year, the U.S. government spends billions of dollars to control drug use and to enforce laws enacted to protect society from the dangers created by drug use. Some people believe that the war on drugs has been effective, but they assert that government agencies and communities are not fighting hard enough to stop drug use and that drug laws are too few and too lenient. Others argue that society has already lost the war on drugs and that the only way to remedy the problem is to end the fighting altogether by ending the criminalization of drug use.

Many conflicting views exist on whether or not legislation has had the intended result of reducing the problems of drug use. Many argue that legislation and the criminalization of drugs have been counterproductive in controlling drug problems. Some suggest that the criminalization of drugs has actually contributed to and worsened the social ills associated with drugs. Proponents of drug legalization maintain that the war on drugs, not drugs themselves, is damaging to American society. They also argue that the strict enforcement of drug laws damages American society because it drives people to violence and crime, corrupts law enforcement officials, and overburdens the court system, thus rendering it ineffective. Furthermore, the criminalization of drugs fuels organized crime, allows children to be pulled into the drug business, and makes illegal drugs themselves more dangerous because they are manufactured without government standards or regulations. Hence, drugs may be adulterated or of unidentified potency. Legalization advocates also argue that legalization would take the profits out of drug sales, thereby decreasing the value of and demand for drugs.

In addition to the tangible costs, some legalization advocates argue, drug prohibition on the part of the federal government is an immoral and impossible objective. To achieve a "drug-free society" is self-defeating and a misnomer because drugs have always been a part of human culture. Furthermore, prohibition efforts indicate a disregard for the private freedom of individuals because they are employed under the assumption that individuals are unable to make their own choices.

People who favor legalizing drugs feel that legalization would give the government more control over the purity and potency of drugs and that it would allow the international drug trade to be regulated more effectively. Legalization, they argue, would also take the emphasis off of law enforcement policies and allow more effort to be put toward education, prevention, and treatment. Decriminalization advocates assert that most of the negative implications of drug prohibition would disappear.

Opponents of this view maintain that drug legalization is a very dangerous idea. Legalization, they argue, will drastically increase drug use. If drugs are more accessible, more people will turn to drugs, and the upsurge in drug use will come at an incredibly high price: Society will be overrun with drug-related accidents, loss in worker productivity, and hospital emergency rooms filled with drug-related emergencies; drug treatment efforts would be futile because users would have no legal incentive to stop taking drugs; users may prefer using drugs over rehabilitation; and education programs may be ineffective in dissuading children from using drugs.

Legalization advocates claim that drug abuse is a "victimless crime" in which the only person affected is the drug user. Legalization opponents argue that this notion is both ludicrous and dangerous because drug use has dire repercussions for all of society. Also, regulations to control drug use have a legitimate social aim to protect society and its citizens from the harm of drugs. Maintaining criminalization is not immoral or a violation of personal freedom to individuals opposed to legalization. Rather, criminalization allows a standard of control to be established in order to preserve human character and society as a whole.

In the following selections, Ethan Nadelmann and Jann S. Wenner explain their argument for legalizing drugs. James A. Inciardi and Christine A. Saum describe the detrimental effects that would occur with the decriminalization of drugs.

YES

Ethan Nadelmann and Jann S. Wenner

TOWARD A SANE NATIONAL DRUG POLICY

The war on drugs is over. After eight decades of interdiction, prohibition and punishment, the results are in: There are now more than 330,000 Americans behind bars for violating the drug laws. We are spending over $20 billion per year on criminal-justice approaches, but illegal drugs are available in greater supply and purity than ever before. Cynical phrases such as *zero tolerance* and *drug-free society* substitute for thoughtful policies and realistic objectives. It's time for a change.

We have ignored the dear lessons of history. Prohibition, the 18th Amendment to the Constitution, financed the rise of organized crime and filled miserably as social policy. Likewise, the war on drugs has created new, well-financed and violent criminal conspiracies and failed to achieve any of its goals.

It's time for Americans to look seriously at other options. No one has found *the answer* to the drug problem, but there are alternatives to spending tens of billions each year on a policy that is better at filling prisons and spreading AIDS than curing addictions. When Surgeon General Joycelyn Elders spoke out in December 1993 in favor of studying alternatives, it came as no surprise that drug-policy reactionaries screamed. But more interesting were the voices of support mom around the country: Mayor Sharon Pratt Kelly of Washington and Mayor Frank Jordan of San Francisco have joined former secretary of state George Shultz, Mayor Kurt Schmoke of Baltimore and a number of prominent Americans from across the political spectrum in speaking out for an alternative.

* * *

Despite the fact that there is no evidence that pot has ever caused a single death and that there is clear evidence that cannabis is actually useful in treating certain medical conditions, the federal government continues to spend millions of dollars each year to eradicate plants and harass users. In 1992, according to the FBI, 535,000 people were arrested for possession, sale or manufacture of marijuana. In six cases, life sentences were imposed.

This is the drug war at its most absurd. Paramilitary raids composed of state police, Drug Enforcement Administration (DEA) operatives and National Guardsmen fly over public and private lands, their helicopters skimming the tops of private homes. Citizens are detained at gunpoint, and houses and property worth hundreds of thousands of dollars are forfeited to local police departments for no other reason than the existence of small numbers of marijuana plants.

The DEA's global presence stands at an all-time high. U.S. military units and border-patrol forces scramble around Bolivia and Peru, destroying easily replaced makeshift laboratories. The U.S. Navy, Air Force, Coast Guard and Customs Service patrol the seas in search of illicit shipments. U.S. diplomats lean on European governments to throw their money into the kitty for perennial crop-substitution programs.

To what effect? Certainly not any reduction in the flow of drugs into the United States. Law-enforcement authorities readily admit that cocaine imports appear to be as high as ever. Heroin exports to the United States, meanwhile, are rising to unprecedented levels as Asian gangsters and Afghan terrorists consolidate their networks and the ever resourceful Colombians enter the business.

In late 1991, the General Accounting Office reported that the Pentagon's interdiction efforts, which cost U.S. taxpayers close to $1 billion during the previous two years, had had no impact on the flow of drugs. For at least a generation, law-enforcement officials have recited the claim that they seize "only 10 percent" of drug shipments into the United States. The fact is, despite this dismal rate, they haven't the slightest idea what percentage they're seizing.

The drug war has been most efficient at filling up the country's prisons and jails: In all, there are 440,000 prisoners in local jails, 840,000 in state prisons and another 87,000 in federal prisons. (Add to that 2.7 million people on probation and more than 500,000 on parole.) This represents by far the highest proportion of the American population incarcerated in our history, as well as the highest proportion incarcerated of any country in the world.

* * *

Much of the increase in prison population can be explained entirely in terms of the war on drugs. More than 60 percent of federal prison inmates are incarcerated for violations of federal drug laws. One in five are first-time petty offenders, in many cases naive young people who ran into sophisticated entrapment procedures. According to a Justice Department study ordered by Janet Reno, 16,316 federal prisoners who have no previous incarcerations, crimes or high-level drug activity on their records are serving an average of six-year sentences for drugs. Two out of three are in prison because of mandatory sentencing laws. More than half of new incarcerations in New Jersey state prisons in 1990 were for drug-law violations, 46.7 percent in New York, 32 percent in Pennsylvania, and 53 percent in Washington, D.C. Although no one has actually added up the numbers, it is safe to estimate that one-third of a million people are now behind bars for violating drug laws and two to three times that many are on probation or parole for the same reason.

These grim statistics don't reveal the entire cost of the government's war against its own citizens. A complete total would have to include the drug dealers incarcerated for crimes of violence as well as the one-third of robbers and burglars who reported in a survey sponsored by the Justice Department's Bureau of Justice Statistics that they had committed their crimes to obtain money for drugs.

The drug war takes most of its collateral casualties from the inner cities. Here, drugs are a fact of life, even if many customers live far away in protected communities. Though illegal-drug use has fallen in some inner cities, there are still intolerable levels of violence associated with competitive drug dealing.

If our prohibition policies really made a difference in terms of reducing illicit-drug use in the country, there might be some grounds for the claim that this tremendous expenditure of dollars and lives is worth it. But all the evidence suggests that the simple deterrence model of tough enforcement and incarceration has not had the desired impact on drug availability in the inner city or the small town. The ambitious street sweeps of drug dealers and ever more pervasive undercover operations have simply made it that much easier for urban young people to step into the shoes of those whose jobs they covet.

The costs incurred by America's orgy of incarceration are impressive. But they pale, at least in human terms, next to the costs exacted by the spread of AIDS by and among illicit-drug users, their sexual partners and their babies. Most U.S. states, as well as the vast majority of foreign countries, allow people to buy syringes over the counter. Nine states, however, don't. Those nine are nearly the same as those with the worst illicit-drug-use problems and the highest number of drug-related AIDS cases.

Both common sense and a host of scientific studies suggest that making syringes available over the counter, creating needle-exchange programs and sponsoring outreach programs to maintain contact with hard-core drug users are cheap and relatively effective ways of reducing the spread of AIDS among drug users. National and state commissions on AIDS, as well as international health organizations, routinely advocate these programs. Virtually all European countries, including some that punish drug dealing as severely as rape and murder, have instituted such measures. But in the United States, cowardly politicians who know better have combined with inner-city leaders obsessed with the rhetoric and images of genocidal plots to oppose such programs.

What it all adds up to is a contemporary variant of the Crusades—a war to purge America of illicit drugs and any one who makes, sells or uses them. Forget compromise. Forget tolerance. And for that matter, forget any attempt at cost-benefit analysis. Forget as well the fact that virtually all societies in the history of human civilization have used psychoactive substances—whether it's marijuana or wine.

* * *

It's time for a new drug policy. The choices are far more complex than prohibition vs. legalization. What we need to do now is start learning what works in other countries and start relying a little more on common sense and decency. We need to stop demonizing illicit-drug users and remind ourselves that they are citizens and human beings. We need to stop filling our prisons with petty dealers and unlucky users and focus our criminal-justice resources on those who commit violent and predatory crimes. And we need to stop believing that abstinence is the sole solution to drug use.

The easy way to begin is with small steps—ones that reduce the harmful effects of drug use and drug policies without completely eliminating our current system of prohibition.

* * *

First, we should immediately decriminalize the sale and possession of small amounts of marijuana and make it easily available by prescription to those suffering from cancer, AIDS, multiple sclerosis and other diseases. Eleven states decriminalized marijuana during the 1970s, with no noticeable effects on consumption rates. California has saved more than $1 billion in criminal-justice costs by decriminalizing pot.

No drug, including marijuana, is completely safe—but as the DEA's own administrative law judge Francis Young declared in 1988, marijuana is possibly "one of the safest therapeutically active substances known to man." Though 36 states have called for the legalization of marijuana for medical treatment, the federal government refuses to remove pot from a Schedule 1 listing as a dangerous narcotic.

* * *

What about hard drugs like heroin? The first steps of a harm-reduction-based policy are easy and virtually risk-free. Hundreds of studies and 25 years of experience have proved that getting heroin

addicts to switch to methadone can reduce heroin consumption, crime and AIDS and help former users to get and keep their lives together. But methadone is now the most tightly regulated drug in the pharmacopeia, according to Ernest Drucker, professor of epidemiology and social medicine at Montefiore Medical Center-Albert Einstein College of Medicine, in the Bronx, N.Y. It continues to get a bad rap from powerful politicians and drug-treatment bigwigs who insist that abstinence is the only cure. They're wrong, just like those who insist that the only way to deal with teenage-pregnancy is by telling kids to remain "sex-free."

What we need is a wide range of methadone programs and outlets: from full-service programs that help recovering drug users get their lives together and find jobs to "low threshold" programs that reach out to the most down-and-out addicts on the streets. We should allow private physicians and public-health clinics to write prescriptions for methadone and allow their clients to pick the drug up at a local pharmacy. Methadone could be dispensed from mobile vans—as Baltimore and Boston have begun to do. And most important, we should not kick people out of methadone programs if they relapse and continue taking illegal drugs. All the evidence shows that they, and we, are better off if they maintain some link with health services. Simply stated, we should treat drug addicts who want methadone like we treat diabetics who need insulin and depressed Americans who want Prozac.

Virtually every public health commission and organization—from the Centers for Disease Control and Prevention and the National Academy of Sciences to the World Health Organization—has suggested that needle exchanges can play an important role in reducing the transmission of HIV by and among drug injectors. In some European cities, addicts can exchange dirty needles in local pharmacies, health clinics, vending machines and even police stations. We should do the same. The policy is risk-free.

* * *

What about cocaine? It's helpful to remember that the crack epidemic, a devastating plague, but one that is passing, was not prevented by strict prohibition. Indeed, the drug laws may well have *created* crack, just as Prohibition produced 190-proof bathtub gin. And just as the repeal of Prohibition didn't legalize moonshine, so the repeal of drug laws doesn't have to mean legalizing crack. The world is full of drugs that are less dangerous and more attractive than crack. We can begin by testing low-potency cocaine products—coca-based chewing gum or lozenges, for example, or products like Mariani's wine and the Coca-Cola of the late 19th century—which by all accounts were as safe as beer and probably not much worse than coffee. If some people want to distill those products down to something more potent, let them. But most people won't want to buy it, just as few Americans wanted to keep buying 190-proof alcohol once beer, wine and liquor became legally available.

There's much more we can do to reduce the negative consequences of both drug use and our drug policies without junking the whole prohibition system. But we can't do it successfully unless we put our punitive predispositions and abstentious goals on the back burner. Drug-treatment programs should be user-friendly, as other medical services are supposed to be, rather than like adolescent hazing rituals. A good harm-reduction program teaches sex workers how to get uncooperative clients to use condoms and saves the moralizing for later. It teaches illegal drug injectors how to inject safely, so that they don't end up in emergency rooms or dead, and then lets them know there's a drug-treatment slot available when they're ready.

From all accounts, policies like these work. Free needles, readily available methadone and other harm-reduction programs hold no attractions for kids trying to decide whether to use drugs or not. And these policies are more effective in undermining illegal drug markets, cutting crime and improving public health than anything yet devised in the United States.

* * *

Repeal immediately all mandatory-minimum-sentencing laws for drug-law offenders. It's hard to find a respected jurist, from Chief Justice William Rehnquist on down, who supports either current mandatory minimum requirements or the Draconian penalties he or she is required to impose on petty drug offenders. "Three strikes, you're out" is catchy sloganeering, and it may even make sense for murderers and hired assassins, but it's a ludicrous approach for drug offenders.

Virtually everything we're suggesting here is already happening in many European cities. None of it's revolutionary. In fact, quite the opposite, virtually everything we're suggesting can be described as *evolutionary*, relatively risk-free and less expensive than our current policies. All the available evidence indicates that a switch from a war-on-drugs approach to a harm-reduction strategy will save lives, reduce disease, cut crime and contribute to safer, healthier, more livable cities.

* * *

When all is said and done, however, the best drug policies are those that rely not on prohibition but on regulatory approaches wisely conceived and implemented. We harbor no illusions regarding the political prospects of repeal in the short term. But once Americans realize that most of our drug problems are a result of current policies, drug prohibition will crumble just as alcohol prohibition did 61 years ago.

One often forgotten lesson of Prohibition is that it was followed not by a uniform national policy but by "local option." When, in 1933, the 21st Amendment to the Constitution repealed Prohibition, the states went their own ways: Some opted state monopolies, others for licensing schemes, and some chose to remain dry. Some legalized all alcoholic beverages, others just beer and wine. Some imposed high taxes, others low taxes.

We need local solutions to local problems. What the federal government needs to do is repeal many of the laws and regulations that stifle local initiatives and block any movement away from the war on drugs. Let towns, cities, counties and states experiment with new approaches. It's the only way to find out what really works.

Any good nonprohibitionist drug policy has to contain three central ingredients. First, possession of small amounts of any drug for personal use has to be legal. Second, there have to be legal means by which adults can obtain drugs of certified quality, purity and quantity. These can vary from state to state and town to town, with the Food and Drug Administration playing a supervisory role in controlling quality, providing information and assur-

ing truth in advertising. And third, citizens have to be empowered in their decisions about drugs. Doctors have a role in all this, but let's not give them all the power.

A drug policy with these ingredients would decimate the black market for drugs and take out of the hands of drug lords the $50 billion to $60 billion in profits they earn each year. The nation would gain billions of dollars in law-enforcement savings and tax revenues, which could then be used to treat America's most serious problem: the miserable life prospects of millions of poor, undereducated Americans growing up in decaying, crime-ridden inner cities.

The only respectable argument against such a policy is that it would result in a substantial increase in drug use. We don't see why. All the evidence, as well as common sense, indicates that the vast majority of Americans don't need drug-prohibition laws to keep from becoming junkies. Some African American leaders, like Rep. Charles Rangel of New York, cry genocide, but they forget that drug prohibition has already proved a failure and a disaster in urban ghettos. Other Americans ask, "What about our children?" but they forget that virtually any kid—in any city, town or suburb—who wants to try drugs can find them easily enough right now. And still others say, "What about the message it would send?" but they forget that our current response—inane anti-drug efforts like "Just Say No" and "This Is Your Brain on Drugs," along with our incredibly cruel laws, send far worse messages: that kids are stupid, that drug users are less than human and that people who do no harm to others deserve to lose their freedom.

A society cannot long afford to have its laws widely and openly broken. The urge to use some form of mind-altering substance is deeply ingrained in human nature. Attempting to legislate it out of existence can only lead us to grant government the kind of power it should not have in a free society. The drug laws in this country are outdated. The arguments against decriminalization are tired and invalid. Our fear that it would result in a massive wave of new addicts is unfounded. The institution of common-sense harm-reduction proposals would eliminate much of the inner-city violence associated with competitive drug dealing and allow billions of dollars to be rechanneled for economic assistance for job training, day care and better schools.

In the inner cities, where the front-line battles of the drug war are waged daily, the situation is desperate. The disintegration of the family structure, the dire job outlook, inadequate education and government abandonment have created communities where the drug trade is guaranteed to flourish. Drug prohibition has created a permanent underclass of unemployable inner-city youths whose lives have become hopelessly interwoven with drug crime and who in turn are becoming parents to another generation of dysfunctional children. Can we let this damage continue? Isn't it time to stop moralizing about drugs and put an end to policies that are destroying the nation?

NO

James A. Inciardi and
Christine A. Saum

LEGALIZATION MADNESS

Frustrated by the government's apparent inability to reduce the supply of illegal drugs on the streets of America, and disquieted by media accounts of innocents victimized by drug-related violence, some policy makers are convinced that the "war on drugs" has failed. In an attempt to find a better solution to the "drug crisis" or, at the very least, to try an alternative strategy, they have proposed legalizing drugs.

They argue that, if marijuana, cocaine, heroin, and other drugs were legalized, several positive things would probably occur: (1) drug prices would fall; (2) users would obtain their drugs at low, government-regulated prices, and they would no longer be forced to resort to crime in order to support their habits; (3) levels of drug-related crime, and particularly violent crime, would significantly decline, resulting in less crowded courts, jails, and prisons (this would allow law-enforcement personnel to focus their energies on the "real criminals" in society); and (4) drug production, distribution, and sale would no longer be controlled by organized crime, and thus such criminal syndicates as the Colombian cocaine "cartels," the Jamaican "posses," and the various "mafias" around the country and the world would be decapitalized, and the violence associated with drug distribution rivalries would be eliminated.

By contrast, the anti-legalization camp argues that violent crime would not necessarily decline in a legalized drug market. In fact, there are three reasons why it might actually increase. First, removing the criminal sanctions against the possession and distribution of illegal drugs would make them more available and attractive and, hence, would create large numbers of new users. Second, an increase in use would lead to a greater number of dysfunctional addicts who could not support themselves, their habits, or their lifestyles through legitimate means. Hence crime would be their only alternative. Third, more users would mean more of the violence associated with the ingestion of drugs.

These divergent points of view tend to persist because the relationships between drugs and crime are quite complex and because the possible outcomes of a legalized drug market are based primarily on speculation. However, it is

From James A. Inciardi and Christine A. Saum, "Legalization Madness," *The Public Interest*, no. 123 (Spring 1996). Copyright © 1996 by National Affairs, Inc. Reprinted by permission of the author and *The Public Interest*.

possible, from a careful review of the existing empirical literature on drugs and violence, to make some educated inferences.

CONSIDERING "LEGALIZATION"

Yet much depends upon what we mean by "legalizing drugs." Would all currently illicit drugs be legalized or would the experiment be limited to just certain ones? True legalization would be akin to selling such drugs as heroin and cocaine on the open market, much like alcohol and tobacco, with a few age-related restrictions. In contrast, there are "medicalization" and "decriminalization" alternatives. Medicalization approaches are of many types, but, in essence, they would allow users to obtain prescriptions for some, or all, currently illegal substances. Decriminalization removes the criminal penalties associated with the possession of small amounts of illegal drugs for personal use, while leaving intact the sanctions for trafficking, distribution, and sale.

But what about crack-cocaine? A quick review of the literature reveals that the legalizers, the decriminalizers, and the medicalizers avoid talking about this particular form of cocaine. Perhaps they do not want to legalize crack out of fear of the drug itself, or of public outrage. Arnold S. Trebach, a professor of law at American University and president of the Drug Policy Foundation, is one of the very few who argues for the full legalization of all drugs, including crack. He explains, however, that most are reluctant to discuss the legalization of crack-cocaine because, "it is a very dangerous drug. . . . I know that for many people the very thought of making crack legal destroys any inclination they might have had for even thinking about drug-law reform."

There is a related concern associated with the legalization of cocaine. Because crack is easily manufactured from powder cocaine (just add water and baking soda and cook on a stove or in a microwave), many drug-policy reformers hold that no form of cocaine should be legalized. But this weakens the argument that legalization will reduce drug-related violence; for much of this violence would appear to be in the cocaine- and crack-distribution markets.

To better understand the complex relationship between drugs and violence, we will discuss the data in the context of three models developed by Paul J. Goldstein of the University of Illinois at Chicago. They are the "psychopharmacological," "economically compulsive," and "systemic" explanations of violence. The first model holds, correctly in our view, that some individuals may become excitable, irrational, and even violent due to the ingestion of specific drugs. In contrast, taking a more economic approach to the behavior of drug users, the second holds that some drug users engage in violent crime mainly for the sake of supporting their drug use. The third model maintains that drug-related violent crime is simply the result of the drug market under a regime of illegality.

PSYCHOPHARMACOLOGICAL VIOLENCE

The case for legalization rests in part upon the faulty assumption that drugs themselves do not cause violence; rather, so goes the argument, violence is the result of depriving drug addicts of drugs or of the "criminal" trafficking in drugs. But, as researcher Barry Spunt points out,

"Users of drugs do get violent when they get high."

Research has documented that chronic users of amphetamines, methamphetamine, and cocaine in particular tend to exhibit hostile and aggressive behaviors. Psychopharmacological violence can also be a product of what is known as "cocaine psychosis." As dose and duration of cocaine use increase, the development of cocaine-related psychopathology is not uncommon. Cocaine psychosis is generally preceded by a transitional period characterized by increased suspiciousness, compulsive behavior, fault finding, and eventually paranoia. When the psychotic state is reached, individuals may experience visual, as well as auditory, hallucinations, with persecutory voices commonly heard. Many believe that they are being followed by police or that family, friends, and others are plotting against them.

Moreover, everyday events are sometimes misinterpreted by cocaine users in ways that support delusional beliefs. When coupled with the irritability and hyperactivity that cocaine tends to generate in almost all of its users, the cocaine-induced paranoia may lead to violent behavior as a means of "self-defense" against imagined persecutors. The violence associated with cocaine psychosis is a common feature in many crack houses across the United States. Violence may also result from the irritability associated with drug-withdrawal syndromes. In addition, some users ingest drugs before committing crimes to both loosen inhibitions and bolster their resolve to break the law.

Acts of violence may result from either periodic or chronic use of a drug. For example, in a study of drug use and psychopathy among Baltimore City jail inmates, researchers at the University of Baltimore reported that cocaine use was related to irritability, resentment, hostility, and assault. They concluded that these indicators of aggression may be a function of drug effects rather than of a predisposition to these behaviors. Similarly, Barry Spunt and his colleagues at National Development and Research Institutes (NDRI) in New York City found that of 269 convicted murderers incarcerated in New York State prisons, 45 percent were high at the time of the offense. Three in 10 believed that the homicide was related to their drug use, challenging conventional beliefs that violence only infrequently occurs as a result of drug consumption.

Even marijuana, which pro-legalizers consider harmless, may have a connection with violence and crime. Spunt and his colleagues attempted to determine the role of marijuana in the crimes of the homicide offenders they interviewed in the New York State prisons. One-third of those who had ever used marijuana had smoked the drug in the 24-hour period prior to the homicide. Moreover, 31 percent of those who considered themselves to be "high" at the time of committing murder felt that the homicide and marijuana were related. William Blount of the University of South Florida interviewed abused women in prisons and shelters for battered women located throughout Florida. He and his colleagues found that 24 percent of those who killed their abusers were marijuana users while only 8 percent of those who did not kill their abusers smoked marijuana.

AND ALCOHOL ABUSE

A point that needs emphasizing is that alcohol, because it is legal, accessible, and inexpensive, is linked to violence to a far greater extent than any illegal drug. For example, in the study just cited, it was found that an impressive 64 percent of those women who eventually killed their abusers were alcohol users (44 percent of those who did not kill their abusers were alcohol users). Indeed, the extent to which alcohol is responsible for violent crimes in comparison with other drugs is apparent from the statistics. For example, Carolyn Block and her colleagues at the Criminal Justice Information Authority in Chicago found that, between 1982 and 1989, the use of alcohol by offenders or victims in local homicides ranged from 18 percent to 32 percent.

Alcohol has, in fact, been consistently linked to homicide. Spunt and his colleagues interviewed 268 homicide offenders incarcerated in New York State correctional facilities to determine the role of alcohol in their crimes: Thirty-one percent of the respondents reported being drunk at the time of the crime and 19 percent believed that the homicide was related to their drinking. More generally, Douglass Murdoch of Quebec's McGill University found that in some 9,000 criminal cases drawn from a multinational sample, 62 percent of violent offenders were drinking shortly before, or at the time of, the offense.

It appears that alcohol reduces the inhibitory control of threat, making it more likely that a person will exhibit violent behaviors normally suppressed by fear. In turn, this reduction of inhibition heightens the probability that intoxicated persons will perpetrate, or become victims of, aggressive behavior.

When analyzing the psychopharmacological model of drugs and violence, most of the discussions focus on the offender and the role of drugs in causing or facilitating crime. But what about the victims? Are the victims of drug- and alcohol-related homicides simply casualties of someone else's substance abuse? In addressing these questions, the data demonstrates that victims are likely to be drug users as well. For example, in an analysis of the 4,298 homicides that occurred in New York City during 1990 and 1991, Kenneth Tardiff of Cornell University Medical College found that the victims of these offenses were 10 to 50 times more likely to be cocaine users than were members of the general population. Of the white female victims, 60 percent in the 25- to 34-year age group had cocaine in their systems; for black females, the figure was 72 percent. Tardiff speculated that the classic symptoms of cocaine use—irritability, paranoia, aggressiveness—may have instigated the violence. In another study of cocaine users in New York City, female high-volume users were found to be victims of violence far more frequently than low-volume and nonusers of cocaine. Studies in numerous other cities and countries have yielded the same general findings —that a great many of the victims of homicide and other forms of violence are drinkers and drug users themselves.

ECONOMICALLY COMPULSIVE VIOLENCE

Supporters of the economically compulsive model of violence argue that in a legalized market, the prices of "expensive drugs" would decline to more affordable levels, and, hence, predatory crimes would become unnecessary. This argument is based on several specious assumptions. First, it assumes that there is empirical support for what has been referred to as the "enslavement theory of addiction." Second, it assumes that people addicted to drugs commit crimes only for the purpose of supporting their habits. Third, it assumes that, in a legalized market, users could obtain as much of the drugs as they wanted whenever they wanted. Finally, it assumes that, if drugs are inexpensive, they will be affordable, and thus crime would be unnecessary.

With respect to the first premise, there has been for the better part of this century a concerted belief among many in the drug-policy field that addicts commit crimes because they are "enslaved" to drugs, and further that, because of the high price of heroin, cocaine, and other illicit chemicals on the black market, users are forced to commit crimes in order to support their drug habits. However, there is no solid empirical evidence to support this contention. From the 1920s through the end of the 1960s, hundreds of studies of the relationship between crime and addiction were conducted. Invariably, when one analysis would support the posture of "enslavement theory," the next would affirm the view that addicts were criminals first and that their drug use was but one more manifestation of their deviant lifestyles. In retrospect, the difficulty lay in the ways that many of the studies had been conducted: Biases and deficiencies in research designs and sampling had rendered their findings of little value.

Studies since the mid 1970s of active drug users on the streets of New York, Miami, Baltimore, and elsewhere have demonstrated that the "enslavement theory" has little basis in reality. All of these studies of the criminal careers of drug users have convincingly documented that, while drug use tends to intensify and perpetuate criminal behavior,

it usually does not initiate criminal careers. In fact, the evidence suggests that among the majority of street drug users who are involved in crime, their criminal careers are well established prior to the onset of either narcotics or cocaine use. As such, it would appear that the "inference of causality"—that the high price of drugs on the black market itself causes crime—is simply false.

Looking at the second premise, a variety of studies show that addicts commit crimes for reasons other than supporting their drug habit. They do so also for daily living expenses. For example, researchers at the Center for Drug and Alcohol Studies at the University of Delaware who studied crack users on the streets of Miami found that, of the active addicts interviewed, 85 percent of the male and 70 percent of the female interviewees paid for portions of their living expenses through street crime. In fact, one-half of the men and one-fourth of the women paid for 90 percent or more of their living expenses through crime. And, not surprisingly, 96 percent of the men and 99 percent of the women had not held a legal job in the 90-day period before being interviewed for the study.

With respect to the third premise, that in a legalized market users could obtain as much of the drugs as they wanted whenever they wanted, only speculation is possible. More than likely, however, there would be some sort of regulation, and hence black markets for drugs would persist for those whose addictions were beyond the medicalized or legalized allotments. In a decriminalized market, levels of drug-related violence would likely either remain unchanged or increase (if drug use increased).

As for the last premise, that cheap drugs preclude the need to commit crimes to obtain them, the evidence emphatically suggests that this is not the case. Consider crack-cocaine: Although crack "rocks" are available on the illegal market for as little as two dollars in some locales, users are still involved in crime-driven endeavors to support their addictions. For example, researchers Norman S. Miller and Mark S. Gold surveyed 200 consecutive callers to the 1-800-COCAINE hotline who considered themselves to have a problem with crack. They found that, despite the low cost of crack, 63 percent of daily users and 40 percent of non-daily users spent more than $200 per week on the drug. Similarly, interviews conducted by NDRI researchers in New York City with almost 400 drug users contacted in the streets, jails, and treatment programs revealed that almost one-half of them spent over $1,000 a month on crack. The study also documented that crack users—despite the low cost of their drug of choice—spent more money on drugs than did users of heroin, powder cocaine, marijuana, and alcohol.

SYSTEMIC VIOLENCE

It is the supposed systemic violence associated with trafficking in cocaine and crack in America's inner cities that has recently received the attention of drug-policy critics interested in legalizing drugs. Certainly it might appear that, if heroin and cocaine were legal substances, systemic drug-related violence would decline. However, there are two very important questions in this regard: First, is drug-related violence more often psychopharmacological or systemic? Second, is the great bulk of systemic violence related to the distribution of crack? If most of the drug-related violence is psychopharmacological in nature, and if systemic violence is typically related to crack—the drug generally excluded from consideration when legalization is recommended—then legalizing drugs would probably *not* reduce violent crime.

Regarding the first question, several recent studies conducted in New York City tend to contradict, or at least not support, the notion that legalizing drugs would reduce violent systemic-related crime. For example, Paul J. Goldstein's ethnographic studies of male and female drug users during the late 1980s found that cocaine-related violence was more often psychopharmacological than systemic. Similarly, Kenneth Tardiff's study of 4,298 New York City homicides found that 31 percent of the victims had used cocaine in the 24-hour period prior to their deaths. One of the conclusions of the study was that the homicides were not necessarily related to drug dealing. In all likelihood, as victims of homicide, the cocaine users may have provoked violence through their irritability, paranoid thinking, and verbal or physical aggression—all of which are among the psychopharmacological effects of cocaine.

Regarding the second question, the illegal drug most associated with systemic violence is crack-cocaine. Of all illicit drugs, crack is the one now responsible for the most homicides. In a study done in New York City in 1988 by Goldstein and his colleagues, crack was found to be connected with 32 percent of all homicides and 60 percent of all drug-related homicides. Furthermore, although there is evidence that crack sellers are more violent than other drug sellers, this violence is not confined to the drug-selling context—violence potententials appear to precede involvement in selling.

Thus, though crack has been blamed for increasing violence in the marketplace, this violence actually stems from the psychopharmacological consequences of crack use. Ansley Hamid, a professor of anthropology at the John Jay College of Criminal Justice in New York, reasons that increases in crack-related violence are due to the deterioration of informal and formal social controls throughout communities that have been destabilized by economic processes and political decisions. If this is the case, does anyone really believe that we can improve these complex social problems through the simple act of legalizing drugs?

DON'T JUST SAY NO

The issue of whether or not legalization would create a multitude of new users also needs to be addressed. It has been shown that many people do not use drugs simply because drugs are illegal. As Mark A.R. Kleiman, author of *Against Excess: Drug Policy for Results*, recently put it: "Illegality by itself tends to suppress consumption, independent of its effect on price, both because some consumers are reluctant to disobey the law and because illegal products are harder to find and less reliable as to quality and labeling than legal ones."

Although there is no way of accurately estimating how many new users there would be if drugs were legalized, there would probably be many. To begin with, there is the historical example of Prohibition. During Prohibition, there was a decrease of 20 percent to 50 percent in the number of alcoholics. These estimates were calculated based on a decline in cirrhosis and other alcohol-related deaths; after Prohibition ended, both of these indicators increased.

Currently, relatively few people are steady users of drugs. The University of Michigan's *Monitoring the Future* study reported in 1995 that only two-tenths of 1 percent of high-school seniors are daily users of either hallucinogens, cocaine, heroin, sedatives, or inhalants. It is the addicts who overwhelmingly consume the bulk of the drug supply—80 percent of all alcohol and almost 100 percent of all heroin. In other words, there are significantly large numbers of nonusers who have yet to even try drugs, let alone use them regularly. Of those who begin to use drugs "recreationally," researchers estimate that approximately 10 percent go on to serious, heavy, chronic, compulsive use. Herbert Kleber, the former deputy director of the Office of National Drug Control Policy, recently estimated that cocaine legalization might multiply the number of addicts from the current 2 million to between 18 and 50 million (which are the estimated numbers of problem drinkers and nicotine addicts).

This suggests that drug prohibition seems to be having some very positive effects and that legalizing drugs would not necessarily have a depressant effect on violent crime. With legalization, violent crime would likely escalate; or perhaps some types of systemic violence would decline at the expense of greatly increasing the overall rate of violent crime. Moreover, legalizing drugs would likely increase physical illnesses and compound any existing psychiatric problems among users and their family members. And finally, legalizing drugs would not eliminate the effects of unemployment, inadequate housing, deficient job skills, economic worries, and physical abuse that typically contribute to the use of drugs.

POSTSCRIPT

Should Drugs Be Legalized?

Part of this debate concerns whether or not drug legalization is a rational and productive option. Many people question whether or not the purported benefits of legalization would outweigh the potential risks. Legalization advocates feel that we should not abandon the war on drugs but that we need instead to toughen and broaden laws. Prevention, education, and treatment are necessary and will be effective only if regulation and control exist.

Nadelmann and Wenner assert that utilizing the criminal justice system to eradicate drug problems simply does not work. They argue that international control efforts, interdiction, and domestic law enforcement are ineffective and that many problems associated with drug use are the consequences of drug regulation policies. They also contend that drug prohibition imposes on personal liberties. They maintain that decriminalization is a feasible and desirable means of dealing with the drug crisis.

Inciardi and Saum charge that the advantages of maintaining illegality far outweigh any conceivable benefits of decriminalization. They profess that if drug laws were relaxed, the result would be more drug users and, thus, more drug addicts and more criminal activity. Legalization also opens the door for more drug-related social problems, such as disorders in infants of addicted mothers, psychiatric disorders, AIDS and tuberculosis, homelessness, automobile accidents, and family violence. Inciardi and Saum conclude that society cannot afford to soften its position on legalization.

Legalization proponents argue that drug laws have not worked and that the drug battle has been lost. They believe that drug-related problems would be significantly reduced if legalization were implemented. Despite potential risks, advocates believe that legalization is worth considering. Opponents contend that anyone who values human life would not regard legalization as acceptable. Citing alcohol and tobacco as examples, legalization opponents argue that decriminalizing drugs would not decrease profits from the sale of drugs (the profits from cigarettes and alcohol are incredibly high). Moreover, using the same examples, opponents argue that legalizing a drug does not make its problems disappear (alcohol and tobacco still have extremely high addiction rates as well as a myriad of other problems associated with their use).

Many European countries have systems of legalized drugs, and most have far fewer addiction rates and lower incidences of drug-related violence and crime than the United States. This does not mean that the European experience can be generalized to the United States. Legalization in the United States could still be a tremendous risk because drug problems could escalate and recriminalizing drugs would be difficult. This was the case with Prohibition in the 1920s, which, in changing the status of alcohol from legal to illegal, produced numerous crime- and alcohol-related problems.

Another aspect of the debate revolves around the moral considerations of drug criminalization. Legalization advocates believe that adults should be allowed to make their own descisions about drug use and that criminalization is a violation of personal freedom. Should adults be allowed to use drugs even though the serious health, social, and economic risks are known? On the other hand, should the government be allowed to police the personal habits of its citizens? Are drug users criminals? Should they be kept in prisons alongside murderers and on taxpayers' money? As America's drug problem continues, these and other questions persist.

Many good articles debate the pros and cons of drug legalization. These include "Drug Legalization: Time for a Real Debate," by Paul Stares, *The Brookings Review* (Spring 1996); "Legalization of Narcotics: Myths and Reality," by Joseph Califano, *USA Today* (March 1997); and "Drug Policy: Should the Law Take a Back Seat?" by Virginia Berridge, *The Lancet* (February 3, 1996). Also, the February 12, 1996, issue of *The National Review* has a number of prominent individuals discussing whether or not the war on drugs has been lost.

ISSUE 2

Should the United States Put More Emphasis on Stopping the Importation of Drugs?

YES: Barry McCaffrey, from *The National Drug Control Strategy, 1997* (1997)

NO: Mathea Falco, from "U.S. Drug Policy: Addicted to Failure," *Foreign Policy* (Spring 1996)

ISSUE SUMMARY

YES: Barry McCaffrey, director of the Office of National Drug Control Policy, argues that the importation of drugs must be stopped to reduce drug use and abuse. If the supply of drugs being trafficked across American borders was reduced, then there would be fewer drug-related problems. He maintains that a coordinated international effort is needed to combat the increased production of heroin, cocaine, and marijuana.

NO: Mathea Falco, president of Drug Strategies, a nonprofit policy institute, asserts that the emphasis should not be on curtailing the availability of drugs but on factors that contribute to Americans' use of drugs. She notes that blaming other countries for drug-related problems in the United States is one way for politicians to deflect criticism from themselves. Moreover, she argues, people involved in the drug trade in other countries have little incentive to end their involvement.

Since the beginning of the 1990s, overall drug use in the United States has increased. Up to now, interdiction has not proven to be successful in slowing the flow of drugs into the United States. Drugs continue to cross U.S. borders at record levels. This point may signal a need for stepped-up international efforts to stop the production and trafficking of drugs. Conversely, it may illustrate the inadequacy of the current strategy. Should the position of the U.S. government be to improve and strengthen current measures or to try an entirely new approach?

Some people contend that rather than attempting to limit illegal drugs from coming into the United States, more effort should be directed at reducing the demand for drugs and improving treatment for drug abusers. Foreign countries would not produce and transport drugs like heroin and cocaine into the United States if there were no market for them. Drug policies, some people maintain, should be aimed at the social and economic conditions underlying domestic drug problems, not at interfering with foreign governments.

Many U.S. government officials believe that other countries should assist in stopping the flow of drugs across their borders. Diminishing the supply of drugs by intercepting them before they reach the user is another way to eliminate or curtail drug use. Critical elements in the lucrative drug trade are multinational crime syndicates. One premise is that if the drug production, transportation, distribution, and processing functions as well as the money laundering operations of these criminal organizations can be interrupted and eventually crippled, then the drug problem would abate.

In South American countries such as Peru, Colombia, and Bolivia, where coca—from which cocaine is processed—is cultivated, economic aid has been made available to help the governments of these countries fight the cocaine kingpins. An alleged problem is that a number of government officials in these countries are corrupt or fearful of the cocaine cartel leaders. One proposed solution is to go directly to the farmers and offer them money to plant crops other than coca. This tactic, however, failed in the mid-1970s, when the U.S. government gave money to farmers in Turkey to stop growing opium poppy crops. After one year the program was discontinued due to the enormous expense, and opium poppy crops were once again planted.

Drug problems are not limited to the Americas. Since the breakup of the Soviet Union, for example, there has been a tremendous increase in opium production in many of the former republics. These republics are in dire need of money, and one source of income is opium production. Moreover, there is lax enforcement by police officials in these republics.

There are many reasons why people are dissatisfied with the current state of the war on drugs. For example, in the war on drugs, the *casual* user is generally the primary focus of drug use deterrence. This is viewed by many people as a form of discrimination because the vast majority of drug users and sellers who are arrested and prosecuted are poor, members of minorities, homeless, unemployed, and/or disenfranchised. Also, international drug dealers who are arrested are usually not the drug bosses but lower-level people working for them. Finally, some argue that the war on drugs should be redirected away from interdiction and enforcement because they feel that the worst drug problems in society today are caused by legal drugs, primarily alcohol and tobacco.

The following selections address the issue of whether or not the war on drugs should be fought on an international level. Barry McCaffrey takes the view that international cooperation is absolutely necessary if we are to stem the flow of drugs and maintain world order. Mathea Falco feels that an international approach to dealing with drugs avoids the real issues that have led to drug abuse.

YES

Barry McCaffrey

THE NATIONAL DRUG CONTROL STRATEGY, 1997

INITIATIVES TO SHIELD OUR FRONTIERS

America's place in the world—its status as global leader, economic giant, and bastion of democracy—ensures that extraordinary numbers of people will come to our shores, air terminals, and borders on various modes of transport. According to the U.S. Customs Service, each year sixty million people enter our country on more than 675,000 commercial and private flights. Another six million come by sea and 370 million by land. In addition, 116 million vehicles cross the land borders with Canada and Mexico. More than 90,000 merchant and passenger ships dock at our ports, carrying more than nine million shipping containers and four hundred million tons of cargo, while another 157,000 smaller vessels visit our many coastal towns. Amid voluminous trade, drug traffickers seek to hide illegal substances that destroy our citizens and ruin neighborhoods. Through concerted effort, we can limit illegal drugs entering our country from abroad while maintaining open, free-flowing commerce, tourism, and international exchange that help make our nation great.

Preventing Drug Trafficking Across the Southwest Border
If a single geographic region were to be identified as a microcosm of America's drug problem, it would be the U.S.–Mexican border. Cocaine, heroin, methamphetamine, and marijuana all cross into the United States here, hidden among the eighty-four million cars, 232 million people, and 2.8 million trucks that the Customs Service estimates cross the thirty-eight ports of entry spanning nearly two thousand miles. American and Mexican ranchers often are harmed by violent bands of drug runners openly crossing their property. Border areas suffer from disproportionate levels of crime and violence due to the abundance of illegal drugs. The general population is terrified by increasingly sophisticated organizations that ply their vicious trade across what is otherwise a historic setting that marks the conflux of two great nations and their cultures.

From Barry McCaffrey, Office of National Drug Control Policy. *National Drug Control Strategy, 1997*. Washington, DC: Government Printing Office, February 1997. Notes omitted.

The current situation must be changed. Significant reinforcements have been committed to the substantial resources already focused on the southwest border. Approximately a thousand Border Patrol agents and 150 Immigration and Naturalization inspectors, 625 U.S. Customs Service agents and inspectors, fifty Drug Enforcement agents, seventy FBI agents, and additional Deputy U.S. Marshals will be added in fiscal year 1997. Advanced technological equipment, sophisticated sensors, and long-range infrared night-vision devices have been installed near the border. A variety of intelligence agencies have been tracking the flow of illegal drugs, enhancing interdiction operations, and pursuing drug-trafficking organizations. The Southwest Border Initiative, Southwest Border Council, Southwest Border HIDTA [High Intensity Drug Trafficking Area], Joint Task Force-Six, OCDETF, and the Attorney General's Executive Committee and Operation Alliance have stepped up activities, expanding coordination with state and local agencies. Bilateral working groups have been established with Mexico to achieve the rule of law.

However, illegal drugs are still crossing the border. This tough problem is complicated by illegal immigration, corruption, and questions of jurisdiction, policy, and law. To meet these challenges, we are pursuing an overarching framework to complement individual inspection and interdiction operations, focus resources, provide timely and accurate information that can secure evidence for specific cases, and anticipate strategic and tactical activities of drug traffickers. We will also coordinate efforts among many agencies devoted to the issue, harness technologies in an integrative fashion so that one system complements the other, and work more closely with Mexicans for the common good.

Closing the Caribbean "Back Door"

The DEA estimates that the second-most-significant drug trafficking route into the U.S. is through the Caribbean, specifically Puerto Rico and the U.S. Virgin Islands. Puerto Rico is a natural point of entry because of its central location amid major lines of commerce and transportation and the absence of customs inspections for domestic cargo moving between the island and U.S. mainland. The consequences of this trafficking have been devastating for Puerto Rico, the Virgin islands, and many island nations of the Caribbean. Cocaine sold in Puerto Rico is cheaper than anywhere else in the United States. Violent gangs control nearly a thousand drug-distribution points throughout the island and victimize more than three hundred public housing areas. Puerto Rico has the second highest per capita murder rate in the United States.

In response to the threat posed by international drug trafficking in the Caribbean, the United States established the Puerto Rico–U.S. Virgin Islands High Intensity Drug Trafficking Area (HIDTA) in 1994. To combat drug trafficking and money laundering, HIDTA brings together twenty-six agencies and more than six hundred federal, state, and local personnel forming ten task forces and an intelligence coordination center. During FY '96, HIDTA participants arrested 417 individuals, confiscated 14,500 kilograms of cocaine, and seized eight million dollars in assets and currency.

The United States Coast Guard and United States Customs Service have also worked to constrict this illegal drug route into the United States. Their operations feature expanded marine and air enforcement, more cargo examinations, and frequent searches of small vessels. From March 1 through December 31, 1996, the Customs Service's Operation Gateway produced the seizure of 28,507 pounds of cocaine, 3,060 pounds of marijuana, sixty-two pounds of heroin, and $2.2 million and 129 arrests in the Puerto Rico/U.S. Virgin Islands area. In the last three months of 1996, the Coast Guard seized seven vessels, 13,897 pounds of cocaine, forty pounds of heroin, and made nineteen arrests. Interdiction can help stop drugs from entering our country.

We continue to work closely with our Caribbean allies to guard the approaches to Puerto Rico and deny narcotraffickers safe haven anywhere in the region while complying with international law. We currently have bilateral enforcement agreements in place with sixteen countries in or bordering the Caribbean. Negotiations are underway with an additional six countries, and we are working to expand agreements that help protect island nations possessing small law-enforcement establishments from the onslaught of international criminal organizations that violate their sovereignty and corrupt their economies and democratic institutions. Multinational counterdrug operations in the Caribbean provide an additional force multiplier. For example, British, French, and Dutch Naval forces participate in fully coordinated operations helping to block smuggling routes out of South America.

Addressing Other Drug Entry Points

The greater our success at interrupting drug trafficking along any particular border, the more traffickers attempt to introduce illegal drugs elsewhere. South Florida, for example, continues to be a key site for drugs coming into the U.S. and for money moving out —despite the successful disruption of the air bridge that brought cocaine during the last decade from Colombia to the southeastern United States. Mexican coastal ports are entry points for drugs being smuggled northward across our southwest border, necessitating interdiction operations on key trafficking routes through the eastern Pacific and western Caribbean. New York City remains the primary port of entry for Southeast Asian heroin. Ports in the Pacific Northwest and along the Pacific coast—as well as the border with Canada and any airport that handles international cargo or passengers —are vulnerable to drug trafficking.

Consequently, we must develop a comprehensive, coordinated capability that allows the federal government to focus resources in response to shifting drug-trafficking threats. We must be proactive in efforts to keep drug traffickers from penetrating our sovereign territory. Existing organizations and initiatives— like the three Joint Inter-Agency Task Forces (East, West, South), the Domestic Air Interdiction Coordination Center, Joint Task Force-Six, and Operation Alliance, which address the southwest border problem, as well as HIDTAs and other cooperative interagency efforts— must remain the building blocks for this effort.

INITIATIVES TO REDUCE DRUG AVAILABILITY

Only sustained commitment can reduce the supply of illegal drugs. The basic principles of supply reduction are straightforward. A five-stage grower-to-user chain links the drug producer in a foreign land with the consumer in the United States. The stages are: cultivation, processing, transit, wholesale distribution, and retail sales on the street. The U.S. government's international drug control programs target the first three links in this chain: cultivation, processing, and transit. International drug control programs have demonstrated that they can be particularly effective when they focus on severing the chain at the source. When drug crops or synthetic drug laboratories are eliminated, fewer drugs enter the system. This approach is analogous to removing a tumor before it metastasizes.

Opposing international criminal organizations that traffic in drugs at all stages of their operation and in all their operating environments is essential. The global drug trade has spawned large trafficking organizations with an almost limitless capacity to subvert the economic and political systems of underdeveloped countries. In our own hemisphere, the two countries that have faced the longest struggle against drug traffickers—Colombia and Mexico—have been plagued by widespread drug corruption. Efforts to break these organizations must be supported by public information that depicts the true nature of drug traffickers, endorses the elements countering them, and supports the rule of law.

The success of our international drug control policies depends on the political will and institutional capability of other countries to implement programs that reduce and ultimately eliminate cultivation of illicit drug crops and suppress the production, trafficking, and abuse of illegal drugs. Consequently, we are convinced that our drug control programs must be complemented by efforts to strengthen democratic institutions in key drug producing and transit countries.

Encouraging Other Nations to Confront Drug Production and Trafficking

The Certification Process.   One way to pressure foreign governments to stand up against drug trafficking organizations is through periodic public scrutiny of their counterdrug record. The U.S. government does so through the annual process of certifying the counterdrug performance of narcotics producing and transit countries. Performance is evaluated in terms of cooperation with U.S. efforts, or unilateral efforts to comply with the goals and objectives of the 1988 United Nations Convention Against Illicit Traffic in Narcotics, Drugs, and Psychotropic Substances.

This annual certification process gives the President an international platform for candid, public evaluation of major drug source and transit countries. While denial of certification carries important foreign assistance sanctions as well as a mandatory U.S. vote against multilateral development banks lending money to such countries, the major sanction is public opprobrium at failing the standard. This process has proved increasingly effective. It has fostered the development of realistic performance benchmarks and increased cooperation in important countries.

Bilateral Cooperation with Mexico. The principal mechanism for counterdrug cooperation with Mexico is the High Level Contact Group on Drug Control formed in March 1996. This bilateral group of senior officials meets periodically while subordinate working groups are in continuous contact. The Contact Group on Drug Control operates at the cabinet level and has instituted a number of broad initiatives, including a shared assessment of the drug threat and a binational counterdrug strategy. Key elements of that strategy include: measures to strengthen border security, actions to ensure criminals cannot escape justice in one country by flight to another, improved information sharing, reduction of drug use in both countries, anti–money laundering initiatives, cooperation to interrupt drug shipments destined for both Mexico and the U.S., and concentration of law enforcement efforts on trafficking organizations that operate in both countries.

Progress, while not uniform across the board, has been significant. The criminal drug organizations that operate in both our countries are ruthless, violent, flexible, and defiant of national sovereignty. The corrupting power of thirty billion dollars of illegal drug money is an enormous threat to the democratic institutions of both Mexico and the United States. Notable successes include: the Mexican government's passage of important anti-crime legislation, U.S. training for anti-drug units of Mexican police and Armed Forces as well as in money laundering investigations for investigators and prosecutors from the Mexican Treasury and Attorney General's office. Mexico continues to implement one of the world's most successful drug crop eradication programs. Drug seizures by Mexican authorities increased significantly in 1996; heroin seizures were up 78 percent and cocaine seizures up 21 percent.

To build on these successes, we must continue working with our counterparts to insulate law enforcement organizations from corruption and build Mexican counterdrug capabilities. A major bilateral concern is the cross-border activity of Mexican trafficking organizations and their ability to hold Mexican author-

ities at bay. Finally, we must be cognizant of sovereignty concerns in this complex relationship as we broaden the bilateral counterdrug effort. Drug traffickers have developed complex infrastructures and multiple routes in Mexico over the better part of a decade. These criminal organizations can be pursued, but success will take a long-term commitment on the part of dedicated, honest, and courageous Mexican authorities and sustained, cooperative efforts by the United States.

Making Cocaine Less Available

Cocaine is currently our most dangerous illicit drug. It is responsible for more addiction, health problems, economic dislocation, and social costs than any other illegal substance. It is also more vulnerable to international supply reduction than other foreign-produced drugs. Our national efforts against coca cultivation and the production and trafficking of cocaine are guided by Presidential Decision Directive 14, the Western Hemisphere counterdrug strategy. U.S. anti-cocaine activities fall into the following three categories: reduction of cultivation, interdiction, and actions against trafficking organizations.

Reduction of Cultivation. Nearly all the cocaine consumed in the United States is produced from coca crops grown in Bolivia, Colombia, and Peru. In 1995, enough coca was grown on 214,800 hectares of land in these three countries to produce 780 metric tons of cocaine for the world market. Eighty percent of the cocaine in the United States comes from Peruvian coca crops. A top international drug policy priority is support for the efforts of Bolivia, Colombia, and Peru to reduce coca cultivation. Our forthcoming regional initiative, whose goal is nothing less than complete elimination within the next decade of cultivation of coca destined for illicit cocaine production, will focus on alternative economic development in Peru. These efforts will recognize that drug cultivation in source countries is an important means of employment and income for some of the poorest members of society. To be successful, drug crop reduction programs must include measures to resolve socio-economic factors that promote the cultivation of illegal drug crops.

Interdiction. Since 1993, global seizures averaged 270 metric tons of cocaine, leaving approximately five-hundred tons potentially available for consumption each year. U.S. cocaine seizures by themselves averaged 112 tons a year over the same period.

Within South America, a sustained, U.S.–supported interdiction effort continues to disrupt the air, river, maritime, and land transportation of cocaine base from Bolivia and Peru to Colombia. By the end of 1996, Peru and Colombia seized or destroyed dozens of drug trafficker aircraft, resulting in a two-thirds reduction in the number of detected trafficker flights over the Andean ridge region compared with the number of flights detected before the denial program was launched in early 1995. As coca cultivation subsequently exceeded drug trafficker transportation capabilities, average coca prices in Peru dropped by 50 percent over the same time period. We have demonstrated that interdiction efforts in the source country zone can disrupt trafficking patterns significantly. Our challenges now are to work with host nations to: restrict further the air movement of coca products between and within Bolivia, Peru, Brazil, and Colombia; block drug traf-

fickers from developing alternative river, ground, and maritime routes; and assist South American nations in preventing drug trafficking organizations from violating their sovereign air, land, and sea space.

In the "transit zone" of the Caribbean, Central America, Mexico, and the eastern Pacific waters, U.S. interdiction seeks to prevent traffickers from moving cocaine. An effective transit zone interdiction program requires flexible, in-depth, intelligence-driven defenses. Drug traffickers are adaptable, and they will react to our successes by shifting routes and changing modes of transportation. We must be equally flexible and give the traffickers no quarter as we respond to their moves. This objective will require that we—in concert with our regional allies—maintain a "defense in depth," taking aggressive action in source countries, throughout the transit zone, and at our borders.

International coordination and cooperation are important components of our interdiction effort. U.S. interdiction agencies do not by themselves have sufficient resources to address the trafficking threat. Bilateral or multilateral agreements, sharing intelligence and information, and conducting combined operations with our allies can multiply the effectiveness of the regional interdiction effort. Improving the interdiction capabilities of committed nations will also increase the effectiveness of our transit zone efforts. Finally, technology and intelligence can help us employ limited assets against high pay-off targets.

Actions Against Trafficking Organizations. Even after the arrest of major Cali Mafia leaders, Colombian drug syndicates continue to be the preeminent cocaine producing and trafficking organizations. They purchase the majority of semi-finished cocaine base from Bolivian or Peruvian farmers. Along with Mexican poly-drug traffickers and others, they increasingly move the illicit drug to the United States and elsewhere. The power, wealth, and sophistication of Colombian, Mexican, and other drug syndicates pose enormous threats to governmental and judicial institutions in many Western hemisphere countries.

Our successes against these and other international criminal organizations have been increasing. U.S.–supported Colombian law enforcement efforts have resulted in the arrest or surrender of the top seven leaders of the Cali drug cartel. U.S. support for other nations helped disrupt and dismantle trafficking organizations, including the Jose Castrillon organization based in Colombia and Panama. This crime syndicate was responsible for the maritime shipment of several multi-ton loads of cocaine destined for the United States. While the sentences announced to date by the Colombian government have been inadequate considering the magnitude of the crimes committed, cocaine traffickers are operating in an increasingly hostile environment. Our international cocaine control strategy will continue to include an across-the-spectrum attack on these criminal organizations.

Making Heroin Less Available

Efforts against production and trafficking of heroin are guided by the President's heroin control policy of November 1995 (PDD-44). Potential global heroin production has increased about 60 percent in the past eight years to about 360 metric tons. Heroin is not just an American problem. U.S. demand (estimated between four and thirteen metric tons) is equivalent to only a fraction of that potential.

The heroin interdiction challenge is enormous. Central governments in the two major source countries, Afghanistan and Burma, have limited powers. U.S. access and influence there is also extremely limited. Trafficking organizations are highly cohesive and difficult to penetrate. They use multiple trafficking routes and methods. Heroin flows through East Asia, the Middle East, the Former Soviet Union, Nigeria, South Africa, and South America, following the paths of least resistance and avoiding law enforcement. Heroin is a low bulk, high value commodity. An individual courier traveling aboard a commercial airliner can use body-carry techniques and ingestion to conceal several million dollars worth of heroin. Larger multi-kilogram amounts have been found hidden in commercial cargo shipments. Consequently, the worldwide seizure of morphine base/heroin in 1995 consisted of only thirty-two metric tons while U.S. seizures were just 1.3 metric tons. The recent increase in heroin production in Colombia underscores the diffuse nature of the international heroin challenge. Just a few years ago, Colombia was an insignificant producer of heroin. Now, its potential heroin production (six tons in 1995) represents a significant portion of the estimated U.S. demand. South American heroin is being sold in the U.S. at higher purity levels and lower prices than South East Asian heroin to garner larger market shares, and is in some areas becoming an important source of heroin.

The United States will work through diplomatic and public channels to promote international awareness of the heroin threat, help strengthen law enforcement efforts in heroin source and transit countries, bring cooperative law enforcement to bear against processing and trafficking, act against illegal financial systems that bankroll heroin trafficking activities, and promote the United Nations International Drug Control Program (UNDCP) and other multilateral and regional engagement in opium poppy and heroin control programs in source countries where U.S. bilateral influence is limited by political and security constraints. America will support continuing programs by Colombia and Mexico to eradicate opium poppy and will move promptly against any other illicit opium poppy cultivation encountered in the Western hemisphere.

Countering the Methamphetamine Threat

Methamphetamine abuse is a significant problem on the West Coast and in the Southwest and Midwest; it is also moving eastward. This drug is problematic because it is easily manufactured, inexpensive, and incredibly addictive. Methamphetamine is the "poor man's cocaine" and has the potential to assume national prominence if its use is not curtailed. Current law enforcement efforts against the production and distribution of methamphetamine are guided by the *Department of Justice National Methamphetamine Strategy* released in April 1996. This document serves as the basis for an expanded response that integrates treatment and prevention initiatives.

The principal foreign source of methamphetamine is Mexico. Mexican trafficking groups use existing cocaine smuggling networks to funnel methamphetamine into the United States. Through the High Level Contact Group on Drug Control, the United States will continue supporting Mexican government efforts to identify and destroy methamphetamine production, storage, or shipment activities and act against criminal organizations engaged in this traffic. The U.S. will also cooperate with other industrialized countries, the U.N. Drug Control Program, and multilateral organizations to limit international commerce in methamphetamine precursors and prevent illicit diversion or trafficking in domestic or foreign methamphetamines.

Domestically, the drug is produced in clandestine laboratories using toxic and highly explosive mixtures of hydriotic acid, phosphene gas, and red phosphorous. These chemicals are either smuggled into the country or illegally diverted from legitimate sources. The Methamphetamine Control Act of 1996 addressed this problem by controlling precursor chemicals and increasing criminal penalties for possession and distribution. Meth labs are mostly short-term, "one-batch" facilities commonly established in rural or sparsely populated areas to preclude detection as a result of the chemicals' odors. Nevertheless, federal and state lab seizures are increasing as a result of law enforcement attention to this emerging drug threat.

Measuring and Reducing Domestic Cannabis Cultivation

Marijuana remains the most-commonly-used illegal drug in the United States. Much of the marijuana smoked in the U.S. is cultivated domestically—commercially, privately, outdoors, and indoors. However, we have no accurate estimate of the extent of domestic marijuana cultivation. Our domestic cannabis crop reduction efforts must be supported by accurate information about drug crop locations and potentials. The Office of

National Drug Control Policy will coordinate the development of a domestic marijuana crop measurement program.

Controlling the Diversion of Drug-essential Chemicals

The production of illegal drugs requires enormous quantities of precursor chemicals. Clearly, drug production can be curtailed if the necessary precursor chemicals can be prevented from being diverted for this purpose. The importance of controlling chemicals has been internationally accepted. Article 12 of the 1988 United Nations Convention Against Illicit Traffic in Narcotic Drugs and Psychotropic Substance establishes the obligation for parties to the treaty to control their chemical commerce to prevent diversion to illicit drug manufacture. The Convention lists twenty-two chemicals as most necessary to drug manufacture and, therefore, subject to control.

International cooperation between enforcement and regulatory agencies is essential to the prevention of diversion of precursor chemicals. Information exchange to verify the legitimacy of proposed transactions in regulated chemicals is the key element to such cooperation. The United States continues to urge adoption of chemical control regimes by governments that do not have them. Our goal is to continue and expand the cooperation until sharing of information on proposed transactions in regulated chemicals is routine. We need to demonstrate that all sources of information must be queried, not only those in the exporting and importing countries, and that information sharing can occur without jeopardizing commercial confidentiality.

NO

Mathea Falco

U.S. DRUG POLICY: ADDICTED TO FAILURE

As Americans struggle to define their national security interests in the post–Cold War world, drug control enjoys strong political support from both parties. When asked to rank "very important" foreign policy goals, 85 per cent of the American public place "stopping the flow of drugs" at the top of the list, according to the 1995 Chicago Council on Foreign Relations national survey. For that reason, international drug-control programs will survive the congressional assault on the foreign affairs budget. Voter opposition to foreign aid does not yet extend to eradication and interdiction programs intended to stem the flow of drugs from abroad. Indeed, U.S.-supported antidrug programs in Latin America now represent almost 20 per cent of total American foreign assistance to the region, compared with only 3 per cent a decade ago.

The popular view that other countries are largely responsible for America's drug problems has deep historic roots. When the first drug laws were adopted early in this century, drugs were associated with immigrant groups and minorities: opium with Chinese laborers in the West; cocaine with blacks; and marijuana with Mexican immigrants in the Southwest. These drugs were seen as foreign threats to America's social fabric, undermining traditional moral values and political stability. Today the perceived link between foreigners and drugs still prompts the U.S. government to use diplomacy, coercion, money, and even military force to try to stop drugs from entering the country.

The supply-side approach is logically compelling. If there were no drugs coming in, the argument goes, then there would be no drug problem. And even if foreign drugs cannot be eliminated entirely, the laws of the marketplace dictate that reducing the supply will drive up the price, which in turn will deter potential users from trying drugs and force addicts to either go "cold turkey" or seek treatment. The critical assumption is that curtailing foreign supplies is the most effective way to cut drug abuse in the United States.

This supply-side approach to drugs has powerful political appeal. Blaming foreigners for America's recurring drug epidemics provides convenient if distant targets for public anger that might otherwise be directed toward

From Mathea Falco, "U.S. Drug Policy: Addicted to Failure," *Foreign Policy*, no. 102 (Spring 1996).

elected officials. Getting foreign farmers to stop growing drug crops seems easier than curbing America's appetite for drugs. Moreover, intercepting incoming drugs in the air or on the high seas appears to be the kind of technological challenge Americans are uniquely capable of meeting. If our scientists could land men on the moon, then surely we can shut off the drug traffic.

The supply-side approach to drug control has been thoroughly tested by both Republican and Democratic administrations. President Richard Nixon, faced with rising heroin and marijuana use in the late 1960s, closed a key U.S.-Mexican border crossing to convince Mexico to take action against illegal drug production. He also stepped up diplomatic pressure against Turkey, a major opium source for the notorious "French Connection" heroin traffickers, and provided narcotics-control assistance to Mexico and Turkey. Presidents Gerald Ford and Jimmy Carter continued programs of crop eradication, substitution, and overseas law-enforcement spending tens of millions of dollars during the 1970s.

At the end of the seventies, Turkey was no longer a significant source far illegal heroin, although the government allowed some farmers to grow opium for the international pharmaceutical industry. Due to intensive aerial opium eradication, Mexico's share of the U.S. heroin market declined sharply, from between 70 and 80 per cent in 1975 to 30 per cent in 1979. During the same period, heroin addiction in the United States also declined, in large part because addicts faced with rising heroin prices went into treatment, which was then widely available.

Unfortunately, the success of these supply-reduction programs was limited and brief. Production in other regions quickly expanded to fill American demand: Southeast Asia's Golden Triangle (Burma, Laos, and Thailand) and South Asia's Golden Crescent (Afghanistan, Iran, and Pakistan) became primary heroin sources. By 1983, Mexico had again become a major supplier, as opium cultivation spread to more remote areas only nominally controlled by the government.

President Ronald Reagan gave unprecedented resources to supply-control efforts. Just as he intended to shield the United States from Soviet missiles through the Strategic Defense Initiative, so, too, did Reagan try to seal the borders against the flow of drugs that threatened the nation's security. Funding for interdiction and international supply-control programs jumped from $416 million in 1981 to $1.6 billion in 1987, constituting about one-third of total federal antidrug spending.

President George Bush followed similar policies. In September 1989, in his first televised presidential address, Bush announced that, "we will for the first time make available the appropriate resources of America's Armed forces. We will intensify our efforts against drug smugglers on the high seas, in international airspace, and at our borders."

The Defense Department initially resisted congressional efforts to enlist the military in the drug war. However, when faced with major budget cuts after the collapse of the Soviet Union, the Defense Department embraced a drug-fighting mission, protecting some endangered programs by reclassifying them as drug-related. For example, over-the-horizon radar systems designed to guard against Soviet missiles overflying Canada were redirected southward to watch for drug-smuggling aircraft. By 1991, the Defense

Department had captured the largest share of the $2 billion drug-interdiction budget.

Although President Bill Clinton has generally endorsed his predecessors' emphasis on curtailing drug supplies, voices within the administration and the Congress express increasing skepticism about the effectiveness of America's international drug war. In September 1993, a National Security Council (NSC) interagency review concluded that interdiction had not succeeded in slowing the flow of cocaine, confirming the findings of several previous General Accounting Office (GAO) studies. Although interdiction funding had been cut substantially in the Bush administration's last budget, funding fell further under Clinton, dropping to approximately $1.3 billion by 1995.

The NSC policy review argued that stopping drugs close to their source of production might prove a more effective strategy than traditional interdiction efforts. Funding for overseas narcotics-control programs had declined from an estimated $660 million in 1992 to about $330 million in 1994. Following the NSC recommendation, the administration requested substantial increases in the fiscal 1995 budget for source-country programs, but the Democratic-controlled Congress refused to fund them. Noting that Congress had approved the $2.2 billion five-year Andean Strategy, begun in 1989 under the Bush administration to help Bolivia, Colombia, and Peru reduce illicit drug activities, the House Appropriations Committee's 1995 report on foreign operations concluded that

> there are no signs that actual levels of cocaine reaching U.S. shores has changed.... We thus find ourselves continuing to march steadily down a path towards devoting more and more resources to helicopters, vehicles, police and army bases, and weaponry, while not doing enough to fund comprehensive economic solutions.... The program has done little in its country programs to ensure sustainability, and thus the Committee has no confidence that the reforms achieved so far will stick.

The new Republican Congress has sharply criticized Clinton's shift away from interdiction, calling this a litmus test of his determination to combat drugs. In July 1995, the House of Representatives voted to eliminate the White House Office of National Drug Control Policy (ONDCP), which develops the administration's annual drug strategy and coordinates federal antidrug efforts. While the Senate subsequently restored ONDCP under threat of presidential veto, its budget was cut by one-third. Critics contended that ONDCP's budget would be better spent on interdiction. According to Senator Richard Shelby (R-Alabama), his appropriations subcommittee "voted to terminate" ONDCP in order to provide "full funding for ... drug interdiction efforts with the $10 million in savings."

Congressional enthusiasm for interdiction does not extend to source-country programs, which two key House committee chairmen characterized as "tried-and-failed crop eradication and alternative development initiatives" in an open letter to Clinton in 1995. Congress cut $98 million from the Clinton administration's requested $213 million for the State Department's source-country efforts in the fiscal 1996 budget.

SUPPLY-CONTROL SCORECARD

Since 1981, American taxpayers have spent $23 billion on international drug control. Yet drug supplies have increased substantially both at home and abroad. Worldwide opium production has more than doubled in the past decade and now exceeds 3,400 tons per year, the equivalent of 340 tons of heroin. From 1984 to 1994, coca production almost doubled, although the United States provided more than $2 billion in narcotics-control assistance to Bolivia, Colombia, and Peru, the world's largest coca producers. Meanwhile, drug prices in the United States have fallen precipitously. Heroin now sells for less than half its 1981 street price, and heroin purity exceeds 60 per cent in many cities, compared with only 7 per cent in 1981. Cocaine prices have dropped by two-thirds. The administrator of the Drug Enforcement Administration (DEA), Thomas Constantine, testified before the House International Relations Subcommittee on the Western Hemisphere in March 1995 that "drug availability and purity of cocaine and heroin are at an all-time high."

Some congressional critics blame the apparent failure of interdiction on a lack of resources, arguing that budget cuts of one-third since 1992 have hindered federal efforts to intercept foreign drug traffic. Others blame Clinton's strategic shift away from efforts to interrupt drug traffic through the Caribbean, Central America, and Mexico in favor of trying to eliminate the *production* of drugs in Bolivia, Colombia, and Peru. In June 1995, Joseph Kelley, a top analyst for international affairs at the GAO, testified that the U.S. international antidrug effort suffers from weak management and poor coordination.

The underlying problem, however, is not operational. Increased resources and better implementation will not make foreign supply-control efforts more successful in driving up drug prices in the United States. The supply-side strategy is fatally flawed for several reasons, which follow.

The economics of drug cultivation mitigate against sustained reductions in supply. Drug crops can be grown very cheaply almost anywhere in the world, and poor farmers have strong economic incentives to adapt to changing conditions. If one production area is wiped out, lost crops can easily be replaced. In Peru, for example, a fungal infestation of coca crops in the early 1990s pushed cultivation into more remote, previously uncultivated areas of the Huallaga Valley. In the 1970s in Mexico, the government's opium-eradication campaign drove farmers to change their cultivation techniques, growing opium poppies in much smaller patches under large-leafed crops, such as banana trees, which made aerial detection difficult.

The number of countries producing drugs has significantly increased in the past two decades. Although coca is a traditional crop in Bolivia, Colombia, and Peru, it is now being grown in other South American countries, and worldwide poppy cultivation continues to expand. In the Central Asian republics, opium is an important source of revenue, while cocaine traffickers in Colombia are diversifying into heroin from locally grown opium poppies. (Before 1991, Colombia had never grown opium.) Marijuana is essentially a weed grown in every temperate region of the world, including many parts of the United States.

Drug crops are the mainstay of many poor countries, where farmers have few comparable alternatives. In Bolivia, for example, where the per capita gross national product (GNP) is $770 a year, an acre of coca yields about $475 annually, compared with $35–$250 for crops such as bananas and grapefruit—if there are buyers. In Kyrgyzstan, per capita GNP was only $610 in 1994, but a pound of opium brings $400 in local markets or can be bartered for canned goods, cooking oil, and other commodities.

The real but brief success of U.S. efforts to reduce Turkish and Mexican drug production in the 1970s has not been matched. Despite continuing U.S. pressure, source-country governments have been unable or unwilling to undertake sustained drug-eradication campaigns. The reductions in cultivation that do occur are symbolic, since the eradicated crops tend to be more than offset by new plantings. For example, from 1987 to 1993, the Bolivian government devoted $48 million in U.S. aid to pay farmers to eradicate 26,000 hectares of coca. During the same period, Bolivian farmers planted more than 35,000 new hectares of coca. Some observers have concluded that U.S. eradication efforts in Bolivia are little more than a coca support program at U.S. taxpayers' expense.

The only successful example of a large-scale reduction in illicit drug cultivation in recent years occurred in Thailand, where rapid economic growth has produced opportunities more lucrative than opium farming. After decades of supplying the world heroin market, Thailand now imports opium from neighboring Burma to support its own addicts. However, some Thais continue to play a significant role in international drug trafficking and money laundering.

The United States consumes a relatively small portion of worldwide drug production. In 1993, Americans used eight metric tons of heroin, less than 4 per cent of worldwide production, according to the DEA. The U.S. cocaine market absorbs less than one-third of total global production. Domestic marijuana consumption accounts for 817 tons per year: As much as half of that total is grown illegally in the United States.

The great bulk of foreign drug production is consumed in countries other than the United States—often in the regions where the drug crops are grown. Burma, Laos, and Thailand, for example, have almost 500,000 opium and heroin addicts, while India, Iran, and Pakistan account for several million more. According to the World Health Organization, drug abuse is regarded as an emerging "public health and social problem" in Central and East European countries. Cocaine supply appears to be on the rise; heroin addiction is also either increasing or maintaining high levels throughout Europe. In recent years, the abuse of coca paste (known as *basuco*) and cocaine has become a major problem in the South American producer and transit countries. Even if the U.S. demand for drugs declined precipitously, foreign drug suppliers have ready markets in every region of the world and would not stop production.

America's annual drug demand can be supplied from a relatively small growing area and transported in a few airplanes. The illegal drugs Americans consume are grown worldwide and can be cultivated on very little acreage. A poppy field roughly the area of northwest Washington, D.C.—25 square miles—can supply the American heroin market for a year. The annual demand for cocaine can be met from coca fields less than one-quarter the size of Rhode Island, or about 300 square miles.

Effectively reducing the flow of drugs into the United States is exceedingly difficult not only because America's borders are long and porous, but because relatively small amounts of heroin and cocaine are involved. Three DC-3A or five Cessna Caravan turboprop planes could carry the nation's annual heroin supply, while three Boeing 747 cargo planes or 12 trailer trucks could transport the necessary cocaine.

The price structure of the drug market severely limits the potential impact of interdiction and source-country programs. By far, the largest drug-trade profits are made at the level of street sales, not in foreign poppy or coca fields or on the high seas. The total cost of cultivating, refining, and smuggling cocaine to the United States accounts for less than 12 per cent of retail prices here. RAND estimates that the total cost of growing and importing heroin accounts for an even smaller fraction of the retail price. Even if the United States were able to seize half the cocaine coming from South America—or eradicate half the coca crop—the price of cocaine in U.S. cities would increase by less than 5 per cent. Thus, massive interdiction and drug-eradication efforts are far less effective in making drugs more expensive than is enforcement directed at U.S. street markets. Police patrols aimed at increasing the "hassle" factor that drug dealers and drug buyers face exert a much greater impact in discouraging domestic drug abuse and drug crime. These patrols also help deter street violence related to drug dealing.

CONCENTRATE ON DOMESTIC DEMAND

After a century of criticizing other countries for being the source of America's drug problem, it is time to recognize that any lasting solutions lie here at home. In the continuing debate over the supply-side drug strategy, we should remember that the steepest declines in drug use occurred during a period when drug availability was rapidly increasing. In 1982, the National Household Survey showed that 23.3 million Americans used illicit drugs. By 1991, when drug prices hit record lows, only 12.5 million people reported illicit drug use. This dramatic decline reflected public awareness that drugs were harmful as well as growing social disapproval of drug use. Following the death of sports star Len Bias from a cocaine overdose in 1986, cocaine use declined by half, particularly among better-educated Americans inclined to respond to health information.

Unfortunately, these downward trends have now reversed. Marijuana use among eighth graders has doubled since 1992, and illicit drug use among high school seniors is climbing for the first time in a decade. Recent surveys reveal that a majority of both teenagers and adults view drugs as less harmful than they did four years ago. This shift in public attitudes presages further increases in drug problems, particularly among young people for whom the 1980s are ancient history.

Moreover, the drugs of choice in the recent upsurge are primarily domestic, not foreign. Teenagers are using marijuana, LSD, and amphetamines—all of which are produced illegally within the United States. Younger children are turning to common household substances, such as glue, solvents, and aerosols, that are virtually impossible to control. In 1995, one in five eighth graders reported using these inhalants, which produce instant highs and can be lethal.

Experience has shown that reducing demand is the key to sustained progress against drug abuse. A 1994 RAND study, *Controlling Cocaine: Supply Versus Demand Programs*, found that treatment is far more effective than either interdiction or source-country programs in reducing cocaine consumption. Specifically, $34 million invested in treatment reduces annual cocaine use by the same amount as $366 million invested in interdiction or $783 million in source-country programs.

Most Americans do not realize that treatment works—not always, and often not the first time, but eventually. National studies that have followed tens of thousands of addicts through different kinds of programs report that one of the most important factors is the length of time in treatment. One-third of those who stay in treatment longer than three months are drug-free a year after leaving treatment. The success rate jumps to two-thirds when treatment lasts a year or longer. And some programs that provide intensive, highly structured therapy report even better results.

Yet since the early 1980s, treatment has been a low priority nationwide as drug interdiction and enforcement have dominated state and federal spending. In 1995, treatment represented only one-fifth of the more than $13 billion federal drug budget compared with one-quarter 10 years earlier, well before the cocaine epidemic created millions of new addicts. About 40 per cent of the nation's drug addicts cannot get treatment due to inadequate funding for treatment facilities.

Education is the key to protecting our children from drugs, no matter where the offending substances are produced. In the past decade, prevention programs have been developed that significantly reduce new drug use among teenagers. These programs, built on social-learning theory, teach children how to recognize pressures that influence them to smoke, drink, and use drugs and how to resist these pressures through role-playing in the classroom. The impact of these programs is much greater when prevention includes families, media, and the community in a comprehensive effort to discourage drug use. Nonetheless, Congress cut funding for in-school drug education by reducing the Safe and Drug Free Schools Program budget for 1996 from $441 million to $200 million—less than one-sixth the total federal budget for interdiction.

TOWARD A NEW DRUG POLICY

Since America's international drug strategy has not reduced drug problems in this country, should the United States support *any* international efforts to control the illicit drug trade? Yes, to the extent that global cooperation can be effective against the multinational drug networks that undermine the stability of political and financial institutions throughout the world. For example, countries formerly controlled by the Soviet Union in Central Asia and Eastern Europe, as well as Russia itself, are being weakened by the activities of transnational criminal drug syndicates. Many burgeoning entrepreneurs in the newly independent republics have learned that hard drugs are a ready substitute for hard currency in international markets. Opium production in Tajikistan, Turkmenistan, and Uzbekistan has doubled since 1990. Law enforcement in the former Soviet Union is now sporadic at best and is already riven by rampant corruption. In many areas, drug traffickers operate unchallenged.

In this hemisphere, the power of the drug traffickers directly threatens two important democracies, Colombia and Mexico. Although the arrests of the Cali drug lords in August 1995 were an important victory for the Colombian government in its bloody war against the cocaine cartels, Colombia continues to be the world's primary cocaine producer. Evidence that President Ernesto Samper Pizano and some of his Cabinet ministers may have taken cartel money has severely strained Colombia's relations with the United States. Continuing allegations of corruption raise doubts about the government's viability.

The "Colombianization" of Mexico, where drug traffickers penetrated the highest levels of the former Salinas administration and may be involved in high-level assassinations, directly threatens U.S. economic and political interests. Recent revelations that Raul Salinas de Gortari banked at least $84 million in drug money in Switzerland while his brother was president have rocked public confidence in the political system that has governed Mexico for more than 60 years. Although the current president, Ernesto Zedillo, has pledged to clean up drug corruption, he may not have sufficient power to do so. Shortly after Zedillo's most recent pledge, in November 1995, a jet owned by the Cali cartel, loaded with cocaine, landed in Baja California. Witnesses report that the plane was unloaded by uniformed Mexican federal police, who subsequently attempted to conceal the fuselage. The cocaine, estimated to be worth $100 million, has "disappeared."

The failure of American efforts to curtail the flow of drugs into the United States should not cause us to abandon the effort at a time when drug traffic is growing rapidly. The passage of the North American Free Trade Agreement (NAFTA) raised concerns among many in this country that Mexican traffickers would now be able to operate unchecked across the border. Outspoken NAFTA opponents, such as California Democratic senator Dianne Feinstein, have threatened to overturn the treaty largely because of these concerns. Although border controls have very little practical impact on drug availability in America, tough inspections send an important political message that the United States will not tolerate traffickers. The U.S. decision in December 1995 to delay NAFTA's unrestricted-trucking provisions reflects the administration's concern about negative public reaction to removing existing restraints—however weak—on cross-border traffic.

The globalization of national economies broadens the reach of the traffickers, who conduct annual business estimated to be valued at $180 to $300 billion worldwide. In this rapidly evolving scenario, the United States has much to share with other countries in the areas of narcotics intelligence, law enforcement, judicial reform, education, and treatment. For example, DEA intelligence was critically important in facilitating the Colombian government's arrests of the Cali cartel leaders. The FBI, the DEA, and other U.S. enforcement agencies are currently training their Russian counterparts in crime-control techniques, including the surveillance of drug networks.

In addition, the United States can take a leading role in improving international efforts to undermine the money-laundering activities that safeguard the profits of drug traffickers. More than 100 governments have ratified the 1988 United Nations Convention

Against Illicit Traffic in Narcotic Drugs and Psychotropic Substances, a worldwide framework for attacking money laundering and bank secrecy. But a dozen governments representing major financial centers have yet to ratify the convention, and enforcement by participating governments remains inconsistent. While some progress has been made in opening up traditional safe havens for drug money—such as Switzerland and the Bahamas—money laundering is increasing in the rapidly growing East Asian and Pacific financial centers. In his October 1995 speech at the United Nations's 50th anniversary, President Clinton highlighted the need for greater international cooperation against money laundering, threatening economic sanctions against countries that refuse to adopt antilaundering measures.

The computer-aided expansion of world trade and financial services complicates monitoring and enforcement for even the most capable governments. Indeed, according to the State Department, "U.S. financial systems continue to be exploited, at levels probably not approached by any other country." Major banks and investment firms in the United States have been implicated in money laundering, and, in June 1995, three former Justice Department officials were indicted for obstructing justice and assisting the Cali cartel in laundering its profits. By pursuing such major corruption cases, the United States can set an example for other countries beset by high-level involvement in drug trafficking. Still, the $375 million combined budget of the U.S. Organized Crime Drug Enforcement Task Forces—an interagency program that investigates and prosecutes high-level drug traffickers—remains less than one-fourth the level of federal spending on interdiction and international supply-control programs.

International narcotics control, if no longer subject to the elusive counts of drugs eradicated or seized, can serve America's larger interests in strengthening democratic institutions and freeing countries from the grip of criminal organizations. The arrests of the Cali cartel may not have made an appreciable difference in cocaine's availability in the United States, but they are an encouraging indication of that government's determination to fight the drug traffickers. Still, it is important to remember that lasting answers to America's drug problem lie here at home, not abroad. Providing drug-prevention programs for every school child will curb domestic drug abuse more than trying to reduce overseas drug crops. In the final analysis, offering treatment to the nation's addicts will do more to reduce drug consumption than additional drug seizures at the source of production, on the high seas, or at the border.

POSTSCRIPT

Should the United States Put More Emphasis on Stopping the Importation of Drugs?

The drug trade spawns violence; people die from using drugs or by dealing with people in the drug trade; families are ruined by the effects of drugs on family members; prisons are filled with people who were and probably still are involved with illegal drugs; and drugs can devastate aspirations and careers. The adverse consequences of drugs can be seen everywhere in society. How should the government determine the best course of action to follow in remedying the negative effects of drugs?

Two paths that are traditionally followed involve reducing either the supply or the demand for drugs. Four major agencies involved in the fight against drugs in the United States—the Drug Enforcement Administration (DEA), the Federal Bureau of Investigation (FBI), the U.S. Customs Service, and the U.S. Coast Guard—have seized thousands of pounds of marijuana, cocaine, and heroin during the past few years. Drug interdiction appears to be reducing the availability of drugs. But what effect does drug availability have on use?

Annual surveys of high school seniors indicate that availability is not a major factor in drug use. Throughout the 1980s, drug use declined dramatically even though marijuana and cocaine could be obtained easily. According to the surveys, the perceived harm of these drugs, not their availability, is what affects students' drug use. As individuals' perceptions of drugs as harmful increase, usage decreases; as perceptions of harm decrease, usage increases. The extent to which the government's antidrug campaign contributes to the perceived harm of drugs cannot be easily determined.

Efforts to prevent drug use may prove fruitless if people have a natural desire to alter their consciousness. In his 1989 book *Intoxication: Life in the Pursuit of Artificial Paradise* (E.P. Dutton), Ronald Siegel contends that the urge to alter consciousness is as universal as the craving for food and sex.

Articles that examine international efforts to deal with the issue of drugs include "Global Reach: The Threat of International Drug Trafficking," by Rensselaer Lee, *Current History* (May 1995); "Worldwide Drug Scourge," by Stephen Flynn, *The Brookings Review* (Spring 1993); and "Passing Grades: Branding Nations Won't Resolve the U.S. Drug Problem," by Mathea Falco, *Foreign Affairs* (September/October 1995). Christina Jacqueline Johns's book *Power, Ideology, and the War on Drugs: Nothing Succeeds Like Failure* (Praeger Press, 1992) describes the pitfalls of an international approach to addressing drug-related problems.

ISSUE 3

Should All Employers Be Allowed to Drug Test Their Employees?

YES: William J. Judge, from "Drug Testing: The Legal Framework," in Robert S. Wright and Deborah George Wright, eds., *Creating and Maintaining the Drug-Free Workforce* (McGraw-Hill, 1993)

NO: Judith Wagner DeCew, from "Drug Testing: Balancing Privacy and Public Safety," *Hastings Center Report* (March–April 1994)

ISSUE SUMMARY

YES: Attorney William J. Judge asserts that companies should have the right to test their employees for drugs because of the high costs of drug use for American businesses. If there is "reasonable suspicion," Judge believes, drug testing is warranted. He maintains that companies that have implemented drug testing programs have seen a marked decline in on-the-job accidents.

NO: Philosophy professor Judith Wagner DeCew questions the accuracy and effectiveness of drug testing and is concerned that the practice is intrusive and violates individuals' right to privacy. She also contends that a link between drug use and unsafe job performance has not been clearly established.

In 1986 President Ronald Reagan first called for a drug-free federal work-place, ordering all federal employees in "sensitive" jobs to submit to random drug testing. The goal was to begin attacking the drug problem from the demand side and to involve all employees, both public and private, in the fight against drugs. Today, an overwhelming percentage of major corporations in the United States require drug testing as a condition of employment, and government agencies, including the military, have adopted the practice of random urine testing to screen its personnel for illicit drugs.

The impetus for random drug testing was a 1987 collision between an Amtrak train and a Conrail train near Baltimore, Maryland, which claimed the lives of 16 people. Because both the Conrail engineer and brakeman had used marijuana just prior to the wreck, the cause of the crash was immediately tied to drug use, even though the warning indicators on the Conrail train were malfunctioning at the time. This was a strong indication to many that drug testing was needed—if not for the sake of deterring employees from using illicit drugs for their own well-being, then to ensure the safety of others.

The Fourth Amendment of the U.S. Constitution guarantees citizens the right to be protected from unreasonable searches and seizures. With regard to drug testing, this should protect citizens from being tested unless probable cause, or a reason to suppose that an individual is engaged in criminal behavior, is shown. Many people feel that random drug testing is unreasonable because it involves testing even those employees who are not drug users and who have shown no cause to be tested. In addition, drug tests may not clearly differentiate between on-the-job drug use and off-duty drug use. Many people contend that an infringement of personal liberties and an unwarranted invasion of privacy for the sake of the government's drug battle agenda are at stake.

Others believe that all people suffer from individuals' use of illicit drugs. For example, the public pays higher prices due to lost productivity from work-related accidents and job absenteeism caused by drug use. Also, innocent people are often directly victimized by individuals on drugs who inadvertently make dangerous mistakes. From this perspective, random drug tests are not unreasonable searches. Proponents for drug testing contend that the inherent dangers of drug use, particularly while on the job, necessitate drug testing. Accidents and deaths can and do occur because of drug-induced losses of awareness and judgment. The fact that a majority of the Americans who use illicit drugs are employed has convinced many that random drug testing at the workplace should be mandatory.

In the following selections, William J. Judge argues that the benefits of drug testing outweigh the drawbacks. Judge feels that the importance of discouraging drug use and making the workplace safer takes precedence over the concern of whether or not someone's right to privacy has been violated. Logically, if one does not use illegal drugs, then drug testing should not be a concern to that individual.

Judith Wagner DeCew argues that drug testing, especially urine testing, does not prove that one is under the influence of an illegal substance while at work. For example, a person who uses marijuana, which is the most commonly used illegal drug, can test positive for the drug up to 30 days after it was last used. DeCew further argues that the evidence suggesting a correlation between drug use and unsafe job performance is unconvincing. She maintains that the Constitution upholds individual liberties over government agendas and that drug testing sacrifices the American public's right to protection under the Fourth Amendment. Although drug use is a problem in society, DeCew concludes, drug testing is not the fairest and most efficient way of dealing with the problem.

YES

William J. Judge

DRUG TESTING: THE LEGAL FRAMEWORK

INTRODUCTION

Drug testing is a sensitive subject. Thousands of lawsuits have been filed by individuals who believe that their constitutionally protected rights were violated when forced to submit to a drug test or who feel that they were falsely accused of alcohol or drug use and, as a result, suffered some loss. Because of the contentious nature of employee drug and alcohol testing, not only employers, but collection sites, laboratories, and medical review officers performing drug or alcohol tests are "at risk" of loss resulting from errors or omissions in the performance of their various tasks. A verified positive drug or alcohol test can immediately affect the donor's career and reputation. Because those terminated for suspected drug use find it particularly difficult to secure other employment, the loss of a job for a positive drug test is tantamount to the death penalty of employment.

There is, however, another side to the testing question. Too often employers ignore the problem of drug or alcohol use at work or fail to take reasonable steps to detect drug use. An employer that fails to detect drug or alcohol use can face liability if a drug-or alcohol-using employee injures someone while performing his or her duties. Today, the best insurance for employers may be in taking action to prevent accidents triggered by drug or alcohol use by employees.

Employers, collection site operators, laboratories, and other service providers are at risk of lawsuit even if they performed their tasks properly. Steps can be taken, however, that limit the risk of loss inherent in the performance of these various tasks. *While there can be no guarantee that lawsuits will not occur,* these steps are designed to *minimize* the risk of a lawsuit and *to maximize* the likelihood of success if sued.

Those thinking of implementing an employee drug program have many questions: "Is it wisest to utilize drug testing as a means of detecting problems or as a deterrent to employee drug or alcohol use?" "Isn't drug testing too controversial?" "Will I be sued if I choose to test my employee or independent workers?"

Clearly, drug testing is controversial and complex. It is, however, a far safer means of dealing with the problem of drug and alcohol use by employees than to do nothing. *To ignore the problem is to invite disaster.*

BACKGROUND

Employee drug and alcohol use continues to cost American businesses billions of dollars annually. This cost is incurred through increased absenteeism, tardiness, theft, on-the-job injuries, and reduced productivity. Many employers fail to recognize that drugs and alcohol are in their workplace. But one recent survey shows that as many as 64 percent of the employed individuals questioned (50 percent full-time) are admitted current users. As many as 20.1 percent of those full-time employees questioned admitted using marijuana *on the job.*

While existing evidence is anecdotal or the result of unscientific study, it would be difficult to deny that drugs and alcohol have an impact on one's ability to safely perform assigned tasks. One example is tragically illustrative. In 1987 outside Chase, Maryland, a Conrail/Amtrak train accident killed 16 people and injured scores of others. The Conrail engineer admitted smoking marijuana just before the collision.

A number of companies have found a significant reduction in on-the-job accidents after employee drug and alcohol programs were instituted. Utah Power and Light Company conducted an exhaustive study of its employee drug use prevention program and concluded that the reduction in the number of on-the-job vehicle accidents saved it $281,000 between 1985, when the drug testing program was initiated, and 1987 after deducting testing costs. Georgia Power Company's analysis of its testing program resulted in an estimated savings of between $294,000 and $1.7 million by discharging and replacing 198 employees who had failed for-cause drug tests between 1983 and 1987. The overwhelming majority of employers with drug and alcohol programs point to improved workplace safety as a significant benefit from drug testing.

Increasingly, employers are including employee drug testing in their programs as a way to further limit the risks posed by employee drug and alcohol use. While the propriety of drug testing continues to be debated, evidence of the positive impact of testing is emerging. Recent studies of employer drug and alcohol testing programs demonstrate that the costs of employee drug and alcohol use can be contained. These costs can be further reduced by recognizing the value drug testing can have as a defense to workers' compensation claims.

GOVERNMENT ACTION

The federal government and several state governments have recognized the value of employee drug programs. Currently, nine federally mandated drug-free workplace initiatives are under way, and an additional program was recently proposed by the Department of Energy for employees of private contractors. These initiatives include drug testing for employees of businesses regulated by the six agencies of the Department of Transportation, for private employers contracting with the Department of Defense, and for employees of contractors regulated by the Nuclear Regulatory Commission. In addition, the Anti-Drug Abuse Act of 1988 requires certain federal contractors and grant recipients to establish employee drug awareness programs and to exercise "good faith" to maintain a drug-free workplace. A number of states have adopted similar legislation.

Some states have targeted specific areas where employee drug or alcohol use has been shown to have a particularly damaging effect. The states of Arkansas and Louisiana have enacted legislation that defines drug or alcohol use or being "under the influence of intoxicants" as misconduct and that either prohibits an employee discharged for such misconduct from receiving unemployment benefits or limits the amount that can be collected. The states of Florida, Georgia, and Missouri have recently enacted laws that limit or eliminate the workers' compensation benefits of an injured drug-alcohol-positive employee. The states of Iowa and Ohio also enacted laws recently that deny benefits for injuries "caused by" the use of intoxicants. The state of Texas now requires all employers who have 15 or more employees and who maintain workers' compensation insurance coverage to "adopt a policy designed to eliminate drug abuse and its effects in the workplace."

LITIGATION RISK

As noted above, drug testing is controversial. Following the initiation of employee drug testing by the federal government in 1988, more than 60 lawsuits were filed attempting to enjoin the government from proceeding. Such a high level of controversy can be explained by recognizing that drug testing sets two fundamental interests on a collision course—the individual's right of privacy against the employer's responsibility to provide and maintain a safe workplace. The courts were faced with the task of balancing those two interests.

The balance has for the most part favored the need to maintain safety over the limited privacy interest of the workers. This period of resolving the dispute between two interests can be viewed as the first phase in the evolution of legal issues posed by employee drug testing.... [T]wo additional phases of legal issues are living with drug testing day to day and the proper employer response to a positive drug test....

To limit these risks, an employer should take time to thoroughly examine the various regulations issued by the federal agencies mandating testing and state laws that restrict such actions. Additionally, every employer should have an appreciation for the legal framework within which drug testing functions. Becoming a legal scholar is not necessary, but you and your supervisors will better appreciate the serious nature of the decisions to be made. There is no substitute for training and education—*You must be prepared!*

LEGAL ISSUES RELATED TO DRUG TESTING...

Phase One: "Can You Test?"
The first "phase" of legal issues arising out of employee drug testing stems from the question, "Can you test employees for drugs?" Essentially what is being asked is whether drug testing is legal—can employers do it? The simple answer is yes. But there are no simple answers in the field of drug testing. Whether an employer can legally require employees to submit to drug testing depends upon

the answer to many complex—some still unanswered—questions. Among the many issues facing employers as they begin to develop a drug testing program are the following questions:

1. Is the program constitutional?
2. Must the employer bargain with the union?
3. Must the employer follow both federal and state law?

Is the Program Constitutional?   The constitutionality—or legality—of an employer's drug testing program involves the debate between the individual's claimed right of privacy and the employer's demand that the employee submit to drug testing. The resolution of this debate, and the constitutionality of the employer's drug testing program, depends upon who that employer is (government or private employer), who is subject to testing (safety-sensitive employees or all employees), when those subject to testing will be tested (only when there is "suspicion" or randomly), how the testing will be performed, and what will be done with the results. The answer to these questions will be used by a court to determine the legality an employer's drug testing program. The first question that a court reviewing the program must answer, however, is whether the Constitution even applies.

State Action Required.   The restrictions of the United States Constitution *only* apply to *state actors.* Who are state actors? State actors are the government, one of its agencies, or a private company or individual acting at the direction of the government (i.e., in compliance with a federal or state law or as a subcontractor). *Otherwise, individuals and private employers*

are not state actors! Why is this important? Only state actors are limited by the Constitution. The concept of privacy exists only if the Constitution applies. Therefore, unless the employer requiring the employee or applicant to submit to a drug rest is a state actor, there will be no limits on who, when, how, or where an individual may be tested, because without state action the right of privacy does not exist. An employee of a strictly private employer cannot bring a lawsuit based upon the right of privacy and hope to convince the court to enjoin the testing because the prerequisite state or federal action does not exist.

The Fourth Amendment.   Employers compelled by government agencies to institute a drug testing program are bound by the limits of the United States Constitution. The United States Supreme Court in 1989 concluded that private employers implementing drug testing "at the behest of" the federal government are "state actors" to whom the Constitutional limitations apply. The regulations upheld by the Court in *Skinner v. Railway Executives Association* are similar to those which will serve as the basis of most employer programs. It is appropriate, therefore, to have some sense of the Constitution's application to drug testing.

First, it must be understood that a drug test is a search. Therefore, the limitation on government searches found in the Fourth Amendment to the Constitution apply. The Fourth Amendment provides in part as follows:

[t]he right of the people to secure in their persons, houses, papers and effects, against unreasonable search and seizure shall not be violated. . . .

Essentially, this means we all have the right to be left alone. Whether privacy exists as a matter of law depends upon a subjective and an objective test. Subjectively, the individual asserting the right must be able to demonstrate that he is treating the subject of the search (e.g., a work locker or desk, a purse, a home) privately. If anyone and everyone is allowed access to a work locker, any limited privacy that may have existed is considered to be waived. Objectively, it must be shown that we as a society (through the courts as our representative) would agree that it was reasonable for the individual to treat the subject of the search privately. One who keeps illicit drugs in a work locker cannot reasonably expect to be protected from a search for such items. Privacy, therefore, may exist, but under the circumstances of the case it may not be protectable.

If both tests are met, then the court will conclude that the concept of privacy exists. The court must then decide if that privacy, under the circumstances, is protectable. The search is protectable only if the government fails to prove the reasonableness of the search.

No government agent can require an individual to submit to a search unless reason exists for that search and the search is conducted in a reasonable manner. The obvious question, then, is what is a reasonable search? To be legal, a search must be reasonable at its inception and as carried out. To be reasonable at its inception, the government must establish a legitimate interest in the search. For example, the Supreme Court in *Skinner* concluded that the Federal Railway Administration's interest in maintaining the safety of rail travel was legitimate and justified the need for its drug testing regulations.

If the search is found to be needed, the method used to conduct the search must also be found to be reasonable. The Court in *Skinner* found the methods adopted by the Federal Railway Administration to, likewise, be reasonable. The Court was convinced that the scientific methods employed along with the steps taken to ensure the individual's sense of dignity established the reasonableness of the search.

If privacy is shown to exist and the government also proves it has a legitimate need for the search (drug tests) and that the method of searching is reasonable, how does the court decide who wins? The judge must balance the competing interests. (Refer to Fig. 1.)

The left column in Fig. 1 represents circumstances where privacy can exist. As you proceed down the column from the situation where luggage is subject to a search to the search of a home or bodily fluids, your expectation that privacy is protectable by a court is enhanced. Simply put, your home is more protectable than your luggage or your purse, and you expect the courts, when asked, to take appropriate action (i.e., issue an injunction) to protect your privacy. If the government wishes to search your home, significant proof of a reasonable need must be shown. Less proof is required to search your purse.

When the search is a drug test at work, it can be seen that the privacy interest is not as protectable as that at home. The privacy expectation is limited. When balanced against the government's significant need to protect safety at work, the majority of courts have found in favor of the government and upheld the testing regulations. But as you proceed down the right side of the column in Fig. 1, going from preemployment

Figure 1

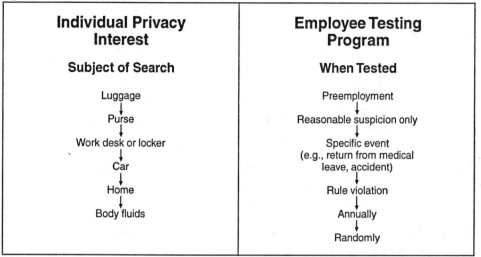

and reasonable suspicion testing to random testing, the level of invasion into the individual's privacy is enhanced; random testing is the ultimate invasion into privacy. Why? Because, generally under the Fourth Amendment a search is not reasonable unless based upon some level of suspicion. By definition, random testing involves no suspicion. But the United States Supreme Court in *Skinner* made it clear that where the government interest to be protected is sufficient, drug testing can occur even where no level of suspicion exists.

NO

Judith Wagner DeCew

DRUG TESTING: BALANCING PRIVACY AND PUBLIC SAFETY

Recent increases in the use of illegal drugs and problems related to that use have raised a variety of public health and safety concerns and have led many to propose drug testing as one of the best ways to combat the proliferation of drug use. Although my focus is testing for drugs, it is worth noting that similar calls for increased testing have arisen due to the spread of the human immunodefidency virus (HIV) and the threat it poses to those exposed to it. Clearly, these public health and safety concerns conflict with the privacy claims of those being targeted for testing. Nevertheless, many view the public safety threat as serious enough to override completely any individual privacy interests. Indeed, public opinion polls indicate that there is wide spread support for a variety of testing programs, even those that are random and mandatory.[1]

But it is misleading to view a public policy decision about when and how to conduct drug tests as a simple choice between privacy and public safety. What is less often mentioned is that the issues surrounding testing programs are far more complex than the foregoing suggests. It is both difficult and unwise to reach conclusions about whether testing programs are justified without specifying what type of testing is being proposed (e.g., blood, urine), what is being tested for (e.g., alcohol, drugs, HIV infection), who is initiating the tests (e.g., government agencies, employers, insurance companies), the goals of the tests and the likelihood that they will reduce or eradicate the problem, the harm that would result without the tests, the costs of the proposed testing program, the accuracy of the type of test under consideration, whether confirmatory tests will be added, whether the testing will be mandatory or voluntary, whether the tests will be random or will selectively target particular groups, whether an identifiable showing of suspicion or performance decline will prompt the tests, and how test results will be used and distributed. Furthermore, one must assess which goals of a particular drug-testing program are achievable, and must balance those against the consequences of the testing. The crucial question is to determine when that balance provides adequate moral justification for the testing.

From Judith Wagner DeCew, "Drug Testing: Balancing Privacy and Public Safety," *Hastings Center Report*, vol. 24, no. 2 (March–April 1994), pp. 17–23. Copyright © 1994 by The Hastings Center. Reprinted by permission.

My aim is to address many of these issues by setting out the various arguments and constitutional considerations both in favor of and against certain testing programs. While it should be clear from the above list of concerns relating to drug and HIV tests that broad generalizations are difficult to make, I shall discuss how major public health and safer goals can be addressed seriously while still taking precautions to protect privacy vigorously. Drug abuse should not be tolerated in the workplace or when it threatens the safety of others. But care must be taken to limit the extent to which drug testing intrudes on people's privacy. The ideal is to use the technology selectively, with adequate moral justification, and with enough safeguards and precautions to ensure that testing is done thoughtfully and responsibly.

ARGUMENTS IN FAVOR OF DRUG TESTING

Both the government and private employers argue that they have a significant interest in testing citizens and employees for a wide variety of reasons: (1) to fight the "drug war" by weeding out users and curbing drug use; (2) to insure safety by revealing conditions that pose a serious threat to co-workers or the public; (3) to maintain an unimpaired and effective work force; (4) to identity those who will be unable to work in the future; (5) to reduce the costs of employee health care plans; and (6) to maintain public confidence in the integrity and trustworthiness of their operations. Insurers argue in addition that testing is necessary because it is fundamentally unfair to require relatively healthy policyholders to subsidize the costs of health care and life insurance benefits for those with high mortality risks, and because banning insurer testing might leave the industry financially unable to afford to offer individual insurance policies at all.[2] Taken together, these provide strong political, moral, and economic reasons to consider seriously the option of drug testing in some form.

Moreover, the alarming levels of drug abuse in America are estimated to be very costly. The illegal narcotics traffic of about $27 to $110 billion each year correlates with the rising crime rate. In fact, studies showing that "drug use is very much a characteristic of serious and violent offenders" and that "increasing or reducing the level of drug abuse is associated with a corresponding increase or reduction in criminality" may have provided the earliest theoretical justification for initiating drug testing programs.[3] A further consequence is increased medical expenses and rehabilitation costs for drug users.

It has also been claimed that the industrial costs of drug abuse are enormous:

> In human terms they include lost jobs, injuries, illnesses, and deaths. In economic terms they include property damage, tardiness, absenteeism, lost productivity, quality control problems, increased health insurance costs, increased worker's compensation costs, the cost of replacing and training new employees, and employee theft.[4]

According to government estimates, drug abuse cost employers in the United States $33 billion in 1985. More recently, government officials have claimed that these costs are as high as $60 to $100 billion.[5]

Drug testing is taken seriously as a partial solution to the growing drug problem because of the purported results of urinalysis programs instituted by many agencies and employers. The

Barcelona Olympics renewed the testing controversy and focused public attention on the athletes who had been disqualified for failing drug tests and on official claims that the tests do deter athletes from taking performance-enhancing drugs. Private companies report that the effects of drug testing programs include increased employee productivity, enhanced job efficiency; significant declines in lost work time and accident rates, and decreased hazards to other employees and the public. If correct, these findings suggest that employer-initiated testing is an efficient way of addressing employee drug abuse and may he a useful deterrent in other contexts as well.

Indeed, drug testing is now commonplace for many workers. In 1986 President Reagan authorized testing all federal job applicants and ordered random testing of federal employees in positions referred to as "safety sensitive." Random urinalysis is utilized for job applicants and sometimes current employees at numerous private businesses, including IBM, DuPont, Exxon, Lockheed, Federal Express, AT&T, the *New York Times*, some Wall Street firms, and over 25 percent of Fortune 500 companies as well.[6] Testing in the trucking industry, for rapid transit and airline workers, law enforcement officials, and athletes is widespread. And recent court cases continue to address the constitutionality of testing teachers, postal workers, customs officials, criminal suspects, prisoners, and many others. The tests are so pervasive that according to the National Institute on Drug Abuse (NIDA) as many as 15 million working Americans had their urine tested for illegal drugs in 1990.[7] Interestingly, these high numbers increase the amounts of money involved, and so have made drug testing a very profitable business.

THREATS TO PRIVACY

Despite its popularity, there is good reason to question the justifiability of drug testing. Supreme Court Justice Antonin Scalia, for example, has referred to the practice as a "needless indignity." Drug testing clearly intrudes on individual privacy in a number of distinct ways. One central concern is the technological and physical intrusiveness into a person's biological functions in the actual procedures used for collecting samples. If a blood test is used, it necessarily involves puncturing the skin. If a urinalysis is utilized, the sample must sometimes be gained under direct observation to guard against drug-free substitutions and falsification of results. The additional psychological intrusion of urinating on demand, under surveillance, is not minimal. And critics point out that there are less intrusive ways to identify drug abusers—mainly, observation to detect impairment.

Moreover, besides confirming or disconfirming the presence of drugs in the body, analysis of blood and urine samples may reveal numerous physiological facts about the party being tested that he or she may not want shared with others. Tests can reveal such conditions as the use of contraceptives, pregnancy, epilepsy, manic depression, diabetes, schizophrenia, and heart trouble, for example.

Revelations of this sort are particularly troubling because they raise the privacy question concerning how the results of drug tests are handled. In some testing programs, individuals are not even notified that their samples will be tested. If they are notified and then are informed of the results, it is usually not clear who else has access to the results and what controls there are for maintaining the confidentiality of the information the test reveals. Disclosure of information from drug tests can be embarrassing, can lead to loss of employment and financial loss, discrimination, and further disclosures. There is a serious worry that the individual loses control over any information gained from the tests. Moreover, it is not unreasonable to maintain that employees, for example, should be free from scrutiny during their nonworking hours as long as their activities are not affecting their performance.

FURTHER ARGUMENTS AGAINST TESTING

Opponents of drug testing also focus on the limitations of the testing procedures, arguing that the tests are highly inaccurate. One worry is the sensitivity of the tests. Many types of tests, opponents argue, yield inaccurate results as often as 60 percent of the time. Even if the tests are more highly accurate, they claim, innocent parties will be harmed because most tests produce a large number of false positives, results indicating drug use when there has been none. Such false positives can arise from the use of medications, or passive inhalation of marijuana smoke, for example. Critics worry, moreover, that the technology employed for many drug tests allows false negatives as well, and they cite the human error of lab personnel that further implicates the accuracy of results.

A related issue involves the problems of interpreting the results of drug tests. Most tests set a threshold level that is deemed to establish drug use. But there are few standards for determining how or where that level should be set. Moreover, a true positive may indicate an isolated instance of drug use in the past, not a habitual pattern; interpretation of results does not usually differentiate the two or reveal when the drug was used.

Another serious concern is that the tests cannot establish whether a subject is under the influence of a drug at the time the test is administered, and the tests are incapable of determining if and how much drug use impairs the individual's performance level or actually affects his or her behavior. There is general agreement in the scientific community that "testing does not discriminate between drug use that impairs performance and drug use that does not impair performance. It does not even determine impairment at the time of the test."[8] At best, what is established is whether a person's body contains traces of chemicals that may indicate previous use. Short of this, tests may merely indicate involuntary exposure or an error in procedure. Notably, then, test results may only show nonperformance-related conditions that are arbitrary for determining employment or the quality of performance.

Finally, critics worry that tests justified for people in safety sensitive positions can be abused because of the malleability of the term 'safety sensitive.' Legislators or employers may expand the definition so that it becomes a camouflage for unprincipled random testing.

TESTS AND ACCURACY CONCERNS

The most commonly administered drug tests are conducted through urinalysis, in part because these are less intrusive than blood tests and in part because they are less expensive to administer. Urinalysis tests can be divided into two types. The most frequently used are administered as presumptive screening tests. The most common involves the enzyme multiplied immunoassay technique (EMIT), others the radioimmunoassay (RIA) and the thin layer chromatography (TLC) tests. These tests are intended to be used easily, rapidly and inexpensively, to identify specimens that most likely contain the sought-after substances. One limit of immunoassay tests is that they are designed to detect only one drug or metabolite or a few closely related ones. The (sometimes erroneous) assumption is that a positive test identifies a user—of marijuana, cocaine, or amphetamines, for example—and a negative test shows a nonuser. Although relatively inexpensive, the screening tests are recognized to be nonspecific and insensitive.

For those programs that add confirmatory tests, a second and more accurate procedure, gas chromatography—mass spectrometry (GC/MS) assessment is also used. In these cases, a sample is reported positive only if both the screening and confirmatory tests are positive. But confirmatory tests are complex, slow to complete, and more expensive than immunoasay tests. A single (GC/MS) test costs $75 or more. And it is worth noting that confirmatory methods for some drugs are not readily available.

The reliability of the immunoassay screening test is undermined by many factors alluded to above. The high rate of false positives cited by critics can arise from temperature changes in the sample or the presence of substances other than the ones being sought. Positive cannabinoid results have been obtained from urine samples of people who have taken anti-inflammatory drugs such as ibuprofen (Advil, Motrin, etc.) or naproxen, and similar medications might affect the results of tests for barbiturates. Cold remedies such as Contac or Sudafed can

suggest the presence of amphetamines, and positive tests for morphine can be obtained from taking drugs containing codeine, including many popular cough syrups. A metabolite of cocaine was measured in a subject who had had one cup of an herbal tea which was alleged to have contained decocainized coca leaves, but in fact had about 5 mg. of cocaine per tea bag.[9] Thus critics conclude,

> a positive urine test, regardless of the absolute concentration of the sample, provides no information on the amount of drug ingested or inhaled, the time or duration of exposure, or the behavioral effect of the drug. A positive test, if confirmed, may establish exposure, but it does not confirm drug abuse or intoxication, either at the time the sample was obtained or any time prior to that; conversely, a negative test does not rule out abuse or intoxication.[10]

False positive and negative test results indicate the importance of conducting confirmatory tests on samples. But the cost and time required limit the extent to which confirmatory tests are used. Moreover, even a combination of screening and confirmatory tests is susceptible to glaring deficiencies. The threshold or cutoff value that separates positive and negative test results varies depending on the amount of the drug being tested for. If the cutoff is set too low, then a confirmatory test may not actually confirm the result of the initial screening test. If the cutoff is set too high, some positive specimens may be missed, but confirmations will be more reliable. "Decisions on choosing cutoffs depend on how many false negatives, false positives, and unconfirmed test results are economically and scientifically acceptable."[11] When testing donors for blood banks, clearly allowing more false positives is preferable to allowing any false negatives. But in other contexts the balance is less clear, and value judgments may differ more widely.

Another difficulty is that for those who wish to work at it there are ways to defeat the tests. Those who practice timed abstinence or who ingest large amounts of fluids can dilute the concentration of a drug in urine to below the cutoff amount. Adding salt, vinegar, bleach, liquid soap, blood, or another interfering substance can adulterate samples and produce false negative results that do not rule out abuse.

Quality control in the lab also calls into question the accuracy of test results. Critics claim that technicians are often given minimal training. There can be procedural mishaps as simple as misidentifying a sample, and technicians may not know how to interpret the findings. Signs of a single instance of marijuana use, for example, can persist in urine samples for days or even weeks, but lab technicians might not recognize the importance of including such information along with a positive result. Private laboratories claim that their work is 95 to 99 percent accurate, but they have given little documentation for their claims, nor have the results of proficiency testing for labs been made available.[12]

To the extent drug tests produce false negatives, they are ineffective in identifying users. For those who test positive falsely, the implications for reputation, employment, and freedom may be grave indeed. It is widely agreed that blood tests more accurately measure evidence of intoxication or abuse for alcohol and other drugs. Because concentrations in the blood are usually proportional to concentrations in the brain, blood tests will also be more likely to measure performance capacity with greater reliability. In addition, blood tests are taken directly from individuals by lab personnel, so with trustworthy technicians, tampering with specimens is almost impossible. But analyses of blood specimens are also more difficult, complex, and costly. Moreover, because blood concentrations peak and decrease very rapidly, and back calculations in time are rarely possible for most drugs, there is often just a short window of time when a blood test will be useful.

REVIEWING THE THREAT TO PUBLIC SAFETY

Given the many difficulties associated with drug tests, it is worth reconsidering the extent of the evidence that urine tests, even with confirmatory testing, will result in improvement in health, safety, and performance. While such claims are made regularly, it is difficult to find confirmatory data. It is also difficult to assess the extent of the deterrent effect of drug test programs. Many in the medical field argue bluntly that "[o]bjective biomedical science tells us that urine testing is of no value in coping with illicit drug use.[13]

Even for transportation accidents, where it is claimed there is evidence that drug impairment plays a major role, evaluations of the findings are unclear. After nearly every plane or rail crash there is (often sensational) publicity about drug tests for pilots and engineers. It is rare, however, for the data to show evidence that employees were impaired by drugs other than alcohol, or that random urine drug testing would have prevented the accident. It has been pointed out that "[f]or testing to be fully effective, every worker would have to be tested daily for every drug that might impair performance, the results would have to be available before he started work, and he would have to be under constant surveillance while at work to make sure he did not use a drug while working."[14]

It is worth noting that marijuana accounts for a huge majority of positive findings nationwide—perhaps as many as 90 percent—because it is the most widely used illegal drug and because it persists in urine for a month or more, compared to two days for most drugs. Yet because of its persistence, many of those true positive drug tests have little or no implication for performance difficulty. Finally, a 1989 NIDA report contradicted claims of increasing illegal drug use. According to the report, illegal drug use has been decreasing for ten years, and the decline accelerated over the latter five of those years.[15]

Thus the correlation between drug use and unsafe or risky job performance is not definitely established. Nevertheless, there are studies that show a significant correlation between positive drug tests and poorer scores on certain general measures of job performance, such as absenteeism and dismissal for other reasons. In addition, studies of airline pilots under simulated conditions indicate diminished ability to perform various maneuvers with prior drug use, including marijuana. Thus there is at least some evidence of a correlation between drug use and performance, particularly in one safety sensitive occupation, suggesting a possible role for appropriately targeted drug tests. One challenge, then, is to determine when drug testing will actually contribute to the goals of public health and safety.

CONSTITUTIONAL GUIDELINES AND THE COURTS

The first two cases on drug testing to reach the Supreme Court were argued in 1988. From the decisions issued the following year, it is clear that the Court held that urine tests are a significant intrusion into a fundamentally private domain.[16] Since then, virtually every court that has addressed the issue has found that urinalysis and blood tests intrude on privacy as a search and seizure forbidden under the Fourth Amendment. Courts have mainly focused on the privacy invasions involved, first, in the process of urination and the manner in which the specimen is obtained, and second, in the individual's interest in safeguarding the confidentiality of the information contained in the sample. While drug tests might also violate the Fifth Amendment guarantee against self-incrimination, the Fourteenth Amendment protection of due process, and constitutional privacy interests, courts have nevertheless taken the privacy claims of the Fourth Amendment to be the most forceful constitutional threats.

Courts have been somewhat divided over how intrusive unobserved urine testing is. But they have generally agreed that compulsory urinalysis infringes on an individual's expectation of privacy both in the process and in the loss of control over information. Nevertheless, case law currently indicates that some drug screening is constitutionally permissible. Fourth Amendment protection is not absolute, and the courts have traditionally used a two-part test to decide when the government has infringed on an individual's Fourth Amendment privacy. First, the individual must show a "subjective expectation of privacy," and second, the expectation must be "one that society considers reasonable."[17]

The key, then, is the determination of when drug tests are "reasonable." No court has held testing to be a violation of the Fourth Amendment when there is a showing of "reasonable suspicion" that the individual has been using illegal drugs. But the Supreme Court also allowed testing of any customs officials in positions directly involving the interdiction of drugs or where firearms were required to be carried in the line of duty. The evolving legal standard is that reasonable suspicion be required except for random testing upheld for public employees in safety sensitive positions, law enforcement positions, or where employees have access to classified materials.

It is not surprising that courts have taken Fourth Amendment privacy seriously in the context of drug tests. Historically, stomach pumping, strip searches, and body cavity checks to gain evidence have been judged unconstitutional. By analogy, although United States banks are surely concerned to insure that their employees are not embezzlers, that does not entitle them to search all bank employees and their homes on the chance that they may uncover a dishonest employee.[18]

It is troubling, however, that many courts have refused to address concerns about testing error, and have avoided discussions of the implications of false positives and false negatives. Moreover, protection against warrantless and unreasonable searches does not apply in the private sector, and most private sector drug testing programs have survived legal challenge thus far. Nonconstitutional state regulations are largely absent. The few that have been enacted form a patch-work of conflicting guidelines. Some, such as Utah's, promote employer interests by allowing random testing of all employees. Others have been more sensitive to employee interests, but the great majority of states have no guidelines at all. Still, the model of the courts embracing a basic concern with protecting Fourth Amendment privacy may indicate that those initiating testing programs that do not take sufficient care to address privacy intrusions will face an increasing risk of liability.

ETHICAL JUSTIFICATIONS

Certainly there is a very real problem of drug abuse in this country. Yet drug testing in the workplace may not be the most effective way of tackling the problem. I have explained the various privacy interests at stake for test subjects, including the intrusion of the testing procedure, the revelation of additional medical information, and the difficulties arising from false results and from mismanagement of the information gained. I have also reviewed concerns over the accuracy of screening tests, the difficulty of interpreting results, the expense and difficulty of confirmatory tests, the lack of information on performance ability, and concerns that tests may not ferret out those who are a threat to others. These considerations lead to worry that drug tests cannot adequately protect others from harm as intended. They also provide compelling arguments that widespread and random drug testing is unnecessarily intrusive, unwise, and inefficient.

It might seem, therefore, that we have reached the inevitable conclusion that drug testing is never morally justifiable. I believe such a conclusion would be too hasty, however. That a practice is difficult to justify does not make it impossible to justify in all cases. The key moral issues involve determining when the interests of others are significant enough to outweigh the threats to test subjects and when the achievable goals outweigh the negative consequences of testing. Although I cannot address every conceivable case, I believe that in carefully circumscribed circumstances, drug testing can be defended as morally justifiable. But even then, I will defend testing only when administered with stringent procedural safeguards.

Some cases seem absolutely clear. My sense is that most would agree that tests should be permissible and perhaps even mandated for potential blood donors. The expectation is that donated blood will be clean, and the interests of those needing transfusions are highly significant. The condition is often life-threatening, and the risk of harm to the recipient is immediate and certain. Moreover, such testing is not random, but targets only those wishing to donate blood.

In less clear cases, what considerations can override the privacy invasions and other deleterious consequences of testing? The practice can be justified if there is a substantial and demonstrable likelihood that a significant drug problem exists, and if the testing program targets those potentially causing the problem in the hope that it can be alleviated. That is, I believe the concerns with testing enumerated above are significant enough to require substantial evidence of an existing drug problem and a reasonable expectation of resolving it, before testing becomes morally defensible.

If there is probable cause or reasonable suspicion to believe there is a drug use problem, such as substantial evidence of frequent use or abuse of drugs by a group or individual over a significant amount of time, and if it can be shown likely to be affecting the safety of customers (e.g., passengers), co-workers, or products, then random testing and follow-up to single out those risking the welfare of others gains ethical force. Thus I support, for instance, the Supreme Court's decision in *Skinner v. Railway Labor Executives Association* to allow tests of railway workers where there was evidence of frequent alcohol and drug use and a demonstrated connection between use and accidents. In that particular case it seemed that the safety threat was clear, substantial (at minimum 23 percent of the railway workers were found to be "problem drinkers"), and the subjects formed a targeted group that, if it became drug-free, could decrease the railway accident rate significantly.

Additionally, when individuals or groups show some evidence of performance impairment and the likelihood of a serious accident or defective product is considerably heightened by it, drug testing may also be morally justified. Even if it is not certain that the impairment is due to drug use, the individual's behavior can be worrisome enough to defeat claims that they must not be intruded upon. The presumption of a person's innocence is, in such cases, rightly called into question. A drug test, administered with procedural safeguards, can help determine if drug use is indeed contributing to the performance difficulty observed. In sum, the studies concerning difficulties with drug tests do not rule out testing when some causal showing, performance impairment, or reasonable suspicion of drug use exists.

In contrast, however, absent such evidence, drug testing programs instituted to accomplish general deterrence of drug use, or based on generalized claims about the need to fight the "war on drugs," do not carry sufficient moral justification to outweigh all the negative consequences and difficulties of drug testing. With no showing of a significant problem there is too little evidence that there will be any deterrent effect or any progress made to combat drug use. Thus I find insufficient ethical justification for the Supreme Court's judgment in *National Treasury Employees v. Von Raab*, which upheld random testing of customs workers by virtue of the job they held, even though there was almost no evidence of a drug problem either by individuals or across a section of the group of customs workers.

One difficulty of mandating testing for persons in positions that count as safety sensitive is that it is difficult to assure that this is an accurate, not merely expedient, classification. Moreover, people holding positions where they are required to carry firearms or have access to classified material have already been subjected to extensive background checks. The Court in *Raab* appealed to a generalized compelling interest that customs employees not use drugs even when off duty, and to the extraordinary safety and national security hazards of drug use among customs officials. But combined with the admission that customs is largely drug-free and that previous drug use was not the reason for establishing the testing program, those appeals lose moral force. The actual purposes cited for the testing were to deter drug use among employees in the specified positions and to keep drug users from being promoted into such positions. It was claimed that customs officials who use drugs are more susceptible to bribery and that those in jobs where they may use firearms depend uniquely

on their judgment and dexterity, both of which could be compromised by drug use. One major difficulty, however, was that there was at best a potential for harm to others, yet no clear threat of harm. Second, there was virtually no evidence that any customs officials had a drug problem and so no reason to suppose that there was any need to deter any of them, or that testing could reduce drug use. There was minimal likelihood the testing program would have any impact at all.

I have argued that several criteria must be met for drug testing programs to be deemed morally justifiable. The most basic is that a significant drug problem must actually be apparent, through a causal showing, performance impairment, or other reasonable suspicion. We might well consider, therefore, whether a less objectionable alternative focusing more directly on performance can effectively protect the public from harm. Some have argued, for example, that state-of-the-art employee assistance programs, combined with proper education of supervisory personnel, can be as effective as or more effective than drug testing in minimizing harm to others.

This is a provocative suggestion, and it may be that, when fully developed, the implementation of such programs ultimately will be able to supersede drug testing even in the cases where I have defended it. At present, however, there are a number of difficulties with advocating such programs in place of any drug testing at all. First, the educational process of supervisors is critical, and it could take much time to develop and implement it adequately. It would be a mistake to underestimate the scope of the education necessary for such programs to be successful. Second, employee assistance programs could be economically more costly and thus less feasible than drug testing programs. Small businesses, for example, may find it prohibitive to introduce adequate employee assistance programs for only a few isolated cases. Third, it is difficult to see how to mandate procedural safeguards for employees when the programs are individualized and run by supervisory personnel. Some may worry about what recourse or appeal mechanism an employee has if a supervisor is distrustful or is erroneously convinced of an employee's abuse. Drug testing programs have the virtue, perhaps, of being more easily subject to federal regulations protecting test subjects' interests uniformly.

Ideally and more characteristically, however, employee assistance programs are set up so supervisory personnel only refer employees for assessment by health care professionals and for treatment recommendations. The object of these assistance programs is not intended to be a determination of wrongdoing. Rather, the goal is to provide treatment recommendations to employees who are chemically dependent or substance abusers, with the assurance of continued employment if treatment is successful. Perhaps the most notable difficulty with these programs is the lack of hard evidence that a high percentage of chemically dependent employees are actually identified and then treated.

PROCEDURAL SAFEGUARDS AND RECOMMENDATIONS

Even in the narrowly circumscribed cases when drug testing can ethically be justified on my view, I believe it is necessary to mandate precautions to protect privacy and minimize error. To be effective, these should be embodied in federal guidelines that are backed up with sanctions for violations and that recommend combining test results with follow-up assessments of performance.

To reiterate, we should mandate that drug tests be conducted only after there is evidence of a reasonable probability of drug abuse. Reasonable suspicion might be indicated if there is perceived impairment, deficient output or performance, major unexplained change in attitude, or other behavior arousing suspicion. When reasonable suspicion is required to justify testing, there is less intrusion into workers' privacy, the testing program is less vulnerable to constitutional attack, and supervisors are forced to oversee more fully the performance of those in their charge.

Even when fully justified, drug testing plans should be explained in writing, and those who might be tested should be made aware of the reasons for the testing program. They will then know whether the testing will involve direct observation, whether it will be voluntary or mandated as a condition of employment, and so on. We might also require that employees be informed in advance whether a testing program is to be random or required as a condition of employment.

Due to the inadequacies and inaccuracies of various types of tests, we should require that whoever initiates a testing program give confirmatory tests for those with positive results. If the initial screening is selective, as I have argued it should be, the cost of confirmatory testing will not be prohibitive. People testing positive should be allowed an opportunity to explain the test results and to have the sample retested at an independent laboratory.

We can hope that the testing technology being developed by Roche, Abbott, and others will continue to improve. Methods are being did covered to discern from a test if a common medication has been the cause of a false positive result. The possibility of less intrusive and more accurate tests—using saliva or hair samples, for example—is also under investigation. In the meantime, it seems reasonable to require laboratories to justify the thresholds used for determining positive and negative readings on tests. Laboratories ought also to be required to state the length of time the drug remains in the system, the test's inability to determine performance limitations, and similar relevant information. This will set the results in perspective and will help explain what they mean. It might also be reasonable to mandate laboratory procedures such as requiring documentation of all handling of a sample and requiring all samples to be divided into two containers, one for analysis and one for freezing in case the results are contested later.

Finally, detailed guidelines must be bet up to protect the confidentiality of the information gained from tests. It seems that with computer data banks of medical information it may be almost impossible to guarantee confidentiality. But it can certainly be a legal requirement, with strong sanctions for noncompliance, that test results not be used for any purpose other than that originally articulated, and that test information not be released without permission to anyone other than the individual tested. Confidentiality can be further enhanced by requiring "anonymous" testing, which marks samples by coded numbers rather than names.

This may appear to be a burdensome list of requirements to impose on testing programs. But the requirements not only protect individual privacy, they also encourage government and employers to use testing only when it is most likely to be helpful in averting public harm. Time, energy, and money not used on widespread random tests could then be better spent on monitoring performance through observation, controlling alcohol abuse on the job, and limiting illegal drug traffic in the United States.

My goal has been to recognize the benefits of drug testing when there is probable cause or clear substantial evidence of abuse, with likely correlation to a safety threat and a reasonable possibility of achieving the desired effects. Mass testing without suspicion is intrusive, inefficient, often inaccurate, and a waste of resources. I have suggested restrictions aimed at maximizing privacy and accuracy of results while still allowing identification of those who use illegal drugs.

REFERENCES

1. See, for example, the data cited in Michael R. O'Donnell, "Employee Drug Testing—Balancing the Interests in the Workplace: A Reasonable Suspicion," *Virginia Law Review* 74 (1988): 969–1009, at 971–72.
2. Nancy Perkins, "Prohibiting the Use of the Human Immunodeficiency Virus Antibody Test by Employers and Insurers," *Harvard Journal on Legislation* 25 (1988): 275–315, at 297–303.
3. Cathryn Jo Rosen and John S. Goldkamp, "The Constitutionality of Drug Testing at the Bail Stage," *Journal of Criminal Law and Criminology* 80 (1989): 114–76, at 117.
4. Edward S. Adams, "Random Drug Testing of Government Employees: A Constitutional Procedure," *University of Chicago Law Review* 54 (1988): 1335–72, at 1337, citing Thomas Geidt.
5. John Horgan, "Test Negative," *Scientific American* 262 (March 1990): 18–19, at 18.
6. Adams, "Random Drug Testing," p. 1337. Steven Wisotsky claims testing is practiced at as many as 80 percent of Fortune 500 companies, in his "A Society of Suspects: The War on Drugs and Civil Liberties," *Policy Analysis* 180 (1992): 1–49, at 12.
7. Horgan, "Test Negative," p. 18.
8. Alan R. Westin et al., "College and University Policies on Substance Abuse and Drug Testing," *Academe* 78, no. 3 (1992): 17–23, at 20.

9. Arthur J. McBay, "Drug-Analysis Technology: Pitfalls and Problems of Drug Testing," *Clinical Chemistry* 33, no. 11 (1987): 33B–40B, at 34B.

10. David J. Greenblatt and Richard I. Shader, "Say 'No' to Drug Testing," *Journal of Clinical Psychopharmacology* 10, no. 3 (1990): 157–59, at 158.

11. McBay, "Drug-Analysis Technology," p. 34B.

12. McBay, "Drug-Analysis Technology," P. 37B.

13. Greenblatt and Shader, "Say 'No' to Drug Testing," p. 157.

14. Arthur J. McBay, "Drugs and Transportation Safety," *Journal of Forensic Sciences* 35 (1990): 523–29, at 523.

15. Horgan, "Test Negative," p. 19.

16. National Treasury Employees Union v. Raab, 109 S. Ct. 1384 (1989); Skinner v. Railway Labor Executives Association, 109 S. Ct. 1402 (1989).

17. Katz v. United States, 389 U.S. 347, 361 (1967).

18. The analogy is from Phyllis T. Bookspan, "Jar Wars: Employee Drug Testing, the Constitution, and the American Drug Problem," *American Criminal Law Review* 26 (1988): 359–400, at 388.

POSTSCRIPT

Should All Employers Be Allowed to Drug Test Their Employees?

As a follow-up to the discussion of whether or not to allow random drug testing, one needs to ask what should be done with people who test positive for drugs. Should they be fired or helped? Is the purpose of drug testing to eliminate workers who use drugs or to help them? Do companies have the right to punish workers for activities engaged in away from the job? Aside from the legal issues, how reliable are drug tests?

Many questions surround the legalities of drug testing. Over the years, the courts have been divided over whether or not drug testing is reasonable and whether or not it constitutes a search under the Fourth Amendment. Most courts have concluded that a mandatory urine, blood, or breath test can be considered a search under the Fourth Amendment; the focus now is on the extent to which drug searches may be unreasonable.

Advocates of random drug testing argue that testing at the workplace will prevent illicit drug use and associated problems. Proponents believe that it is not a violation of civil rights when the government acts to protect all citizens from the problems of illicit drug use. But drug tests are not always accurate. To avoid a positive result, some drug users submit another person's urine or put salt and detergent in their own samples, which affect the accuracy of the test. People on both sides of the argument contend that more reliable tests are needed if drug testing is to be allowed.

Drug testing raises other questions: How should drug test results be recorded at work? Should testing be implemented at the work site or at a "neutral" location? Who should be allowed access to employees' files regarding test results? How could employees be assured of their privacy? In addition, will job discrimination or employee stigmatization come about from positive test results?

An excellent overview of drug use in the workplace is presented in Michael D. Newcomb's "Prevalence of Alcohol and Other Drug Use on the Job: Cause for Concern or Irrational Hysteria?" *Journal of Drug Issues* (Summer 1994). The merits of drug testing are discussed in John Honour's article "Testing for Drug Abuse," *The Lancet* (July 6, 1996). The prevalence of drug testing is reviewed in "Prevalence of Drug Testing in the Workplace," by Tyler Hartwell et al., *Monthly Labor Review* (November 1996). The legality of the Fourth Amendment, especially as it relates to testing political candidates for drugs, is discussed in the article "Fourth Amendment—Mandatory Drug Testing—Eleventh Circuit Upholds Suspicionless Drug Testing for Political Candidates," *Harvard Law Review* (vol. 110, 1996).

ISSUE 4

Do Needle Exchange Programs Reduce the Spread of AIDS?

YES: Editors of *Consumer Reports,* from "Can Clean Needles Slow the AIDS Epidemic?" *Consumer Reports* (July 1994)

NO: Office of National Drug Control Policy, from "Needle Exchange Programs: Are They Effective?" *ONDCP Bulletin No. 7* (July 1992)

ISSUE SUMMARY

YES: The editors of *Consumer Reports* assert that needle exchange programs in several European countries have successfully slowed the transmission of AIDS. The editors further argue that needle exchange programs not only reduce the spread of AIDS among adults but also curtail the risk of children developing the disease.

NO: The Office of National Drug Control Policy, an executive agency that determines policies and objectives for the U.S. drug control program, sees needle exchange programs as an admission of defeat and a retreat from the ongoing battle against drug use, and it argues that compassion and treatment are needed, not needles.

Both selections presented here refer to intravenous drug use as a factor in the escalating incidence of AIDS (acquired immunodeficiency syndrome). One point needs to be clarified: Any type of drug injection, whether it is intravenous (mainlining), intramuscular, or just below the surface of the skin (skin popping), can result in the transmission of AIDS. Technically, what is transmitted is not AIDS but the human immunodeficiency virus (HIV), which ultimately leads to the development of AIDS.

Until a cure for AIDS is found or a vaccine against HIV is developed, the relationship between AIDS and injecting drugs will remain a cause of great concern. Illegal drug injection is the second leading cause of AIDS in the United States. The federal government has estimated that over 16,000 people developed AIDS as a result of injecting drugs. This figure does not take into account the number of intravenous drug users who have infected their sexual partners. In 1992 new pediatric AIDS cases—over half of which are related to drug injection—increased more than 13 percent from the 1991 figures.

No one disagrees that the spread of AIDS is a problem and that the number of people who inject drugs is a problem. The issue that needs to be addressed is, What is the best course of action to take to reduce drug injection and the transmission of AIDS? Is it better to set up more drug treatment facilities, as the Office of National Drug Control Policy (ONDCP) suggests, or to allow people who inject drugs access to clean needles?

One concern of needle exchange opponents is that endorsement of these programs convey the wrong message concerning drug use. Instead of discouraging drug use, they feel that such programs merely teach people how to use drugs or encourage drug use. Needle exchange advocates point to studies showing that these programs have not resulted in an increase of intravenous drug users. Other studies indicate that many drug users involved in needle exchange programs drop out and that drug users who remain in the programs are not as likely to share needles in the first place.

Proponents of needle exchange programs argue that HIV is easily transmitted when needles are shared and that something needs to be done to stem the practice. Opponents argue that whether or not needle exchange programs are available, needles will be shared. Three reasons cited by drug users for sharing needles are (1) they do not have access to clean needles, (2) they do not own their own needles, and (3) they cannot afford to buy needles. If clean needles were readily available, would drug addicts necessarily use them? Some studies show that people who inject drugs are concerned about contracting AIDS and will alter their drug-taking behavior if presented with a viable alternative.

Although needle exchange programs may result in the use of clean needles and encourage people to obtain treatment, they do not get at the root cause of drug addiction. Drug abuse and many of its concomitant problems stem from inadequate or nonexistent employment opportunities, unsafe neighborhoods, underfunded schools, and insufficient health care. Some argue that until these underlying causes of drug abuse are addressed, stopgap measures like needle exchange programs should be implemented. Needle exchange programs, however, may forestall the implementation of other programs that could prove to be more helpful.

Needle exchange programs generate a number of legal and social questions. Since heroin and cocaine are illegal, giving needles to people for the purpose of injecting these drugs contributes to illegal behavior. Should people who are addicted to drugs be seen as criminals or as victims who need compassion? Should drug users, especially drug addicts, be incarcerated or treated? The majority of drug users involved with needle exchange programs are members of minority groups. Could needle exchange programs promote the continuation of drug use and, hence, the enslavement of minorities rather than a turn to healthier alternatives?

In the following selections, the editors of *Consumer Reports* address the benefits of needle exchange programs and respond to some of the criticisms of these programs. The ONDCP points out the inadequacies of previous research regarding needle exchange programs and argues that these programs exacerbate drug abuse problems by facilitating drug use.

YES

Editors of *Consumer Reports*

CAN CLEAN NEEDLES SLOW THE AIDS EPIDEMIC?

Early in the AIDS epidemic, even before the virus that causes it was identified, it was clear the mysterious disease was spreading rapidly among drug users. Soon it was also appearing in their sexual partners and their children. AIDS is now among the 10 most common causes of death in American children under five. In New York State, it is the second leading cause of death in black children under five, and the leading cause of death in Hispanic children of that age. Just east of upper Manhattan, in the South Bronx, almost 5 percent of all children under 13 years old—an estimated 4,000 in number—are infected with the AIDS virus.

Moreover, the number of children affected is rising rapidly. New cases of pediatric AIDS in 1992 rose 13.4 percent over 1991, some 13 times the rate of increase among drug injectors themselves. Among women of child-bearing age infected sexually (primarily by addicts), the rate is rising even faster. In 1992, 2,442 women were diagnosed with AIDS contracted sexually, a 17 percent jump over 1991 and the highest increase for any group. For the first time, the annual number of such cases surpassed that of women who inject drugs. Overall, the number of drug-related AIDS victims among those who have never injected drugs now exceeds 15,000.

AN ESCALATING EPIDEMIC

Human immunodeficiency virus, or HIV, the agent that causes AIDS, is transmitted by sexual intercourse, by injection or transfusion of HIV-tainted blood or blood products, and from an infected mother to her fetus or newborn. One-third of the 339,000 AIDS cases reported to the U.S. Centers for Disease Control and Prevention (the CDC) by late 1993 have been associated directly or indirectly with injecting heroin, cocaine, or both. Some 60 percent of all those affected have died—a greater number of fatalities than the nation experienced in Vietnam.

In striking contrast to health-care workers, who have rarely been infected with HIV in thousands of needle-stick exposures to it, drug injectors have rapidly acquired the infection. Laws restricting possession of injection equipment, under penalty of imprisonment, encourage the sharing of needles and syringes. And frequent injections—often three to four times a day among heroin users and even more among cocaine users —raise the risk of encountering contaminated equipment.

Intravenous drug use has become the most important factor in the spread of AIDS in the U.S. Although the majority of AIDS cases to date has occurred among homosexual and bisexual men, the percentage of drug-related cases has been increasing while that for homosexual and bisexual men has declined in each of the last three years.

Surging epidemics among drug injectors are not the norm among Western nations. Several European countries and Australia have blunted the spread of AIDS far more successfully than the United States has. Where the U.S. has relied primarily on punishment and advertising campaigns of the "just say no" variety to combat drug use, most Western nations have stressed more direct forms of disease prevention.

TO MITIGATE HARM

Even before the threat of AIDS was apparent, the Netherlands sought to prevent transmission of hepatitis B, a common blood-borne infection, by allowing addicts to exchange used needles and syringes for new, sterile ones. As the risk of AIDS grew, cities such as Amsterdam expanded their needle-exchange programs. The government's harm-reduction measures also included regular medical examinations for addicts, distribution of methadone and condoms, and referral to hospitals.

Such efforts appear to be working. In a study published in the *American Journal of Public Health* in 1991, researchers at the Municipal Health Service in Amsterdam reported that HIV infection rates in a group of 622 drug injectors had remained stable over four consecutive years. Overall, the study reported, 75 cases of AIDS had occurred among heterosexual drug addicts in the Netherlands from the start of the epidemic to the end of 1989. That represents a disease incidence rate of about 1 percent. In the U.S., the comparable incidence rate over the same period among heterosexual drug users was 2.4 percent, or 24,212 cases. Since the end of 1989, moreover, the number of drug-related AIDS cases in the U.S. has more than tripled.

In contrast to U.S. practice, Dutch officials have traditionally been less punitive toward users, preferring to emphasize a public-health approach to the problem. Yet countries less tolerant of drug use than the Netherlands, including Australia, the United Kingdom, Germany, Sweden, and others have introduced needle-exchange programs and a broad range of services geared to reduce HIV transmission.

In Edinburgh, Scotland, for example, officials decided to let physicians prescribe, free and on demand, oral versions of nearly any drug used by addicts. Those receiving the drugs had to avoid using needles and agree to regular drug and medical counseling. The object was to reduce risky drug-taking behavior first and then seek to overcome drug dependency.

The initial program site opened in 1988 at Royal Edinburgh Hospital. In a news dispatch from Edinburgh last year, correspondent William E. Schmidt of the *New York Times* reported that the program "has not only reduced the number of addicts injecting drugs from thousands to only a few hundred, but has also effectively halted the spread of HIV via contaminated needles." After peaking in the mid-1980s at an average of 120 new infections a year, the number steadily declined to just 8 in 1992. In addition, Schmidt reported, heroin use and local crime rates had declined as well.

The reported rate of AIDS cases in Britain is 2 per 100,000 people— among the lowest in Europe and well below the U.S. rate of 18.5 per 100,000 in 1992. According to World Health Organization officials in Geneva, the low incidence in part reflects ambitious and early government programs to intervene, including provision of clean injection equipment to addicts.

Indeed, almost all Western nations make sterile injection equipment legally accessible to drug injectors. Sweden is the only Western European country that restricts pharmacy sales of syringes, but it sanctions needle-exchange programs. Several countries, including Germany, Norway, and the Netherlands, also allow syringes to be dispensed in vending machines, particularly in areas frequented by drug users. Even Canada and Australia, which historically have taken punitive approaches to illicit drug use, provide funding for needle-exchange and permit pharmacy sales to users.

AGAINST THE TIDE

Unlike its counterparts abroad, the U.S. has striven to keep clean injection equipment out of the hands of addicts. Layers of Federal and state law block access to such equipment or make its possession a crime, often forcing drug injectors to share whatever is available, whether it's clean or contaminated.

Ten states—including several with the greatest number of drug addicts, such as California, Illinois, New Jersey, and New York—require a medical prescription for purchasing injection equipment. In those states, addicts commonly buy such equipment from drug dealers. Some sellers purchase their supplies out of state; others acquire needles stolen from hospitals or doctors' offices, scavenge them from hospital trash bins, or secure them through forged prescriptions or from diabetics. According to drug researchers in New York City, many sellers will resell used and unsterilized needles as new ones.

Addicts who manage to secure sterile injection equipment then confront another set of laws. Forty-six states and the District of Columbia have statutes based on the Federal Model Drug Paraphernalia Act of 1979, which shows states how to strengthen laws that prohibit addicts from possessing injection equipment. Fear of arrest for simply possessing a needle or syringe is one of the chief reasons addicts share equipment.

In 1979, the threat of AIDS had not yet surfaced. By the mid-1980s, though, the soaring rate of infection among drug injectors was becoming apparent. Yet, instead of urging states to relax their laws on drug paraphernalia, the Federal Government acted to tighten them further. In October 1986, it enacted the Mail Order Drug Paraphernalia Control Act, which prohibits the sale or transport of drug paraphernalia through the mails or "by other interstate conveyance." The title of the Act suggests a focus on mail-order businesses, but the law's actual wording supports a much broader reach. Specifically, if state or local government were to permit gaps in their drug-paraphernalia laws, the Act provides a basis for Federal agencies to intervene.

As the AIDS epidemic intensified, the Government took further steps to block access to sterile injection equipment. Under three different Presidents, Congress passed eight separate bills with provisions that bar or inhibit Federal funding for needle-exchange.

THE WRONG MESSAGE

Distributing needles "undercuts the credibility of society's message that drug use is illegal and morally wrong," declared Robert Martinez, director of the Office of National Drug Control Policy under President Bush. "In response to the AIDS epidemic, there are those who are ready to sound a retreat in the war on drugs by distributing clean needles to intravenous drug users," said Martinez in his agency's July 1992 Bulletin. "I believe this would be a serious mistake. We must not lose sight of the fact that illegal drugs still pose a serious threat to our nation. Nor can we allow our concern for AIDS to undermine our determination to win the war on drugs."

Like Martinez, a number of prominent black legislators have expressed strenuous opposition to needle-exchange programs. Fearing that access to injection equipment will only fuel the cycle of addiction, crime, and violence decimating their communities, they have frequently joined conservatives to block Federal financing for such projects.

Representative Charles B. Rangel, Democrat of New York, for example, used his leverage when chair of the House Select Committee on Narcotics to bar funding of needle-exchange programs. Instead, he urged Federal support for drug-treatment programs with a broad range of services.

Last fall, scientists at the University of California's Berkeley and San Francisco campuses completed a major study of needle-exchange for the CDC, including interviews with numerous supporters and opponents of the programs in 13 cities. They found that African-Americans, like other Americans, differ widely in their views on needle-exchange.

In contrast to Representative Rangel, for example, black legislators in California have proposed bills to legalize and fund needle-exchange programs in the state. Black mayors in Baltimore, New Haven, Conn., New York City, and Washington, D.C., have also backed such programs in their cities. Surveys of Harlem families in 1989 and 1990 found 54 percent of all respondents in favor of providing clean syringes to drug injectors.

"The most consistent and often most vocal community opposition... has emanated from the more established African-American community and church officials," the University of California scientists reported. Despite the severe impact of AIDS in African-American communities (about 47 percent of all drug-related cases), black ministers in particular have fought vehemently against needle-exchange. Many view it as a policy that condones drug use and merely perpetuates addiction among blacks—a trifling substitute for the drug-treatment services their communities desperately need.

Federal funding for drug treatment, of course, has been a stepchild for years. In three out of every four cities that offer treatment, waiting lists of up to six months are typical, the U.S. Food and Drug Administration has reported.

Nationwide, there are generally more than 100,000 drug users on waiting lists at any given time.

JUST SAY NO, OR ELSE

Even as cocaine use soared in the 1980s along with AIDS, the Government's primary response was the Reagan Administration's "Just Say No" campaign. As some drug experts point out, that amounts to a policy of doing nothing. Taking drugs is viewed as a criminal act, and AIDS is part of the package criminals can expect for injecting them. At the same time, the Reagan Administration chose to just say no itself to any increase in funds for treatment, actually cutting outlays back from $332-million in 1980 to $234-million by 1986. Funding has increased significantly since then, but it still falls far short of addressing the need.

Eventually, activist groups such as the National AIDS Brigade and ACT-UP began distributing needles to addicts as explicit acts of civil disobedience. The largest needle-exchange program in the nation, for example, Prevention Point in San Francisco, was launched by a roving team of volunteers defiantly pushing a baby carriage filled with sterile injection equipment through the city.

Initially, most such programs were small, "underground" projects, lacking legal sanction but tolerated by local authorities troubled by the spread of the epidemic. Legally organized programs first appeared in Tacoma, Wash., in 1988, and in Portland, Ore., and Seattle in 1989.

Not until recently, however, have any good-sized, officially sanctioned programs been established in inner-city locales where both drug addiction and AIDS are rife. But the situation is changing, in part because of the impact of a needle-exchange project operating in New Haven, Conn.

A COMMUNITY RESPONDS

Like officials in Edinburgh, community leaders in New Haven realized in the mid-1980s that the city had a significant drug-related epidemic. More than 60 percent of its reported AIDS cases could be traced to drug injection, particularly in poor and minority areas of the city. In 1986, a mayoral committee representing diverse constituencies was formed to foster community cooperation in forging a rational response to the AIDS threat.

State legislators were ultimately persuaded to fund a pilot needle-exchange program exempt from drug-paraphernalia laws. Enacted in May 1990, the bill also mandated that the program be evaluated. The state health department chose professor Edward H. Kaplan of Yale University's schools of management and of medicine to conduct an independent appraisal.

Evaluating needle-exchange programs has long proved formidable, partly because of the chance that self-reported accounts of drug use could be unreliable. Addicts dependent on a program might conceivably report what they think interviewers want to hear; such self-reports are hard to verify in a scientific way. Thus, even though a variety of studies, both here and abroad, have shown favorable results for needle-exchange, opponents of the programs have commonly attacked the reliability of the findings.

Accordingly, Kaplan devised an evaluation method that departed entirely from previous studies. Instead of interviewing participants, the program would "interview" the needles. They would be tracked by special codes assigned to the syringes themselves and to the participants who picked them up and returned them. Random samples of the returned needles would then be tested for traces of HIV contamination.

The evaluation relied on mathematical techniques to estimate HIV infection rates. The approach was similar to one used to study the spread of malaria, which spreads from humans to mosquitoes and back to humans. In this instance, contaminated injection equipment replaced the mosquito. Overall, the method avoided any dependence on self-reports by addicts or changes in their behavior. It was the behavior of the *needles* that mattered.

LISTENING TO THE NEEDLES

As the project progressed, random testing of the needles for traces of HIV showed a significant decline in contamination rates. Of 579 program needles tested by March 1991, 50.3 percent were positive for HIV, down from 67.5 percent for a baseline sample of 160 street needles serving as a comparison. Eventually, the contamination rate in program needles fell to 40.5 percent.

On the basis of the contamination rates, the circulation time of the needles, and other data, the mathematical model estimated that the program reduced HIV transmission rates by 33 percent among those who participated.

Two major studies conducted for the Government—one by the General Accounting Office, the investigative arm of Congress, and one by the University of California for the CDC—have scrutinized the New Haven evaluation in detail. Both found it to be scientifically valid.

"Overall, it is a remarkably efficient and sound method for estimating [needle-exchange] effects," the University of California study stated. Both studies also concluded that the 33 percent drop in HIV transmission rates was an underestimate, because of the intentionally conservative criteria incorporated in the mathematical model. (Those who left the program to enter drug treatment, for example, were simply recorded as dropouts.)

The model indicated a drop in new HIV infections from six per year to four per year for every 100 drug injectors in the program. On that basis, Kaplan estimated that 20 infections had been prevented over the first two years of the program. The current Federal estimate of the cost of treating a person with HIV, from the time of infection until death, is approximately $119,000. In its first two years of operation, the New Haven program cost only about $150,000 annually while saving at least $2-million for the health-care system.

BEYOND HIV

Other results of the program, however, may ultimately prove as important as the savings in lives and money. For one thing, there was no evidence of any increase in injecting drug use in New Haven as a result of the program. Secondly, one of every six addicts who joined the program subsequently entered drug treatment. Moreover, the racial and ethnic makeup of those who did was far different from the primary white clientele at many treatment centers. Among those who left the program to seek treatment, 41 percent were black, 25 percent were Hispanic, and 34 percent were white. By comparison, those already in treatment at the time in New Haven were 63 percent white, 27 percent black, and only 9 percent Hispanic.

Advocates of needle-exchange often contend that it reaches people who are ordinarily wary of official government programs, including drug treatment. The New Haven experience appears to bear that out. The implication is that a well-run needle-exchange program can serve an outreach function, attracting addicts who distrust the establishment system and usually shun it. Thus, needle exchange needn't be an alternative to drug treatment; it can be a bridge to it.

As a result of the New Haven findings, Connecticut has enacted legislation expanding the needle-exchange to Bridgeport and Hartford. And in July 1992, the state decriminalized the possession of injection equipment. Drug users may now buy up to 10 syringes at a time without a prescription and carry such equipment on their person without being subject to arrest. Last fall, the state of Maine rescinded its prescription law as well.

The University of California study —the most comprehensive to date on needle-exchange—recommended repeal of all such prescription laws as well as all drug-paraphernalia laws "as they apply to syringes." It also urged the Government to repeal the ban on Federal funds for needle-exchange and expand access to treatment.

The war on drugs is arguably no nearer solution today than when President Nixon first declared it in 1971. While there are no easy answers, a civilized nation must curtail the mounting number of AIDS casualties from friendly fire.

"Federal funding is critical," says drug expert Dr. Don C. Des Jarlais, who is directing an evaluation of New York City's needle-exchange programs. "Most state governments are in worse shape than the Federal Government. Without Federal funds, we are really going to be limited in what we can accomplish in this epidemic."

NO

Office of National Drug
Control Policy

NEEDLE EXCHANGE PROGRAMS:
ARE THEY EFFECTIVE?

When President Bush took office, most Americans regarded the use of illegal drugs as the most serious problem confronting the Nation. Since that time, the Nation has made substantial progress in reducing drug use. But now, in response to the AIDS epidemic, there are those who are ready to sound a retreat in the war against drugs by distributing clean needles to intravenous drug users in the hope that this will slow the spread of AIDS. I believe this would be a serious mistake. We must not lose sight of the fact that illegal drugs still pose a serious threat to our Nation. Nor can we allow our concern for AIDS to undermine our determination to win the war on drugs.

In 1988, 14.5 million Americans and nearly two million young people, aged 12–17, were using drugs. In response to the devastation caused by drug use, the President boldly announced the first National Drug Control Strategy in a televised address to the Nation in 1989. That Strategy was a landmark document. Not only did it establish a coherent, coordinated policy for the national effort against drugs, but it committed unprecedented new resources for fighting drug use.

The Strategy is working; the use of illegal drugs by Americans is declining. Between 1988 and 1991, almost two million fewer Americans were using drugs, a drop of almost 13 percent. And by 1991, about half a million fewer young people were current users of drugs, a drop of 27 percent. Since 1985, the number of Americans using drugs has fallen by over 10 million.

Key to the success of the Strategy has been increasing Americans' intolerance of illicit drugs. But, for those already caught in the deadly web of addiction, we must act with compassion. The Administration therefore vigorously supports efforts to provide effective drug treatment to those who want it and can benefit from it, and has increased finding for drug treatment from $1.1 billion in 1989 to a proposed $2.1 billion for 1993.

Our gains against drug use have been hard-won, and this is no time to jeopardize them by instituting needle exchange programs. Despite all the arguments made by proponents of needle exchange, there is no getting around

From Office of National Drug Control Policy, Executive Office of the President, "Needle Exchange Programs: Are They Effective?" *ONDCP Bulletin No. 7* (July 1992). Some notes omitted.

the fact that distributing needles facilitates drug use and undercuts the credibility of society's message that using drugs is illegal and morally wrong. And just as important, there is no conclusive evidence that exchange programs reduce the spread of AIDS.

The Administration's concerns about needle exchange are widely shared. Recently, for example, the Congress extended a prohibition on the use of most Federal drug treatment funds to support needle exchange programs. And in June 1992, the National Association of State Alcohol and Drug Abuse Directors informed every member of Congress of its support for continuing this prohibition. Also, in February 1992, the National District Attorneys Association passed an official policy position condemning needle exchange.

The Administration will continue to work with the Congress, and with State and local officials to support alternatives to needle exchange, including expanded and improved drug treatment and aggressive outreach programs. These efforts will provide addicts with something that needle exchange programs cannot: hope and a chance for real recovery from drug addiction.

NEEDLE EXCHANGE PROGRAMS IN THE UNITED STATES

Intravenous Drug Use and HIV/AIDS.[1] Intravenous drug users in the United States are one of the groups most at risk for contracting AIDS. AIDS prevention and education programs, which have had a measurable effect on the behavior of other high-risk groups, have not been so successful with intravenous drug users. In fact, the Centers for Disease Control estimates that about 32 percent of the diagnosed AIDS cases in this country, involving nearly 70,000 individuals, resulted from intravenous drug use or sexual contact with intravenous drug users. In addition, intravenous drug use is responsible for half of the AIDS cases among women.

AIDS is spread among intravenous drug users primarily through the sharing of hypodermic syringes, or "needles," and other drug-using paraphernalia (e.g., cotton and water) that have been contaminated with the AIDS virus, and secondarily by high-risk sexual behavior. Thus, intravenous drug users pose a threat not only to themselves, but to their sexual partners and offspring as well. In fact, 58 percent of all reported pediatric AIDS cases are associated with intravenous drug use.

Faced with the growing link between intravenous drug use and AIDS, some cities and communities have instituted or are contemplating programs to provide clean needles to addicts in the hope that this will help reduce the sharing of needles, and hence, the spread of the HIV virus.

Needle Exchange Programs. Needle exchange programs provide free, clean needles to intravenous drug users in an attempt to reduce the likelihood that they will share needles with other users. Some programs operate from fixed locations such as city government offices or pharmacies. Others are mobile, using outreach workers in vans, on foot, and at temporary sites. Some programs provide a new needle only in exchange for an old one, while others provide at least one "starter" needle. Most programs limit the number of needles that can be exchanged at any one time. Some programs provide needles to persons only if they have a verifiable history of drug injection, and most have age limits. Most programs are privately funded; others are supported with State or municipal government funds.[2]

Needle exchange programs also differ in scope. Some only exchange needles, while others are more comprehensive and provide counseling, referral to testing and drug treatment, bleach to clean needles, and safer sex information.

Needle Exchange and the Law. In 39 States and the District of Columbia, sterile needles can be purchased inexpensively without a prescription in many pharmacies.[3] In most of the remaining 11 States, a prescription is required. However, four of the 11 are considering legislation that would broaden access to needles. Only one State, Alabama, is considering legislation that would restrict accessibility by making it a criminal offense for those other than licensed pharmacists or practitioners to sell needles.

Forty-nine States, the District of Columbia, and numerous local jurisdictions have laws to prohibit the sale and distribution of drug paraphernalia. The majority of these laws conform with the Model Drug Paraphernalia Act, which was released by the Drug Enforcement Administration in August 1979. The Model Drug Paraphernalia Act would make it a crime to possess, deliver, or manufacture needles with the intent to violate anti-drug laws. Therefore, operating needle exchange programs may be a violation of the law in many States and local jurisdictions. Furthermore, operating such programs may subject municipalities to civil liability in some jurisdictions.

What the Research Shows. Several studies on the efficacy of needle ex-change programs have been conducted in the United States and abroad. Some of these studies have been cited by proponents of needle exchange as evidence that such programs work. However, all of the needle exchange programs studied have yielded either ambiguous or discouraging results. Moreover, the methodology used to conduct these studies has been flawed. For example:

- Many studies make long-term projections of addict behavior based on short-term results;
- Many use a small or insufficient sample size and then project results to larger populations;
- Despite claims that needle sharing was reduced, none of the studies conducted objective tests (e.g., analysis of blood types on returned needles) to determine whether needles were shared;
- Most do not use valid comparison or control groups; and
- Most have program staff, rather than independent evaluators, conduct client interviews on which the findings of the studies are based.

There are four other significant problems with the research. First, needle exchange programs are plagued by high levels of attrition. Programs may have initial contact with intravenous drug users who are at the highest risk of sharing needles and contracting AIDS, but only as few as 20 percent may return for a second or third visit.

Second, needle exchange programs tend to attract and retain a self-selecting group of older, long-term intravenous drug users who are less likely to share needles than less experienced, more promiscuous users. Therefore, positive reports on the effectiveness of exchange programs may be due *more* to the behavior of this less risky subset of the intravenous drug using population and *less* to the availability of clean needles.

Third, programs offering needle exchange often provide bleach for cleaning needles, referrals to testing and treatment, and other services. However, the research conducted to date has not isolated the specific impact that exchanging needles has had on reducing the transmission of AIDS compared with these other factors. Most researchers have simply attributed positive results to needle exchange.

The fourth weakness with the research relates to the dynamics of addiction. No matter what addicts promise when they are not on drugs, they may still share needles when they shoot up heroin or cocaine. In many cases it is simply part of the ritual of taking drugs. More often, a drug-induced state overwhelms rational thinking. Many addicts know that they can get AIDS from dirty needles. Yet hazards to their health—even deadly ones—do not weigh heavily on their minds. Rather, they are primarily concerned with the instant gratification of drugs.

To expect an individual locked in the grip of drug addiction to act responsibly by not sharing needles is unrealistic. Such a change in behavior requires self-discipline and a willingness to postpone gratification and plan for the future—all of which are contrary to the drug-using lifestyle. The fact that addicts can purchase clean needles cheaply, without prescription, in many pharmacies in most States, but often fail to do so, is evidence of their irresponsible behavior.[4] In fact, the only proven way to change an addict's behavior is through structured interventions, such as drug treatment.

The New Haven Study. A 1991 interim study of a needle exchange program in New Haven, Connecticut, is cited by many needle exchange advocates as evidence of the benefits of needle exchange. The study asserts numerous positive findings, most of which are not supported by the data.

The study states that retention rates stabilized after a high attrition rate early in the program. But, of the 720 addicts who initially contacted the New Haven program over an eight-month period, only 288 (40 percent) returned at least once to exchange a used needle (Figure 1). The New Haven study defines the 288 returning intravenous drug users as "program participants," but does not distinguish between those who exchanged needles once and those who exchanged needles more frequently.[6] The loose definition of "program participation" exaggerates the program's reported retention rate and calls into question the claim that participation in the program stabilized. In addition, the study does not provide information on the 288 individuals who remained in the program and whether they shared needles before the program started. In fact, the study reports that of the 720 addicts who contacted the program, 436 (61 percent) reported never sharing needles before the program began (Table 1).

The study also states that about half of the 10,180 needles distributed by the program between November 1990 and June 1991 were returned, and that an additional 4,236 "street" or nonprogram needles were brought in for exchange. However, the study fails to account for the 4,917 needles—50 percent of those given out—that were not returned. Based on this information, the study claims that the circulation time for needles was

Figure 1

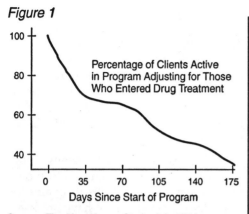

Percentage of Clients Active in Program Adjusting for Those Who Entered Drug Treatment

Days Since Start of Program

Source: The New Haven Study, July 1991.

Table 1

Extent of Needle Sharing Reported at Initial Contact With Program

How Often Shared Works		
Always (100%)	16	(2%)
Almost Always (67–99%)	16	(2%)
Half the Time (34–66%)	43	(6%)
Sometimes (1–33%)	196	(27%)
Never (0%)	436	(61%)
(Missing)	13	(2%)

Source: The New Haven Study, July 1991.

reduced and that fewer contaminated needles were appearing in public places. However, no data are presented to directly support such conclusions.

The authors also report that 107 intravenous drug users (about 15 percent of those who contacted the program) entered treatment over an eight-month period through contact with the New Haven program, but there are no data on how many of these individuals were "program participants" (e.g., had exchanged needles more than once). Therefore, the study does not present any basis for correlating the *exchange* of needles to entry into drug treatment. Also, no data on treatment retention or completion are presented.

The study also claims that intravenous drug use in the community did not increase. Although this may be true, it is not supported by convincing data. The study indicates that 92 percent of those who initially contacted the program were experienced users who had been injecting drugs for one year or more. The study uses this statistic to demonstrate that the availability of free needles did not entice individuals to begin using intravenous drugs. However, there is no evidence to

verify that experienced users did not use needles distributed by the program to initiate new users. The study also cites an unchanged rate in drug arrests as evidence that no increase in intravenous drug use occurred due to the program. However, the New Haven program had only been in operation for two months and had been contacted by fewer than 200 addicts at the time statistics on drug arrests were recorded. Therefore, it is unlikely that the program could have had any impact on the rate of drug arrests.

The most striking finding of the New Haven study—that the incidence of new HIV infections was reduced by one-third among those participating in the program—is based on tenuous data. The study indicates that 789 needles—581 from the program, 160 from the street, and 48 from a local "shooting gallery"[7] —were tested for the presence of HIV.[8] The tests found that program needles were much less likely to be HIV positive than street or gallery needles. The tests also indicated that "dedicated" program needles (e.g., those returned by the original recipient) were much less likely to be HIV positive than other program needles. Based on this information, the study concludes that "dedicated" needles were not shared, *although no tests were conducted to determine if different blood types appeared on the needles or the blood type on the needle matched that of the program participant.* Without conducting such tests, accurate conclusions as to whether needles were shared cannot be drawn, and a reduction in the spread of HIV cannot be attributed to needle exchange.

Finally, the study projects that expanding the availability of clean needles to New Haven's entire intravenous drug using population would also reduce the incidence of new HIV infections by one-third. The projection is based on a highly complex mathematical model involving eight different factors that are supported by numerous assumptions, estimates, probabilities, and rates. While the model may be valid, its projections are based on the tenuous assumption that the 288 intravenous drug users "participating" in the New Haven program are representative of the general intravenous drug using population. However, the high attrition rate of the New Haven program demonstrates that such an assumption cannot be made.

FOREIGN NEEDLE EXCHANGE PROGRAMS

In recent years, other countries—most notably the Netherlands and the United Kingdom—have established needle exchange programs. Studies of these programs have also produced mixed results. Most reflect the problems noted in existing research on needle exchange. Many report anecdotal or other unquantified information. Furthermore, some base "success" on the number of needles distributed.

In Amsterdam, a program started in 1984 reported that the number of participants grew more than tenfold in four years. The program also reported that during the first four years participants shared fewer needles, the HIV prevalence rate among intravenous drug users stabilized, and instances of Hepatitis B decreased.

In England, about 120 exchange programs distribute approximately four million needles annually. These programs reportedly reach users who have not been in contact with drug treatment services, decrease needle sharing, and increase contact with other social services by participants.

Sweden's three needle exchange sites reported after three years that no project participant had become infected with HIV, that needle sharing had declined, and that many users not previously in contact with drug treatment had been attracted to the program.

Although generally positive, the reports on these programs are scientifically weak and present very few objective indicators of success. All claim that needle exchange reduced the number of needles shared, but none of the programs conducted the tests (e.g., blood-type tests) necessary to make that determination.

In addition, the attrition rates in foreign programs are extremely high. A 1989 study of 15 needle exchange programs in England and Scotland reported that only 33 percent of intravenous drug users who initially contacted the programs returned up to five times. As in the United States, needle exchange programs in other countries are more likely to attract and retain intravenous drug users who are already predisposed not to share needles, and who therefore are at lower risk of contracting AIDS than other, less cautious, users.

ALTERNATIVES TO NEEDLE EXCHANGE

The challenges to society presented by drug use and HIV/AIDS require the steady development of scientific understanding and the promotion of effective interventions. Requested Federal funding for AIDS prevention, treatment, research, and income maintenance in 1993 is $4.9 billion—a 69 percent increase since 1990 (Figure 2). The President's National Drug Control Strategy supports using a portion of these funds for research, experiments, and demonstrations to seek out high-risk drug users; to encourage and support their entry into drug treatment; and to provide them with information on the destructiveness of their behavior and ways to change it. The Strategy also supports efforts to expand the capacity and effectiveness of drug treatment for intravenous drug users.

Outreach Programs. The most effective method of reducing the spread of AIDS among intravenous drug users is to treat successfully their drug addiction. However, Federal studies estimate that more than 40 percent of intravenous drug users have never been in treatment, even though many have used drugs intravenously for more than 10 years. Therefore, it is essential to continue efforts to aggressively recruit intravenous drug users into treatment.

Since 1987, the Department of Health and Human Service's National Institute on Drug Abuse has funded projects in more than 40 cities to help identify intravenous drug users and persuade them to enter treatment. In these cities, squads

Figure 2

Federal Funding for HIV/AIDS, 1990–1993

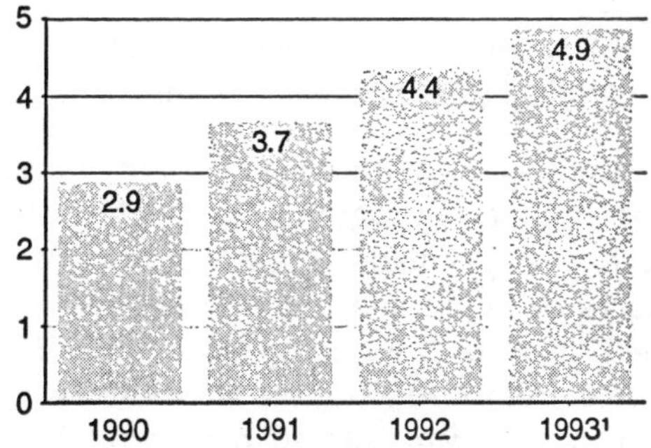

¹Requested

Source: Office of Management and Budget, 1992

of outreach workers contact addicts and encourage them to avoid sharing needles and other risky behaviors and to enter treatment. Outreach workers also provide addicts with information on the threat of AIDS and dispense materials (e.g., bleach and condoms) to reduce the risk of HIV infection.

Between 1987 and 1992, outreach workers contacted approximately 150,000 intravenous drug users. Of these, 45,000 addicts (54 percent of whom reported regularly sharing needles) and 9,500 sexual partners were provided with information on treatment, counseling and methods for reducing the risk of infection. Program participants were assigned to standard and enhanced interventions. Follow-up surveys were conducted six months after the assignments were made, and the results of those surveys indicated that:

- 31 percent of the intravenous drug users had enrolled in formal drug treatment programs;
- 38 percent were sharing needles less frequently;

- 44 percent had begun to always clean their needles, always use a new needle, or had stopped injecting completely; and
- 47 percent had stopped injecting or reduced their frequency of injection.

The success of this effort demonstrates that outreach programs are highly effective in persuading intravenous drug users to avoid sharing needles and to seek treatment. By comparison, only 15 percent of those who contacted the New Haven program entered treatment. The Federal government will continue to support outreach programs by awarding approximately 60 grants in 1992 and 1993.

The Centers for Disease Control also administers an extensive outreach program for preventing the spread of the HIV virus among intravenous drug users. This program, which is operated through State departments of health and community-based organizations, offers intravenous drug users counseling, testing, and referral to treatment. An evaluation of the program will be completed in about two years.

Expanding Treatment Capacity. The Federal government continues to support expanded treatment capacity for intravenous drug users, primarily through the Alcohol, Drug Abuse and Mental Health Services Block Grant program, which requires States to use at least 50 percent of their drug allotment for outreach and treatment of these drug users. Also, the Capacity Expansion Program, which was created by the Bush Administration in Fiscal Year 1992, will increase the number of drug treatment slots for areas and populations in the greatest need of treatment, including intravenous drug users. If Congress fully funds this program in Fiscal Year 1993 (the Administration has requested $86 million), an additional 38,000 addicts—many of whom will be intravenous drug users—will be provided with drug treatment.

Medications Development. The Federal government is continuing its efforts to develop medications to treat heroin addiction. New pharmacological therapies, such as LAAM (a longer-acting alternative to methadone), depot naltrexone, and buprenorphine, are showing considerable promise in treating heroin addiction and should be available within the next few years.[9] In addition, performance standards and clinical protocols are being developed for methadone treatment programs to enhance their safety and effectiveness in treating heroin addiction.[10]

CONCLUSION

The rapid spread of AIDS has prompted officials of some of America's cities to institute programs that distribute clean needles to intravenous drug users. Such programs are questionable public policy, however, because they facilitate addicts' continued use of drugs and undercut the credibility of society's message that drug use is illegal and morally wrong. Further, there is no compelling research that needle exchange programs are effective in preventing intravenous drug users from sharing needles, reducing the spread of AIDS, or encouraging addicts to seek drug treatment.

Research does show, however, that aggressive outreach efforts are an effective way to get intravenous drug users to end their high-risk behavior and seek treatment. Therefore, the National Drug Control Strategy will continue to support such outreach programs. It also will continue to support expanded treatment capacity for high-risk populations, including intravenous drug users; the development of medications for treating heroin addiction; and the exploration of other options that may offer intravenous drug users a real chance for recovery.

NOTES

1. Human Immunodeficiency Virus/Acquired Immunodeficiency Syndrome.

2. Federal law prohibits the use of Alcohol, Drug Abuse, and Mental Health Services Block Grant funds—the major source of Federal support for drug treatment—to pay for needle exchange programs.

3. In some States, such as California, needles may be sold without prescription for the administration of insulin or adrenaline if the pharmacist can identify the purchaser and records the purchase.

4. Syringes cost about $.30 each. For example, in a recent study of pharmacies in St. Louis, Compton et al. found the cost of a package of 10, 28-gauge, 100-unit insulin syringes to range from $1.92 to $4.28.

See Compton, W., et al. "Legal Needle Buying in St. Louis," *American Journal of Public Health*, April 1992, Vol. 82, No. 4.

5. In Fiscal Year 1992, the National Institute on Drug Abuse awarded a grant to Yale University to conduct a rigorous evaluation of the New Haven program over a three-year period. Results of the evaluation will be available in 1995.

6. Researchers estimate that intravenous heroin users on average inject two or more times a day, heavy users four to six times a day. Intravenous cocaine users invariably inject more frequently. There is very little data yet available on the number of injections an average user gets from a needle before it is discarded, although a 1989 California survey of 257 users found a mean of 22.5 uses (with 27 reporting one use and 15 reporting over 100).

7. A "shooting gallery" is a communal injection site notorious for inadequate sterilization of injection equipment.

8. The study does not specify the method used to select program and street needles or whether they are considered random or representative samples.

9. LAAM is a longer-acting alternative to methadone, depot naltrexone is a long-acting heroin blocker, and buprenorphine is being investigated for treating individuals addicted to both heroin and cocaine.

10. Methadone is a synthetic medication used to treat heroin addicts by relieving withdrawal symptoms and craving for heroin for 24 hours. Methadone is only administered as part of a supervised treatment program.

POSTSCRIPT

Do Needle Exchange Programs Reduce the Spread of AIDS?

The implementation of needle exchange programs arouses several ethical and practical concerns. Opponents challenge the wisdom of giving drug addicts needles to inject themselves with illegal drugs. They ask, What might impressionable adolescents think if the government funds programs in which drug addicts are given needles? Some people reason that those who inject drugs into their bodies know the risks and should live with the consequences of their actions. Others wonder whether the distribution of needles will lead to an increase or a decrease in drug use.

Whether or not needle exchange programs will help slow down the spread of AIDS is extremely relevant because people who inject drugs are the primary sources for heterosexual transmission of AIDS to sexual partners. Also, many pregnant drug users end up infecting their fetuses either through their own or their sexual partners' drug use. Individuals who inject cocaine are more likely to infect sexual partners than heroin users because cocaine heightens perceptions of sexual arousal. Also, the immune systems of drug addicts are impaired not only by their addictions but by their typically poor environment as well. With a weakened immune system, one can contract HIV more easily.

One potential advantage of needle exchange programs is that needles may be safely discarded after they have been used. Unsafely discarded needles may accidentally prick someone (including nonusers) and lead to HIV transmission. A second potential benefit is that when people come to needle exchange sites, they can be encouraged to enter drug treatment programs. It is not always easy to reach the drug-injecting population; one place to reach these individuals is where they exchange needles.

Despite the difficulties of studying people who inject drugs, long-term studies are needed to determine the impact of needle exchange programs on (1) the incidence of AIDS, (2) the continuation or reduction of drug use, (3) whether or not these programs attract new users to the drug culture, (4) the likelihood of program participants entering drug treatment programs, and (5) the impact on other high-risk behaviors. Preliminary studies into the effectiveness of needle exchange programs are contradictory. One such program was introduced in Tacoma, Washington, and needle sharing declined 30 percent. Programs in New York City and New Haven, Connecticut, resulted in fewer reports of HIV infection without an increase in drug use. Conversely, in a program in Louisville, Kentucky, nearly two-thirds of people who inject drugs continued to share needles. In Louisville, however, needles are obtained through a prescription, which may have a different effect in the long run than receiving needles through an exchange program. If needle exchange programs are implemented, who should organize and finance them? Is this the responsibility of government? Should public funds be used? Would these programs save taxpayers money in the long run?

In "Prevention of HIV/AIDS and Other Blood-Borne Diseases Among Injection Drug Users: A National Survey on the Regulation of Syringes and Needles," *JAMA* (*Journal of the American Medical Association*) (January 1, 1997), Gostin et al. discuss how "syringe exchange programs may reduce the spread of AIDS with little impact on crime." In "Needed: A Zero-Tolerance Policy on AIDS," *Drug Policy Letter* (Summer 1995), Peter Lurie describes how thousands of lives are sacrificed due to governmental denial of federal funds for needle exchange programs.

Wallace Mandell and his associates report on the effects of needle exchange programs on the incidence of needle sharing in "Correlates of Needle Sharing Among Injection Drug Users," *American Journal of Public Health* (June 1994). John Watkins examines the impact of needle exchange programs on the use of drugs in "Syringe and Needle Exchange as HIV/AIDS Prevention for Injection Drug Users," *JAMA* (*Journal of the American Medical Association*) (January 12, 1994).

ISSUE 5

Should Pregnant Drug Users Be Prosecuted?

YES: Paul A. Logli, from "Drugs in the Womb: The Newest Battlefield in the War on Drugs," *Criminal Justice Ethics* (Winter/Spring 1990)

NO: Sue Mahan, from *Crack Cocaine, Crime, and Women: Legal, Social, and Treatment Issues* (Sage Publications, 1996)

ISSUE SUMMARY

YES: Paul A. Logli, an Illinois prosecuting attorney, argues that it is the government's duty to enforce every child's right to begin life with a healthy, drug-free mind and body. Logli maintains that pregnant women who use drugs should be prosecuted because they may harm the life of their unborn children.

NO: Writer Sue Mahan asserts that the prosecution of pregnant drug users is unfair because poor women are more likely to be the targets of such prosecution. Instead of treating these women as criminals, Mahan believes that both society and these women would be better served by providing them adequate prenatal care and treatment. Fear of prosecution may dissuade them from seeking prenatal care.

The effects that drugs have on a fetus can be mild and temporary or severe and permanent, depending on the extent of drug use by the mother, the type of substance used, and the stage of fetal development at the time the drug crosses the placental barrier and enters the bloodstream of the fetus. In recent years, there has been a dramatic increase in the number of drug-exposed babies born in the United States, and medical experts are beginning to understand the health consequences that these children face. Both illegal and legal drugs, such as cocaine, crack, marijuana, alcohol, and nicotine, are responsible for increasing incidents of premature births, congenital abnormalities, fetal alcohol syndrome, mental retardation, and other serious birth defects. The exposure of the fetus to these substances and the long-term involuntary physical, intellectual, and emotional effects are disturbing. In addition, the medical, social, and economic costs to treat and care for babies who are exposed to or become addicted to drugs while in utero (in the uterus) warrant serious concern.

In recent years, attempts have been made to establish laws that would allow the incarceration of drug-using pregnant women on the basis of "fetal abuse."

Some cases have been successfully prosecuted: mothers have been denied custody of their infants until they enter appropriate treatment programs, and criminal charges have been brought against mothers whose children were born with drug-related complications. The underlying presumption is that the unborn fetus should be afforded protection against the harmful actions of another person, specifically the use of harmful drugs by the mother.

Those who profess that prosecuting pregnant women who use drugs is necessary insist that the health and welfare of the unborn child is the highest priority. They contend that the possibility that these women will avoid obtaining health care for themselves or their babies because they fear punishment does not absolve the state from the responsibility of protecting the babies. They also argue that criminalizing these acts is imperative to protect fetuses or newborns who cannot protect themselves. It is the duty of the legal system to deter pregnant women from engaging in future criminal drug use and to protect the best interests of infants.

Others maintain that drug use and dependency by pregnant women is a medical problem, not a criminal one. Many pregnant women seek treatment, but they often find that rehabilitation programs are limited or unavailable. Shortages of openings in chemical dependency programs may keep a prospective client waiting for months, during which time she will most likely continue to use the drugs to which she is addicted and prolong her fetus's drug exposure. Many low-income women do not receive drug treatment and adequate prenatal care due to financial constraints. And women who fear criminal prosecution because of their drug use may simply avoid prenatal care altogether.

Some suggest that medical intervention, drug prevention, and education are needed for pregnant drug users instead of prosecution. Prosecution, they contend, drives women who need medical attention away from the very help they and their babies need. Others respond that prosecuting pregnant women who use drugs will help identify those who need attention, at which point adequate medical and social welfare services can be provided to treat and protect the mother and child.

In the following selections, Paul A. Logli, arguing for the prosecution of pregnant drug users, contends that it is the state's responsibility to protect the unborn and the newborn because they are least able to protect themselves. He charges that it is the prosecutor's responsibility to deter future criminal drug use by mothers who violate the rights of their potential newborns to have an opportunity for a healthy and normal life. Sue Mahan insists that prosecuting pregnant drug users is counterproductive to improving the quality of infant and maternal health. The threat of arrest and incarceration will decrease the likelihood that pregnant drug users will seek out adequate prenatal care.

YES

Paul A. Logli

DRUGS IN THE WOMB: THE NEWEST BATTLEFIELD IN THE WAR ON DRUGS

INTRODUCTION

The reported incidence of drug-related births has risen dramatically over the last several years. The legal system and, in particular, local prosecutors have attempted to properly respond to the suffering, death, and economic costs which result from a pregnant woman's use of drugs. The ensuing debate has raised serious constitutional and practical issues which are far from resolution.

Prosecutors have achieved mixed results in using current criminal and juvenile statutes as a basis for legal action intended to prosecute mothers and protect children. As a result, state and federal legislators have begun the difficult task of drafting appropriate laws to deal with the problem, while at the same time acknowledging the concerns of medical authorities, child protection groups, and advocates for individual rights.

THE PROBLEM

The plight of "cocaine babies," children addicted at birth to narcotic substances or otherwise affected by maternal drug use during pregnancy, has prompted prosecutors in some jurisdications to bring criminal charges against drug-abusing mothers. Not only have these prosecutions generated heated debates both inside and outside of the nation's courtrooms, but they have also expanded the war on drugs to a controversial new battlefield—the mother's womb.

A 1988 survey of hospitals conducted by Dr. Ira Chasnoff, Associate Professor of Northwestern University Medical School and President of the National Association for Perinatal Addiction Research and Education (NAPARE) indicated that as many as 375,000 infants may be affected by maternal cocaine use during pregnancy each year. Chasnoff's survey included 36 hospitals across the country and showed incidence rates ranging from 1 percent to 27 percent. It also indicated that the problem was not restricted to urban populations

From Paul A. Logli, "Drugs in the Womb: The Newest Battlefield in the War on Drugs," *Criminal Justice Ethics*, vol. 9, no. 1 (Winter/Spring 1990), pp. 23–39. Copyright © 1990 by *Criminal Justice Ethics*. Reprinted by permission of The Institute for Criminal Justice Ethics, 899 Tenth Avenue, New York, NY 10019-1029. Notes omitted.

or particular racial or socio-economic groups. More recently a study at Hutzel Hospital in Detroit's inner city found that 42.7 percent of its newborn babies were exposed to drugs while in their mothers' wombs.

The effects of maternal use of cocaine and other drugs during pregnancy on the mother and her newborn child have by now been well-documented and will not be repeated here. The effects are severe and can cause numerous threats to the short-term health of the child. In a few cases it can even result in death.

Medical authorities have just begun to evaluate the long-term effects of cocaine exposure on children as they grow older. Early findings show that many of these infants show serious difficulties in relating and reacting to adults and environments, as well as in organizing creative play, and they appear similar to mildly autistic or personality-disordered children.

The human costs related to the pain, suffering, and deaths resulting from maternal cocaine use during pregnancy are simply incalculable. In economic terms, the typical intensive-care costs for treating babies exposed to drugs range from $7,500 to $31,000. In some cases medical bills go as high as $150,000.

The costs grow enormously as more and more hospitals encounter the problem of "boarder babies"—those children literally abandoned at the hospital by an addicted mother, and left to be cared for by the nursing staff. Future costs to society for simply educating a generation of drug-affected children can only be the object of speculation. It is clear, however, that besides pain, suffering, and death the economic costs to society of drug use by pregnant women is presently enormous and is certainly growing larger.

THE PROSECUTOR'S RESPONSE

It is against this backdrop and fueled by the evergrowing emphasis on an aggressively waged war on drugs that prosecutors have begun a number of actions against women who have given birth to drug-affected children. A review of at least two cases will illustrate the potential success or failure of attempts to use existing statutes.

People v. Melanie Green   On February 4, 1989, at a Rockford, Illinois hospital, two-day-old Bianca Green lost her brief struggle for life. At the time of Bianca's birth both she and her mother, twenty-four-year-old Melanie Green, tested positive for the presence of cocaine in their systems.

Pathologists in Rockford and Madison, Wisconsin, indicated that the death of the baby was the result of a prenatal injury related to cocaine used by the mother during the pregnancy. They asserted that maternal cocaine use had caused the placenta to prematurely rupture, which deprived the fetus of oxygen before and during delivery. As a result of oxygen deprivation, the child's brain began to swell and she eventually died.

After an investigation by the Rockford Police Department and the State of Illinois Department of Children and Family Services, prosecutors allowed a criminal complaint to be filed on May 9, 1989, charging Melanie Green with the offenses of Involuntary Manslaughter and Delivery of a Controlled Substance.

On May 25, 1989, testimony was presented to the Winnebago County Grand Jury by prosecutors seeking a formal indictment. The Grand Jury, however, declined to indict Green on either charge. Since Grand Jury proceedings in the State of Illinois are secret, as are the jurors' deliberations and votes, the reason for the decision of the Grand Jury in this case is determined more by conjecture than any direct knowledge. Prosecutors involved in the presentation observed that the jurors exhibited a certain amount of sympathy for the young woman who had been brought before the Grand Jury at the jurors' request. It is also likely that the jurors were uncomfortable with the use of statutes that were not intended to be used in these circumstances.

It would also be difficult to disregard the fact that, after the criminal complaints were announced on May 9th and prior to the Grand Jury deliberations of May 25th, a national debate had ensued revolving around the charges brought in Rockford, Illinois, and their implications for the ever-increasing problem of women who use drugs during pregnancy.

People v. Jennifer Clarise Johnson On July 13, 1989, a Seminole County, Florida judge found Jennifer Johnson guilty of delivery of a controlled substance to a child. The judge found that delivery, for purposes of the statute, occurred through the umbilical cord after the birth of the child and before the cord was severed. Jeff Deen, the Assistant State's Attorney who prosecuted the case, has since pointed out that Johnson, age 23, had previously given birth to three other cocaine-affected babies, and in this case was arrested at a crack house. "We needed to make sure this woman does not give birth to another cocaine baby."

Johnson was sentenced to fifteen years of probation including strict supervision, drug treatment, random drug testing, educational and vocational training, and an intensive prenatal care program if she ever became pregnant again.

SUPPORT FOR THE PROSECUTION OF MATERNAL DRUG ABUSE

Both cases reported above relied on a single important fact as a basis for the prosecution of the drug-abusing mother: that the child was born alive and exhibited the consequences of prenatal injury.

In the Melanie Green case, Illinois prosecutors relied on the "born alive" rule set out earlier in *People v. Bolar*. In *Bolar* the defendant was convicted of the offense of reckless homicide. The case involved an accident between a car driven by the defendant, who was found to be drunk, and another automobile containing a pregnant woman. As a result, the woman delivered her baby by emergency caesarean section within hours of the collision. Although the newborn child exhibited only a few heart beats and lived for approximately two minutes, the court found that the child was born alive and was therefore a person for purposes of the criminal statutes of the State of Illinois.

The Florida prosecution relied on a live birth in an entirely different fashion. The prosecutor argued in that case that the delivery of the controlled substance occurred after the live birth via the umbilical cord and prior to the cutting of the cord. Thus, it was argued, that the delivery of the controlled substance occurred not to a fetus but to a person who enjoyed the protection of the criminal code of the State of Florida.

Further support for the State's role in protecting the health of newborns even against prenatal injury is found in the statutes which provide protection for the fetus. These statutes proscribe actions by a person, usually other than the mother, which either intentionally or recklessly harm or kill a fetus. In other words, even in the absence of a live birth, most states afford protection to the unborn fetus against the harmful actions of another person. Arguably, the same protection should be afforded the infant against intentional harmful actions by a drug-abusing mother.

The state also receives support for a position in favor of the protection of the health of a newborn from a number of non-criminal cases. A line of civil cases in several states would appear to stand for the principle that a child has a right to begin life with a sound mind and body, and a person who interferes with that right may be subject to civil liability. In two cases decided within months of each other, the Supreme Court of Michigan upheld two actions for recovery of damages that were caused by the infliction of prenatal injury. In *Womack v. Buckhorn* the court upheld an action on behalf of an eight-year-old surviving child for prenatal brain injuries apparently suffered during the fourth month of the pregnancy in an automobile accident. The court adopted with approval the reasoning of a New Jersey Supreme Court decision and "recognized that a child has a legal right to begin life with a sound mind and body." Similarly, in *O'Neill v. Morse* the court found that a cause of action was allowed for prenatal injuries that caused the death of an eight-month-old viable fetus.

Illinois courts have allowed civil recovery on behalf of an infant for a negligently administered blood transfusion given to the mother prior to conception which resulted in damage to the child at birth. However, the same Illinois court would not extend a similar cause of action for prebirth injuries as between a child and its own mother. The court, however, went on to say that a right to such a cause of action could be statutorily enacted by the Legislature.

Additional support for the state's role in protecting the health of newborns is found in the principles annunciated in recent decisions of the United States Supreme Court. The often cited case of *Roe v. Wade* set out that although a woman's right of privacy is broad enough to cover the abortion decision, the right is not absolute and is subject to limitations, "and that at some point the state's interest as to protection of health, medical standards and prenatal life, becomes dominant."

More recently, in the case of *Webster v. Reproductive Health Services*, the court expanded the state's interest in protecting potential human life by setting aside viability as a rigid line that had previously allowed state regulation only after viability had been shown but prohibited it before viability. The court goes on to say that the "fundamental right" to abortion as described in *Roe* is now accorded the lesser status of a "liberty interest." Such language surely supports a prosecutor's argument that the state's compelling interest in potential human life would allow the criminalization of acts which if committed by a pregnant woman can damage not just a viable fetus but eventually a born-alive infant. It follows that, once a pregnant woman has abandoned her right to abort and has decided to carry the fetus to term, society can well impose a duty on the mother to insure that the fetus is born as healthy as possible.

A further argument in support of the state's interest in prosecuting women who engage in conduct which is damaging to the health of a newborn child is especially compelling in regard to maternal drug use during pregnancy. Simply put, there is no fundamental right or even a liberty interest in the use of psycho-active drugs. A perceived right of privacy has never formed an absolute barrier against state prosecutions of those who use or possess narcotics. Certainly no exception can be made simply because the person using drugs happens to be pregnant.

Critics of the prosecutor's role argue that any statute that would punish mothers who create a substantial risk of harm to their fetus will run afoul of constitutional requirements, including prohibitions on vagueness, guarantees of liberty and privacy, and rights of due process and equal protection....

In spite of such criticism, the state's role in protecting those citizens who are least able to protect themselves, namely the newborn, mandates an aggressive posture. Much of the criticism of prosecutorial efforts is based on speculation as to the consequences of prosecution and ignores the basic tenet of criminal law that prosecutions deter the prosecuted and others from committing additional crimes. To assume that it will only drive persons further underground is to somehow argue that certain prosecutions of crime will only force perpetrators to make even more aggressive efforts to escape apprehension, thus making arrest and prosecution unadvisable. Neither could this be accepted as an argument justifying even the weakening of criminal sanctions....

The concern that pregnant addicts will avoid obtaining health care for themselves or their infants because of the fear of prosecution cannot justify the absence of state action to protect the newborn. If the state were to accept such reasoning, then existing child abuse laws would have to be reconsidered since

they might deter parents from obtaining medical care for physically or sexually abused children. That argument has not been accepted as a valid reason for abolishing child abuse laws or for not prosecuting child abusers....

The far better policy is for the state to acknowledge its responsibility not only to provide a deterrant to criminal and destructive behavior by pregnant addicts but also to provide adequate opportunities for those who might seek help to discontinue their addiction. Prosecution has a role in its ability to deter future criminal behavior and to protect the best interests of the child. The medical and social welfare establishment must assume an even greater responsibility to encourage legislators to provide adequate funding and facilities so that no pregnant woman who is addicted to drugs will be denied the opportunity to seek appropriate prenatal care and treatment for her addiction.

ONE STATE'S RESPONSE

The Legislature of the State of Illinois at the urging of local prosecutors moved quickly to amend its juvenile court act in order to provide protection to those children born drug-affected. Previously, Illinois law provided that a court could assume jurisdiction over addicted minors or a minor who is generally declared neglected or abused.

Effective January 1, 1990, the juvenile court act was amended to expand the definition of a neglected or abused minor....

those who are neglected include... any newborn infant whose blood or urine contains any amount of a controlled substance....

The purpose of the new statute is to make it easier for the court to assert jurisdiction over a newborn infant born drug-affected. The state is not required to show either the addiction of the child or harmful effects on the child in order to remove the child from a drug-abusing mother. Used in this context, prosecutors can work with the mother in a rather coercive atmosphere to encourage her to enter into drug rehabilitation and, upon the successful completion of the program, be reunited with her child.

Additional legislation before the Illinois Legislature is House Bill 2835 sponsored by Representatives John Hallock (R-Rockford) and Edolo "Zeke" Giorgi (D-Rockford). This bill represents the first attempt to specifically address the prosecution of drug-abusing pregnant women....

The statute provides for a class 4 felony disposition upon conviction. A class 4 felony is a probationable felony which can also result in a term of imprisonment from one to three years.

Subsequent paragraphs set out certain defenses available to the accused.

> It shall not be a violation of this section if a woman knowingly or intentionally uses a narcotic or dangerous drug in the first twelve weeks of pregnancy and:
> 1. She has no knowledge that she is pregnant; or 2. Subsequently, within the first twelve weeks of pregnancy, undergoes medical treatment for substance abuse or treatment or rehabilitation in a program or facility approved by the Illinois Department of Alcoholism and Substance Abuse, and thereafter discontinues any further use of drugs or narcotics as previously set forth.

... A woman, under this statute, could not be prosecuted for self-reporting her addiction in the early stages of the pregnancy. Nor could she be prosecuted under this statute if, even during the subsequent stages of the pregnancy, she discontinued her drug use to the extent that no drugs were present in her system or the baby's system at the time of birth. The statute, as drafted, is clearly intended to allow prosecutors to invoke the criminal statutes in the most serious of cases.

CONCLUSION

Local prosecutors have a legitimate role in responding to the increasing problem of drug-abusing pregnant women and their drug-affected children. Eliminating the pain, suffering and death resulting from drug exposure in newborns must be a prosecutor's priority. However, the use of existing statutes to address the problem may meet with limited success since they are burdened with numerous constitutional problems dealing with original intent, notice, vagueness, and due process.

The juvenile courts may offer perhaps the best initial response in working to protect the interests of a surviving child. However, in order to address more serious cases, legislative efforts may be required to provide new statutes that will specifically address the problem and hopefully deter future criminal conduct which deprives children of their important right to a healthy and normal birth.

The long-term solution does not rest with the prosecutor alone. Society, including the medical and social welfare establishment, must be more responsive in providing readily accessible prenatal care and treatment alternatives for pregnant addicts. In the short term however, prosecutors must be prepared to play a vital role in protecting children and deterring women from engaging in conduct which will harm the newborn child. If prosecutors fail to respond, then they are simply closing the doors of the criminal justice system to those persons, the newborn, who are least able to open the doors for themselves.

NO

Sue Mahan

CRIMINALIZATION OF PREGNANCY

ANALYSIS OF JUDICIAL ALTERNATIVES

Criminalization

A large number of criminal actions against cocaine-abusing pregnant women originate in Florida, reflecting a punitive approach to crack mothers. There are more pregnant women in prison in Florida than in any other state, and a number of babies are born while their mothers are incarcerated in the state (Maguire & Pastore, 1994).

Criminally prosecuting mothers who give birth to drug-dependent babies conflicts with the stated public policy underlying Florida's child welfare laws. The Florida legislature's paramount concern in providing comprehensive protective services for abused and neglected children is supposed to be "to preserve the family life of the parent and children, to the maximum extend possible, by enhancing the parental capacity for adequate child care." Instead, enforcing a punitive policy actually results in lower parental capacity to provide for adequate child care. Criminal prosecutions needlessly destroy the family by incarcerating the mother when alternative measures could both protect the child and stabilize the family (Spitzer, 1987).

This contradiction between goals and application of one state's policy on pregnant substance abusers is typical. Discrepancies among policies, legislation, and case law concerning crack babies in many states resulted from public confusion and hasty responses that accompanied the fear of the crack epidemic spreading across the United States in the late 1980s.

Public policy, procedure, and laws designed to control women who use drugs during their pregnancy can be classified into three types: narcotics laws, criminalization laws, and informant laws. All three types of law focus on punishing a mother for drug use so that the fetus will be protected.

Narcotics laws apply existing prohibitions against drug possession and distribution to pregnant women. Both men and women lose their liberty when they are convicted for illegal drug use; pregnant women may lose their liberty for longer. The intent of existing narcotics laws has been expanded so

From Sue Mahan, *Crack Cocaine, Crime, and Women: Legal, Social, and Treatment Issues* (Sage Publications, 1996), pp. 38–49. Copyright © 1996 by Sage Publications, Inc. Reprinted by permission. References omitted.

that women can be charged with delivering a controlled substance to a minor when the recipient is a fetus or newborn infant.

Criminalization laws are recently drafted statutes that specifically define behaviors such as fetal endangerment or fetal abuse. Many authors have called this fetal abuse path in policy a legal "slippery slope" (Bagley & Merlo, 1995). Fetal abuse laws have two important limitations. They define a fetus as a child, but court decisions have not supported the concept of a fetus as a separate entity. They also hold the rights of a fetus as above the rights of a pregnant woman to make decisions about her own body.

Informant laws are those most often used to take away the rights of the mother. Informant laws require health care workers or other treatment providers to report suspected or actual drug use by pregnant women. Women who are routinely subjected to drug testing or the testing of their newborns are likely to be poor and either black or Hispanic.

Fetal Abuse as Child Abuse

When pregnant mothers are charged with "child abuse" before their babies have been born, there may be some question about how the behavior is defined in the law. In most statutes, reference is made to nonaccidental harm inflicted on children by those responsible for their care. Three issues arise from thee statutes: the meaning of "nonaccidental," the proof of harm, and whether fetuses are to be considered as children.

Child abuse laws are enacted at the state level. Their purpose is to protect infants and children from abuse and neglect perpetrated by parents or guardians. When someone reports to a state's division of child protective services that a child is being abused or neglected, a worker usually will conduct a preliminary investigation. If abuse or neglect is substantiated, the worker may petition the court for temporary custody of the child.

In many states, child protective service agencies have petitioned the courts in order to get protective custody of fetuses. In these actions, it has been affirmed that the child (fetus) is or will be abused or neglected. The Supreme Court, however, upheld that for state child protection laws to apply to the unborn fetus, the laws must specifically define a "fetus" as a "child," or it must be clear that the state legislature intended an unborn fetus to be considered a child under the child abuse and neglect laws (*Webster v. Reproductive Health Services*, 1989).

Some state divisions of child protective services have tried to obtain protective custody of a fetus in order to get custody of the child upon birth. New Jersey enacted a child protection statute that is applicable to an unborn fetus. The statute provides,

> Whenever it shall appear that any child within this state is of such circumstances that his welfare will be endangered unless proper care or custody is provided, an application *may be filed* seeking that the Bureau of Children's Services accept and provide such care or custody of such child as the circumstances may require. The provisions of this section shall be deemed to include an application on behalf of an unborn child. (NJ Stat. Ann. §30:4C-11)

When a charge of improper parenting or delivery of a controlled substance is based on using illicit substances while pregnant, the question that must be addressed by the court is whether fetal abuse is child abuse. Most states do not recognize fetal abuse as child abuse (Kantrowitz, 1989). The following is Florida's statute (1993) with regard to child abuse; many states have similar statutes.

> Whoever, willfully or by culpable negligence, deprives a child of, or allows a child to be deprived of, necessary food, clothing, shelter, or medical treatment, or who, knowingly or by culpable negligence, permits physical or mental injury to a child, and in so doing causes great bodily harm, permanent disability, or permanent disfigurement to such child, shall be guilty of a felony of the third degree. (Sec. 827.04(1))

At the district level, some courts of appeal have held that a child abuse statute does not include a fetus and, therefore, that the defendant cannot be prosecuted for child abuse based on introduction of drugs into her own body during gestation (*State v. Gethers*, 1991). A New York City court also held that a defendant cannot be charged with endangering the welfare of a child based on acts that endanger the unborn (*The People of the State of New York v. Melissa A. Morabito*, 1992). The Kentucky Supreme Court decided that the offense of criminal child abuse does not extend to the defendant's use of drugs while pregnant (*Commonwealth v. Welch*, 1993).

Many cases of drug-exposed and drug-addicted infants reach the dependency side of the juvenile court. The first point of entry of drug-exposed infants and their families into the juvenile court system is often immediately after birth. Many hospitals routinely perform neonatal toxicology screens when maternal substance abuse is suspected. Based on a positive toxicology test, the hospital may report the results to the child protective services agency, which in turn may ask the juvenile court to prevent he child's release to the parents while an investigation takes place. Child neglect is an issue with "boarder babies" being abandoned by their parents. Crack addiction is said to have led to the creation of a large number of babies being boarded in maternity, pediatric, and other settings because they have been abandoned by, or taken away from, their parents (Levy & Rutter, 1992). Babies being abandoned may be directly related to threats of civil and criminal action and to fear of authorities on the part of childbearing addicts. Threat of court action against pregnant drug users may also be indirectly responsible for harm inflicted from unprofessional abortions and lack of adequate care during pregnancy.

Courts have ruled that the use of drugs during pregnancy is by itself sufficient basis to trigger a child-abuse report and to support juvenile court dependency jurisdiction (Sagatun, 1993).

Such cases, however, seldom are upheld on appeal. For example, the Court of Appeals of Ohio decided that the juvenile court has no jurisdiction to regulate the conduct of a pregnant adult for the purpose of protecting the health of her unborn child (*Cox v. Court of Common Pleas*, 1988).

Although the sate may justify coercion of cocaine mothers on the basis of its interest in protecting the fetus, it does not undertake any duty to ensure the necessary care for the woman's body. Instead, when pregnant addicts are handled by the court, the duty for protecting the fetus is imposed entirely on the pregnant woman. A wide variety of acts or conditions on the part of a pregnant woman could pose some threat to her fetus, including failure to eat well; using nonprescription, prescription, or illegal drugs; engaging in sexual intercourse; exercising or not exercising; smoking; drinking alcohol; and even ingesting something as common as caffeine. Other threats, such as physical harm resulting from accident or disease and working or living near toxic substances, also are significant when it comes to imposing responsibility (Kasinsky, 1993).

Harm and danger to a potential life may be greatest from an environment over which the mother has little control. The perils of pollution and ecological damage to unborn children, which are the responsibility of the state, remain unconsidered in child abuse and neglect issues (Mariner, Glantz, & Annas, 1990).

These environmental risks are likely to be high for those pregnant women who also are at the greatest risk of being criminalized for substance abuse.

Delivery of a Controlled Substance to a Minor

Women can be charged with delivery of a controlled substance to a minor when blood test results are positive for cocaine at the moment of birth. This action presumes that health care personnel will provide information and that the mother has no right to privacy. The state can require a physician to administer a toxicology test to a pregnant women without her consent if there is a compelling interest that outweighs her Fourth Amendment right to privacy from government intrusion. The state statute, however, must be strictly worded for the protection of infant rights over the rights of the mother (Appel, 1992).

The state of Missouri has one such strictly worded statute. Its wording includes the following:

[N]eglect also includes prenatal exposure to a controlled substance... used by the mother for a non-medical purpose, as evidenced by withdrawal symptoms in the child at birth, results of a toxicology test performed on the mother at delivery or the child at birth, or medical effects or developmental delays during the child's first year of life that medically indicate prenatal exposure to a controlled substance.

In addition any

person with responsibility for the care of children, [who] has reasonable cause to suspect that a child has been or may be subjected to conditions or circumstances which would reasonably result in abuse or neglect, including the use of a controlled substance by a pregnant women for a non-medical purpose,... shall immediately report or cause a report to be made to the Missouri division of family services. (Missouri Senate Bill No. 756, 1990)

Many medical and legal experts criticize the practice of administering toxicology tests to nonconsenting pregnant women. These experts believe that toxicology tests given without the knowledge or consent of the patient violate their professional trust (Appel, 1992). Such tests raise the issues of discrimination, consent, and confidentiality. They often target women who cannot afford prenatal care or who can afford only to go to public hospitals or clinics. These women are labeled "high risk" and are tested routinely without their consent. Those who can afford private care remain effectively insulated from this form of state intrusion (Robin-Vergeer, 1990).

Hair analysis also has been used in some studies to detect gestational cocaine exposure. Samples of hair are collected from the mothers, and meconium, urine, and hair are also collected from newborns ("Best Way," 1992; Marques, Tipetts, &

Branch, 199). Intrusiveness and right to privacy issues are important with hair analysis, as with urine and blood testing.

Florida, along with many other states, passed a statute in 1987 calling for state intervention when infants are born drug dependent. It was argued that although legislators may not have the right to protect the unborn, they must make an effort to protect the quality of life for children born to drug-dependent mothers. Hospital workers are required to notify the state department of Health and Rehabilitative Services immediately whenever babies are born with drugs in their systems. Child dependency proceedings can then be initiated to remove the child from parental custody (Spitzer, 1987). Throughout the United States, special prosecutors handling child abuse cases have made it clear that no woman, whether she is pregnant or not, has the right to use cocaine. In this area, they see no reason for concern about legal rights (Curriden, 1990).

Jennifer Johnson was the first woman in the United States to be convicted for delivery of a controlled substance to a minor on the birth of a baby with traces of cocaine in her system. The Florida Supreme Court did not uphold the conviction.

Likewise, the circuit court in Michigan held that the use of cocaine by pregnant women, which may result in postpartum transfer of cocaine through the umbilical cord to their infants, is not the type of conduct that the legislature intended to be prosecuted under the *delivery of cocaine* statutes (*People v. Hardy*, 1991).

The court decisions are, no doubt, a reaction to the obvious limits of the criminal approach to the problem of cocaine pregnancies. In order to have proof of delivery of a controlled substance to the new-born child, the child must be born alive. In addition, evidence of delivery of cocaine must rest on blood tests done at the moment of birth. Positive results indicate cocaine use very close to the delivery. There is no way to prove delivery of cocaine to the fetus in the first or second trimester of pregnancy, although the damage to the developing child from drug use may be great during the early stages and long before the moment of birth.

Medical personnel may avoid reporting cocaine use by pregnant women because they believe that, out of fear of prosecution, mothers will stay away from prenatal care (Mills & Bishop, 1990). Some prosecutors disagree. Those who favor criminal sanctions say that the fear of pregnant addicts avoiding prenatal care is not a sufficient concern to interfere with the action of the state to protect the unborn. From this perspective, if laws against crack mothers should not be enforced because they might keep pregnant addicts from seeking prenatal care, then child abuse laws should not be enforced either. Child abuse penalties may deter parents from obtaining medical care for abused children out of fear of criminal consequences in the same ways that crack abuse penalties may deter mothers from seeking medical care for themselves while pregnant (Logli, 1990).

Although the state's motive in prosecuting pregnant women may be to provide an incentive for them to stop using drugs, drug treatment is largely unavailable to them. Their pregnancy acts as a disqualifying factor for most programs (Kasinsky, 1993).

Manslaughter

Pregnant drug users may be charged with manslaughter even though the statutes were intended for third party criminal culpability. For example, the Florida criminal code makes the willful killing of an unborn quick child, by any injury *to the mother* of such child that would be murder if it resulted in the death of such mother, to be deemed manslaughter, a felony in the second degree (Florida Criminal Code 782.09, 1992). The law does not mention injury done *by the mother* to herself, yet there have been cases after the second trimester in which infants were stillborn and their mothers were charged with manslaughter. The court must decide that the death resulted from cocaine use for a crack mother to be convicted of manslaughter.

Attributing the stillbirth of an infant to cocaine abuse and considering this to be manslaughter comes from a "reasonable person" perspective about the law. The rationale behind this approach is that pregnant women are being asked only to act reasonably. If a women elects to have unprotected sex, and once pregnant elects not to have an abortion, she takes on the additional responsibilities to see that, as far as possible, the child will be born healthy (Curriden, 1990). This may not seem so reasonable to a pregnant crack user.

The pregnant addict may not realize that she is pregnant until far into the first trimester and after significant risk of damage to the fetus already has been incurred. She may expect that if she uses cocaine, she is likely to have a spontaneous abortion. Although the numbers of spontaneous miscarriages among cocaine-abusing pregnant women are high, using the drug may not bring about the results she sought, and instead an unhealthy infant may result.

Finally, holding responsible for the health birth of the child the pregnant mother who carries her fetus to full term, rather than electing to have an abortion, assumes that safe, no-cost abortions are available to all women in the first few weeks of pregnancy. Legal, medically authorized abortions are not free to any female who wants to have one. Adequate prenatal health care is not easily available to all pregnant women, either. Without them, pregnant addicts in the throes of a lifestyle of compulsion are not likely to take care of their own health and well-being or to be responsible for that of their unborn children.

It is doubtful whether manslaughter charges would ever result in a conviction for a cocaine mother if tested in a jury trial. It is even more unlikely that the charge would be upheld in an appeal to a higher court. The case law is clear: The legal conception of "person" does not include a fetus (Spitzer, 1987). The Supreme Court has held that at no state of development is a fetus a "person" with legal rights separate from those of the mother (Paltrow, 1990). When cocaine mothers have been convicted of manslaughter, it was the result of their guilty pleas without the deliberation of public trials.

Involuntary Detention

Punishment, rehabilitation, and deterrence all have been used to justify involuntary detention of pregnant addicts, along with education and protection for the "infant" (Mills & Bishop, 1990). For some, detention is the key element in treating pregnant cocaine addicts to reduce the severity of the effects of cocaine use on the fetus (New York Senate Committee on Investigations, Taxation and Government Operations, 1989). According to *The New York Times*, when medical doctors who were maternal-fetal specialists were surveyed in 1986, more than half of them agreed that pregnant women who refuse medical advice and endanger the life of the fetus should be detained in hospitals and forced to follow their physicians' orders (Lewin, 1987). Some law enforcement agents and state prosecutors have justified the detention of pregnant cocaine addicts in jails and lock-up facilities for this reason, not necessarily because of punishment or retributive goals.

In effect, the state has taken custody of a child before it is born (Gest, 1989). In other words, the mother-fetus relationship can cause conflict because the treatment of one involves the mistreatment of the other. There is an understood obligation to the mother's health and well-being, but with involuntary detention, the health and well-being of the fetus comes first, although this is not a legally recognized obligation (Nelson & Milliken, 1988).

Some public officials and researchers have suggested that drug users can be civilly committed to a drug treatment program while they are pregnant. Involuntary civil commitment is a process whereby an individual is found to pose a danger to herself or others and is forced to undergo care. Conditions that usually subject a person to civil commitment include mental illness, developmental retardation, mental retardation, alcoholism, drug dependency, or some combination of these factors. Approximately 75% of the states have some statutory provision governing the involuntary commitment of drug-dependent persons (Garcia & Keilitz, 1990). In these states, the laws limit involuntary civil commitments to drug-dependent persons in need of treatment and care, who are likely to be dangerous to themselves or others, or who are unable to meet their basic needs for sustenance, shelter, and self-protection. Pregnant drug users may be subject to laws that find them to be dangers to themselves because of their actions, or maternal addiction may be deemed to endanger an "other" with protectable rights. Addicts may lose their maternal rights as well as their rights to liberty in civil proceedings because they are considered dangerous, even though no criminal charge can be made.

When pregnant drug users are charged with any offense, they can be subject to the discretionary orders of the judge before whom they appear. For example, judges throughout the country are sentencing pregnant drug offenders to enter drug treatment facilities. Prosecutors are also arguing successfully that release from jail or prison be made conditional on completion of drug treatment. Judicial discretion also can affect the length of sentence imposed. Sometimes judges impose longer sentences on pregnant drug users. In 1993, 489 pregnant women were being held in state corrections institutions (in 47 states for which there were reports), and 105 pregnant inmates were in federal custody. During that year, there were 789 reported births in inmates (Maguire & Pastore, 1994). Many more went uncounted because inmates delivered in community facilities and then returned to the state or federal prison to complete their sentences. These are only a small proportion of the pregnant women being detained. The number of pregnant inmates serving terms in county jails and local facilities is not available. It is likely that most crack addicts are sentenced to misdemeanor terms in local corrections facilities to detain them until their babies are born.

Jailing pregnant drug users may not reduce harm to the fetus at all. In jail, where the mother may be experiencing extreme stress, there actually may be an increased chance of fetal distress. In addition, pregnant women may not get adequate medical care. Health care providers within the criminal justice system are neither well equipped nor prepared to handle obstetrics.

When judges tailor a woman's sentence to her reproductive status, the resulting harsher treatment has an impact not only for the individual being sentenced but for all women in general. Women who suffer from drug or alcohol dependency and AIDS do not exist in a social, political, and economic vacuum, yet when policy calls for criminalization and medicalization for these problems, each individual is treated without consideration of her environmental concerns. The conditions of poverty, discrimination, unemployment, inadequate health care services, and violence against women are not addressed. General social problems underlying the symptoms confronted in criminal courts and crisis health care treatment are ignored (Bagley & Merlo, 1995).

Women who do seek help for drug addiction during pregnancy cannot get it. Two-thirds of the hospitals surveyed by the House Select Committee reported they had not drug treatment programs to which their pregnant patients could be referred; none reported the availability of special programs geared to providing comprehensive drug treatment and prenatal care (Kasinsky, 1993). Without treatment, prosecutions are simply punitive stopgaps, and reporting laws force poor women of minority groups to surrender their children (Humphries, 1993).

Fetal Endangerment

Fundamental Rights. The use of narcotics and cocaine already is illegal. Many states have found it sufficient simply to enforce already existing laws rather than add penalties for pregnant women. When laws make actions criminal that only women can commit, the laws are, by their nature, discriminatory.

Prosecutions by the criminal justice system for drug use have been of predominantly poor women of minority backgrounds who have given birth to drug-exposed babies. Between 1987 and 1991, at least 165 women in 26 states were arrested on criminal charges because of their drug behavior during pregnancy. Tens of thousands more women have had their children removed from them and taken into custody by welfare agencies. Poor women have been prosecuted by a largely white social welfare establishment; more than half of all the recent prosecutions of pregnant women were of women of color (Kasinsky, 1993).

Women are being prosecuted for behavior that *may be* harmful without proof that the behavior *has been* harmful. The failed duty of these women is failure to avoid risk, not failure to avoid harm (Reed, 1993).

Rights of Women. There has been increasingly outspoken opposition of public health organizations to prosecutions of cocaine-addicted pregnant women (Paltrow, 1990). The very nature of the problem mandates that whatever action criminal justice authorities may take will be possible only with the cooperation and support of health care providers.

Health care providers are being asked to supply information to legal and criminal authorities if pregnant patients are using cocaine. It is not clear by what judicial standard a mother may have her acts of commission and omission while pregnant made subject to state scrutiny (Paltrow, 1990). Health care providers are being asked to take on a role outside the purview of their professions. As informants for the state, they are also acting in potential violation of patients' rights.

Rather than a focus on criminalization of pregnant addicts, a more comprehensive and complex policy is needed. Instead of filtering pregnant substance abusers through the costly process of criminalization, women in need of care can be identified by outreach workers in their neighborhoods. Some drug treatment programs have employed former addicts as outreach workers. Workers go to laundromats, grocery stores, and crack houses searching for pregnant women on drugs. These neighborhood workers are more likely than others to be effective in encouraging pregnant women to seek care and helping them find appropriate drug treatment, health care, and family services (Appel, 1992).

When compared with that of other industrialized countries, the infant mortality rate is high in the United States, and the rate of infant death has climbed since the 1970s. Despite a high standard of living, the United States ranks low on this significant indicator of quality of life. Improving the status of the nation in this important area will come only when all pregnant women are provided with qual-

ity prenatal care and assistance before and throughout their pregnancies. Making infant mortality a priority for change means addressing the multiple health care problems of all childbearing women (Merlo, 1993).

Structural Issues.   To some, laws relating to family life are important because of their direct effect in coercing compliance. The real importance of these laws is that they set the outer limits of what the community regards as morally tolerable (Johnson, 1990). Prohibitory laws show that concern is not really focused on the well-being of infants, nor that of their mothers. Drastic action toward cocaine mothers and other substance abusers reflects public fear and loathing toward crack cocaine. The risks faced by pregnant women in the workplace and in substandard housing without adequate health care are not considered; instead, responsibility for the fetus is made a personal responsibility.

In assessing blame, criminal law focuses on the past. A wiser approach is to look toward the future, in which the well-being of both the mother and the child should be of equal importance to a society that has an interest in producing future generations of healthy people.

POSTSCRIPT

Should Pregnant Drug Users Be Prosecuted?

Babies born with health problems as a result of their mothers' drug use is a tragedy that needs to be rectified. The issue is not whether or not this problem needs to be addressed, but what course of action is best. The need for medical intervention and specialized treatment programs serving pregnant women with drug problems has been recognized. The groundwork has been set for funding and developing such programs. The Office of Substance Abuse Prevention is funding chemical dependency programs specifically for pregnant women in several states.

Mahan argues that drug use by pregnant women is a medical problem that requires medical, not criminal, attention. She supports the notion that pregnant drug users and their drug-exposed infants are victims of drug abuse. She also feels that there is an element of discrimination in the practice of prosecuting women who use drugs during pregnancy because these women are predominantly low-income, single, members of minorities, and recipients of public assistance. Possible factors leading to their drug use—poverty, unemployment, poor education, and lack of vocational training—are not addressed when the solution to drug use during pregnancy is incarceration. Moreover, many pregnant women are denied access to treatment programs.

Prosecution proponents contend that medical intervention is not adequate in preventing pregnant women from using drugs and that criminal prosecution is necessary. Logli argues that "eliminating the pain, suffering and death resulting from drug exposure in newborns must be a prosecutor's priority." He insists that the criminal justice system should protect newborns and, if legal cause does exist for prosecution, then statutes should provide protection for the fetus. However, will prosecution result in more protection or less protection for the fetus? In essence, if a mother stops using drugs for fear of prosecution, then the fetus benefits. If the mother avoids prenatal care because of potential legal punishment, then the fetus suffers.

If women can be prosecuted for using illegal drugs such as cocaine and narcotics during pregnancy because they harm the fetus, then should women who smoke cigarettes and drink alcohol during pregnancy also be prosecuted? The evidence is clear that tobacco and alcohol place the fetus at great risk; most discussions of prosecuting drug users, however, overlook women who use these drugs. Also, there is evidence that secondhand smoke may be a health hazard. Should people be prosecuted if they smoke around pregnant women?

In "Punishment, Treatment, Empowerment: Three Approaches to Policy For Pregnant Addicts," *Feminist Studies* (Spring 1994), Iris Marion Young contends that punishing pregnant addicts may be both racist and sexist and that women need to be empowered. A series of articles in *Alcohol Health and Research World* (vol. 18, no. 1, 1994) address the effects of alcohol on the fetus, strategies for preventing fetal alcohol syndrome, and the economic impact of fetal alcohol syndrome. Two additional articles that examine this issue are "Crack in the Cradle: Social Policy and Reproductive Rights Among Crack-Using Females," by John Lieb and Claire Strek-Elifson, *Contemporary Drug Problems* (Winter 1995) and "How Social Policies Make Matters Worse: The Case of Maternal Substance Abuse," by Maureen Norton-Hawk, *Journal of Drug Issues* (Summer 1994).

ISSUE 6

Is Harm Reduction a Desirable National Drug Policy Goal?

YES: Peter Reuter and Jonathan P. Caulkins, from "Redefining the Goals of National Drug Policy: Recommendations from a Working Group," *American Journal of Public Health* (August 1995)

NO: Robert L. DuPont and Eric A. Voth, from "Drug Legalization, Harm Reduction, and Drug Policy," *Annals of Internal Medicine* (1995)

ISSUE SUMMARY

YES: Peter Reuter of the University of Maryland and Jonathan P. Caulkins of Carnegie-Mellon University support efforts to reduce the violence and disease associated with drugs and the drug trade by minimizing the harm caused by drugs.

NO: Professor Robert L. DuPont of Georgetown University and Professor Eric A. Voth of the University of Kansas argue that there is insufficient evidence that a policy of harm reduction is beneficial and that the notion of harm reduction is just another way for some people to rationalize legalizing drugs.

There is little debate as to whether or not drug use has the potential to cause adverse physical and psychological effects upon the user. Moreover, the families and communities of drug users are affected as well. It would be desirable if people always did that which was good for themselves, their families, and their communities. However, people do not always act in health-promoting ways. Tens of millions of people engage in unhealthy behaviors such as ingesting cocaine, smoking marijuana, chewing tobacco, drinking large quantities of alcohol, inhaling solvents, smoking cigarettes, and injecting heroin. The question is not whether drug use is harmful to the individual or whether drug use is the cause of many of the problems in our society. Rather, one needs to ask: What strategy is most likely to limit or reduce problems resulting from drug use? Is it better to teach people how to use drugs in order to reduce or minimize the personal and social hazards associated with drugs, or is it better to strive for drug abstinence and limit access to drugs?

There are various approaches that can be taken to address drug use. One approach focuses on harm reduction. Another approach focuses on supply reduction. The harm reduction approach attempts to minimize the dangers of drug use. The premise behind this approach is that since millions of people take drugs and that many will continue to take drugs regardless of whether or not they are legal, it is logical to teach people how to lessen the problems associated with using drugs. A harm reduction approach attempts to curtail drug-related problems while also trying to diminish drug use. Reducing the demand for drugs is an important component of this approach. The concept of harm reduction applies not only to the individual but to society as well.

Even if individuals do cause harm to themselves, are there policies that can be enacted to limit the risks that drugs pose to other members of society? Harm reduction opponents claim that all members of society would be better served by improving and expanding enforcement of existing drug laws. Harm reduction advocates point out that current restrictive policies that strive for supply reduction by emphasizing drug enforcement, prosecution, and interdiction have been ineffective and that alternatives need to be explored.

Some of the goals of harm reduction include reducing violence related to the drug trade, lowering death rates directly attributable to drugs, reducing infectious diseases caused by drug use, and preventing the ravages of drugs from affecting family members. Another benefit may be economical in that less money would go for enforcement and prosecution, although more funds would be needed for drug prevention, education, and treatment. On the other hand, harm reduction may result in greater drug use and more people seeking drug treatment. Harm reduction opponents maintain that stiff drug laws act as important deterrents. Moreover, many people arrested for drug-related offenses receive treatment for their drug abuse while incarcerated.

Opponents of harm reduction feel that its advocates are hypocritical and point out that its advocates demand more stringent policies regarding tobacco advertising, smoking restrictions, and driving while under the influence of alcohol, while calling for a reduction in the penalties for illegal drug use. It is true that tobacco and alcohol cause more deaths and disabilities. Is it not possible that a policy of harm reduction would increase the number of deaths and disabilities from illegal drugs?

Using the Netherlands to illustrate their point, drug prohibition proponents state that, following decriminalization of marijuana in that country, there was an increase in shootings, robberies, and car thefts, and a rise in the rate of drug addiction. Even if the evidence demonstrated that decriminalization of marijuana in the Netherlands had beneficial effects, would it mean that marijuana decriminalization in the United States would have the same effect? Can the experience in the Netherlands be generalized to the United States?

The following selections debate whether or not a policy of harm reduction would lessen the adverse health and social effects that come from using illegal drugs. Peter Reuter and Jonathan P. Caulkins believe that current, restrictive policies have failed. Robert L. DuPont and Eric A. Voth feel that a policy of harm reduction would increase the negative consequences of drugs and that restrictive policies toward drug use are necessary since they deter their use.

YES

**Peter Reuter and
Jonathan P. Caulkins**

REDEFINING THE GOALS OF NATIONAL DRUG POLICY

INTRODUCTION

Policy goals matter for many reasons, such as mobilizing popular support, creating occasions for social learning, and developing accountability in government organizations. Here we focus on the ability of U.S. national drug-policy goals to generate targets that guide programmatic choices. A goal should identify an important value for society. Ideally, a set of goals should include all such values—and only such values—that are likely to be affected by policy decisions, and in so doing should generate priorities.

The Office of National Drug Control Policy is mandated to publish an annual *National Drug Control Strategy*, which sets forth the national goals for drug policy. Unfortunately, the goals of the agency have been narrowly focused on prevalence. Although the first Clinton administration *Strategy*, released in February 1994, differs substantially in focus and rhetoric from those of the Bush administration, it reaffirms the traditional theme of "one overarching goal—the reduction of drug use."[1(p61)]

The principal goal for drug policy should instead be to reduce the harms to society arising from the production, consumption, distribution, and control of drugs. Total harm (to users and the rest of society) can be expressed as the product of total use and the average harm per unit of use and thus can be lowered by reducing either component. Attention has been focused on the first; greater attention to the second would be beneficial.

This report briefly reviews the recent history of drug policy in terms of both goals and programs. It then suggests a new set of goals and discusses what indicators might be used to assess progress. Lastly, it presents some programmatic recommendations flowing from these goals and indicators.

BACKGROUND: POLICY AND GOALS, 1989 TO 1992

The Bush administration's first *Strategy* enunciated a clear, overriding goal for drug control—namely, to reduce the use of illicit drugs: "The highest priority of our drug policy must be a stubborn determination further to reduce the overall level of drug use nationwide—experimental first use, 'casual' use, regular use and addiction alike."(p8) In conformity with that goal and with the legislative requirement of the 1988 Anti-Drug Abuse Act that the strategy include "long-range goals for reducing drug abuse in the United States" and "short-term measurable objectives which the Director determines may be realistically achieved in [a] two-year period,"(section 1005) this *Strategy* targeted reductions in various survey-based measures of the prevalence of drug use. Of nine goals, five were reductions in National Household Survey on Drug Abuse measures, such as the percentage of 12- to 17-year-olds reporting use of cocaine within the last month. No specific health goals (e.g., reductions in the number of drug-affected births) were included. Neither were tobacco and alcohol included, except for reductions in drinking by those under age 21, which was added to the list of goals in 1992.

In practice, federal policy from 1989 to 1992, like state and local policy, continued its emphasis on law enforcement. In fact, the number of drug-related incarcerations over the last 15 years has increased much more dramatically than the number of persons in drug treatment. Although federal expenditures for treatment have grown rapidly (e.g., from $900 million in 1988 to $1.9 billion in 1992), state and local governments have slacked in their efforts so that total treatment funding has actually grown slowly. Thus, in 1990, more than 100,000 persons were sentenced to state prison for drug offenses, compared with fewer than 10,000 in 1980.[2] In contrast, drug treatment admissions less than doubled between 1980 and 1992 (reaching about 1.5 million) although there was probably a larger increase in the numbers needing such treatment.

Since 1985, as law enforcement has intensified, the prevalence of drug use has fallen substantially.[3] The proximate cause for this seems to be increased concern with the dangers of drug use rather than decreased availability of drugs or (except possibly for marijuana) rising prices.[4] Little research has been done to explain the change in attitude.[5]

Although overall prevalence has fallen sharply, the same cannot be said of heavy or problem use. Certainly, the number of emergency room admissions for drug-related problems has risen,[6] the percentage of criminal arrestees testing positive for drugs has declined only modestly (again, except for marijuana),[7] and there has not seemed to be any evidence of reductions in the amount of damage related to illicit drugs. An increasing number and percentage of reported acquired immunodeficiency syndrome (AIDS) cases have involved injection drug use (although the long lag time for the appearance of AIDS complicates the task of determining when the virus was contracted), and the occurrence of tuberculosis and hepatitis seems to be growing among the drug dependent.[8,9]

Furthermore, reductions in the prevalence of occasional drug use will only slightly ameliorate these drug-related problems in the next few years. The history of heroin use illustrates the problem. The number of addicts in 1985 was close to that in 1975, even though incidence rates for heroin use fell sharply after 1973. Most of the 1975 addicts were still addicted in 1985.[10] Heavy cocaine use may prove to be similarly resilient.

THE OBJECTIVES OF CURRENT NATIONAL DRUG POLICY

Based on experience since 1985, the rhetorical and policy-oriented emphasis on making drug use less acceptable and drugs less available, as well as the focus on drug prevalence as the dominant indicator of program success, has probably outlived its usefulness. More attention needs to be given now to the problems associated with frequent or high-risk use and to some of the most risky sequelae. Although the Clinton administration's new policy takes important steps in this direction, it still comes up short.

The most important step forward is that "[T]he 1994 *Strategy* expands the focus away from casual and intermittent drug use and places it more appropriately on the most difficult and problematic drug-using population—hardcore drug users."[1(p61)] In particular, the plan calls for a significant expansion in treatment and a reduction in enforcement's share of total federal expenditures. Unfortunately, it also calls for a 21.7% increase in spending on source country control, the least promising programmatic area.[11]

The Clinton *Strategy's* focus on problem users is another step forward. The Bush *Strategies* lacked such a focus, so rhetoric and resources were inefficiently deployed against aspects of drug use that caused relatively fewer problems for society. However, the Bush *Strategies* were coherent (albeit poorly directed in our opinion), whereas the Clinton *Strategy* can perhaps be best described as cluttered. It lists 14 goals and 64 bulleted objectives, some of which are more sensible than others.

It is commendable, for example, that the second objective is to "reduce the adverse health and social consequences of illicit drug use."[1(p65)] On the other hand, another objective is to "[B]etter define the size and scope and work aggressively to suppress domestic marijuana production and trafficking [sic]."[1(p69)] Not only is this vague and oriented toward process rather than outcome, but there is no measure whatsoever associated with this objective.

The 64 objectives do not flow from a single vision but rather are merely an unprioritized list. Some items on the list are good; some are bad; some are vacuous. They do not, however, do much to direct policy.

As an alternative, we suggest considering two simple goals: harm reduction and use reduction. This would facilitate development of a strategy that is both coherent and focused on the most important aspects of the problem.

INTEGRATING THE GOALS OF HARM AND USE REDUCTION

Use reduction is inadequate as the only guiding principle for drug policy because it is unidimensional and tends to overlook real differences among drugs, drug use patterns (including modes of administration), populations, and the many harms associated with drug distribution, enforcement, and control as opposed to drug use. In terms of harms, shifting a drug injector to a less dangerous form of drug use may be more important than persuading an occasional user of marijuana to cease consumption. At a programmatic level, use reduction invites a focus on the most easily deterred users, generally those at least risk of harming themselves or others, and a neglect of the most problematic users, those whose desistance can be achieved only at substantial cost. Generally speaking, use reduction slights drug treatment efforts, which lower the total number of users only moderately but may have a substantial impact on the total amount of drug-related damage.

Conceptually, harm reduction is much more attractive. Each policy or programmatic decision is assessed for its expected impact on society. If a policy or program is expected to reduce aggregate harm, it should be accepted; if it is expected to increase aggregate harm, it should be rejected. The prevalence of drug use should play no special and separate role. However, the harm reduction philosophy itself is intrinsically unacceptable to those who oppose drug use on moral grounds, can be stalled by an inability to quantify and compare various kinds of harm, and may be difficult to sell politically. Furthermore, reducing use—when harm per use does not rise—is one way of reducing harm. Hence, we recommend that both harm and use reduction goals be pursued and, thus, that the 1988 Anti-Drug Abuse Act be amended to focus goals on reducing drug abuse and related harms, and not just on abuse.

General harm reduction goals include reducing violence related to drug distribution, lowering mortality and morbidity (particularly the prevalence of infectious diseases) among the drug dependent, reducing the harms borne by innocent others (including family members), and reducing the costs stemming from and created by drug control interventions themselves. Clearly, these are broad categories that can be broken down into more specific subgoals, such as lowering the incidence of human immunodeficiency virus related to needle use, the incidence of tuberculosis among the drug dependent, and the number of homicides related to cocaine selling. Thus, whereas

use reduction can be seen as a pragmatic and measurable goal toward the ultimate end of reducing harm and is particularly appropriate for adolescents, harm reduction may be seen as the primary goal for adult populations.

The goals should reflect the integration of all psychoactive substances, regardless of legal status. For example, instead of trying to reduce the number of infants damaged by their mothers' illicit drug use during pregnancy, the appropriate goal should be to reduce the number of infants damaged by any substance abuse (including alcohol and cigarettes), given that the relevant programs and high-risk populations overlap.

We do not suggest that every goal falls within a framework that combines use and harm reduction. For example, minimizing the invasion of privacy that is a by-product of drug enforcement does not directly relate to reducing the prevalence of drug use or the harm done by drug abuse. Likewise, neither use nor harm reduction addresses the need for programs to be equitable (e.g., in their treatment of different ethnic and economic groups). Equity, like a number of other values (e.g., privacy and procedural fairness), should be a major consideration in making decisions about achieving goals.

INDICATORS

It is clearly desirable to incorporate indicators and other quantitative information into policy-making. Yet it would be a mistake to tie policy too closely to indicators for the simple reason that there are so few good indicators available. Existing data on harms may reasonably be termed "woeful"; no plausible measures exist for the number of child abuse or neglect cases related to drug abuse or for the share of homicides related to drug distribution, and information about lost productivity and property crime attributable to drug use is weak.[12] Some surveys contain items on perceptions of harms incurred by respondents and their intimates; these may provide a useful start in developing indicators and tracking their trends, but they have been underused to date.

The weakness of the indicators does not preclude the pursuit of harm reduction policies. Indeed, in other countries, data are even less available, yet at least some countries, such as the Netherlands, have implemented harm reduction policies that are highly regarded.[13] Since policy decisions are informed not just by data but also by intuition, anecdote, expert judgment, and (we hope) reason, a paucity of data does not reduce policymaking to coin tossing. Indicators can and should serve policy, but they should not be allowed to drive it.

POLICY AND PROGRAM RECOMMENDATIONS

We do not aim to be comprehensive in our recommendations here but to suggest some of the changes for both federal and lower levels of government that flow from having explicit harm reduction goals.

Inclusion of Alcohol and Tobacco

A major step toward developing sounder policy with respect to drugs would be to use that label for alcohol and nicotine (as the scientific literature already does), and to make an augmented Office of National Drug Control Policy responsible for coordinating federal policy toward alcohol and nicotine as part of the overall national drug control strategy. This extension of that agency's responsibility might reduce its ability to unite political constituencies under a banner of moral indignation, but that may actually be a desirable outcome and is, in our opinion, outweighed by other considerations. Alcohol and nicotine account for the vast majority of drug-related negative health outcomes and economic costs,[14] and for a large part of the drug-related dangers faced by juveniles.[15] Alcohol (but not nicotine) also plays a major role in causing violent crime and disrupting families, schools, and neighborhoods.

Including alcohol and cigarettes would allow integrated policy and ensure that all drugs are given proper emphasis in the key decisions about health care and crime control. For example, alcohol treatment can reduce crime; decisions about funding such treatment should reflect that gain. Similarly, well-designed drug enforcement at the local level can help reduce the spread of sexually transmitted diseases. The integration would also allow society to be tougher on alcohol and cigarettes, as it would help diminish the power of alcohol and cigarette producers to impede regulation.

Merging authority for illicit drugs with that for alcohol and tobacco does not have to result in the former receiving less attention. As enumerated above, the damages caused by illicit drugs are many, and few of those damages are given appropriate weight in decisions about the levels and programmatic forms of funding for control measures. For example, the gains to a community from reduced drug market-related disorder are not currently factored into evaluations of treatment effectiveness. However, once these illicit drugs are viewed as part of the family of psychoactive substances that cause a wide variety of individual and social damages, the potential reductions in tuberculosis, hepatitis, and sexually transmitted diseases, as well as in community quality of life, can be given full consideration. Finally, we believe that the integration will help ensure that for illicit drugs, the public will be alerted to the distinction between use and harm, while for alcohol and tobacco, the public will be reminded that all use has some risk of harm.

Programmatic Design

Secondary prevention is underused, yet it is a low-cost intervention that may have high payoffs. For example, doctors and other health care professionals rarely include questions about the use of alcohol, cigarettes, and illicit drugs when taking medical histories. However, evidence from research in the alcohol field suggests that even a 5-minute lecture, along with provision of information leaflets, can make a difference.[16]

Similarly, efforts to inform current users about harms associated with different modes of drug use should be encouraged. Just as the government now funds programs to reduce the risk of harm from adolescent sexual behavior while encouraging abstinence, so must it strive to apprise determined users about less harmful ways (e.g., mode of administration, time, and setting) of using drugs. Needle exchange programs, for which evaluations provide increasingly strong evidence, are just one example of this kind of program.[17,18]

The concerns with communicable diseases associated with frequent use of illicit drugs suggest aggressive screening and prophylaxis for tuberculosis (and probably other diseases as well) particularly targeted at drug-positive arrestees and drug treatment clients. These are the highest-risk populations, and their involvement in the criminal justice system provides an opportunity for increasing their compliance with medical regimes.

Drug enforcement at all levels should be more targeted toward harm reduction goals. Similarly, prosecutors and courts should seek means of using arrest as a way of pushing drug-involved offenders to abstinence, with incarceration as a threat rather than the first choice; the well-regarded Miami drug court represents such an innovation,[19] which has also been a staple of Dutch enforcement.

Federal Programs That Deal With Illicit Drugs

Source-country drug control programs seem to be very ineffective in raising the price of illegal drugs, and they offer few other benefits as well.[11] Slightly weaker but similar statements can be made about interdiction.[20] At least for cocaine, treatment compares very favorably with these programs and even with domestic enforcement in its ability to reduce consumption per dollar spent on the effort.[21] Some prevention programs also appear to be cost-effective.[22] Hence, expenditures for more carefully targeted treatment and prevention efforts should be increased. Additionally, federal enforcement should shift resources away from marijuana and toward heroin; and investigative agencies should give higher priority to the violence of organizations than to the quantity of drugs they ship.

The primary budget issue, however, is not so much balancing federal drug expenditures across different categories; rather, it is raising the priority of treatment and prevention within the health and education budgets and lowering it within the enforcement budget.[23] This is true in other levels of government as well.

Drug enforcement may account for as much as one third of national law enforcement expenditures; drug treatment, on the other hand, accounts for less than 1% of the nation's health care expenditures, and drug prevention accounts for a similarly minuscule share of national educational and community development expenditures.

Federal sentences for drug offenders are often too severe; they offend justice, serve poorly as drug control measures, and are very expensive to carry out. Prison costs form the most rapidly increasing element of the federal drug budget, and this trend will likely continue unless action is taken promptly. More than 40% of drug offenders serving 5-year sentences in federal prisons are relatively minor participants in the business.[24] This results in both an inefficient use of federal prison space and an important sense of inequity about federal drug enforcement. Congress should review the harsh mandatory minima that it imposed in 1986 and 1988, particularly for those caught selling small amounts of crack and for low-level participants (e.g., drivers and couriers) in large-scale transactions. The U.S. Sentencing Commission should review its guidelines to allow more attention to the gravity of the offense and not simply to the quantity of the drug. Federal prosecutors should be discouraged from bringing minor drug offenders into federal court.

In theory, harm reduction, unlike use reduction, is compatible with legalization. However, there is no evidence that legalization is, in fact, a harm-minimizing strategy, and no analytic approach offers promise of resolving that issue in the near future.

Any time that multiple objectives are identified for policy, weights or priorities have to be assigned to each. Although determining those weights is beyond the scope of this paper, moving from the rhetoric of a "drug-free America," a common slogan since the mid-1980s, to a policy focused on reducing the damage created by the production, distribution, consumption, and control of drugs could help ensure a more balanced policy.

REFERENCES

1. *National Drug Control Strategy.* Washington, DC: The White House; 1994.
2. *Prisoners in 1992.* Washington, DC: Bureau of Justice Statistics; 1993.
3. *National Household Survey on Drug Abuse: Main Findings.* Rockville, Md: National Institute on Drug Abuse; (annual).
4. Bachman JG, Johnston LD, O'Malley PM, Humphrey RH. Explaining the recent decline in marijuana use: differentiating the effects of perceived risks, disapproval and general lifestyle factors. *J Health Soc Behav.* 1988;29:92–112.
5. Johnston L, O'Malley P, Bachman J. *Drug Use, Drinking and Smoking: National Survey Results from High School, College and Young Adult Populations: 1975–1991.* Rockville, Md: National Institute on Drug Abuse; 1992.
6. *Drug Abuse Warning Network.* Series I. Rockville, Md: National Institute on Drug Abuse; (annual).
7. *Drug Use Forecasting: 1992 Annual Report.* Washington, DC: National Institute of Justice; 1993.
8. U.S. AIDS cases reported through December 1992. *HIV/AIDS Surveill.* 1994;6(2).
9. Screening for tuberculosis and tuberculous infection in high-risk populations. *MMWR.* 1990;39(RR-8):1–12.
10. Hser Y, Anglin MD, Powers K. A twenty-four year follow-up of California narcotic addicts. *Arch Gen Psychiatry.* 1993;50:577–584.
11. Kennedy M, Reuter P, Riley KJ. A simple economic model of cocaine production. *Math Comput Modelling.* 1993;17:19–36.
12. *Crack Babies.* A Report of the Office of the Inspector General, Office of Evaluation and Inspections. Washington, DC: U.S. Dept of Health and Human Services, Office of the Inspector General; 1990. OEI-03-89-01540.
13. Engelsman E. Dutch policy on the management of drug-related problems. *Br J Addict.* 1989;84:211–218.
14. Rice D, Kelman S, Miller L. Estimates of economic costs of alcohol and drug abuse and

mental illness, 1985 and 1988. *Public Health Rep.* 1991;106:280–292.

15. Pernanen K. *Alcohol in Human Violence.* New York, NY: Guilford Press; 1991.

16. Institute of Medicine. *Broadening the Base of Treatment for Alcohol Problems.* Washington, DC: National Academy of Sciences; 1990.

17. DesJarlais D, Friedman S. AIDS and legal access to sterile injecting equipment. *Ann Am Acad Polit Soc Sci.* 1992;521:42–65.

18. Kaplan E. Needle exchange or needless exchange? The state of the debate. *Infect Agents Dis.* 1992;1:92–98.

19. Miami's drug court: a different approach. Washington, DC: National Institute of Justice; 1993.

20. Caulkins JP, Crawford G, Reuter P. Simulation of adaptive response: a model of drug interdiction. *Math Comput Modelling.* 1993;17:37–52.

21. Rydell CP, Everingham S. *Controlling Cocaine: Supply Versus Demand Programs.* Santa Monica, Calif: RAND; 1994.

22. Caulkins JP, Fitzgerald N, Model K, Willis HL. *Preventing Drug Use among Youth through Community Outreach: The Military's Pilot Outreach Programs.* Santa Monica, Calif: RAND; 1994.

23. Kleiman MAR, *Against Excess: Drug Policy for Results.* New York, NY: Basic Books; 1992.

24. *Special Report to Congress: Mandatory Minimum Sentences in the Federal Criminal Justice System.* Washington, DC: U.S. Sentencing Commission; 1991.

NO

Robert L. DuPont
and Eric A. Voth

DRUG LEGALIZATION, HARM REDUCTION, AND DRUG POLICY

BACKGROUND

Two alternative policy options shape the current debate about how to move forward in addressing the Nation's problems with drug use(1). One school of thought, broadly labeled as *prohibition*, supports widening interdiction, treatment and prevention efforts while keeping drugs such as marijuana, cocaine, LSD, and heroin illegal. A conflicting viewpoint labeled *legalization* supports the elimination of restrictive drug policy while trying to limit the harms associated with non-medical drug use. Understanding the history of drug control in the United States places into perspective today's debate about drug policy options, which include legalization and the related policy called *harm reduction*(2).

Modern drug prohibition began in the 19th century when medicinal chemistry began to produce an enormous array of potent and habituating drugs. This array included heroin, which was first sold in the United States in 1898. These drugs were sold as ordinary items of commerce along with a popular new drink, cocaine-containing Coca-Cola. Physicians at that time prescribed addicting drugs freely to their patients producing a large group of medical addicts. The use of drugs such as cocaine originated with legitimate medical indications. Drug use by the public later grew rapidly to include the compulsive use, illegal activity to support the non-medical use, and consumption despite clear medical and social consequences.

This era of indiscriminate sale and use of addictive drugs ended during the first two decades of the 20th century with a new social contract embodied in the Pure Food and Drug Act of 1906(3), which dealt with the labeling of drugs. In 1914, The Harrison Narcotics Act(4), prohibited the sale of narcotics. The Volstead Act along with the 18th Amendment to the Constitution in 1919 prohibited the sale of alcohol. These laws were part of a broad reform movement in the United States which also included the rights of women to vote.

From Robert L. DuPont and Eric A. Voth, "Drug Legalization, Harm Reduction, and Drug Policy," *Annals of Internal Medicine*, vol. 123 (1995), pp. 461–465. Copyright © 1995 by the American College of Physicians. Reprinted by permission.

Under this new social contract, habituating drugs were not available except through a physician's prescription, and then they were used sparingly in the treatment of illnesses other than addiction. In 1933 alcohol was removed from the group of strictly controlled or prohibited substances. In 1937 marijuana was added to the list of prohibited substances because of a sudden increase in the use of the drug(5). The patent drug epidemic had begun with morphine and heroin in the final decade of the 19th century and ended with an explosive increase in the use of cocaine during the first decade of the 20th century.

The social contract for drugs of abuse and supporting laws served the country well by virtually ending the first drug abuse epidemic. The American drug control laws proved to be a model throughout the world during the first two-thirds of the 20th century. The use of habituating drugs, which had been out of control at the end of the 19th century, was dramatically reduced in the United States from 1920–1965(5).

The nation was lulled into complacency by the great and prolonged success of this drug abuse policy. American public and policy leaders entered a period of amnesia for the tragic consequences of widespread drug use. By the 1960's, most Americans had no personal memory of the earlier American addiction epidemic. Strict non-alcohol drug prohibition was respected broadly until the ascendant youth culture integrated drugs as a central element of its new lifestyles.

Marijuana, the hallucinogens, and cocaine became widely defined as *marginally addictive* or *soft* drugs.(6) Their use grew to be the focus of a call for legalization based on unsubstantiated claims that they were *no worse than alcohol and tobacco.* The substantial health and addiction problems currently recognized to result from the use of crack cocaine and marijuana, and extensive research now available on the harmful effects of many drugs are testimony to how society was misled in the 1960's(7). These effects include but are not limited to addiction, vehicular trauma, disease, suicide, and specific negative physical effects of drugs themselves(8–15).

LEGALIZATION OF ILLEGAL DRUGS

During recent years, the drug legalization movement has gained modest public support by attempting to associate opponents of drug legalization with the negative public perceptions of alcohol prohibition and by labeling the opponents of legalization as prohibitionists. For purposes of this discussion, prohibition is a restrictive policy which maintains legal restrictions against non-medical use or sale of addicting drugs as covered under the Controlled Substances Act(16).

Drug legalization is neither a simple nor singular public policy proposal. For example, drug legalization could at one extreme involve a return to wide-open access to all drugs for all people as was seen at the end of the 19th century. Partial legalization could entail such changes in drug policy as making currently illegal drugs available in their crude forms to certain types of medical patients. It might include the maintenance of addicts on heroin or their drug of choice, handouts of needles to addicts without the requirement of cessation of drug use, or marked softening in sentencing guidelines for drug-related offenses short of frank legalization.

The evidence of the negative global experience with the legal substances tobacco and alcohol is overlooked by most supporters of drug legalization. The data on alcohol and tobacco support the view that legalization of drugs leads to large increases in the use of the legalized drugs and to higher total social costs. These added costs are mostly paid in lost productivity, illness, and death. About 125,000 deaths annually in the United States are attributed to alcohol, while tobacco is estimated to cause 420,000 deaths annually. The deaths resulting from all illicit drugs combined total less than 10,000 annually. The social costs from alcohol use in the United States are estimated at $86 billion, while the costs of prohibiting illegal drug use (including enforcement and incarceration) are annually $58 billion(17,18). The social costs of smoking tobacco are estimated to be $65 billion annually(17). If one of the goals of a drug policy is to reduce the harm to society resulting from drug use, then alcohol and tobacco must be a top priority within this strategy.

Considering the numbers of users of illegal and legal drugs in the United States and the trends in the rates of use from 1985 to 1991 (Table 1), it becomes apparent that prohibitive drug policy actually has maintained lower levels of use compared to relatively widely available habituating substances. Equally important are the rates of use of illicit drugs which have fallen faster in comparison to the rates of legal drug use(19).

Substantial progress was made in the reduction of adolescent drug use from 1978 to 1992 (Table 2). That success was due to a relatively clear national message and broad-based anti-drug efforts in both the public and private sectors. Since 1992, a recent rise in adolescent drug use and more accepting attitudes toward drug use(20) has occurred. While the causes are multifactoral, the reduction of government and media anti-drug efforts coupled with increases in pro-drug media campaigns have played a role.

HARM REDUCTION

While reducing the harm caused by drug use is a universal goal of all drug policies, policy proposals which are currently termed *harm reduction* include a creative renaming for the dismantling of legal restrictions against drug use and sale. The essential components of legalization policies are couched within the concept termed *harm reduction*. Much of the driving force behind the harm reduction movement also centers around personal choice and *safe* drug use habits.(21)

Paradoxically, some public policy attempts at reducing the harms associated with use of alcohol and tobacco involve tightening restrictions on events such as intoxicated driver legislation and smoking restrictions(22), while current harm reduction proposals involving illegal drugs, to the contrary, generally involve softening the restrictions on use of illegal drugs.

The current proposals for harm reduction focus heavily on reduction or elimination in criminal penalties for drug offenses, softening of sentencing guidelines, addict maintenance programs, needle exchange programs for intravenous drug users, and removal of workplace drug testing programs(23). The efficacy of any of these modalities is yet to be established.

Table 1

Drug Use in the United States Prior 30 Days (in Millions)

	1985	1993	Decline
Drugs Legal for Adults			
Alcohol	113	103	9%
Cigarettes	60	50	17%
The Most Widely Used Drugs That Are Illegal for All Ages			
Marijuana	18	9	50%
Cocaine	6	1.3	78%

Source: U.S. Department of Health and Human Services, Public Health Service, National Institutes of Health. *National Survey Results on Drug Use, from the Monitoring the Future Study 1975–1993.* NIH Publication No. 94–3809, 1994.

Harm reduction policy as it is represented in the current policy debate, also attempts to mitigate the negative effects of non-medical drug use without reducing the use of illegal drugs. It is based on the assumption that most of the harm caused by non-medical drug use is the result of the societal efforts to stop drug use rather than the result of drug use itself. Those harms are considered generally to be associated with arrests and legal consequences from illegal behavior and incarceration(24). While harm reductionists contend that essentially innocent drug users are targeted by prohibition, only 2% of federal inmates are incarcerated for possession-related crime while 48% are incarcerated for trafficking. Despite the clear deterrent effect of legal penalties, some positive outcomes can be attributed to the criminal justice system. For example, 35% of drug-related inmates obtain treatment while incarcerated(25).

The Netherlands has been the international model for decriminalization and harm reduction. Their experience with decriminalization has included an increase in crime and drug use associated with decriminalization. From 1984 to 1992 cannabis use among pupils in

the Netherlands has increased 250%. Between 1988 and 1993, the number of registered addicts has risen 22%. Reflecting the decriminalization of marijuana, the number of marijuana addicts has risen 30% from 1991 to 1993 alone. As we see in the United States, the harms of increased drug use go beyond the user alone. Since the onset of tolerant drug policy in that country, shootings have increased 40%, hold ups have increased 69%, and car thefts have increased 62%(26).

In the United States we experimented briefly with the decriminalization of marijuana. That temporary softening of drug policy resulted in a statistically significant increase in emergency room drug mentions as compared to metropolitan areas not having decriminalization(27).

The current and still dominant drug policy seeks to curb drug use and the associated harms by using the legal system and other means such as workplace drug testing and treatment to reduce non-medical drug use in society. In contrast to the advocates of harm reduction or legalization, supporters of the current restrictive drug policy emphasize that most drug-related harm

Table 2

Drug Use Rates: Marijuana

| | Percent of High School Seniors Use of Marijuana | | | | | | | |
	1978	1986	1987	1988	1991	1992	1993	1994
Last 12 Mos	50.2	39.0	36.0	33.1	23.9	21.9	26.0	30.7
Last 30 Days	37.1	23.4	21.0	18.0	13.8	11.9	15.5	19.0
Daily	10.7	4.0	3.3	2.7	2.0	1.9	2.4	3.0

Source: U.S. Department of Health and Human Services, Public Health Service, National Institutes of Health. *National Survey Results on Drug Use, from the Monitoring the Future Study 1975–1993.* NIH Publication No. 94–3809, 1994.

is the result of drug use and not simply the result of the prohibition of drugs(28).

The legalizers and the prohibitionists find some common ground in the support of drug education and treatment. Supporters of restrictive drug policy teach avoidance of non-medical drug use entirely, and harm reductionists support teaching *responsible use* of currently illegal drugs. Many harm reductionists admit that they seek the ultimate legalization of illegal drugs, especially marijuana. A distinct subset of harm reductionists support harm reduction because of the element of decriminalization which takes legal pressure off of their own drug use. Those individuals seek to manipulate drug policy to justify their own drug using behaviors.

Clearly, all forms of legalization, including harm reduction, are strategies ultimately aimed at softening public and governmental attitudes against non-medical drug use and the availability of currently illegal drugs.

COSTS OF DRUG POLICY

Those who support legalization correctly point out that prohibiting the use of our currently illegal drugs is an expensive strategy. Table 3 demonstrates the sources of overall costs produced by the use of legal drugs as compared to illegal drugs. These data also illustrate the fact that restrictive drug policy shifts the costs of drug use related to health and productivity to the criminal justice system.

Augmenting a restrictive drug policy by broadening the drug treatment available to addicts may be a beneficial and cost-effective policy decision. A recent study by Rand estimates that the current societal costs and actual costs of controlling cocaine use alone total $42 billion annually ($13 billion for control costs and $29 for societal costs). Rand also estimated that the net control and societal costs related to cocaine could be reduced to $33.9 billion(29) by maintaining our current enforcement policies and adding to it treatment for all addicts. The Rand study further concluded that treatment is effective in reducing the costs to society not only by reducing the demand for drugs, but in removing the addict from drugs for sustained periods of time.

The supporters of restrictive drug policy must acknowledge that prohibition alone does not end either the use of prohibited drugs or the high cost to society resulting from the use of these drugs. Furthermore, drug prohibition achieves its goals at a substantial cost in the form of

Table 3

Economic Costs of Addiction in the United States 1990

	Illicit Drugs	Alcohol	Tobacco
Total Cost (Billions)	$66.9	$98.6	$98.6
Medical Care (%)	3.2 (4.8)	10.5 (10.7)	20.2 (28)
Lost Productivity (%)	8.0 (11.9)	36.6 (37.1)	6.8 (9.0)
Death (%)	3.4 (5.1)	33.6 (34.1)	45 (63.0)
Crime (%)	46.0 (68.8)	15.8 (16.0)	0.0 (0.0)
AIDS (%)	6.3 (9.4)	2.1 (2.1)	0.0 (0.0)

Source: Institute for Health Policy, Brandeis University. *Substance Abuse: The Nation's Number One Health Problem—Key Indicators for Policy.* Prepared for the Robert Wood Johnson Foundation, Princeton, NJ, 1998.

maintaining the criminal justice system and some restriction of personal choice. Prohibiting the use of some drugs is undeniably costly, but it is well worth the cost given the fact that the overall level and the total societal costs of drug use are reduced.

DRUG POLICY OPTIONS

Recognizing the range of options available within legalization and drug prohibition policies, it is important to look at the big picture of drug policy. We must ask if prohibiting the consumption of some drugs is effective in reducing social costs, or *harm*, and if restrictive policy is cost-effective. Two models for drug policy exist which help provide answers to these questions.

The first model looks back at life in the United States one hundred years ago to a time when habituating drugs were sold like toothpaste or candy. The problems with freely available habituating drugs at the end of the 19th century were judged by Americans at that time to be unacceptable. In the context of today's debate on drug policy, recall that prohibition policies were the result of a nonpartisan out-

cry over the serious negative effects of uncontrolled drug use. In other words, the prohibition of marijuana, heroin, and cocaine did not cause widespread drug use in the United States. Rather, widespread use of those drugs caused their prohibition. Furthermore, non-alcohol drug prohibition was successful in reducing drug use, and it was almost universally supported by all political parties in the United States and throughout the world for half a century.

To a large extent, alcohol prohibition was also successful from a health perspective while it lasted. As examples, deaths from cirrhosis of the liver fell from 29.5 per 100,000 in 1911 to 10.7 in 1929. Admissions to state mental hospitals for alcohol psychosis fell from 10 per 100,000 in 1919 to 4.7 in 1928 (30). The main failure of alcohol prohibition was in attempting to remove availability of alcohol from the public after it had been legal, accepted, and deeply integrated into society for many years. Our currently illegal drugs do not share that same level of acceptance and integration.

The second model compares the costs generated by the drugs which are now legal for adults to those which are not.

This entails comparing the social costs resulting from the use of alcohol and tobacco (legal drugs), to marijuana, cocaine, heroin, and other illegal drugs. Alcohol and tobacco produce more harm than all of the illegal drugs combined because they are so widely used. They are more widely used because they are legal. Being legal substances, they enjoy greater social acceptance, widespread advertising, and glorification. The national experience with alcohol and tobacco does not represent an attractive alternative to the prohibition of drug use as it is currently practiced in the United States and other countries throughout the world.

Because of the deep integration of alcohol and tobacco into society, prohibiting their use is unrealistic politically. However, major constraints on their use such as total elimination of advertising, high taxation, restriction on smoking locations, designated drivers programs, and product liability by manufacturers and distributors of these products show some promise in reducing the harm produced by these legal drugs(23).

RECOMMENDATIONS

The relevant policy question is whether legalization or reducing the restrictions on the availability of drugs would increase the number of drug users and total social harm produced by the use of currently illegal drugs. The available data demonstrate that legalization would increase the use of currently prohibited drugs(3,20,26,27).

Legalization or decriminalization creates a particular risk among young people whose social adaptation and maturation are not yet complete. This fact can be illustrated by comparing the levels of the use of currently legal drugs by young

Table 4

Prevalence of Drug Use in the United States High School Seniors, 1993 (Percent)

Drug	Lifetime Use	Last 30 Days
Any Illicit Drug	43	18
Marijuana	35	16
Cocaine	6	1.3
Alcohol	87	51
Cigarettes	62	30

Source: U.S. Department of Health and Human Services, Public Health Service, National Institutes of Health. *National Survey Results on Drug Use, from the Monitoring the Future Study 1975–1993.* NIH Publication No. 94–3809, 1994.

people (alcohol and tobacco) to the levels of illegal drugs. The use of all or these drugs is illegal for youth, yet the drugs that are legal for adults are more widely used by youth than the drugs which are illegal for both adults and youth (Table 4).

What is needed today is not the dismantling of restrictive drug policies. Instead, a strong national policy with the goal of reducing the harm of drug use through harm prevention (implementing drug prevention programs) and harm elimination through broader interdiction and rehabilitation efforts(31,32,33). This new policy should strengthen efforts to reduce the use of alcohol and tobacco as well as currently illegal drugs. In so doing, this policy should take aim at the especially vulnerable parts of the community with a special emphasis on the young.

If those who seek to reform drug policy and harm reduction are sincere in their intent, they would focus their efforts on alcohol and tobacco where there exists an abundant need for harm reduction and leave the currently illegal drugs illegal.

Unless those who subscribe to the notion of harm reduction move ahead to harm prevention and harm elimination, the global costs associated with any form of drug use will continue to rise. Relaxation of the restrictive policies surrounding the use of currently illegal drugs should only be considered in the context of programs which can first prove drastic and lasting reductions in alcohol and tobacco use. Real harm reduction involves prohibiting illegal drugs while concurrently working to prevent and treat their use. We do not need new experiments to tell us what we already have learned from legal alcohol and tobacco. Those experiments have already been done at the cost of great human suffering.

REFERENCES

1. DeLeon G, Some Problems with the Anti-Prohibitionist Position on Legalization of Drugs. *Journal of Addictive Diseases*, 1994;13:35–57.

2. U.S. General Accounting Office, General Government Division. *Confronting the Drug Problem—Debate Persists on Enforcement and Alternative Approaches*, GAO/GGD-93-82. Report to the Chairman, Committee on Government Operations, House of Representatives. Washington, D.C.: United States General Accounting Office, General Government Division, 1993.

3. Pure Food and Drug Act of 1906, Public Law 59-384.

4. Harrison Narcotics Act. Public Law 63-47.

5. Musto DF, *The American Disease—Origins of Narcotic Control*. New York, Oxford University Press, 1987.

6. Brecher EM, ed. *Licit and Illicit Drugs*. Boston, Little, Brown, and Co, 1972:267–306, 335–451

7. U.S. Department of Health and Human Services. *Drug Abuse and Drug Abuse Research—The Third Triennial Report to Congress from the Secretary*, Department of Health and Human Services. Washington, D.C.: Superintendent of Documents, U.S. Government Printing Office, DHHS Publication no. (ADM) 91-1704, 1991.

8. Berman AL, Schwartz RH, Suicide Attempts Among Adolescent Drug Users. *AJDC*, 1990; 144:310–314.

9. Rivara FP, Mueller BA, Fligner CL, Luna G, Raisys VA, Drug Use in Trauma Victims. *The Journal of Trauma*, 1989; 29:462–470.

10. Soderstrom CA, Dischinger PC, Sinith GS, McDuff DR, Hebel JR, Gorelick DA, Psychoactive Substance Dependence Among Trauma Center Patients. *JAMA*, 1992;267: 2756–2759.

11. Committee on Drug Abuse of the Council on Psychiatric Services, Position Statement on Psychoactive Substance Use and Dependence: Update on Marijuana and Cocaine. *Am J Psychiatry*, 1987;144:698–702.

12. Polen MR, Sidney S, Tekawa IS, Sadler M, Friedman GD, Health Care Use by Frequent Marijuana Smokers Who Do Not Smoke Tobacco. *Western Journal of Medicine*, 1993;158:596–601.

13. Nahas GG, Latour C, The Human Toxicity of Marijuana. *The Medical Journal of Australia*, 1992; 156:495–497.

14. Schwartz RH, Marijuana: An Overview. *Pediatric Clinics of North America*, 1987;34: 305–317.

15. Council of Scientific Affairs, American Medical Association. Marijuana: Its Health Hazards and Therapeutic Potentials. *JAMA*, 1981;246:1823–1827.

16. Controlled Substances Act, 21 U.S.C. 811.

17. Institute for Health Policy, Brandeis University. *Substance Abuse: The Nation's Number One Health Problem—Key Indicators for Policy*. Princeton, NJ: Robert Wood Johnson Foundation, October, 1993.

18. U.S. Department of Justice, Bureau of Justice Statistics. Chapter III, Section 5—The Costs of Illegal Drug Use. In *Drugs, Crime, and the Criminal Justice System*, NCJ-133652, 126–127. U.S. Department of Justice, Bureau of Justice Statistics, 1992.

19. U.S. Department of Health and Human Services, Substance Abuse and Mental Health Services Administration. *National Household Survey on Drug Abuse: Main Findings 1991*, DHHS Publication No. (SMA) 93-1980. Rockville, MD: U.S. Department of Health and Human Services, Substance Abuse and Mental Health Services Administration, Office of Applied Studies, 1993.

20. U.S. Department of Health and Human Services, Public Health Service, National Institutes of Health. *National Survey Results on Drug Use, from the Monitoring the Future Study 1975–1993*. NIH Publication No. 94-3809, 1994.

21. Erickson PG, Prospects of Harm Reduction for Psychostimulants. In Nick Heath, ed. *Psychoactive Drugs and Harm Reduction: From Faith to Science*. London: Whurr Publishers, 1993:196.

22. Gostin LO, Brandt AM, Criteria for evaluating a ban on the advertisement of cigarettes. *Journal*

of the American Medical Association, 1993;269:904–909.

23. Nadelman E., Cohen P, Locher U, Stimson G, Wodak A, and Drucker E, Position Paper on Harm Reduction. *The Harm Reduction Approach to Drug Control: International Progress.* The Lindesmith Center, 888 Seventh Ave, New York, NY 10106. 1994.

24. Kleiman MAR, *The Drug Problem and Drug Policy: What Have We Learned from the Past Four Years.* Testimony to the United States Senate Committee of the Judiciary, April 29, 1993.

25 Maguire K, ed. *Sourcebook of Criminal Statistics,* Bureau of Justice Statistics, U.S. Department of Justice. 1992:491.

26. Gunning KF, Dutch National Committee on Drug Prevention. Personal Communication. September 22, 1993.

27. Model KE, The Effect of Marijuana Decriminalization on Hospital Emergency Room Drug Episodes: 1975–1978. *Journal of the American Statistical Association,* 1993; 88: 737–747.

28. Kleber HD, Our Current Approach to Drug Abuse—Progress, Problems, Proposals. *NEJM,* 1994;330:361–365.

29. Rydell CP, Everingham SS, *Controlling Cocaine: Supply Versus Demand Programs.* Santa Monica, Ca.:Rand 1994.

30. Gold MS, *The Good News About Drugs and Alcohol.* New York, Villard Books, 1991: 245.

31. Board of Trustees, The American Medical Association. Drug Abuse in the United States: Strategies for Prevention. *JAMA,* 1991;265: 2102–2107.

32. Romer D, Using Mass Media to Reduce Adolescent Involvement in Drug Trafficking. *Pediatrics,* 1994;93: 1073–1077.

33. Voth E, Drug Policy Options. Letter to the Editor in *JAMA,* 1995;273:459.

POSTSCRIPT

Is Harm Reduction a Desirable National Drug Policy Goal?

One could argue against the concept of harm reduction on the grounds that it is immoral: Where is the morality in downplaying people's use of illegal drugs while prioritizing ways to minimize its dangers? If a drug is illegal, then any use could be construed as harmful. By virtue of the illegality of drugs, the only way to minimize both personal and social risk is simple: do not use drugs. Harm reduction opponents conclude that to abstain from drug use is the only way to ensure the safety of drug use.

Another concern regarding the harm reduction approach is that some people, especially children and young adults, may get the wrong impression or receive a mixed message regarding drug use. If the federal government promotes the concept of harm reduction, young people may feel that drug use is, in the end, not that harmful.

In their article, Reuter and Caulkins do not argue in favor of drug use. They contend, however, that many of the personal and social problems emanating from drug use can be curtailed by developing a policy of harm reduction. Reuter and Caulkins maintain that focusing on a program in which the primary goal is to eliminate access to drugs is inadequate because it overlooks differences among drugs, the extent of drug use, and the different types and groups of people who are using drugs. For example, they feel that persuading a person to switch from injecting drugs to a less dangerous form of drug use is more important than persuading an occasional marijuana user to cease use.

DuPont and Voth feel that the evidence does not support a policy of harm reduction. They contend that lessening or abolishing criminal penalties for drug offenses, promoting needle exchange programs, and eliminating workplace drug testing has not been proven to diminish drug-related problems. Deviating from a course of action that emphasizes reducing the supply of drugs and prohibiting their use is wrong, according to DuPont and Voth. They feel that a harm reduction approach would exacerbate the problems.

For an overview of the federal government's drug policy in the United States, one should read the National Drug Control Strategy, published annually by the Office of National Drug Control Policy. This publication outlines efforts that have been enacted toward reducing drug use and lists future goals as well. An article that advocates the harm reduction approach is "Harm Reduction: An Emerging New Paradigm for Drug Education," by David Duncan et al., *Journal of Drug Education* (vol. 24, 1994). In "Just Say Maybe," *Forbes* (June 17, 1996), Richard C. Morais examines the impact of marijuana decriminalization in the Netherlands.

ISSUE 7

Should Tobacco Products Be More Closely Regulated?

YES: Margaret Kriz, from "Where There's Smoke...," *National Journal* (May 7, 1994)

NO: John Hood, from "Anti-Smoking War Could Deny Consumers Choice," *Consumers' Research* (June 1994)

ISSUE SUMMARY

YES: Writer Margaret Kriz maintains that current restrictions on tobacco products are minimal compared to restrictions of other products. She blames the tobacco industry for turning the debate over regulation into a smokers' rights issue, and she argues that public concern over the health effects of smoking justify sensible regulation of tobacco products.

NO: John Hood, vice president of the John Locke Foundation in Raleigh, North Carolina, argues that the tobacco industry is already heavily regulated, that smokers should have the freedom to choose to smoke, and that the Food and Drug Administration (FDA) is attempting to intrude too much into the lives of individuals.

Most people, including those who smoke, recognize that tobacco is a dangerous product. Because of tobacco's reputation as an addictive substance that jeopardizes people's health, many activists are requesting that more stringent restrictions be placed on it. As it stands now, cigarette packages are required to carry warnings describing the dangers of tobacco products. Tobacco products cannot be advertised on television or radio. And laws restricting minors from purchasing tobacco products are being more vigorously enforced than they have ever been. The U.S. Food and Drug Administration (FDA), however, feels that enforcement needs to be tightened even more.

In defense of the tobacco industry, advocates point to benefits associated with nicotine, the mild stimulant that is the chief active chemical of tobacco. In previous centuries, for example, tobacco was used for a variety of ailments, including skin diseases, internal and external disorders, and diseases of the eyes, ears, mouth, and nose. Tobacco and its smoke was often employed by Native Americans for sacramental purposes. For users, nicotine provides a sense of euphoria, and smoking is a source of gratification without impairing thinking or performance. One can drive a car, socialize, study for a test, and engage in a variety of activities while smoking. Nicotine can relieve anxiety and stress, and it can reduce weight by lessening one's appetite and by increasing metabolic activity. Many smokers claim that smoking cigarettes enables them to concentrate better and that abstaining from smoking impairs their concentration.

Critics paint a very different picture of tobacco products, citing some of the following statistics: Tobacco is responsible for about 30 percent of deaths among people between ages 35 and 69, making it the single most prominent cause of premature death in the developed world. The relationship between cigarette smoking and cardiovascular disease, including heart attack, stroke, sudden death, peripheral vascular disease, and aortic aneurysm, is well documented. Even as few as one to four cigarettes daily can increase the risk of fatal coronary heart disease. Cigarettes have also been shown to reduce blood flow and the level of high-density lipoprotein cholesterol, which is the beneficial type of cholesterol.

Cigarette smoking is strongly associated with cancer, accounting for over 85 percent of lung cancer cases and 30 percent of all deaths due to cancer. Cancer of the pharynx, larynx, mouth, esophagus, stomach, pancreas, uterus, cervix, kidney, and bladder have been related to smoking. And studies have shown that smokers have twice the rate of cancer than nonsmokers.

According to smokers' rights advocates, the majority of smokers are already aware of the potential harm of tobacco products; in fact, most smokers tend to overestimate the dangers of smoking. Adults should therefore be allowed to smoke if that is their wish. Many promote the idea that the FDA and a number of politicians are attempting to deny smokers the right to engage in a behavior that they freely choose. On the other hand, tobacco critics maintain that due to the addictiveness of nicotine—the level of which some claim is manipulated by tobacco companies—smokers really do not have the ability to stop their detrimental behavior. That is, it is not really freely chosen behavior. Respondents note that the level of tar and nicotine in cigarettes has dropped almost 70 percent since the 1950s. Moreover, 40 million Americans have stopped smoking since 1964.

There is an economic element associated with this issue. Should taxpayers financially assist smokers who need medical help as a result of their use of tobacco products? Much money is collected on taxes paid by smokers, but several billion dollars go out every year to cover Medicaid costs for smoking-related illnesses. Should such illnesses be covered by government-funded medical programs?

In the following selections, Margaret Kriz argues that tobacco products should be subject to the same rigorous restrictions that are currently placed on other products. John Hood argues that the goal of the FDA is not to restrict tobacco products, but to prohibit them altogether. Hood feels that individuals should have the freedom to choose whether or not they want to smoke and that the government has no right to interfere in this matter.

YES

Margaret Kriz

WHERE THERE'S SMOKE...

In mid-March, a team of investigators from the Health and Human Services Department's Food and Drug Administration (FDA) made history when, for the first time on record, they were allowed to go to a tobacco processing plant and watch cigarettes being made.

The federal regulators, who are investigating whether tobacco companies manipulate the levels of nicotine in cigarettes, got their rare glimpses first at a Philip Morris Co. Inc.'s tobacco processing plant in Richmond, Va., and later at an RJR Reynolds Tobacco Co. factory in Winston-Salem, N.C.

The visits were unprecedented. Tobacco cultivation and cigarette production and advertising are almost totally unregulated by the federal government, despite growing medical evidence linking cigarette smoking to cancer and heart and lung disease in smokers and nonsmokers.

The American Medical Association estimates that 460,000 Americans die from tobacco-related illnesses each year and that tobacco-related illnesses cost the U.S. health care system more than $80 billion a year.

"We regulate all kinds of minor risks, in the form of additives, pesticides and other products that may affect one person in a million," said Scott D. Ballin, a vice president of the American Heart Association and chairman of the Coalition on Smoking OR Health (which represents Ballin's group, the American Cancer Association and the American Lung Association). "Yet we don't regulate tobacco, which kills far more people. It shows the total inconsistencies in the way we apply the law to this product."

As an FDA official put it, "The cheese in Philip Morris's Kraft [General Foods Inc.] division goes through infinitely more regulation than their cigarettes."

During the three decades since Surgeon General Luther L. Terry issued the landmark report that first linked cigarettes to lung cancer, the tobacco industry has wielded enormous political and economic clout with the American public and in Washington.

Americans have been seduced by advertisements that feature scantily clad bathers, rugged cowboys and, now, boldly independent smokers who risk riding on an airplane wing just to enjoy their cigarettes.

More important, David A. Kessler, the FDA's commissioner, suggests that the industry may have hooked its customers by delivering an addictive dose of nicotine in each cigarette.

As the scientific evidence against cigarettes mounted, the tobacco companies tried to neutralize criticism in Washington by pouring millions of dollars into the political war chests of their allies on Capitol Hill and other potentially helpful lawmakers.

But 1994 has proved to be the dawning of a new era of public scrutiny and government oversight of the nation's tobacco industry. Among the signs of change:

In February, McDonald's Corp. banned smoking in its restaurants, joining the growing movement against smoking in public places. Several other restaurant chains promptly followed suit.

Days later, the Defense Department banned smoking at all U.S. military facilities around the world.

In March, Congress passed an education package that prohibits smoking in public schools.

On March 25, the Labor Department issued a preliminary proposal to restrict smoking in all workplaces.

On April 13, the tobacco industry released a long-guarded list of chemicals and other substances that are added to cigarettes. The public disclosure came after a reporter for National Public Radio obtained a copy of the list.

On April 14, the top executives of the seven largest U.S. tobacco companies made history of their own by testifying before Congress for the first time, undergoing six hours of sharp questioning on the health effects of tobacco and business practices within the industry by members of the House Energy and Commerce Subcommittee on Health and the Environment.

In the past two months, Congress and the news media have also focused on internal tobacco company studies that reportedly prove that tobacco is addictive and that the industry has controlled the levels of nicotine in cigarettes. In fact, two former scientists for Philip Morris told Congress on April 28 that after they found evidence in 1983 that nicotine was addictive in test animals, their studies were halted and the results suppressed by company officials.

As the wall of secrecy crumbled, the editorial boards of major newspapers became increasingly critical of the tobacco industry. *The New York Times* has published eight antismoking editorials so far this year, and an editorial in *USA Today* described the tobacco company executives who testified on Capitol Hill as "clowns."

A THREE-FRONT WAR

The fabric of change has been woven primarily from three threads:

- A 1993 scientific study by the Environmental Protection Agency (EPA), which classified secondhand, tobacco smoke as a carcinogen that causes lung cancer and other illnesses in nonsmoking adults and children.

- An FDA investigation, announced in February, into whether nicotine is addictive and should be regulated as a drug.

- The growing grass-roots movement to limit smoking in public and to restrict children's access to cigarettes. It's fueled by the EPA study and by a 1986 Surgeon General's report on the damaging health effects of secondhand smoke.

Riding the wave of public opinion, Congress is considering increasing the 24-cent-a-pack excise tax on cigarettes to $1.25 a pack to pay for health reform. The Clinton Administration supports a 75-cent tax; the industry is fighting all increases.

Congress is also weighing legislation that would ban smoking in public buildings and expand the FDA's authority to regulate all phases of the cigarette industry.

Nevertheless, the tobacco industry hasn't lost its touch.

Forced into a defensive position, it's accusing the Clinton Administration and antismoking forces in Congress of trying to impose a total ban, which public opinion polls show is vastly unpopular.

The industry warns that such a prohibition would result in a black market for cigarettes and further restrictions on prized personal liberties.

Regulation of the tobacco industry "would result in a product that is too expensive to buy, too inconvenient to use and that you can't tell anybody about," Walker Merryman, a vice president of the Washington-based Tobacco Institute, said. "They can't get away with saying that is not prohibition."

But antismoking activists argue that safeguarding public health is more important than preserving the personal freedoms of smokers.

Besides, they ask, does a smoker really have freedom of choice if nicotine is addictive?

"We just want to face reality," said Henry A. Waxman, D-Calif., the chairman of the Health Subcommittee. "The reality is, tobacco kills people. Nicotine is addictive. Advertising influences kids. Environmental tobacco smoke is dangerous. And if we're a rational society, we should be doing things to counteract that."

That message seems to be selling well back home, said Rep. Richard J. Durbin, D-Ill., who authored the 1988 ban on smoking on domestic airline flights and who supports current legislation to restrict smoking.

"Many people like myself have challenged the tobacco companies and found that when you went back home, there were more people supporting you than criticizing you," said Durbin, whose father died of lung cancer when Durbin was 14. "But the tobacco lobby is still a powerhouse. They are not to be underestimated, even though they're under fire today."

A CHANGEOVER ON CAPITOL HILL

When it comes to regulating the tobacco industry, Congress has a long history of pulling its punches. In response to the 1964 Surgeon General's report on smoking and cancer, for example, lawmakers merely required manufacturers to print a health warning on cigarette packages.

"It was an awful piece of legislation, essentially designed in conjunction with the industry to put this mild warning on the package, but to stop the federal regulatory agencies from doing anything more," said antismoking activist Michael Pertschuk, a co-director of the Washington-based Advocacy Institute, which trains public-interest lawyers. Pertschuk was on the staff of the House Interstate and Foreign Commerce Committee when the law was written.

By 1969, lawmakers were willing to go a step further by prohibiting tobacco advertisements on television and radio.

That's about where things stood for more than a decade. Then, in 1984, Jim Repace, a little-known physicist at EPA, independently developed a risk assessment that estimated that secondhand tobacco smoke was causing lung cancer in nonsmokers, too.

Intrigued by Repace's findings, Reagan Administration appointee Joseph A. Cannon, who headed EPA's air pollution office, gave the National Research Council some seed money to develop a more complete study of what has come to be called passive smoking. The fruits of the council's labor became the scientific underpinnings of Surgeon General C. Everett Koop's highly publicized 1986 report that linked passive smoking to lung cancer.

By then, Repace had been reassigned to EPA's newly formed indoor air pollution office, where he pushed for the agency to conduct its own comprehensive scientific study of the health effects of cigarette smoke on nonsmokers.

The conclusions, released in January 1993 by outgoing EPA administrator William K. Reilly, were startling. Exposure to secondhand smoke, the study estimated, causes 3,000 lung cancer deaths among nonsmokers each year and dramatically increases the childhood incidence of asthma, bronchitis, pneumonia and ear infections. The study also said that at least 43 of the hundreds of chemicals added to cigarettes cause cancer in test animals.

"That report was a turning point and began this whole round of scrutiny," EPA administrator Carol Browner said in an interview. "It clearly demonstrated what everyone has suspected for a long time:

People who choose not to smoke are at risk, and they deserve to be protected."

The Clinton Administration followed up on the report with a guide that advised parents to help enact restrictions on smoking in their communities and school districts "to make their children's environment smoke-free."

The Tobacco Institute promptly sued EPA, charging that Congress never gave the agency the authority to issue the study. Rep. Thomas J. Bliley Jr., R-Va., a longtime defender of the tobacco industry, also charged that EPA had skewed the science used to back up its risk estimates.

Despite the industry's protests, the EPA report triggered a domino effect within the Administration. The Defense Department's smoking ban and the Labor Department's proposal to restrict smoking in workplaces are both based on the EPA study.

On Capitol Hill, the EPA risk assessment gave Waxman the scientific ammunition he sought to impose national smoking restrictions. His bill to regulate smoking in public buildings is being considered by his subcommittee but faces tough opposition from tobacco-state lawmakers—including Bliley, the subcommittee's ranking Republican.

"The tobacco industry has invested an enormous amount of time and money in influencing our subcommittee," a member of the subcommittee's staff said. "They've been gearing up for this fight for a long time."

A QUESTION OF HOW, NOT WHETHER?

In 1988, the Coalition on Smoking OR Health filed one in a long series of petitions pushing the FDA to regulate cigarettes.

This time the coalition argued that low-tar, low-nicotine cigarettes should be controlled under the nation's drug laws. It argued that by altering tar and nicotine levels in cigarettes, tobacco companies were marketing a product that promised to mitigate disease—that is, to lower the chances that a smoker would contract lung cancer and heart disease.

That interpretation would place such cigarettes under the purview of the 1938 Federal Food, Drug and Cosmetic Act, which requires the FDA to regulate as drugs products that fall within one of two legal definitions: products that are used to treat or mitigate diseases or that affect the structure or function of the body.

The coalition's petitions went nowhere until 1990, when Kessler took the reigns of the agency. Kessler worried, however, that regulating only low-tar, low-nicotine cigarettes would be sending the wrong message to the American public.

In fall 1992, the FDA shifted gears. Three FDA lawyers approached Kessler with a radically new approach for tackling the tobacco industry: Rather than attacking cigarettes, they said, the government should regulate nicotine as a drug.

Citing tentative evidence that nicotine is addicting and that cigarette companies tinker with the levels of nicotine in cigarettes, they reasoned that nicotine could be regulated as a substance that alters the structure or function of the body.

In a Feb. 25 letter to Ballin, Kessler went public with the FDA's new strategy. "Evidence brought to our attention is accumulating that suggests that cigarette manufacturers may intend that their products contain nicotine to satisfy an addiction on the part of some of their customers," Kessler wrote. "In fact, it is our understanding that manufacturers commonly add nicotine to cigarettes to deliver specific amounts of nicotine."

Some of the accusations were confirmed at the April 14 hearing of Waxman's subcommittee. Under questioning, a Philip Morris executive admitted that the company had suppressed studies showing that animals could become addicted to nicotine and acknowledged that the company packs its low-tar cigarettes with tobacco that contains a higher concentration of nicotine than its regular cigarettes.

While the FDA's lawyers continue to gather evidence against nicotine, its policy makers are beginning to plot their next step.

Under the law, the FDA commissioner can limit the use of or ban a drug that isn't safe. But the aggressive Kessler is seeking broader jurisdiction. At a March 25 hearing of Waxman's subcommittee, Kessler asked for Congress's help in handling the nicotine problem, acknowledging that "if nicotine were removed, the nation would face a host of issues involving the withdrawal from addiction that would be experienced by millions of Americans."

In response, Rep. Mike Synar, D-Okla., introduced legislation that would grant the FDA broad authority over nearly every aspect of cigarette production. "It's no longer a question of whether tobacco is going to be regulated under FDA," Synar said in an interview. "It's a matter of how FDA will regulate it."

PROTECTION V. PROHIBITION

Julia Carol, a co-director of Americans for Nonsmokers' Rights in Berkeley, Calif., is drawing a cartoon for the group's newsletter. It depicts a sleeping giant beginning to awaken, with a little bird musing, "He's awake, but now where's he going?"

The sleeping giant is the federal government, which has long shunned the role of overseer of the nation's tobacco industry. Into that void rushed an army of community activists, who from coast to coast have successfully championed hundreds of local restrictions on smoking in public and bans on cigarette vending machines.

"The most successful element of the whole tobacco control issue is the non-smokers' rights issue," Carol said. "Forget the rhetoric. Forget the TV shows. Forget the articles. Look at what's really changed in America: What you find is that nonsmokers' issues are making headway."

While the tobacco industry has successfully used campaign contributions to influence federal and state lawmakers, "the tobacco industry is not very effective at the grass-roots level," the Advocacy Institute's Pertschuk said. "They're carpetbaggers. They're men in suits from outside when they come into a local community. Local city councils are not as shielded from their neighbors as the state legislatures."

With Congress and the Clinton Administration increasingly interested in regulating the tobacco industry, however, many antismoking activists worry that lawmakers and policy makers in Washington may inadvertently undercut the progress that's been made at the local level.

Local activists fear that the labor Department's attempts to regulate smoking in workplaces, for example, could result in cumbersome regulations that are hard to enforce and preempt more-aggressive local laws.

More troublesome, Carol said, are pro-tobacco lawmakers in the states who are pushing mild smoking-control measures to preempt tougher action at the local level. She described state legislators, who are becoming increasingly dependent on campaign money from the tobacco industry, as the weakest link in the group's efforts to limit smoking.

The current round of tobacco industry bashing could also create a backlash against the nonsmokers' rights movement, Carol warned.

"We've allowed the debate to get shifted to the question of 'Should cigarettes be prohibited?'" she said. "That is how the media is interpreting the whole FDA issue, which in my opinion is extremely dangerous. Americans do not like being told what to do, and they will vote for someone else not to be told what to do."

In fact, tobacco companies are escalating the public relations war by portraying themselves as the underdogs against Washington, antismoking activists warn. "The new mantra against anybody who is for sensible regulation of tobacco products," said Rep. Ron Wyden, D-Ore., "is that they are prohibitionists."

THE SHIFTING TIDE

It's incontestable, the Tobacco Institute's Merryman argues, that the Clinton Administration is more hostile to the tobacco industry than any other Administration in the nation's history.

"First the Clintons announced the smoking ban in the White House," Merryman said. "Then Ira Magaziner's health care group leaked the fact that they wanted to propose a $2 a pack tax increase to fund health care. Clinton settled at 75 cents, but it was a very clear signal that there was a free ride at the federal level for anybody who wanted to hammer on tobacco."

Most Members of Congress, Merryman contended, haven't been converted by the antismoking forces. "I think there's been more attention in the media than on the Hill to these issues," he said. "I don't think there is any significantly increased animosity toward the tobacco industry on the Hill."

In fact, a group of tobacco-state Members recently wrote President Clinton, warning that unless his proposed cigarette tax increase was cut to 48 cents a pack, they wouldn't support his health care reform package.

"It certainly is going to be impossible for Democrats in the Southeast to run for reelection with that tax hanging around their necks," Merryman said. "They simply cannot support it. And if the White House decides that it needs three dozen House Members from the Southeast for a health care plan, then it can't pursue a 75-cent tax increase."

The nation's six tobacco states—Georgia, Kentucky, North Carolina, South Carolina, Tennessee and Virginia—still present a powerful force in Congress. They elect 55 House Members, many of whom have posts on key congressional committees. The industry has also been channeling campaign contributions to members of several crucial committees.

"Most of the major legislation has to go through the Health Subcommittee, where the tobacco lobby has quite a group of friends," Durbin said. "They've also really worked on the Rules Committee, which they understand is key to their future."

The southern bloc isn't the only impediment to the current legislative efforts to control tobacco. Labor unions worry that Waxman's measure to control smoking in all public buildings will divert government resources from their campaign to limit worker exposure to more-dangerous chemical fumes.

Southern lawmakers also point out that the state governments have become dependent on tobacco taxes to finance important police and school programs. Federal smoking control measures and a hefty increase in the federal excise tax are likely to shrink state tobacco revenues, they say.

But the once-impenetrable front of tobacco-state lawmakers may be showing a few cracks. "Public sentiment is turning against the tobacco-state legislators, and they know it," Wyden said. "The politics are starting to shift."

The change is evident in the lawmakers themselves. Only 43 Members of Congress—37 in the House and 6 in the Senate—admitted to being regular smokers in a June 1993 survey by *Roll Call,* a newspaper that covers Capitol Hill. That's half the number of smokers it counted four years earlier.

As fewer voters smoke, even southern lawmakers have dropped their arguments that smoking is safe. "I think it's generally accepted on the Hill that smoking is bad for your health," Virginia's Bliley said. "I think you'd be better off if you didn't smoke, healthwise, just as if you didn't drink, and probably if you didn't eat a lot of red meat. No one can say that smoking is good for your health."

But Bliley, who has 15,000 tobacco-related jobs in his district, argued that regulating smoking should be left to individual businesses, not the government.

Antismoking activist Ballin said that one way to soften the blow from new tobacco controls and higher tobacco taxes would be to earmark some of the tax revenues to help tobacco farmers convert to different crops.

At the same time, federal subsidies to the tobacco industry are coming under closer scrutiny, according to Durbin, who chairs the Appropriations Subcommittee on Agriculture, Rural Development, Food and Drug Administration and Related Agencies. He said that he's systematically challenging a different tobacco subsidy each year, and this year hopes to zero out the $4 million budget for research into tobacco production.

And Durbin predicted that federal aid to the tobacco industry will come under attack during next year's debate over the farm bill. "We spend $25 million–$30 million a year subsidizing the tobacco allotment program," he said. "There are a lot of us that think that is totally inconsistent with our health message that tobacco is dangerous."

Some in Congress see the battle to control tobacco use as a long-term campaign. Synar acknowledged that the best hope for passage of his FDA bill this year would be to attach it as an amendment to a crucial piece of legislation. Waxman is still fighting for subcommittee votes for his smoking restrictions.

Both lawmakers predicted, however, that the growing public concern about the health hazards associated with smoking will eventually break the tobacco industry's hold on Congress and pave the way for tougher federal controls on tobacco.

The Heart Association's Ballin said that the key to beating the tobacco industry lies at the local level. "Members of Congress and someone running to unseat a Member need to be asked where they stand on tobacco control," he said. "Maybe not this year, but in the future that could make a difference."

NO

John Hood

ANTI-SMOKING WAR COULD DENY CONSUMERS CHOICE

Are tobacco products regulated? The average person would no doubt answer yes. In the past two decades, at least 600 local laws have been passed across the country to require non-smoking areas in workplaces, schools, government buildings, public facilities, and restaurants. Every state legislature has taken action against smoking in one form or another. On the federal level, tobacco advertising is heavily regulated—banned from broadcast and saddled with labeling requirements in print. Manufacturers must also live with significant reporting requirements for ingredients and additives. And the Occupational Safety and Health Administration [OSHA] proposed a new rule in March that would ban smoking in virtually all indoor workplaces, including bars and restaurants.

But to many regulators and anti-smoking activists, these numerous restrictions seem almost irrelevant. Former U.S. Surgeon General Antonia Novello once said that tobacco was "the least regulated consumer product" in the country. Tobacco is "a product that is virtually unregulated for health and safety," says Scott Ballin, vice president for public affairs at the American Heart Association. Ballin and other activists have been pressing the U.S. Food and Drug Administration (FDA) for years to assert regulatory authority over tobacco—a move that, given current FDA requirements about the "safety" of products, would almost certainly result in banning virtually all tobacco products. FDA Commissioner David Kessler has recently suggested to a congressional subcommittee that his agency does, indeed, have such authority, given so-called "new" information about the use of tobacco as a drug.

Naturally, tobacco companies, farmers, and smokers' rights groups will fight such a move tooth and nail. Indeed, cigarette manufacturer Philip Morris has already filed a multi-million-dollar libel suit against ABC-TV's "Day One" program for its allegations that tobacco companies add nicotine to cigarettes to foster addiction among consumers.

At stake, however, is not simply the survival of the tobacco industry or tobacco farmers. The real issue is freedom of choice by consumers of all

From John Hood, "Anti-Smoking War Could Deny Consumers Choice," *Consumers' Research* (June 1994). Copyright © 1994 by *Consumers' Research*. Reprinted by permission.

products, not merely cigarettes. Kessler recognizes this implication and stated to Congress that "it is fair to argue that the decision to start smoking may be a matter of choice. But once they have started smoking regularly, most smokers are in effect deprived of their choice to stop smoking." The commissioner is arguing that he, as head of the FDA, must step in to help consumers who can't otherwise help themselves. His intention may be genuine benevolence, but the result of such new regulation would codify and extend the powers of an agency that already limits the freedom of individual consumers to make their own decisions.

A RISKY DECISION

Are smokers the prisoners of nicotine and therefore of the companies that supply their "fix"? Kessler reports that even smokers who develop serious health conditions, presumably as a result of their smoking, remain "in the grip of nicotine." After surgery for lung cancer, he says, almost half of smokers resume smoking. Among smokers who suffer a heart attack, 38% resume smoking while they are still in the hospital.

Overall, Kessler argues that 15 million of the 17 million Americans who try to stop smoking every year fail. But the fact remains that since 1964, more than 40 million people have stopped smoking permanently without any outside intervention or assistance. Over the past decade, domestic consumption of tobacco has dropped both in share (37% of Americans were smokers in 1981, 30% in 1991) and in products (U.S. smokers consumed 640 billion cigarettes in 1981, 500 billion in 1991). Perhaps one reason for this is that, according to statistics from the U.S. Department of Health and Human Services,

levels of tar and nicotine have *fallen* by almost 70% since the 1950s, in nicotine's case, from 2.5 milligrams per cigarette to less than 1 milligram. This fact is difficult to square with conspiracy theories about manufacturers spiking cigarettes with nicotine to keep smokers addicted.

Indeed, the evidence that manufacturers do this is essentially that manufacturers *could* do this. Kessler's case, and that of other anti-smoking partisans, centers almost entirely around patents obtained by tobacco companies for processes which replace nicotine lost during manufacturing. When confronted with strong industry denials that spiking has occurred—as well as evidence showing that there is less nicotine than in the original tobacco leaves from which they are made—Rep. Henry Waxman (D-Calif.) claimed that manufacturers were only playing semantic games. Deliberately restoring some of the nicotine lost during manufacturing is still "playing around with nicotine levels," he said. But tobacco industry officials reply that previous attempts to introduce nicotine-free cigarettes have flopped, and that the presence of the substance clearly affects a smoker's enjoyment of the product.

However, the crucial question in evaluating Kessler's argument is not just whether tobacco companies spike cigarettes, but what should be the operative definition of "addiction." Many of us use the term addiction in loose fashion. We sometimes say we're addicted to coffee, to chocolate, to Cajun cooking, to television. In every case, what we mean is that we value highly the experience of consuming a product or participating in an activity that provides us pleasure, and even that we would be willing to sacrifice other valuable goods—be they money or time—to continue our consumption.

Some of these addictions have a physical component, such as the caffeine in coffee. Others do not.

Using the broadest definition of addiction, most Americans might legitimately be termed "addicts." They could give up their addictions, but it would be distressing for them to do so. Not only are there millions of people who have tried and failed to quit smoking—there are also millions of people who have tried and failed to stop eating fatty foods and sweets, to give up coffee and sodas, to exercise regularly, or to limit the time they spend watching TV. In every case, one can argue that there are health issues at stake (in the case of TV, perhaps mental health issues). At most, tobacco's risks differ only by degree, not by kind; certainly the health risks of alcohol abuse, high-fat diets, and a sedentary lifestyle are themselves most serious. The Center for Science in the Public Interest claims that 445,000 Americans die prematurely each year from poor diet and lack of exercise, compared with 420,000 per year from tobacco use. Alcohol abuse kills around 100,000.

In *Smoking: Making the Risky Decision*, published in 1993, Duke University researcher Kip Viscusi challenges the notion that smokers, as distinguished from people who engage in other personally or socially destructive behavior, are not to be trusted to make their own decisions. "We make choices throughout our lives that are costly to reverse—getting married, choosing a profession, selecting a place to live, and purchasing a car. The fact that reversing such decisions is costly does not imply that such choices are incorrect." Viscusi's research has found that smokers tend to accept and tolerate higher levels of risk in other areas, such as choice of career. They also tend to overestimate, not

underestimate, the risks associated with smoking, reflecting the effectiveness of decades of public service and campaigns on the evils of tobacco.

As long as there are lower-nicotine cigarettes, nicotine patches, chewing gum, and fortitude, some smokers will limit their risk, others will eliminate it altogether by quitting, and still others will choose to continue their habit, most of them knowing the risks they are assuming. Viscusi notes that survey data showing most smokers want to quit but can't are about as reliable as surveys showing that most people want to move to the country or change jobs, even though they never do: "Survey statements in which individuals indicate that they would like to quit smoking, for example, might mean that they would like to smoke without risk. However, the fact that they have continued to smoke even with the availability of chewing gum with nicotine suggests that these statements... should not always be taken at face value."

Obviously, the debate on smoking regulation would change dramatically with the introduction of solid evidence that significant numbers of *nonsmokers* are harmed by tobacco smoke. But... such evidence does not yet exist. Indeed, if the risk the consumption of a substance poses on innocent bystanders is to be the criterion for banning the substance, then bringing back the prohibition of alcohol would be a much higher priority than banning cigarettes, given the former's undeniable role in many of the 44,000 traffic fatalities each year. So far, the highest number of second-hand smoke fatalities the EPA can come up with —by massaging the data well beyond believability—is 3,000 a year. (See also,

"Facts Catch Up With 'Political' Science," CR, May 1993.)

So, the new war against tobacco, predicated on the idea that cigarettes are nothing more than the delivery system for a highly addictive drug, must be waged on behalf of paternalism, not concern for bystanders. To justify a major expansion of federal regulatory authority, Kessler and the Congress should have to prove that smokers cannot help themselves and do not recognize the risks associated with their behavior—and that regulation would resolve these problems.

MUZZLING INFORMATION

Unfortunately, Kessler does not really have to prove these points. Once Congress decides that the FDA has authority to regulate cigarettes, the burden of proof for all health and safety issues shifts to manufacturers and consumers. The government doesn't have to prove that tobacco kills innocent bystanders, or that nicotine can be reduced without affecting the quality of tobacco products, or that new tobacco products are unsafe, to make rulings. Instead, tobacco companies will have to prove that their products are "safe," which under the FDA definition means essentially risk-free, an admittedly impossible standard to meet for these products.

Based as it is on the "guilty until proven innocent" standard, the FDA's scrutiny of new pharmaceuticals has already deprived consumers of products from which they might have obtained great benefit. The average cost of developing a new drug approaches $360 million, according to the U.S. Office of Technology Assessment. A good amount of this cost reflects regulatory compliance. Firms have to file separate ap-

plications, running up to 1,000 pages each, for different treatments by the same drug. The approval process can last up to 12 years. In recent years, the FDA has stymied efforts to bring drugs to market that could have treated patients suffering from Alzheimer's disease, angina, hypertension, gastric ulcers, heart conditions, and AIDS.

The agency has also limited or prohibited advertising of health claims that it doesn't believe are conclusively proven by scientific research. So, despite the fact that many researchers think the regular ingestion of aspirin may help prevent heart attacks, the FDA forbids aspirin manufacturers from telling consumers this. The agency has made similar rulings regarding health claims for vitamins, nutritional supplements, and foods. It even allows health claims for some *foods* containing vitamins—such as vitamin E, vitamin C, and betacarotene—but not for *supplements* containing the same vitamins. These restrictions prevent many consumers from discovering and evaluating information that could help them make healthier choices. As former Federal Trade Commission economist Paul Rubin says, "the FDA behaves as if it has a general aversion to provision of information to consumers by manufacturers."

The FDA "is charged with regulating 'false and misleading' advertising and product labeling. However, the agency has substantial discretion in fulfilling this mission," Rubin adds. "While advertising which is clearly false should be eliminated, the agency uses its mandate to enforce an extremely broad interpretation of misleading [advertising] and thereby muzzles the flow of valuable information to consumers."

Kessler says that because extension of the FDA's authority to tobacco would likely result in an immediate ban, Congress should impose stiff regulations directly on the industry that stop short of an outright ban.

But even enacting legislation to give the FDA specific powers to regulate nicotine content, the manufacturing process, and the introduction of new tobacco products would represent a massive increase in the agency's power over the average American. Once let loose on tobacco, the FDA will probably never be restrained by subsequent legislation, as the drafter of the current anti-smoking bill, Rep. Mike Synar (D-Okla.), has admitted. "We wanted to get the jurisdiction over tobacco into the FDA," he says. "It was simple politics. Once we got the product in there, we wouldn't have to do anything legislatively again."

The question must be asked: Where do we stop? Will the FDA also regulate the fat content of steaks, or require that caffeine be removed from all soft drinks (obviously this can be done, given the prevalence of caffeine-free brands today)? And it's not just the FDA that will be emboldened by congressional action here. Efforts by OSHA, EPA, and other regulators will intensify. Regulatory scrutiny of personal behavior will move beyond the workplace as well. Already courts in 11 states have ordered parents to stop smoking or risk losing custody of their children. Will parents next be forced to comply with diet, exercise, or other behavioral guidelines?

At the core of the new war on tobacco is the notion that federal agencies must not only provide information about the risks of what consumers choose to do, but also substitute their judgment to prevent consumers from choosing the "wrong" things.

Health and safety issues are not so cut and dried. Many popular activities have varying levels of risks and benefits, and consumers differ dramatically in how tolerant they are of risk and how highly they value pleasure or satisfaction. No team of regulators is qualified to make blanket judgments about what is and isn't a good choice for consumers. And when government makes such judgments, the consequences can be significant—ranging from lost satisfaction and pleasure to, in the case of drug approvals, lost lives.

The FDA should become less intrusive, not more. Consumers have good reason to make decisions for themselves, given their disparate interests and needs in a marketplace of one-quarter billion Americans. Given the opportunity and accurate, timely information, most consumers will make choices that maximize their happiness. The FDA's role, like that of other federal agencies, should be to provide such information and let individual Americans, even smokers, take it from there.

POSTSCRIPT

Should Tobacco Products Be More Closely Regulated?

Kriz discusses much data indicating that smoking cigarettes is injurious to human health. He points out that more than 400,000 people die from tobacco-related illnesses each year, costing the U.S. health care system more than $80 billion annually. Hood, however, questions the accuracy of that data. How the data are presented and interpreted may affect how one feels about the issue of placing more restrictions on tobacco products. There is currently a great deal of antismoking sentiment in society. Even Hood does not *recommend* that people use tobacco products; he states only that the consequences linked to it may be exaggerated.

Former U.S. Food and Drug Administration (FDA) commissioner David Kessler argues that smoking is not a matter of choice because smokers become addicted to nicotine. Kessler agrees that the decision to start smoking is a matter of choice, but that once dependency occurs, "most smokers are in effect deprived of the choice to stop smoking." Hood argues that people make all types of choices, and if some choices people make are ultimately harmful, then that is their responsibility.

In "The Human Costs of Tobacco Use," *The New England Journal of Medicine* (April 7, 1994), Carl E. Bartecchi, Thomas D. MacKenzie, and Robert W. Schrier discuss the economic costs of tobacco use and present an analysis of the tobacco industry. In "Tobacco: Enemy Number 1," *Mother Jones* (May/June 1996), Dreyfuss discusses the FDA's attempt to regulate nicotine by identifying it as a drug. In "FDA's Proposed Regulation of the Sale and Promotion of Tobacco Products to Minors," *Public Health Reports* (vol. 111, 1996), Zieve describes the FDA's efforts to control tobacco sales. In "Government Paternalism and Citizen Rationality: The Justifiability of Banning Tobacco Advertising," *International Journal of Advertising* (vol. 9, 1990), John Luik argues that individuals should have the freedom to smoke, even if that behavior is harmful. Smoking is an individual's right, he says, and society should not interfere with this right. In "The Tobacco Lobby: Maintaining Profits, Distorting Issues, Costing Lives," *Priorities* (Summer 1992), William Godshall contends that the tobacco industry should be held responsible for the many deaths associated with tobacco.

On the Internet . . .

The Addiction Research Foundation (ARF)

Located in Toronto, Canada, the Addiction Research Foundation conducts workshops and publishes reports on topics ranging from pharmacology to drug treatment, the incidence of drug use, and drug prevention. *http://www.arf.org/*

The National Center on Addiction and Substance Abuse at Columbia University (CASA)

The National Center on Addiction and Substance Abuse at Columbia University provides access to information, research, and commentary on tobacco, alcohol, and drug abuse issues, including prevention, treatment, and cost data. *http://www.casacolumbia.org/*

Drug Watch International

Drug Watch International is a volunteer, nonprofit information network and advocacy organization that promotes the creation of healthy drug-free cultures in the world and opposes the legalization of drugs. *http://www.DrugWatch.org/*

Action on Smoking and Health (ASH)

Action on Smoking and Health is a national, nonprofit legal action and educational organization that fights for the rights of nonsmokers and addresses the problems associated with smoking. *http://ash.org/*

PART 2

Drugs and Social Policy

With the exception of the debate on marijuana, each of the debates in this section deals with legal drugs. The drugs most frequently used in society are legal drugs. Because of their prevalence, the adverse psychological, social, and physical effects of legal drugs such as tobacco, alcohol, and antidepressants are minimized or discounted. Alcohol and tobacco, however, cause far more deaths and disabilities than all illegal drugs combined. Many people remain concerned about what society's view of alcohol and other legal drugs should be.

Prescription medications and the changing pharmaceutical industry have recently become topics of concern. The trend toward medical self-help raises questions of how much control one should have over one's own health, particularly when it comes to drugs. The current tendency to identify nicotine as an addictive drug and to promote the use of moderate amounts of alcohol to reduce heart disease has generated controversy. In the last several years there has been increasing concern that drugs like Ritalin and Prozac are overprescribed. Also under contention is the issue of whether or not marijuana should be made available through prescription to people who suffer certain diseases for which some have suggested the drug could be beneficial.

■ Should Marijuana Be Legalized as a Medication?

■ Should Doctors Promote Alcohol for Their Patients?

■ Is Nicotine Physically Addictive?

■ Should There Be Tighter Restrictions on the Advertising of Prescription Drugs?

■ Are Too Many Children Receiving Ritalin?

■ Is Prozac Overprescribed?

ISSUE 8

Should Marijuana Be Legalized as a Medication?

YES: Lester Grinspoon, from "Should Marijuana Be Legalized as a Medicine? Yes, It's a Beneficial Drug," *The World and I* (June 1994)

NO: Eric A. Voth, from "Should Marijuana Be Legalized as a Medicine? No, It's Dangerous and Addictive," *The World and I* (June 1994)

ISSUE SUMMARY

YES: Lester Grinspoon, professor of psychiatry at Harvard Medical School, argues that marijuana is a safe, therapeutic drug that has been proven beneficial to patients suffering from chemotherapy nausea, glaucoma, chronic pain, epilepsy, migraine headaches, and AIDS, and he feels that the federal government is unjustifiably prohibiting its use.

NO: Eric A. Voth, medical director of Chemical Dependency Services at St. Francis Hospital in Topeka, Kansas, contends that marijuana is capable of producing many adverse psychological and physical effects and that reports of its medical benefits are invalid because they are based on personal testimony, not on scientific studies.

In 1996 voters of the states of California and Arizona passed referenda to legalize marijuana for medical purposes. Despite the position of these voters, the federal government does not support the medical use of marijuana, and federal laws take precedence over state laws. A major concern of opponents of this law is that legalization of marijuana for medicinal purposes will lead to its use for recreational purposes.

Marijuana, or cannabis, has never achieved the medical status of other drugs, such as morphine or opium. Nonetheless, its medicinal qualities have been recognized for centuries. Marijuana was utilized as far back as 2737 B.C. by Chinese emperor Shen Nung and then some 2,900 years later in A.D. 200 by a Chinese physician who mixed cannabis resin with white wine to make a surgical anesthetic. By the 1890s some medical reports had stated that cannabis was useful as a pain reliever. However, despite its historical significance, the use of marijuana for medical treatment has been a widely debated and controversial topic.

Marijuana has been tested in the treatment of glaucoma, asthma, convulsions, epilepsy, and migraine headaches, and in the reduction of nausea, vomiting, and loss of appetite associated with chemotherapy treatment. Many medical professionals and patients believe that marijuana shows promise in the treatment of these disorders and others, including spasticity in amputees and multiple sclerosis. Yet, others argue that there are other drugs and treatments available that are more specific and effective in treating these disorders than marijuana and that marijuana cannot be considered a medical replacement.

Because of the conflicting viewpoints and what many people argue is an absence of reliable, scientific research supporting the medicinal value of marijuana, the drug and it plant materials remain in Schedule I of the Controlled Substances Act of 1970. This act established five categories, or schedules, under which drugs are classified according to their potential for abuse and their medical usefulness, which in turn determines their availability. Drugs classified under Schedule I are those that have a high potential for abuse and no scientifically proven medical use. Many marijuana proponents have called for the Drug Enforcement Administration (DEA) to move marijuana from Schedule I to Schedule II, which classifies drugs as having a high potential for abuse but also having an established medical use. A switch to Schedule II would legally allow physicians to utilize marijuana and its components in certain treatment programs. To date, however, the DEA has refused.

Currently, marijuana is used medically but not legally. Most of the controversy surrounds whether or not marijuana and its plant properties are indeed of medical value and whether or not the risks associated with its use outweigh its proposed medical benefits. Research reports and scientific studies have been inconclusive. Some physicians and many cancer patients claim that marijuana greatly reduces the side effects of chemotherapy— it has antiemetic qualities that are greater than other prescribed chemotherapy buffers. Many glaucoma patients believe that marijuana use has greatly improved their conditions.

Marijuana opponents argue that the evidence in support of marijuana as medically useful suffers from far too many deficiencies. The DEA, for example, believes that studies supporting the medical value of marijuana are scientifically limited, based on biased testimonies of ill individuals who have used marijuana and their families and friends, and grounded in the unscientific opinions of certain physicians, nurses, and other hospital personnel. Furthermore, marijuana opponents state that the safety of marijuana has not been established by reliable scientific data weighing marijuana's possible therapeutic benefits against its known negative effects.

In the following selections, Lester Grinspoon asserts that the federal government has set up needless political roadblocks to prevent needy individuals from receiving the medicinal benefits of marijuana. Eric A. Voth argues that marijuana should not be legalized for medical purposes, because the current research on marijuana's medicinal benefits is insufficient, based upon unreliable, misconducted scientific studies, and reliant upon anecdotal accounts of marijuana use by individuals who may know little about the possible side effects of the drug.

YES

Lester Grinspoon

SHOULD MARIJUANA BE LEGALIZED AS A MEDICINE? YES, IT'S A BENEFICIAL DRUG

Millions of Americans are needlessly suffering because of an irrational prohibition. They are being criminalized for using a substance that has been known from ancient times to be both remarkably safe and useful. The drug's name is cannabis, usually referred to as marijuana. Of the thousands of Americans who are suffering from chemotherapy nausea, glaucoma, chronic pain, epilepsy, migraine, and the AIDS wasting syndrome, only nine people are allowed to use it as a medicine. And millions who find cannabis useful in non-medical ways are being unnecessarily tortured because an uncaring bureaucracy insists on maintaining the prohibition of a relatively benign substance.

The effort to make cannabis available as a prescription drug was initiated in 1972 by the National Organization for the Reform of Marijuana Laws (NORML) and worked its way through the legal system with excruciating slowness. In 1986 the administrator of the Drug Enforcement Administration [DEA] finally announced that he would hold the public hearings ordered by the courts seven years before. Those hearings, which began in 1986 and lasted two years, involved many witnesses, including both patients and doctors, and thousands of pages of documentation. The DEA's own administrative law judge, Francis Young, reviewed the evidence and rendered his decision in 1988.

Young said that approval by a "significant minority" of physicians was enough to meet the standard of "currently accepted medical use in treatment in the United States" established by the Controlled Substances Act for a Schedule II (prescription) drug. He added that

> marijuana, in its natural form, is one of the safest therapeutically active substances known to man.... One must reasonably conclude that there is accepted safety for use of marijuana under medical supervision. To conclude otherwise, on the record, would be unreasonable, arbitrary, and capricious.

Young went on to recommend that

the Administrator [of the DEA] conclude that the marijuana plant considered as a whole has a currently accepted medical use in treatment in the United States, that there is no lack of accepted safety for use of it under medical supervision, and that it may be lawfully transferred from Schedule I to Schedule II.

The DEA disregarded the opinion of its own administrative law judge and refused to reschedule marijuana.

By the early 1970s, it was becoming increasingly clear that there were no valid scientific reasons for the ban on marijuana. The Prohibition-era notions on which the 1937 Marijuana Tax Act was based—that marijuana caused violent crime, "sexual excess" (whatever that is), and addiction and that it served as a stepping-stone to harder drugs—had been thoroughly discredited.

However, as these arguments lost plausibility, groups opposed to liberalization of the marijuana laws began to talk about "new research" supposedly proving that marijuana caused other kinds of harm. It was in this atmosphere that the federal government provided greatly expanded support, largely through the National Institute on Drug Abuse, for studies designed to uncover new health hazards.

FALSE ALARMS AND REPORTS

Thus we heard in the early 1970s that marijuana destroyed brain cells, caused psychoses, lowered testosterone levels and sperm counts, led to breast development in adolescent males, damaged memory and intellectual functions, compromised the immune system, and caused chromosome breakage, genetic damage, and birth defects. The publica-

tion of these findings followed a typical pattern. Each would be reported in a front-page story with alarmist commentary. Then, over the next few months or years, investigators would report that the finding could not be replicated.

When this contradictory evidence was reported at all, the story would usually appear as a short item in the back pages. The public was often left with the impression that the existence of the latest health hazard had been scientifically demonstrated.

After carefully monitoring the literature for more than two decades, I have concluded that the only well-confirmed deleterious effect of marijuana is harm to the pulmonary system. Smoking narrows and inflames air passages and reduces breathing capacity; some heavy hashish smokers seem to have damaged bronchial cells. Marijuana smoke burdens the lungs with three times more tars (insoluble particulates) and five times more carbon monoxide than tobacco smoke.

The respiratory system also retains more of the tars, because marijuana smoke is inhaled more deeply and held in the lungs longer. On the other hand, even the heaviest marijuana users rarely smoke as much as an average tobacco smoker. So far, not a single case of lung cancer, emphysema, or other significant pulmonary pathology attributable to cannabis use has been reported.

Furthermore, the pulmonary risk can be reduced. One way would be to make marijuana of sufficient potency legally available so that less smoking would be necessary and the lungs would be less exposed to toxins. A higher potency would not necessarily heighten other dangers of marijuana because smokers find it easy to titrate the dose, stopping when they attain the desired effect. Another way to reduce the risk is the use of water pipes and other filtering systems, which are now foolishly discouraged by the law. If marijuana were legal, there would be strong incentives to develop further technologies for the separation of undesirable from desirable constituents of cannabis smoke.

In 1971, I pointed out that because marijuana had been used by so many people all over the world for many thousands of years with so little evidence of significant toxic effect, the discovery of some previously unknown, serious health hazard was unlikely. I suggested that the emphasis in cannabis research should be shifted to its medical uses and its potential as a tool to advance our understanding of brain function. Although few resources have been committed to either of these fields, there have been compelling developments in both.

In 1990, researchers discovered receptors in the brain stimulated by tetrahydrocannabinol (THC), the psychoactive chemical in marijuana. This exciting discovery implied that the body produces its own version of cannabinoids for one or more useful purposes. The first of these cannabinoid-like neurotransmitters was identified in 1992 and named anandamide (*ananda* is the Sanskrit word for bliss). Cannabinoid receptor sites occur not only in the lower brain but also in the cerebral cortex, which governs higher thinking.

MEDICAL AND PSYCHOLOGICAL BENEFITS

These discoveries raise some interesting questions. Could the distribution of anandamide receptor sites in the higher brain explain why so many cannabis users claim that the drug enhances some mental activities, including creativity and fluidity of associations? Do these receptor sites play a role in marijuana's capacity to alter the subjective experience of time? What about the subtle enhancement of perception and the capacity to experience the physical world with some of the freshness and excitement of childhood? Perhaps further research on these receptors will also promote a better understanding of the remarkable medical versatility of cannabis. Such studies seem all the more promising now that cannabis receptors have been found outside the cerebral cord.

Despite conditions that deter medical researchers, medical applications of cannabis have seen considerable progress since the early 1970s under the most unusual and difficult of circumstances. New drugs are generally escorted over the complicated federal regulatory obstacle course by pharmaceutical companies, which devote vast resources to the task of taking a chemical with therapeutic potential and transforming it into a marketable property. For many reasons, including the fact that patent protection is impossible, no drug company is ever likely to undertake this effort on behalf of cannabis. Furthermore, the government has been steadfast in its opposition to recognizing the medical utility of cannabis. Yet ever-larger numbers of people are using marijuana medically.

Several developments have greatly increased interest in cannabis as a medicine. In the early 1970s many people learned that cannabis could relieve the intense nausea induced by cancer chemotherapeutic substances, which were then new. Marijuana often proved to be more effective than legal antinauseants. At about the same time it was discovered that marijuana reliably lowered the pressure on the optic nerve in people suffering from open-angle glaucoma; many patients learned, mostly from one another, that cannabis was more effective than conventional medications in retarding the progressive loss of vision caused by this disorder.

In the mid-1980s, people with AIDS discovered that cannabis relieved the nausea caused by their illness or by the medicines taken to counteract it. In addition, cannabis often improved their appetite and enabled them to stop losing or even to gain weight. Like most medical users of cannabis, AIDS patients have found that smoked marijuana is more effective than the synthetic THC (Marinol) that was made legally available as a prescription drug in 1985.

In the last 20 years, as the medical potential of cannabis has become increasingly clear, I have witnessed the growing frustration of patients who cannot obtain it legally. The U.S. government must accept responsibility for the unnecessary suffering produced by a policy that can only be described as ignorant and cruel and for forcing citizens to engage in criminal activity. Despite government obstructionism, many patients have learned to use marijuana therapeutically and many more are discovering its benefits. Unfortunately, they have to endure the anxiety imposed by the threat of arrest and their feelings about breaking the law, and they are compelled to pay exorbitant street prices for a medicine that should be quite inexpensive.

Experience over the last 20 years has compelled me to take much more seriously the claims of those who believe that cannabis has useful properties that cannot be described as medical. For example, I no longer doubt that marijuana can be

an intellectual stimulant. It can help the user to penetrate conceptual boundaries, promote fluidity of associations, and enhance insight and creativity.

Some people find it so useful in gaining new perspectives or seeing problems from a different vantage point that they smoke it in preparation for intellectual work. I suspect that these people have learned to make use of the alteration in consciousness produced by cannabis. Other ways in which cannabis is useful probably have less to do with learning. It can enhance the appreciation of food, music, sexual activity, natural beauty, and other sensual experiences. Under the right conditions and in the right settings, it can promote emotional intimacy. For almost everyone it has the capacity to highlight the comical in life and catalyze a deep and salutary laughter.

'RELATIVELY BENIGN AND REMARKABLY USEFUL'

Perhaps in part because so many Americans have discovered for themselves that marijuana is both relatively benign and remarkably useful, moral consensus about the evil of cannabis is uncertain and shallow. The authorities pretend that eliminating cannabis traffic is like eliminating slavery or piracy, or like eradicating smallpox or malaria. The official view is that everything possible has to be done to prevent everyone from ever using marijuana. But there is also an informal lore of marijuana use that is far more tolerant.

Many of the millions of cannabis users in this country not only disobey the drug laws but feel a principled lack of respect for them. They do not conceal their bitter resentment of laws that render them criminals. They believe that many people have been deceived by the government, and they have come to doubt that the "authorities" understand much about either the deleterious or the useful properties of the drug. This undercurrent of ambivalence and resistance in public attitudes toward marijuana laws leaves room for the possibility of change, especially because the costs of prohibition are so high and rising. More than 300,000 people a year are arrested on marijuana charges, contributing to the clogging of courts and overcrowding of prisons.

Besides the measurable billions wasted on prohibition, there are costs more difficult to quantify. One of them is lost credibility of government. Young people who discover that the authorities have been lying about cannabis become cynical about their pronouncements on other drugs and disdainful of their commitment to justice. Another frightful cost of prohibition is the erosion of civil liberties. The use of informers and entrapment, mandatory urine testing, unwarranted searches and seizures, and violations of the Posse Comitatus Act (which outlaws the use of military forces for civilian law enforcement) are becoming more common. It is increasingly clear that our society cannot be both drug-free and free.

It is also clear that the realities of human need are incompatible with the demand for a legally enforceable distinction between medicine and all other uses of cannabis. Marijuana use simply does not conform to the conceptual boundaries established by twentieth-century institutions. It enhances many pleasures and has many potential medical uses, but even these two categories are not the only relevant ones. The kind of therapy often used to ease everyday discomforts does not fit any such scheme. In many cases, what laypeople do in prescribing marijuana for themselves is not very different from what physicians do when they provide prescriptions for psychoactive or other drugs.

The only workable way of realizing the full potential of this remarkable substance, including its full medical potential, is to free it from the present dual set of regulations: those that control prescription drugs in general and the special criminal laws that control psychoactive substances. These mutually reinforcing laws establish a set of social categories that strangle its uniquely multi-faceted potential. The only way out is to cut the knot by giving marijuana the same status as alcohol: legalizing it for adults for all uses and removing it entirely from the medical and criminal control systems.

NO

Eric A. Voth

SHOULD MARIJUANA BE LEGALIZED AS A MEDICINE? NO, IT'S DANGEROUS AND ADDICTIVE

To best understand the problems associated with legalizing marijuana, it is useful to examine drug legalization in general and then to discuss the specific pitfalls of legal marijuana.

Advocates generally argue that crime would decrease under legalization, that dealers would be driven out of the market by lower prices, that legalization works in other countries, that government would benefit from the sales tax on drugs, that Prohibition did not work, and that the "war on drugs" has failed.

Examining currently legal drugs provides an insight as to the possible effect of legalizing other drugs. First, alcohol is responsible for approximately 100,000 deaths every year and 11 million cases of alcoholism. Virtually every bodily system is adversely affected by alcoholism. While Prohibition was an unfortunately violent time, many of the hardships of that era were really the result of the Depression. Prohibition did decrease the rate of alcohol consumption; alcohol-related deaths climbed steadily after Prohibition was repealed.

Tobacco use is responsible for 400,000 premature deaths per year. It causes emphysema, chronic bronchitis, heart disease, lung cancer, head and neck cancers, vascular disease, and hypertension, to name a few disorders. The taxes on tobacco come nowhere close to paying for the health problems caused by the drug.

The argument that legalization would decrease crime exemplifies a great lack of understanding of drug abuse. Most drug-associated crime is committed to acquire drugs or under the influence of drugs. The Netherlands has often been heralded by the drug culture as a country where decriminalization has worked. In fact, drug-related holdups and shootings have increased 60 percent and 40 percent, respectively, since decriminalization. This has caused the government to start enforcing the drug laws more strictly.

Because of its powerful drug lobby, the Netherlands has never been able to mount a taxation campaign against its legal drugs. We suffer a similar phenomenon in the United States in that the tobacco lobby has successfully defeated most taxation initiatives against tobacco.

The argument that drug dealers would be driven out of the market by lower prices ignores the fact that legalization will probably result in as many as 250,000 to over two million new addicts. Broader markets, even with lower prices, certainly will not drive dealers out of the market. Our overburdened medical system will not be able to handle the drastic increase in the number of addicts.

MEDICAL MARIJUANA

Richard Cowan, national director of the National Organization for the Reform of Marijuana Laws (NORML), has stated that acceptance of medicinal uses of marijuana is pivotal for its legalization.

In 1972, the drug culture petitioned the Drug Enforcement Administration (DEA) to reschedule marijuana from a Schedule I drug (unable to be prescribed, high potential for abuse, not currently accepted for medicinal use, unsafe) to a Schedule II drug (high potential for abuse, currently accepted for medical use, potential for abuse, but prescribable).

This rescheduling petition was initiated by NORML, the Alliance for Cannabis Therapeutics (ACT), and the Cannabis Corporation of America. Of note is the fact that none of these drug-culture organizations has a recognized medical or scientific background, nor do they represent any accredited medical entity.

After substantial legal maneuvering by the drug culture, the DEA carefully documented the case against the rescheduling of marijuana and denied the petition. To examine the potential for therapeutic uses of marijuana, the DEA turned to testimony from nationally recognized experts who rejected the medical use of marijuana (published in the *Federal Register,* December 29, 1989, and March 26, 1992).

In the face of this expert testimony, the drug lobby could only produce anecdotes and the testimony of a handful of physicians with limited or absent clinical experience with marijuana. (Marijuana has not been accepted as a medicine by the AMA, the National Multiple Sclerosis Society, the American Glaucoma Society, the American Academy of Ophthalmology, and the American Cancer Society.)

The drug culture organizations appealed the DEA's decision. Recently, the U.S. Court of Appeals for the District of Columbia denied their petition to reschedule marijuana. This important decision also sets forth the new guideline that only rigorous scientific standards can satisfy the requirement of "currently accepted medical use." These preconditions are:

1. The drug has a known and reproducible chemistry;
2. Adequate safety studies;
3. Adequate and well-controlled studies proving efficacy; and
4. Qualified experts accept the drug.

In addition, the decision stated, "The administrator reasonably accorded more weight to the opinions of the experts than to the laymen and doctors on which the petitioners relied."

In his 1993 book *Marihuana: The Forbidden Medicine,* the psychiatrist Dr. Lester

Grinspoon assembled a group of anecdotes to justify the rescheduling of marijuana. Similar to the promarijuana lobby during rescheduling hearings, Grinspoon asserts that marijuana should be used to help relieve nausea (during cancer chemotherapy), glaucoma, wasting in AIDS, depression, menstrual cramps, pain, and virtually unlimited ailments. His anecdotes have no controls, no standardization of dose, no quality control, and no independent medical evaluation for efficacy or toxicity.

ONLY ANECDOTES PROVE ITS EFFICACY

The historical uses of marijuana in such cultures as India, Asia, the Middle East, South Africa, and South America are cited by Grinspoon as evidence of appropriate medical uses of the drug. One of Grinspoon's references is an 1860 assertion that marijuana had supposed beneficial effects "without interfering with the actions of the internal organs" (this is inaccurate). Let us not forget that medicine in earlier years was fraught with potions and remedies. Many of these were absolutely useless or even harmful to unsuspecting subjects. This is when our current FDA [Food and Drug Administration] and drug scheduling processes evolved, which should not be undermined.

The medical marijuana campaign gained momentum in February 1990, when a student project, initiated by Rick Doblin, published interpretations of a questionnaire that he had sent to oncologists. Doblin is closely associated with the Multidisciplinary Association for Psychedelic Studies, a drug-culture lobbying organization. This group strongly supports the legalization and medical

uses of the street drugs LSD and MDMA (Ecstasy). Doblins' staff sponsor at Harvard, Mark Kleiman, voiced his support for the legalization of marijuana in his recent book *Against Excess.* Neither author has a medical background, nor do they disclose their intrinsic bias toward the legalization of marijuana.

By manipulation of the statistics, the authors contend that 48 percent of their respondents would prescribe marijuana if legal and 54 percent feel it should be available by prescription. But the researchers fail to relate that the respondents account for only 9 percent of practicing oncologists. Only 6 percent of those surveyed feel that marijuana was effective in 50 percent or more of their patients.

Only 18 percent of the surveyed group believe marijuana to be safe and efficacious. Five percent of those surveyed favor making marijuana available by prescription. These numbers become less significant if compared to the number of all practicing oncologists. Furthermore, this survey was conducted before the release for use of the medication ondansetron (Zofran®), which is extremely effective to relieve the nausea associated with chemotherapy.

Unfortunately, the "results" of this unscientific but well-publicized study incorrectly give the impression that oncologists want marijuana available as medicine. But researchers neither asked if the oncologists had systematically examined their patients for negative effects of marijuana use nor if the oncologists were familiar with the myriad of health consequences of marijuana use. Furthermore, they did not ask oncologists if their attitudes about marijuana were affected by their own current or past marijuana use.

Contrary to the findings of Doblin and Kleiman, Dr. Richard Schwartz determined through a survey of practicing oncologists that THC (the major active ingredient of marijuana) ranked ninth in their preference for the treatment of mild nausea and sixth for the treatment of severe nausea. Only 6 percent had prescribed THC (by prescription or marijuana) for more than 50 patients. It was found that nausea was relieved in only 50 percent of the patients who received THC and that 25 percent had adverse side effects.

COMPLICATIONS OF MARIJUANA USE

According to the 1992 National Household Survey on Drug Abuse, 48 percent of young adults have used marijuana and 11 percent continue to use it. In 1992, 8.2 percent of young adults age 26 to 34 admitted having used marijuana in the last month, a figure that was up from 7.0 percent in 1991. Marijuana remains the most frequently used illegal drug. The chronic use of marijuana has now been demonstrated to lead to higher utilization of the health-care system, a long-suspected phenomenon.

Mental, affective, and behavioral changes are the most easily recognized consequences of marijuana use. Concentration, motor coordination, and memory are adversely impacted. For example, the ability to perform complex tasks such as flying is impaired even 24 hours after the acute intoxication phase. The association of marijuana use with trauma and intoxicated motor vehicle operation is also well established.

Memory is impaired for several months after cessation of use. After chronic use, marijuana addicts admit that their motivation to succeed lessens. Several biochemical models have demonstrated abnormal changes in brain cells, brain blood flow, and brain waves. Pathologic behavior such as psychosis is also associated with marijuana use. The more chronic the use, as would be necessary for treating diseases such as glaucoma, the higher the risk of mental problems.

Despite arguments from the drug culture to the contrary, marijuana is addictive. This addiction has been well described by users. It consists of both a physical dependence (tolerance and subsequent withdrawal) and a psychological habituation. Strangely, in the course of the rescheduling hearings, prodrug organizations admitted that "marijuana has a high potential for abuse and that abuse of the marijuana plant may lead to severe psychological or physical dependence," points that they now publicly deny. Unlike those addicted to many other drugs, the marijuana addict is exceptionally slow to recognize the addiction.

The gateway effect of marijuana is also well established in research. Use of alcohol, tobacco, and marijuana are major risk factors for subsequent addiction and more extensive drug use.

Smoked marijuana contains double to triple the concentrations of tar, carbon monoxide, and carcinogens found in cigarette smoke. Marijuana adversely impairs lung function by causing abnormalities in the cells lining the airways of the upper and lower respiratory tract and in the airspaces deep within the lung. It has been linked to head and neck cancer.

Contaminants of marijuana smoke include certain forms of bacteria and fungi. Users with impaired immunity are at particular risk for disease and infection when they inhale these substances.

Adverse effects of marijuana on the unborn were suspected after studies in Rhesus monkeys demonstrated spontaneous abortion. When exposed to marijuana during gestation, humans demonstrate changes in size and weight as well as neurologic abnormalities. A very alarming association also exists between maternal marijuana use and certain forms of cancer in offspring. Additionally, hormonal function in both male and female children is disrupted.

One of the earliest findings was the negative effect of marijuana on various immune functions, including cellular immunity and pulmonary immunity. Impaired ability to fight infection is now documented in humans who use marijuana. They have been shown to exhibit an inability to fight herpes infections and a blunted response to therapy for genital warts. The potential for these complications exists in all forms of administration of marijuana.

It should be clear that use of the drug bears substantial health risks. In populations at high risk for infection and immune suppression (AIDS and cancer chemotherapy patients), the risks are unacceptable.

SUMMARY

The unfortunate reality is that the drug culture is exploiting the unwitting public and the suffering of patients with chronic illnesses for its own benefit. Under the false and dangerous claims that smoking marijuana is a harmless recreational activity and that it offers significant benefits to those suffering from a variety of tragic ailments, the drug culture seeks to use bogus information to gain public acceptance for the legalization of marijuana.

POSTSCRIPT

Should Marijuana Be Legalized as a Medication?

Lester Grinspoon strongly advocates the legalization of marijuana for medical treatment. He believes that the delay in the medicalization of marijuana stems from arduous and restrictive procedures of the federal government and that the government blocks people in need from receiving medication that is both therapeutic and benign.

From Voth's perspective, promoting marijuana as a medicinal agent would be a mistake because it is not medically useful or safe. Moreover, he feels that the availability of marijuana should not be predicated on personal accounts of its benefits, and he asserts that studies showing that marijuana has medical value suffer from unscientific methodology and other deficiencies. The results of previous research, Voth contends, do not lend strong credence to marijuana's medicinal value.

Some people have expressed concern about what will happen if marijuana is approved for medicinal use. Would it then become more acceptable for nonmedical, recreational use? There is also a possibility that some people would misinterpret the government's message and think that marijuana *cures* cancer when, in fact, it would only be used to treat the side effects of the chemotherapy.

A central question is, If physicians feel that marijuana use is justified to properly care for seriously ill patients, should they promote this form of medical treatment even though it falls outside the law? Does the relief of pain and suffering for patients warrant going beyond what federal legislation says is acceptable? Also, should physicians be prosecuted if they recommend marijuana to their patients? What about the unknown risks of using an illegal drug? Is it worthwhile to ignore the possibility that marijuana may produce harmful side effects in order to alleviate pain or to treat other ailments?

Many marijuana proponents contend that the effort to prevent the legalization of marijuana for medical use is purely a political battle. Detractors claim that the issue is purely scientific—that the data supporting marijuana's medical usefulness are inconclusive and scientifically unsubstantiated.

Several articles discuss whether marijuana should be legalized as a medication. These include "The War Over Weed," by Tom Morganthau, *Newsweek* (February 3, 1997); "Acceptance of Marijuana Therapy Prompts Call for More Research," by Sally Lehrman, *Nature* (November 1996); and "The Battle for Medical Marijuana," by Sarah Ferguson, *The Nation* (January 6, 1997).

In a study conducted by Richard Doblin and Mark Kleiman, "Marijuana as Medicine: A Survey of Oncologists," in Arnold Trebach and Kevin Zeese, eds., *New Frontiers in Drug Policy* (Drug Policy Foundation, 1991), almost half of the oncologists surveyed recommended marijuana to their patients to help them deal with the side effects of chemotherapy. Grinspoon's views on legalizing marijuana for medical purposes are more completely discussed in a book he wrote with coauthor James B. Bakalar entitled *Marijuana, the Forbidden Medicine* (Yale University Press, 1993). In his essay "Before I Go," in Arnold Trebach and Kevin Zeese, eds., *Strategies for Change: New Directions in Drug Policy* (Drug Policy Foundation, 1992), Kenny Jenks describes the legal battles his HIV-positive wife, Barbara, encountered when she tried to use marijuana to help her cope with her disease.

ISSUE 9

Should Doctors Promote Alcohol for Their Patients?

YES: Stanton Peele, from "Should Physicians Recommend Alcohol to Their Patients? Yes," *Priorities* (vol. 8, no. 1, 1996)

NO: Albert B. Lowenfels, from "Should Physicians Recommend Alcohol to Their Patients? No," *Priorities* (vol. 8, no. 1, 1996)

ISSUE SUMMARY

YES: Psychologist Stanton Peele, an expert on alcoholism and addiction, feels that physicians should recommend that their patients drink alcohol in moderate amounts. He maintains that numerous studies demonstrate the benefits of moderate alcohol use in reducing the risk of coronary heart disease, the leading cause of death in the United States.

NO: Albert B. Lowenfels, professor at New York Medical College, feels that recommending moderate alcohol consumption is not prudent, especially since many people come from families with histories of alcohol abuse. Lowenfels believes that it is inappropriate to extol the merits of moderate alcohol use to people who have abstained throughout their lives.

Heart disease is the leading cause of death in the United States, so it is reasonable to assume that people are interested in reducing the risks that lead to heart disease. Magazines are replete with articles describing ways to control factors that are linked with heart disease, such as minimizing the amount of saturated fats we consume, managing stress in our lives, and exercising to counter the effects of a sedentary lifestyle. It has been suggested that it is possible to diminish the likelihood of heart disease through the moderate consumption of alcohol. The relationship between alcohol and heart disease and whether or not physicians should recommend moderate alcohol consumption are the focus of this issue.

Discussions regarding the effects of alcohol usually center on the consequences associated with excessive alcohol use. Alcoholism is a devastating problem; an estimated 10–20 million people are affected by it. Individuals and families are sometimes ruined by the unhealthy use of alcohol. Despite a decline during the previous decade in the number of fatalities linked to driving while intoxicated, almost 20,000 people are killed annually by drivers under the influence of alcohol. Alcoholism is often described as a national epidemic that poses a threat to everyone in society. Is it therefore a wise idea to promote the moderate use of alcohol, even though such behavior may reduce the risk of heart disease?

Many research studies do show a relationship between moderate alcohol use and reduced heart disease. However, critics maintain that the evidence demonstrating the benefits of moderate alcohol use over abstinence are generally based on self-reports that are nonrepresentative and likely inaccurate. For example, people who say they do not drink may actually be drinkers. In addition, people who drink heavily are less likely to participate in studies examining the effects of alcohol.

An important aspect of this debate is what constitutes moderate alcohol use. The concept of moderation varies from one individual to another: To a social drinker, moderation may involve one, two, or three drinks per week. To an alcoholic, moderation is probably much more. To a college student, binge drinking may be viewed as moderate if it is limited to weekends and special occasions. Also, how much alcohol does one need to drink to reduce heart disease? How much is too much? Numerous studies show that two drinks per day are beneficial. However, due to individual and cultural differences, many experts feel that no one definition of moderation is adequate.

Health researcher Stanton Peele concurs that excessive alcohol use entails potential harm, but he contends that it is reasonable to advocate moderate alcohol consumption. Peele feels that educators and public health officials are preoccupied with discussing the negative effects of alcohol; thus, moderate alcohol use is not learned by young people. He also believes that researchers downplay the positive effects of alcohol because they fear that people would drink more than a moderate amount if alcohol's benefits were promoted. Peele contends that this fear is unfounded.

Lowenfels questions the value of promoting moderate alcohol consumption for individuals who have maintained a lifetime of sobriety. He argues that there is no research supporting the benefits of moderate alcohol use for abstainers. Some experts maintain that the evidence demonstrating the benefits of moderate alcohol use over abstinence is misleading because these studies are based on self-reports.

One major concern with regard to promoting moderate alcohol consumption to lessen the likelihood of heart disease is that some people may misconstrue the information. Furthermore, moderate alcohol consumption is clearly harmful in some situations, such as before driving, before operating dangerous equipment, while on medication, and during pregnancy.

In the following selections, Peele argues that there is strong evidence that two alcoholic drinks daily act to mitigate the risk of heart disease and that there may be other benefits from publicly advancing such a message. Albert B. Lowenfels contends that the benefits of moderate alcohol use over abstinence are questionable. He also feels that promoting a moderate use message may lead to other problems, especially for individuals with a family history of heavy drinking.

YES   Stanton Peele

SHOULD PHYSICIANS RECOMMEND ALCOHOL TO THEIR PATIENTS? YES

Whenever I have visited a physician over the last decade, the following scenario has been replayed: We discuss my cholesterol levels (total, LDL and HDL). We review dietary guidelines and other medical recommendations. Then I say, "Don't forget to remind me to drink a glass or two of wine daily." Invariably, the doctor demurs: "That hasn't been proven to protect you against atherosclerosis."

My doctors, all of whom I have respected and liked, are wrong. Evidence has established beyond question that alcohol reduces coronary artery disease, America's major killer. This result has been found in the Harvard Physician and Nurse studies and in studies by Kaiser Permanente and the American Cancer Society (ACS). Indeed, the evidence that alcohol reduces coronary artery disease and mortality is better than the evidence for the statin drugs, the most potent cholesterol-reducing medications.

Drinking to excess does increase mortality from several sources, such as cancer, cirrhosis and accidents. But a series of studies in the 1990s—including those conducted in conjunction with Kaiser, ACS and Harvard—in the U.S., Britain and Denmark, have found that moderate drinking reduces overall mortality.

Nonetheless, many people object to the idea that doctors should inform their patients that moderate drinking may prolong life. They fear that such advice will justify the excessive drinking some patients already engage in, or they worry that encouragement from doctors will push people who cannot handle alcohol to drink.

The view that people are so stupid or malleable that they will become alcohol abusers because doctors tell them moderate drinking is good for them is demeaning and self-defeating. If people can't regulate their own diets, drinking and exercise, then doctors should avoid giving patients any information about their health behavior, no matter how potentially helpful.

Not only can people handle such information on lifestyle, it offers the primary and best way to attack heart disease. Of course, doctors may also prescribe medications. These medications rarely solve underlying problems, however, and they often cause adverse side effects that counterbalance their positive effects. Because they are not a cure, courses of medication, once begun, are rarely discontinued.

People are the best regulators of their own behaviors. Even those who drink excessively often benefit when doctors provide straightforward, accurate information. Clinical trials conducted by the World Health Organization around the world showed that so-called brief interventions, in which medical personnel advised heavy drinkers to reduce their drinking, are the most successful therapy for problem drinking.

But far more Americans drink less, not more, than would be most healthful for them. To fail to inform these patients about the benefits of moderate drinking is both counterproductive and dishonest. Physicians may ask, "How much alcohol do you drink," "Is there any reason that you don't drink (or that you drink so little)," and (to those without religious objections, previous drinking problems, etc.), "Do you know that one or two glasses of wine or beer a day can be good for your health if you can safely consume them?"

Here are the data about alcohol and mortality:

1. In 1995 Charles Fuchs and his colleagues at Harvard found that women who drank up to two drinks a day lived longer than abstainers. Subjects were 85,700 nurses.

2. In 1995, Morten Gronbaek and colleagues found that wine drinkers survived longer than abstainers, with those drinking three to five glasses daily having the lowest death rate. Subjects were 20,000 Danes.

3. In 1994, Richard Doll and his colleagues found that men who drank up to two drinks daily lived significantly longer than abstainers. Subjects were 12,300 British doctors.

4. In 1992 Il Suh and colleagues found a 40 percent reduction in coronary mortality among men drinking three and more drinks daily. The 11,700 male subjects were in the upper 10 to 15 percent of risk for coronary heart disease based on their cholesterol, blood pressure and smoking status. Alcohol's enhancement of high density lipoproteins was identified as the protective factor.

5. In 1990, Paolo Boffetta and Lawrence Garfinkel found that men who drank occasionally—up to two drinks daily —outived abstainers. Subjects were over a quarter of a million volunteers enrolled by the American Cancer Society.

6. In 1990, Arthur Klatsky and his colleagues found that those who drank one or two drinks daily had the lowest overall mortality rate. Subjects were 85,000 Kaiser Permanente patients of both genders and all races.

These data—from large prospective studies of people of both sexes, different occupations, several nations and varying risk profiles—all point to alcohol's life-sustaining effects. This phenomenon is now so well accepted that the U.S. dietary guidelines released in January 1996 recognize that moderate drinking can be beneficial.

The levels of drinking at which alcohol lowers death rates are still open to dispute. The new U.S. guidelines indicate that men should not drink more than two drinks per day and women should not exceed one per day. But the British

Table 1

Temperance, Alcohol Consumption and Cardiac Mortality

Alcohol Consumption (1990)	Temperance Nations[a]	Non-Temperance Nations[b]
total consumption[c]	6.6	10.8
percent wine	18	44
percent beer	53	40
percent spirits	29	16
AA groups/million population	170	25
coronary mortality[d] (males 50–64)	421	272

[a]Norway, Sweden, U.S., U.K., Ireland, Australia, New Zealand, Canada, Finland, Iceland
[b]Italy, France, Spain, Portugal, Switzerland, Germany, Denmark, Austria, Belgium, Luxembourg, Netherlands
[c]Liters consumed per capita per year
[d]Deaths per 100,000 population

Source: Peele S. *Culture, alcohol, and health: the consequences of alcohol consumption among Western nations.* December 1, 1995. Morristown, NJ.

government has set its limits for "sensible drinking" at three to four drinks for men and two to three drinks for women. That abstemiousness increases the risk of death, however, can no longer be doubted. Moreover, alcohol operates at least as effectively as pharmaceuticals to reduce the risk of death for those at high risk for coronary disease.

At one point, researchers questioned whether people who had quit drinking due to previous health problems inflated the mortality rate among abstainers. But this position can no longer be maintained. The studies described above separated drinkers who had quit drinking and who had preexisting health problems from other non-drinkers. The benefits of drinking persisted with these individuals omitted.

At some point, ranging from three to six drinks daily, the negative effects of drinking for cancer, cirrhosis and accidents catch up to and surpass alcohol's beneficial cardiac impact. Moreover, women under 50—who have relatively low rates of heart disease and relatively high rates of breast cancer mortality—may not benefit from drinking.

That is, unless they have one or more cardiac risk factors. Even younger women with such risk factors benefit from light to moderate drinking. And, we must remember, most American women and men have such risk factors. (Fuchs et al. found about three quarters of the nurses in the Harvard study had at least one.) Remember, over all ages, American women are ten times as likely to die of heart disease (40 percent) as of breast cancer (4 percent).

Why, then, do Americans—physicians, public health workers, educators and political leaders—refuse to recognize alcohol's benefits? We might also ask why the United Sates banned the manufacture, sale and transportation of alcoholic beverages from 1920 to 1933. It is probably too obvious to mention that alcohol has never been banned—or prohibition even seriously discussed—in France, Italy, Spain and a number of other European nations.

What is it about America and some other nations that prevents them from considering that alcohol may be good for people? These so-called "temperance" nations see alcohol in a highly negative light. This is true even though nations with higher alcohol consumption have lower death rates from coronary heart disease (see Table 1). Oddly, temperance nations—despite concentrating on alcohol problem prevention and treatment —actually have more drinking problems than those in which alcohol is socially accepted and integrated.

This occurs even though temperance nations drink less alcohol. But they drink a higher percentage of their alcohol in the form of spirits. This drinking is more likely to take place in concentrated bursts among men at sporting events or in drinking establishments. This style of drinking contrasts with that in wine-drinking nations, which encourage socialized drinking among family members of both genders and all ages at meals and other social gatherings. These cultures do not teach people that alcohol is an addictive drug. Rather, moderate drinking is modeled for children and taught to them in the home. Furthermore, these cultures accept that drinking may be good for you. We should, too.

NO

Albert B. Lowenfels

SHOULD PHYSICIANS RECOMMEND ALCOHOL TO THEIR PATIENTS? NO

If physicians were to encourage their patients to drink alcohol, what patients would be the target group? Certainly not heavy drinkers, whose health, job and family may already suffer from alcohol abuse or addiction; the advice for these unfortunate individuals should be to reduce alcohol consumption or, preferably, to abstain entirely from alcohol.

Light and moderate drinkers need no encouragement to drink alcohol; instead, they need advice about safe levels for drinking, the dangers of drinking while driving or operating motorized equipment and, for females, the necessity for abstinence from alcohol prior to conception and during pregnancy.

The only target group, therefore, would be those patients who are nonconsumers of alcohol. Physicians would never advocate alcohol consumption for children, so our advice would be limited to nondrinking adults. The size of this group can be estimated as follows: There are currently about 200 million adults in the United States. Although the exact number of nondrinkers in that population is unknown, a good estimate is about 25 to 30 percent, or at least 50 million persons.

We know that this large group of nondrinkers includes many different subgroups. Some nonconsumers avoid alcohol because they already suffer from an alcohol-related disease. Others abstain because they have a chronic disease and have been advised to avoid alcohol. A third group may have an alcoholic parent and intuitively know they must avoid alcohol. A final group abstains from alcohol because of religious convictions. Clearly, it would be unwise to recommend light or moderate drinking to patients in any of these categories.

What about the residual group of nondrinkers who have no definite reason to avoid alcohol? Would their health improve if they began drinking? To give a thoughtful answer to this important question, we must first review the complex relationship between alcohol and health. What are the detrimental effects of alcohol consumption and what, if any, are its health benefits? This problem has attracted an enormous amount of interest: In the past few years thousands of articles have been published on alcohol and health.

From Albert B. Lowenfels, "Should Physicians Recommend Alcohol to Their Patients? No," *Priorities*, vol. 8, no. 1 (1996), pp. 25, 27, 29. Copyright © 1996 by the American Council on Science and Health. Reprinted by permission of *Priorities*, a publication of the American Council on Science and Health, 1995 Broadway, 2nd Floor, New York, NY 10023-5860.

Alcohol consumers are known to have increased risks for many diseases. These include cirrhosis of the liver; digestive-tract diseases such as ulcers or pancreatitis; several painful and often lethal cancers such as throat cancer, esophageal cancer and liver cancer; and certain neurologic disorders such as blackouts and seizures. In addition, all types of accidents, including fatal car crashes, are more frequent in drinkers than in nondrinkers. Finally, fetal alcohol syndrome, now thought to be the most common cause of mental retardation, occurs only in children of alcohol consumers. While it is true that some of these health problems occur primarily in heavy drinkers, any amount of alcohol may be hazardous for other diseases such as fetal alcohol syndrome, for which a safe, lower limit is unknown.

There is only one well-recognized health "benefit" of alcohol consumption: Health professionals now agree that drinking small amounts of alcohol seems to reduce the risk of coronary heart disease. But is this single gain enough to balance the long list of alcohol-associated health problems?

We could find a convincing answer to the overall impact of alcohol on health if we were able to conduct the following experiment, a prospective randomized trial. Nondrinking adults would be randomly assigned to one of two groups: an alcohol-consuming group in which all the participants would be required to drink a daily glass of fruit juice spiked with about an ounce or two of alcohol, and a second "control" group who would drink only fruit juice without alcohol. The two groups would be followed for 10 to 20 years so that we could compare the death rates in alcohol consumers to the rates in nonconsumers.

For various ethical and practical reasons, this experiment—which would give us badly needed information about the potential health benefits of light or moderate drinking—will never be performed. Therefore, to answer the "to drink or not to drink" question, we're forced to rely upon indirect, weaker evidence from nonrandomized trials—retrospective studies that look back at past alcohol exposure and cross-cultural studies that compare drinking levels and health status among different groups. These types of studies can be plagued by confounding and bias.

If we accept the premise that alcohol protects against certain types of heart disease, will we gain or lose by telling our nondrinking patients they should drink? We know that there are already at least 100,000 alcohol-related deaths each year in the United States. It is difficult to predict the number of heart disease deaths caused by alcohol abstinence, but the number has been estimated to be approximately equal to the number of alcohol-related deaths. Thus a health policy of advocating light or moderate drinking for our abstinent patients would be unlikely to save many lives.

According to a report prepared for the Robert Wood Johnson Foundation, the cost of alcohol addiction for the year 1990 in the United States amounted to almost 100 billion dollars—higher than the estimated 67 billion dollars we spend for illicit drugs and the 72 billion dollars we spend for tobacco addiction. An unpredictable number of new alcohol consumers would eventually turn into heavy drinkers or become addicted to alcohol, requiring additional funds to cover the costs of their alcohol-related problems.

Advocates for moderate drinking often speak of the "French paradox." In the southwest of France—despite high consumption of foods rich in cholesterol, such as buttery sauces, various cheeses and goose liver—the risk of heart disease, particularly in men, appears to be lower than expected. According to moderate-drinking advocates, this "paradox" of a high-cholesterol diet and a low risk of heart disease can be explained by the beneficial, protective effect of copious amounts of alcohol—particularly red wine.

But men in France actually die about two years earlier than do men in Sweden or Norway, even though per capita alcohol consumption in Scandinavia is only about one third the consumption in France. Frenchmen, although they may not be dying of heart disease, are dying of other causes. Drinking alcohol does not guarantee longevity—and it certainly does not provide immunity against death!

And what has been the health experience of groups of individuals who have been lifelong abstainers? Do they die prematurely? Do they suffer from excess heart disease or other illnesses? Fortunatley, such information is available from many reports reviewing the health of Seventh Day Adventists and Mormons—groups that abstain from alcohol on religious grounds. Their survival rates are generally higher than the American average. Avoiding alcohol does not interfere with an active, prolonged, healthy life.

From available statistics we know that there are more female than male nondrinkers. We also know that women are more likely to develop complications of alcohol, such as liver cirrhosis, at lower levels of alcohol intake than men. We therefore can predict that a policy of telling our nondrinking patients to begin drinking would be likely to yield more alcohol-related complications in women than in men.

There are many readily available non-addictive drugs that effectively reduce the risk of coronary-artery occlusion. Why, then, should we recommend a drug that we know leads to loss of control or alcohol addiction in about 10 percent of users? It makes little sense to recommend alcohol as a safeguard against coronary heart disease when there are so many much safer drugs already at hand.

As we focus on the problem of alcohol and public health, we can learn a great deal by reviewing recommendations from organizations with recognized expertise in this area.

In 1991 the World Health Organization assembled a special review group to formulate worldwide alcohol policy. The group's conclusion on drinking and heart disease was this: "Any attempt to put across a message which encourages drinking on the basis of hoped-for gains in coronary heart disease prevention would be likely to result in more harm than benefit to the population."

In the United States, the National Institute on Alcohol Abuse and Alcoholism warns us that vulnerability to alcoholism and alcohol-related pathologies varies among individuals and cannot always be predicted before a patient begins to drink.

Finally, the Christopher D. Smithers Foundations, the largest private philanthropic organization devoted to research on alcoholism in America, does not advocate light or moderate drinking as a public health measure.

Over 2,000 years ago Hippocrates, one of our wisest physicians, reminded us, "Above all, do no harm." Let us remember this prudent advice as we decide what we should tell our patients about alcohol and health.

POSTSCRIPT

Should Doctors Promote Alcohol for Their Patients?

Approximately 10 percent of adults in the United States are alcoholics. The social and economic burdens placed on society as a result of heavy alcohol use are immense. Heavy drinking leads to increased health care costs, accidents, premature death, and reduced productivity in the workplace. In view of the myriad of problems caused by excessive alcohol use, is it prudent to suggest that moderate alcohol consumption should be promoted?

Experts agree that heavy drinking is a problem in society; however, heart disease is also a grave concern. Numerous public health education programs strive to reduce the risk factors associated with heart disease. If it can be shown that moderate alcohol use lessens that risk, wouldn't it make sense to advocate moderate consumption?

An important point to consider is the effect of a program that promotes moderate alcohol use. Would such a program result in heavy drinkers' reducing their alcohol consumption? Or would nondrinkers start drinking and people who are predisposed to alcoholism become alcoholic? Peele feels that none of these effects are likely and, moreover, promoting moderate use, especially among young people, will help them to develop a healthy attitude toward alcohol. Albert B. Lowenfels questions whether or not nondrinkers would obtain lower rates of heart disease if they started drinking moderately.

There are numerous papers and studies that examine the issue of heart disease and moderate alcohol use. An excellent paper by Sally Casswell is "Population Level Policies on Alcohol: Are They Still Appropriate Given That Alcohol Is Good for the Heart?" *Addiction* (1997), which focuses on moderate alcohol use and the elderly. The effects of various types of alcoholic beverages are described in "Review of Moderate Alcohol Consumption and Reduced Risk of Coronary Heart Disease: Is the Effect Due to Beer, Wine or Spirits?" *British Journal of Medicine* (vol. 312, 1996), by Eric B. Rimm et al. Another good article is "What If Americans Drank Less? The Potential Effect on the Prevalence of Alcohol Abuse and Dependence," *American Journal of Public Health* (January 1995), by Loran Archer et al.

In "The Effect of Moderate Alcohol Use on the Relationship Between Stress and Depression," *American Journal of Public Health* (December 1994), Robert Lipton reports that light and moderate drinkers experienced less depression in the presence of stress than heavy drinkers. Jean Kinney and Gwen Leaton warn of the potential dangers of moderate alcohol use in their book *Loosening the Grip: A Handbook of Alcohol Information* (Mosby Publishing, 1995).

ISSUE 10

Is Nicotine Physically Addictive?

YES: Carl Sherman, from "Kicking Butts," *Psychology Today* (September/October 1994)

NO: Richard J. DeGrandpre, from "What's the Hook? Smoking Is More Than a Chemical Bond," *Reason* (January 1997)

ISSUE SUMMARY

YES: Carl Sherman, who writes on health issues, maintains that nicotine is a powerfully addictive drug. Overcoming addiction to tobacco is as difficult as overcoming addiction to alcohol and hard drugs. Most nicotine addicts are incapable of quitting their nicotine use despite the adverse health effects that are known by most smokers. The problem for many people is that cigarettes satisfy emotional needs that are rooted in physiology.

NO: Professor Richard J. DeGrandpre of St. Michael's College contends that cigarette addiction is due to social, cultural, and economic factors and not because of physical dependence on nicotine. DeGrandpre points out that nicotine replacement to help people stop smoking is not especially effective and that it is not just the nicotine that smokers desire when they light up a cigarette. Psychosocial factors are instead responsible for cigarette addiction.

Public health experts agree unanimously that cigarette smoking is dangerous to one's health; indeed, one does not need to be an expert to know that nicotine is harmful. Cigarette smoking is a major contributor to heart disease, lung cancer, and emphysema. This information is not breaking news. The perils associated with smoking were clearly identified in the first U.S. Surgeon General's Report on Smoking and Health, which was published in January 1964. Here the issue being debated, however, is not whether cigarette smoking is harmful. This issue focuses on whether or not nicotine causes physical dependence.

One argument against the notion that nicotine causes physical dependence is that millions of people have successfully stopped using nicotine. It can also be argued that smoking does not usually result in addiction. In a 1994 survey of American households, almost three-fourths of respondents indicated that they had smoked cigarettes at some time, but only slightly more than one-fourth responded that they had smoked within the previous 30 days of the survey. One can conclude from these results that not everyone who begins smoking gets hooked on it. According to DeGrandpre, "50 percent of all Americans who have ever smoked no longer do." It is apparent, says De-Grandpre, that the potential for nicotine to cause dependency is exaggerated. Another argument against the addictiveness of nicotine is that most smokers who are trying to quit are not helped by nicotine replacement therapies, such as nicotine gum and nicotine patches.

Millions of people have been able to quit smoking, and many others have smoked without ever becoming dependent. Does this mean that nicotine does not produce dependency? Many people who have been addicted to alcohol, heroin, and cocaine have stopped using these drugs. Does this mean, however, that these drugs do not produce dependency? Part of the problem rests with how the word *dependency* is defined. One could define dependency as "the inability, not unwillingness, to stop an unhealthy or undesirable behavior even though one wants to stop." By this definition, nicotine can be viewed as addictive since it is unhealthy to use it and many people are incapable of stopping its use even when they try to stop.

Many behaviors could be construed as addictive, from eating behaviors to exercise, watching television, gambling, and shopping. One characteristic of dependency to a substance or a behavior is the presence of withdrawal symptoms. Unlike with alcohol and other depressants, the withdrawal symptoms from nicotine are not life-threatening. Nevertheless, nicotine withdrawal symptoms are very real, although the severity varies among individuals. Nicotine withdrawal symptoms include headaches, insomnia, drowsiness, anxiety, shortened attention span, tremors, aggressiveness, fatigue, and irritability. Moreover, the craving for nicotine may persist for years. In extreme cases, some people become so depressed when they give up smoking that their physicians recommend that they give up the idea of quitting.

Despite the consequences of smoking, people who smoke claim that they derive certain benefits from smoking. For some people smoking helps them concentrate; others like the idea of handling something; smoking may help reduce stress, sadness, and anxiety; some people smoke due to boredom; and some simply derive a sense of pleasure from smoking. Smoking behavior is often precipitated by certain cues. For example, many smokers enjoy a cigarette following a meal, when they drink coffee, when they study, or when they socialize with others. These examples suggest that social or emotional factors contribute to smoking.

In the following selections, Carl Sherman states that nicotine is an extremely addictive drug. Sherman claims that there is a physiological basis for nicotine dependence. Most people who try to stop smoking relapse often and usually make several attempts before they are successful. Richard J. DeGrandpre points to the fact that millions of people in the United States have been able to stop smoking and claims that nicotine's physical addictiveness is overstated. People smoke for reasons other than to satisfy their craving for nicotine.

YES

Carl Sherman

KICKING BUTTS

It may not be a "sin" anymore, but few would dispute that smoking is the devil to give up. Of the 46 million Americans who smoke—26 percent of the adult population—an estimated 80 percent would like to stop and one-third try each year. Two to 3 percent of them succeed. "There's an extraordinarily high rate of relapse among people who want to quit," says Michael Fiore, M.D., M.P.H., director of the Center for Tobacco Research and Intervention at the University of Wisconsin.

* * *

The tenacity of its grip can be matched by few other behaviors, most of which, like snorting cocaine and shooting up heroin, are illegal. Since 1988, nicotine dependence and withdrawal have been recognized as disorders by the American Psychiatric Association, legitimizing the experience of the millions who have tried, successfully and otherwise, to put smoking behind them while kibitzers told them to use more willpower.

It's not just a habit, the medical and scientific communities now fully agree, but an addiction, comparable in strength to hard drugs and alcohol.

In fact, the odds of "graduating" from experimentation to true dependence are far worse for cigarettes than for illicit drugs, which testifies to tobacco's one-two punch of addictiveness and availability: Crack and heroin aren't sold in vending machines and hawked from billboards. Alcohol is as legal and available as cigarettes are, and as big a business, but apparently easier to take or leave alone. The majority of people who drink are not dependent on alcohol, while as many as 90 percent of smokers are addicted.

If nothing else, the persistence of smoking in the face of a devastating rogue's gallery of bodily damage, little of which has been kept secret, attests to the fact that this is no rational life-style decision. "Take all the deaths in America caused by alcohol, illicit drugs, fires, car accidents, homicide, and suicide. Throw in AIDS. It's still only half the deaths every year from cigarettes," says Fiore.

The news, however, isn't all bad. For the last 20 years, the proportion of Americans who smoke has dropped continuously, for the first time in our history. In America today, there are nearly 45 million ex-smokers, about as many as are still puffing away.

These quitters, perhaps surprisingly, are for the most part the same folk who tried and failed before. The average person who successfully gives up smoking does so after five or six futile attempts, says Fiore. "It appears that many smokers need to go through a process of quitting and relapsing a number of times before he or she can learn enough skills or maintain enough control to overcome this addiction."

Never underestimate the power of your enemy. Although nicotine may not give the taste of Nirvana that more notorious drugs do, its effects on the nervous system are profound and hard to resist. It increases levels of acetylcholine and norepinephrine, brain chemicals that regulate mood, attention, and memory. It also appears to stimulate the release of dopamine in the reward center of the brain, as opiates, cocaine, and alcohol do.

Addiction research has clearly established that drugs with a rapid onset —that hit the brain quickly—have the most potent psychological impact and are the most addictive. "With cigarettes the smoker gets virtually immediate onset," says Jack Henningfield, Ph.D., chief of clinical pharmacology research for the National Institute on Drug Abuse. "The cigarette is the crack-cocaine of nicotine delivery."

Physiologically, smoking a drug, be it cocaine or nicotine, is the next best thing to injecting it. In fact, it's pretty much the same thing, says Henningfield. "Whether you inhale a drug in 15 seconds, which is pretty slow for an average smoker, or inject it in 15 seconds, the effects are identical in key respects, he says. The blood extracts nicotine from inhaled air just as efficiently as oxygen, and delivers it, within seconds, to the brain.

* * *

The cigarette also gives the smoker "something remarkable: the ability to get precise, fingertip dose control," says Henningfield. Achieving just the right blood level is a key to virtually all drug-induced gratification, and the seasoned smoker does this adeptly, by adjusting how rapidly and deeply he or she puffs. "If you get the dose just right after going without cigarettes for an hour or two, there's nothing like it," he says.

The impetus to smoke is indeed, as the tobacco companies put it, for pleasure. "But there's no evidence that smoke in the mouth provides much pleasure," says Henningfield. "We do know that nicotine in the brain does."

For many, nicotine not only gives pleasure, it eases pain. Evidence has mounted that a substantial number of smokers use cigarettes to regulate emotional states, particularly to reduce negative affect like anxiety, sadness, or boredom.

"People expect that having a cigarette will reduce bad feelings," says Thomas Brandon, Ph.D., assistant professor of psychology at the State University of New York at Binghamton. His research found this, in fact, to be one of the principal motivations for daily smokers.

Negative affect runs the gamut from the transitory down times we all have several times a day, to clinical depression. Smokers are about twice as likely to be depressed as nonsmokers, and people with a history of major depression are nearly 50 percent more likely than others to also have a history of smoking, according to Brandon.

Sadly, but not surprisingly, depression appears to cut your chance of quitting by as much as one-half, and the same apparently applies, to a lesser extent, to people who just have symptoms of depression.

According to Alexander Glassman, M.D., professor of psychiatry at the Columbia University College of Physicians and Surgeons, the act of quitting can trigger severe depression in some people. In one study, nine smokers in a group of 300 in a cessation program became so depressed—two were frankly suicidal—that the researchers advised them to give up the effort and try again later. All but one had a history of major depression.

"These weren't average smokers," Glassman points out. All were heavily dependent on nicotine, they smoked at least a pack and a half daily, had their first cigarette within a half hour of awakening, and had tried to quit, on average, five times before. It is possible, he suggests, that nicotine has an antidepressant effect on some.

More generally, suggests Brandon, the very effectiveness of cigarettes in improving affect is one thing that makes it so hard to quit. Not only does a dose of nicotine quell the symptoms of withdrawal (much more on this later), the neurotransmitters it releases in the brain are exactly those most likely to elevate mood.

For a person who often feels sad, anxious, or bored, smoking can easily become a dependable coping mechanism to be given up only with great difficulty. "Once people learn to use nicotine to regulate moods" says Brandon, "if you take it away without providing alternatives, they'll be much more vulnerable to negative affect states. To alleviate them, they'll be tempted to go back to what worked in the past."

In fact, negative affect is what precipitates relapse among would-be quitters 70 percent of the time, according to Saul Shiffman, Ph.D., professor of psychology at the University of Pittsburgh. "We invited people to call a relapse-prevention hot line, to find out what moments of crises were like; what was striking was how often they were in the grip of negative emotions just before relapses, strong temptations, and close calls." A more precise study using palm-top computers to track the state of mind of participants is getting similar results, Shiffman says.

Most relapses occur soon after quitting, some 50 percent within the first two weeks, and the vast majority by six months. But everyone knows of people who had a slip a year, two, or five after quitting, and were soon back to full-time puffing. And for each of them, there are countless others who have had to fight the occasional urge, desire, or outright craving months, even years after the habit has been, for all intents and purposes, left behind.

Acute withdrawal is over within four to six weeks for virtually all smokers. But the addiction is by no means *all* over. Like those who have been addicted to other drugs, ex-smokers apparently remain susceptible to "cues," suggests Brandon: Just as seeing a pile of sugar can arouse craving in the former cocaine user, being at a party or a club, particularly around smokers, can rekindle the lure of nicotine intensely. The same process may include "internal cues," says Brandon. "If you smoked in the past when under stress or depressed, the act of being depressed can serve as a cue to trigger the urge to smoke."

Like users of other drugs, Henningfield points out, addicted smokers don't just consume the offending substance to feel good (or not bad), but to feel "right." "The cigarette smoker's daily function becomes dependent on continued nicotine dosing: Not just mood, but the ability to maintain attention and concentration deteriorates very quickly in nicotine withdrawal."

Henningfield's studies have shown that in an addicted smoker, attention, memory, and reasoning ability start to decline measurably just four hours after the last cigarette. This reflects a real physiological impairment: a change in the electrical activity of the brain. Nine days after quitting, when some withdrawal symptoms, at least, have begun to ease, there has been no recovery in brain function.

How long does the impairment persist? No long-term studies have been done, but cravings and difficulties in cognitive function have been documented for as long as nine years in some ex-smokers. "There are clinical reports of people who have said that they still aren't functioning right, and eventually make the 'rational decision' to go back to smoking," Henningfield says.

The conclusion is inescapable that smoking causes changes in the nervous system that endure long after the physical addiction is history, and in some smokers, may never normalize.

* * *

The wealth of recent knowledge about smoking clarifies why it's hard to quit. But can it make it easier? If nothing else, it should help people take it seriously enough to gear up for the effort. "People think of quitting as something short term,

but they should expect to struggle for a couple of months," says Shiffman.

What works? About 90 percent of people who give up smoking do so on their own, says Fiore. But the odds for success can be improved: Programs that involve counseling typically get better rates, and nicotine replacement can be a potent ally in whatever method you use.

In a metaanalysis of 17 placebo-controlled trials involving more than 5,000 people, Fiore found that the patch consistently doubled the success of quit attempts, whether or not antismoking counseling was used. After six months, 22 percent of the people who used the patch remained off cigarettes, compared to 9 percent who had a placebo. Of those who had the patch and a relatively intense counseling or support program, 27 percent were smoke-free.

More than 4 million Americans have tried the patch, which replaces the nicotine on which the smoker has become dependent, to ease such withdrawal symptoms as irritability, insomnia, inability to concentrate, and physical cravings that drive many back to tobacco.

You're likely to profit from the patch if you have a real physical dependence on nicotine: that is, if you have your first cigarette within 30 minutes of waking up; smoke 20 or more a day; or experienced severe withdrawal symptoms during previous quit attempts.

Standard directions call for using the patches in decreasing doses for two to three months. Some researchers, however, suggest that for certain smokers, the patch may be necessary for years, or indefinitely.

"It's already happening," says Henningfield. "Some doctors have come to the conclusion that some patients are best able to get on with their life with nicotine maintenance." One such physician is David Peter Sachs, M.D., director of the Palo Alto Center for Pulmonary Disease Prevention. "I realized that with some of my patients, no matter how slowly I tried to taper them off nicotine replacement, they couldn't do it," says Sachs. "They were literally using it for years. Before you start tapering the dose, you should be cigarette-free for at least 30 days."

His clinical experience leads him to believe that 10 to 20 percent of smokers are *so* dependent that they may always need to get nicotine from somewhere. One study of people using the gum found that two years later, 20 percent of those who had successfully remained cigarette-free were still chewing. The idea of indefinite, even lifetime, nicotine maintenance sounds offensive to some. "Clearly, the goal to aim for is to be nicotine-free," says Sachs. "But if that can't be reached, being tobacco-free still represents a substantial gain for the patient, and for society." And getting nicotine via a patch or gum source means a far lower dose than you'd get from a cigarette. Plus, you're getting just nicotine, and not the 42 carcinogens in tobacco smoke.

Although the once-a-day patch has largely supplanted the gum first used in nicotine replacement, Sachs thinks that for some, the most effective treatment could involve one or both. The patch may be easier to use, but the gum is the only product that allows you control over blood nicotine level. Some people know they'll do better if they stay in control. And would-be quitters who do fine on the patch until they run into a stressful business meeting may stifle that urge to bum a cigarette if they boost their nicotine level in advance with a piece of gum, Sachs says.

* * *

However, nicotine replacement "is not a magic bullet," says Fiore. "It will take the edge off the tobacco-withdrawal syndrome, but it won't automatically transform any smoker into a nonsmoker." Other requisite needs vary from person to person. A standard approach teaches behavioral "coping skills," simple things like eating, chewing gum, or knitting to keep mouth or hands occupied, or leaving tempting situations. Ways people cope cognitively are as important as what they do, says Shiffman.

He advises would-be quitters at times of temptation to remind themselves just why they're quitting: "My children will be so proud of me," or "I want to live to see my grandchildren," for example. Think of a relaxing scene. Imagine how you'll feel tomorrow if you pass this crisis without smoking. Or simply tell yourself, "NO" or "Smoking is not an option."

Coping skills, however, are conspicuously unsuccessful for people who are high in negative affect. Supportive counseling works better. Depression or anxiety may interfere with the ability to use cognitive skills.

One exercise that Brandon teaches patients asks them to inventory—and treat themselves to—things that make them feel good, a substitute for the mood-elevating effect of a cigarette. These might include exercising, being with friends, going to concerts, reading, or taking a nap. "Positive life-style changes that improve mood level" are particularly useful if you use cigarettes to deal with negative emotional states, he says.

Depression treatment is particularly important for those trying to quit smoking. One study found that cognitive therapy significantly improved quit rates for people with a history of depression. Various antidepressants have been effective in small studies, and a large double-blind trial using the drug Zoloft is underway.

Fiore has found that having just one cigarette in the first two weeks of a cessation program predicted about 80 percent of relapses at six months. Even when the withdrawal symptoms are gone, a single lapse can rekindle the urge as much as ever.

In the critical first weeks without cigarettes, a key to relapse prevention is avoiding, or severely limiting, alcohol, which not only blunts inhibitions, but is often powerfully bound to smoking as a habit. Up to one-half of people who try to quit have their first lapse with alcohol on board.

Watch your coffee intake, too. It can trigger the urge to smoke. And nicotine stimulates a liver enzyme that breaks down caffeine, so when you quit, you'll get more bang for each cup, leading to irritability, anxiety, and insomnia—the withdrawal symptoms that undermine quit efforts.

Try to change your routine to break patterns that strengthen addiction: drive to work a different way; don't linger at the table after a meal. And don't try to quit when you're under stress: vacation time might be a good occasion.

And if you do have a lapse? Don't trivialize it, because then you're more likely to have another, says Shiffman. But, "if you make it a catastrophe, you'll reconfirm fears that you'll never be able to quit," a low self-esteem position that could become a self-fulfilling prophecy. "Think of it as a warning, a mistake you'll have to overcome."

Try to learn from the lapse: examine the situation that led up to it, and plan to deal with it better in the future. "And take it as a sign you need to double your efforts," Shiffman says. "Looking back at a lapse, many people find they'd already begun to slack off; early on, they were avoiding situations where they were tempted to smoke, but later got careless."

Don't be discouraged by ups and downs. "It's normal to have it easy for a while, then all of a sudden you're under stress and for 10 minutes you have an intense craving," says Shiffman. "Consider the gain in frequency and duration: the urge to smoke is now coming back for 10 minutes, every two weeks, rather than all the time."

If lapse turns into relapse and you end up smoking regularly, the best antidote to despair is getting ready to try again. "Smoking is a chronic disease, and quitting is a process. Relapse and remission are part of the process," says Fiore. "As long as you're continuing to make progress toward the ultimate goal of being smoke-free, you should feel good about your achievement."

NO

Richard J. DeGrandpre

WHAT'S THE HOOK? SMOKING IS MORE THAN A CHEMICAL BOND

During the presidential election campaign, Bill Clinton successfully cast Big Tobacco as a national enemy, with Bob Dole playing the role of collaborator by downplaying the addictiveness of nicotine. Meanwhile, the Food and Drug Administration has been asserting jurisdiction over cigarettes as "nicotine delivery devices," arguing that tobacco companies intend to hook their customers, just like schoolyard drug pushers. Hundreds of pending lawsuits, including class actions and cases filed by state governments, similarly allege a conspiracy to addict smokers. These developments represent important changes in our attitudes toward cigarettes. Though justified in the name of public health, the increasing emphasis on the enslaving power of nicotine may only make matters worse.

Understanding why requires careful consideration of the conventional wisdom about tobacco addiction, which recycles mistaken assumptions about illicit drugs. During the latter half of this century, the classical model of addiction, derived from observations of narcotic abuse, increasingly has been used to describe the cigarette habit. The classical model states that consumption of certain chemicals causes a physical dependence, either immediately or after prolonged use, characterized by withdrawal symptoms—symptoms that can be avoided or escaped only by further drug use. As Steven Hyman, director of the National Institute of Mental Health, opined recently in *Science*, "Repeated doses of addictive drugs—opiates, cocaine, and amphetamine— cause drug dependence and, afterward, withdrawal."

This cyclical model, in which the drug serves as both problem and solution, offers a simple, easy-to-grasp account of the addiction process, giving the concept great staying power in the public imagination. In the case of smoking, this view of addiction is central to the rationale for regulating tobacco and the concern that the cigarette companies have been doping their products with extra nicotine. But the classical model tends to conceal rather than elucidate the ultimate sources of addiction, and it is just as ill-suited to the cigarette habit as it has always been for understanding illicit drug use.

If a chemical compound can be addictive in the manner described by NIMH Director Hyman, we would expect anyone who regularly uses such a substance to become addicted. Yet only a minority of those who use illicit drugs—whether marijuana, cocaine, or heroin—ever develop a dependence on them. The prevalence of addiction, as defined by the *American Psychiatric Association's Diagnostic and Statistical Manual*, among users of alcohol and cocaine runs about 15 percent and 17 percent, respectively. Even in a sample of 79 regular crack users, Patricia Erickson and her colleagues at Toronto's Addiction Research Foundation found that only about 37 percent used the drug heavily (more than 100 times in their lives), and 67 percent had not used in the past month. A similar pattern holds for tobacco. In the 1994 National Household Survey on Drug Abuse, 73 percent of respondents reported smoking cigarettes at some time, but only about 29 percent reported smoking in the previous month, and not necessarily on a daily basis. Writing in the May/June *Mother Jones*, Jeffrey Klein manages to argue that nicotine enslaves its users and, at the same time, that Tobacco Inc. seeks to recruit young smokers to replace the 1.3 million Americans who quit each year. If nicotine is so relentlessly addictive, how can it be that 50 percent of all Americans who have ever smoked no longer do?

The classical model also suggests that the cigarette habit should be highly amenable to nicotine replacement therapy, such as the nicotine patch. Yet few of the tens of thousands of patch users have actually broken the habit (only about 10 percent to 15 percent succeed). In direct conflict with the classical model, most keep smoking while on the patch, continuing to consume the carcinogens in cigarette smoke while obtaining considerably higher blood levels of nicotine. A 1992 study of nicotine replacement therapy reported in the journal *Psychopharmacology* concluded that the "overall lack of effect [of the patch] on cigarette consumption is perhaps surprising and suggests that in regular smokers the lighting up of a cigarette is generally triggered by cues other than low plasma nicotine levels."

Most people who successfully quit smoking do so only after several failed attempts. If addiction is driven by physical dependence on a chemical—in this case, nicotine—relapse should occur during withdrawal, which for nicotine typically lasts a few weeks. Yet a sizable proportion of relapses occur long after the smoker has suffered through nicotine withdrawal. In fact, studies do not even show a relationship between the severity of withdrawal and the likelihood of relapse. As any former smoker could tell you, ex-smokers crave cigarettes at certain times and in certain situations for months, even years, after quitting. In these cases, the desire to smoke is triggered by environmental cues, not by withdrawal symptoms. This is one reason why people who overcome addiction to illicit substances such as heroin or cocaine often say they had more difficulty breaking the cigarette habit. Because regular tobacco users smoke in a wide array of circumstances (when bored, after eating, when driving) and settings (home, work, car), the cues that elicit the urge are more ubiquitous than for illicit drug use.

These failures of the classical model illustrate how conventional wisdom oversimplifies the dynamics of cigarette smoking. This reductionist view is dangerous because it ignores the psychosocial factors that underlie addiction. In coming to terms with cigarette addiction as a psychosocial process, rather than a simple pharmacological one, we need to distinguish between cigarette addiction and nicotine addiction. Certainly no one (except perhaps the tobacco companies) denies that cigarette smoking can be addictive, if by addiction one means a stubborn urge to keep smoking. But it is quite a different matter to say that nicotine accounts for the addictiveness of smoking. Nicotine withdrawal notwithstanding, nicotine alone is insufficient, and may even be unnecessary, to create cigarette addiction.

This claim can be clarified by two dramatic case studies reported in the *British Journal of Addiction* in 1973 and 1989. The earlier article described a 47-year-old woman with a two-and-a-half-year-long dependence on water, one of several such cases noted by the author. The woman reported a nagging withdrawal symptom—a dry, salty taste in her mouth—that was alleviated by the persistent drinking of water (up to 60 glasses per day). This case of dependence on a nonpsychoactive substance contrasts sharply with the second account, which described an 80-year-old woman who used cocaine without incident for 55 years. The authors reported that "she denies any feelings of euphoria or increased energy after [snorting] the cocaine nor any depression or craving for cocaine when her supplies run out.... She appears to have suffered no ill effects from the prolonged use of cocaine in physical, psychological or social terms." So we see that not every addiction involves drug use and not every instance of drug use involves an addiction.

To say that cigarette addiction is a psychosocial process means that social, cultural, and economic factors play a crucial role in acquiring and keeping a cigarette habit. In fact, the tendency to reduce the cigarette experience to chemical servitude may be one of the most powerful cultural factors driving addiction. Cigarette lore wrongly teaches smokers (and smokers-to-be) that they will suffer badly if they attempt to quit, while at the same time freeing them of responsibility for their drug use once they begin. Such beliefs also help romanticize cigarette smoking, elevating nicotine to a sublime abstraction. This not only reinforces the forbidden fruit effect, it helps transform the habit of smoking into a cult behavior. Smoking thus acquires the kind of meaning that the youth of America are most in search of: social meaning. As Richard Klein writes in *Cigarettes Are Sublime,* "smoking cigarettes is not only a physical act but a discursive one—a wordless but eloquent form of expression."

To counteract the forces that give momentum to drug use, the public meaning of addiction needs to be broadened to include the many, changing facets of the psychosocial realm in which we develop. "Putting people back in charge" of their addictions, as John Leo puts it in *U.S. News and World Report,* will not work if we focus only on the naked individual. Rather than pushing the pendulum of public policy between scapegoating the substance and scapegoating the individual, we should seek a middle ground. Realizing that the addiction process has at least three levels of complexity is a good place to start.

First, at the basic and most immediate level, are the short- and long-term biological processes that underlie the psychological experiences of drug use and drug abstinence. Even with the same drug, these experiences vary greatly across individuals. Scientists and journalists too easily forget that every psychological process is built on biology. Discoveries of biological mechanisms and processes underlying addiction are not proof that the problem is biological rather than social and psychological. Eating rich foods has powerful biological effects in both the short and long run, but we should not therefore conclude that the rise in obesity in the United States is a biological problem. Indeed, attempts to alter the addiction process that emphasize biochemistry (such as the nicotine patch) have met with little success.

At the next level are psychological processes (social, motivational, learning) that, although rooted in biology, are shaped by personal experience. Because each of us has unique life experiences, we do not necessarily interpret the same events in the same way. The reasons for one individual's addiction may be altogether different from the reasons for another's. As the recent Scottish film *Trainspotting* makes clear, stories of addiction are no less complex than any other personal stories. Still, intervention at this level has had some success with users of alcohol or illicit drugs, and several research and treatment institutions are examining methods for "matching" addicts with different treatment strategies based on their social and psychological characteristics.

Drug effects and drug addiction also vary greatly across time and place, implicating cultural factors as the third and most general aspect of drug addiction. These factors are rooted in but not reducible to psychological processes, just as psychological processes are not reducible to biology. Patterns of alcohol use around the world, which show that the prevalence of drinking problems cannot be predicted by consumption alone, illustrate the importance of culture. Italians, for example, historically have consumed large quantities of alcohol with relatively low rates of drunkenness and alcoholism. The effects of alcohol on human behavior—violence, boorishness, gregariousness—also have been shown to vary dramatically across cultures.

Given the cultural role in addiction and the radical changes that have occurred in attitudes about smoking, it is quite possible that the young smokers of today are not at all like the smokers of 50 years ago. Those who begin smoking now do so with the belief that it is addictive, causes poor health (and wrinkles!), and can be deadly. If individuals are willing to start smoking despite such knowledge, it is likely that they will acquire and keep the habit, seeming to confirm the current, politically correct image of addiction. And if this self-fulfilling prophecy is realized, chances are that interventions aimed at the social realm will continue to miss their target and fail to curtail addiction.

POSTSCRIPT

Is Nicotine Physically Addictive?

In the United States, attitudes toward smoking have changed considerably over the last several decades. Smoking in public places was the norm, but smokers are now typically relegated to designated areas. At one time smoking was considered a rite of passage into adulthood. Today, the rate of adult smoking has declined and the rate of teenage smoking has increased. Smoking is becoming a rite of passage into adolescence. In the early part of the twentieth century, women who smoked were scorned and considered immoral. Some women now see smoking as a sign of their independence.

Sherman states that nicotine produces a strong and rapid effect on the central nervous system. He feels that there is a clear physiological basis for nicotine dependency. Nicotine, like alcohol, opiates, and cocaine, affects neurotransmitters in the brain that regulate mood, attention, and memory. Since nicotine can alter emotional states in ways that smokers find desirable, smoking behavior is perpetuated. In the absence of nicotine, many smokers experience a decline in reasoning ability, memory, and attention. One way to overcome these cognitive impairments is by taking in nicotine.

It is possible that people smoke also due to depression. Compared to non-smokers, smokers are twice as likely to suffer from major depression. Unfortunately, depressed individuals who would like to quit smoking have considerably less success than those who are not depressed; perhaps nicotine acts as an antidepressant. Some smokers become so depressed when trying to quit that some physicians recommend that they continue smoking for their mental health. The fact that nicotine elevates mood contributes to the difficulty that smokers encounter when they attempt to stop.

DeGrandpre asserts that if nicotine is as physically addictive as many people believe, then why is not everyone who ever smoked addicted? To say that nicotine causes physical addiction, DeGrandpre states, oversimplifies the dynamics of cigarette smoking and ignores the psychosocial factors that contribute to cigarette addiction. The concept of cigarette addiction is acknowledged by DeGrandpre, but he does not agree with the idea that nicotine is addictive.

Whether or not nicotine is addictive has tremendous legal implications. In the late 1990s terminally ill smokers or families of deceased smokers families claimed that tobacco companies were responsible for their situation and began suing certain companies. Similarly, many states proposed litigation against tobacco companies in order to be compensated for medical treatment they provide to smokers. This raises the question as to whether or not tobacco companies should be held liable if people become addicted to nicotine.

Regardless of whether or not nicotine is physically addictive, one needs to ask how much responsibility smokers should assume for such destructive consequences of smoking.

Two articles that look at the internal workings of the tobacco industry are "Nicotine and Addiction: The Brown and Williamson Documents," *JAMA* (*Journal of the American Medical Association*) (July 19, 1995), by Lisa Bero et al. and "Tobacco: Enemy Number 1," *Mother Jones* (May–June 1996), by Robert Dreyfuss. The relationship between nicotine and depression is studied in "Nicotine Dependence and Major Depression: New Evidence From a Prospective Investigation," *Archives of General Psychiatry*, (January 1993), by Breslau, Kilbey, and Andreski.

ISSUE 11

Should There Be Tighter Restrictions on the Advertising of Prescription Drugs?

YES: David A. Kessler et al., from "Therapeutic-Class Wars—Drug Promotion in a Competitive Marketplace," *The New England Journal of Medicine* (November 17, 1994)

NO: Paul H. Rubin, from "What the FDA Doesn't Want You to Know," *The American Enterprise* (May/June 1991)

ISSUE SUMMARY

YES: David A. Kessler, the former commissioner of the Food and Drug Administration, and his associates contend that tighter restrictions should be placed on advertising by pharmaceutical companies, who often promote drugs with misleading information.

NO: Paul H. Rubin, a former senior advertising economist with the Federal Trade Commission, argues that restrictions on drug advertisements are already excessive and inefficient. Rubin maintains that prescription drug advertising results in lower drug prices and a better-informed public.

One of the most lucrative businesses in the world today is the prescription drug business. Billions of dollars are spent every year for prescription drugs in the United States alone. The only way for consumers to obtain a prescribed drug is through a physician. Drug companies in the United States, however, have begun advertising their products directly to consumers. It is logical for drug companies to advertise to physicians because doctors are responsible for writing prescriptions. But is it logical for pharmaceutical manufacturers to advertise their drugs directly to consumers? Are consumers capable of making informed, rational decisions regarding their pharmaceutical needs? Should there be greater regulation of prescription drug advertising?

An increasing number of individuals are assuming more responsibility for their own health care. In the United States, it is estimated that up to one-third of all prescriptions written by physicians are at the request of patients. Many patients also do not take their prescriptions to pharmacies to be filled. Both of these cases raise the question of whether or not consumers are adequately educated to make decisions pertaining to their pharmaceutical needs or to assess the risks associated with prescription drugs. Evidence suggests that many are not. With the exception of alcohol, for example, prescription drugs cause more accidents in the workplace than illegal drugs.

Some commentators argue that there are several advantages to directly advertising drugs to consumers. One advantage is that direct advertisements make consumers better informed about the benefits and risks of certain drugs. It is not unusual for a person to experience side effects from a drug without knowing that the drug was responsible for the side effects. Advertisements may provide this information. Another advantage for consumers is that they may learn about medications that they may not have known existed. Furthermore, advertising lowers the cost of prescription drugs because consumers are able to ask their physicians to prescribe less expensive drugs than the physicians might be inclined to recommend. Finally, prescription drug advertising allows consumers to become more involved in choosing the medications that they need or want.

Critics argue that there are a number of risks associated with the direct advertising of prescription drugs. One concern is with the content of drug advertisements. Consumers are not always told of the adverse effects of the drugs being advertised, and critics charge that the drugs' benefits are frequently exaggerated. There have been instances in which drugs that have been approved by the Food and Drug Administration (FDA) for one purpose have been promoted for other purposes. For example, Retin-A, which is a medication for acne, has also been promoted as effective for getting rid of wrinkles. Another argument is that the content of advertisements for prescription drugs may be difficult for the average consumer to comprehend.

Critics also express concern with the way in which the information in prescription drug advertisements is presented. Promotions for drugs that appear as objective reports are often actually slick publicity material. In such promotions, medical experts are shown providing testimony regarding a particular drug. What is overlooked by the consumer is that these physicians have financial ties to the pharmaceutical companies. Celebrities—in whom the public often puts a lot of trust despite their lack of medical expertise—are used to promote drugs as well. Finally, the cost of the drugs advertised, a major concern for consumers, is seldom mentioned in the advertisements.

In the following selections, David A. Kessler and his associates argue that more restrictions should be placed on how drug manufacturers promote their products because these companies consistently make false or misleading claims. Paul H. Rubin contends that advertisements for prescription drugs are beneficial to consumers because they lower the cost of drugs and they effectively inform consumers about the benefits of new drugs.

YES

David A. Kessler et al.

THERAPEUTIC-CLASS WARS—DRUG PROMOTION IN A COMPETITIVE MARKETPLACE

In today's prescription-drug marketplace a host of similar products compete for essentially the same population of patients. Between 1989 and 1993, for example, the Center for Drug Evaluation and Research of the Food and Drug Administration (FDA) approved 127 new molecular entities (excluding generic drugs), but only a minority offered a clear clinical advantage over existing therapies.[1] Many of the others are considered "me too" drugs because they are so similar to brand-name drugs already on the market.

The preponderance of "me too" drugs has created a highly competitive marketplace for prescription drugs. Pharmaceutical companies are waging aggressive campaigns to change prescribers' habits and to distinguish their products from competing ones, even when the products are virtually indistinguishable. This occurring in many therapeutic classes—antiulcer products, angiotensin-converting–enzyme inhibitors, calcium-channel blockers, selective serotonin-reuptake–inhibitor antidepressants, and nonsteroidal antiinflammatory drugs, to name a few.

Victory in these therapeutic-class wars can mean millions of dollars for a drug company. But for patients and providers it can mean misleading promotions,[2,3] conflicts of interest,[4-6] increased costs for health care,[7] and ultimately, inappropriate prescribing.[8]

CROWDED THERAPEUTIC CLASSES

Pharmaceutical companies do not usually set out to produce a "me too" drug. However, this is frequently the result of the process of drug development. Often, the FDA receives a spate of Investigational New Drug applications at about the same time for products in the same therapeutic class because several companies develop similar drugs concurrently. Another, more common scenario is that several companies set out to develop new entries in a class in which one drug is already a lucrative breakthrough product. Such was the

From David A. Kessler, Janet L. Rose, Robert J. Temple, Renie Schapiro, and Joseph P. Griffin, "Therapeutic-Class Wars—Drug Promotion in a Competitive Marketplace," *The New England Journal of Medicine*, vol. 331, no. 20 (November 17, 1994), pp. 1350–1353. Copyright © 1994 by The Massachusetts Medical Society. Reprinted by permission.

case, for example, with the H_2-receptor antagonists (Tagamet [cimetidine]) and the serotonin-reuptake–inhibitor antidepressants (Prozac [fluoxetine]). A company may hope that its "me too" product will be an improvement over the current members of a class, but often those hopes are not borne out in clinical trials. Even when a drug fails to offer a clear advantage over existing therapies, a company may nevertheless conclude that it would be profitable to bring it to market.

The economics of the prescription-drug marketplace make this feasible. There are a large number of companies in the marketplace, each with a relatively small share of the market. Merck and Co., the largest pharmaceutical company, controls only 6.2 percent of the U.S. sales market.[9] However, since total sales for U.S. pharmaceutical companies in the United States exceed $58 billion per year, even a small share can mean large revenues. More important, sales in the top 18 therapeutic categories each exceeded $1 billion in 1993,[10] so that even if a "me too" drug has a small market share in a single category, it can generate tens of millions of dollars in sales.

An additional incentive for introducing a similar product is that companies can sometimes charge more for a new drug, even in an already crowded class. Traditional economics might suggest the contrary—that a late entry would have to be priced below its competitors to win a market share. Sometimes this is the case. However, companies also rely on the widely held notion—not always true—that what is newer is better and is therefore worth more. Aggressive advertising campaigns and lack of information among prescribing physicians about comparative costs can facilitate the higher prices of "me too" drugs.

Another factor that encourages the marketing of "me too" drugs is that on the basis of clinical trials a drug can be approved for a single indication, but the sponsor may recognize that other products in the class are widely prescribed for different (unlabeled) indications, with a lucrative market. Thus, a company can complete a New Drug application quickly by testing the drug for one indication and then increase market share on the basis of its association with other products in the class. For example, a company may undertake studies to demonstrate that a new angiotensin-converting–enzyme inhibitor is effective in treating hypertension. But the company may anticipate that the drug will also be prescribed for congestive heart failure, because physicians will assume that angiotensin-converting-enzyme inhibitors, which have a common effect on hypertension, will have the same therapeutic effects in heart failure.

We discuss here three techniques used by drug companies to promote "me too" drugs that are of particular concern to the FDA: "seeding" trials, unsubstantiated claims of superiority over competing products, and "switch" campaigns. In general, the FDA does not have the authority to require the approval of advertising and promotional materials and activities before they are introduced. In most cases, the agency can take action only after the fact, when false or misleading claims are made. When the FDA determines that a manufacturer has made false or misleading claims, it typically sends the company a letter requesting that the claims be corrected. Usually companies comply. When there are recurrent violations or more serious initial violations, the FDA may issue a "warning letter" or begin judicial enforcement through an injunction, a seizure, or criminal prosecution. If warranted, the FDA may request that a manufacturer send a correction notice to prescribers and other parties who may have been influenced by the false or misleading claims. We describe violations that were resolved at the earliest stage, as well as those that required more serious action.

SEEDING TRIALS

Some company-sponsored trials of approved drugs appear to serve little or no scientific purpose. Because they are, in fact, thinly veiled attempts to entice doctors to prescribe a new drug being marketed by the company, they are often referred to as "seeding trials." Features that distinguish such trials from scientifically rigorous studies include the use of a design that does not support the stated research goals, the recruitment of investigators not because they are experts or leading researchers but because they are frequent prescribers of competing products in the same therapeutic class, disproportionately high payments given to "investigators" for their work (although the only work may be to write prescriptions for the drug), sponsorship of the studies by the company's sales and marketing division rather than its research department, minimal requirements for data, and the collection of data that are of little or no value to the company. Typically, these trials involve introducing a new drug in a crowded therapeutic class. The success of such a new product may depend on undoing physicians' comfortable habits of prescribing a competing, more established product.

One example of a seeding trial involved a large project associated with the launch of a new antihypertensive agent, a latecomer to its therapeutic class. The stated objectives of the study were to assess the efficacy and tolerability of this agent in controlling mild-to-moderate hypertension. The sponsor used its sales force to recruit 2,500 office-based "investigators" who were frequent prescribers of drugs in the therapeutic class in question. Each investigator was to enroll 12 patients (for a total enrollment of 30,000) and was offered reimbursement of $85 per patient enrolled, or $1,050 per physician.

The "study" was not capable of achieving even the modest objectives stated. There was no control group, and the study was not blinded. There was thus no possibility that it would generate useful data on efficacy and little likelihood that it would produce data on safety other than the potential for detecting a rare adverse event. The study aroused other types of concern. At the investigators' conference and in the accompanying materials, the sponsor discussed unapproved uses of the product and distinguished it from competing members of the class on the basis of unsubstantiated, and thus misleading, claims. FDA officials informed the sponsor that no data from this trial could be used to promote the product.

In another case, a manufacturer was starting a seeding trial to encourage the use of its product for an unapproved indication. The manufacturer mailed more than 12,000 letters of solicitation to office-based physicians, inviting them to participate in the trial of an anticonvulsant drug to treat panic disorder, an unapproved use of the product. From this group, the manufacturer hoped to recruit 500 investigators, each of whom would enroll five patients in the trial. The investigators were to be paid $500 for their participation, which involved completing a one-page case report for each patient.

The FDA determined that this study violated the Food, Drug, and Cosmetic Act in that it was a thinly disguised promotion of an unapproved use.[11] The manufacturer agreed to discontinue the study.

In their internal operations, certain manufacturers conducting seeding trials of this type do not even pretend that the trials are anything but marketing endeavors. The FDA received a copy of a memorandum sent from the marketing division of one sponsor to its sales representatives about yet another seeding trial, this one of an antihypertensive drug. The memo read in part:

> Make no mistake about it: The [name of drug] study is the single most important sales initiative for 1993. Phase I provides 2,500 physicians with the opportunity to observe in their patients... blood pressure control... provided by [name of drug].... If at least 20,000 of the 25,000 patients involved in the study remain on [name of drug], it could mean up to a $10,000,000 boost in sales. In Phase II, this figure could double.

FALSE AND MISLEADING CLAIMS

A second technique in these therapeutic-class wars is to use promotional materials that make unsubstantiated claims of superiority over competing products. The antiulcer products that are also used to treat gastroesophageal reflux disease constitute a lucrative, highly competitive therapeutic category in which sponsors have sometimes seized on unproved and relatively unimportant differences to distinguish their products from competing ones. The distinctions claimed frequently concern relative safety. The FDA took ac-

tion against a sponsor that engaged in a prolonged and extensive effort to disparage the relative safety of a competing product. The sponsor misrepresented the risk of drug interactions associated with its product relative to the risk with the competing product by making selective use of negative clinical reports and omitting certain important drug interactions associated with its own product. The sponsor also mischaracterized the data to suggest that a competitor's product was associated with negative hemodynamic effects, when those effects had not been documented at therapeutic doses.

In some cases, sponsors have relied on pharmacokinetic distinctions that have unknown clinical relevance, or none. The FDA acted against the sponsor of a newly approved angiotensin-converting–enzyme inhibitor that claimed its product was superior to those of competitors by alleging that its product was the only true once-a-day angiotensin-converting–enzyme inhibitor. This claim not only had no data to support it, but also perversely relied on the absence of data; the sponsor had never studied a twice-daily dosing regimen. In addition, the new product had not been shown to be more effective in achieving 24-hour control of blood pressure than any other long-acting angiotensin-converting–enzyme inhibitor.

Another problem we have encountered is that of advertisements targeting particular populations without substantiating adequately that one product is superior to another. An example is the attempt by some manufacturers of antiulcer medications to promote their products as having superior efficacy in smokers. Warning letters have been sent to the makers of two such products for this reason.

Finally, promotional materials making claims of cost effectiveness and comparative effectiveness have become more and more common. In response to the shift toward managed care and health care reform, manufacturers are increasingly directing their promotional campaigns toward large purchasers of drugs. Increasingly, the focus of these campaigns is cost effectiveness. Although traditionally the FDA has not been involved in cost-effectiveness issues, its responsibility for monitoring prescription-drug advertising has required it to evaluate cost-effectiveness studies that are used to support advertising claims.

Despite the growing interest in cost comparisons, there is still no consensus on how to conduct cost-effectiveness studies.[12,13] What is clear, however, is that cost comparisons must be based on sound clinical data regarding comparative efficacy. The FDA has challenged advertised claims of cost effectiveness that are based on unsubstantiated assumptions about comparative efficacy. In the past year, for example, the agency has objected to an unsubstantiated claim by the manufacturer of an antiepileptic drug that the drug's higher cost was justified by its superior clinical efficacy. Prescribing decisions based on inadequate data on comparative efficacy and cost effectiveness could result in increased, rather than decreased, costs for health care.

SWITCH CAMPAIGNS

Pharmaceutical companies, as well as third-party providers of health care and their agents, are increasingly trying to cause patients to be switched from their originally prescribed medications to "me too" drugs marketed by the companies. These attempts are sometimes referred to as "switch campaigns." When done appropriately, switching can improve the quality of care, lower costs, or both. For example, switching from a brand-name product to a less expensive, bioequivalent generic product can reduce the patient's expense and overall expenditures for health care, without affecting the quality of care.

Other types of switching efforts, however, have potential implications for treatment and cost that merit careful consideration. These include efforts to switch patients to another dosage form of the same product or to another product in the same therapeutic class. Sometimes these campaigns involve payments to pharmacists who convince physicians to change their prescribing patterns.[14] Earlier this year, a group of attorneys general of several states reached settlements with two major pharmaceutical firms with regard to their payments to pharmacists.[15,16]

Switch campaigns are typically premised on claims of superior or equivalent therapeutic outcome, lower cost, or both. Recently, there have been a number of examples in which the therapeutic implications of a proposed switch have not been thoroughly considered, the claims on which the suggested switch is based have proved to be misleading, or both.

In one case, the FDA has taken regulatory action against a pharmaceutical manufacturer for a promotional campaign intended to switch patients from one form of an oral hypoglycemic agent to a newer form of the same molecular entity, with a more bioavailable dosage. The promotional material claimed that the newer form offered better overall treatment of diabetic patients than the older form. The manufacturer also claimed that the switch entailed a modest cost savings for the patient.

The manufacturer asked retail pharmacists who received prescriptions for the older form of the drug to contact the prescribing physicians and request that they change their prescriptions to the newer form. In addition, pharmacists were encouraged to identify patients taking the drug in the older form, to send them information about the new form with a coupon they could redeem with a prescription for the new form, and to urge the patients to contact their physicians and ask to be switched. The pharmacists would receive a payment for each prescription thus switched.

FDA officials determined that this sponsor's claim was misleading in several respects. First, there was no substantiation for the statement that the newer form of the drug offered superior overall benefit. Second, the campaign failed to reveal that there was no exact dosage relation between the newer and older forms of the drug. Therefore, a switch would require retitration and might expose a patient to the risk of a period of poor blood glucose control, as well as to added costs associated with blood glucose monitoring during retitration. Finally, the claim that the newer form of the drug offered patients a cost savings was incomplete, if not overtly misleading. The manufacturer did not mention that the newer form had patent exclusivity beyond the year 2000, whereas the older form would lose its patent exclusivity sooner. Therefore, the slight cost savings associated with the newer form would most likely be offset by a substantially increased cost in the future, because patients would not be able to have their prescriptions transferred as readily to a lower-cost generic version of the older form.

At the FDA we are increasingly concerned with switch campaigns that involve substitutions of a different therapy. Such switches are commonly seen in the case of providers of mail-order drugs who contract with pharmaceutical manufacturers to feature their products at a lower price.[17] The mail-order pharmacists then ask physicians who prescribe competing drugs to switch to the featured products. From a therapeutic perspective, it is not always clear that such switches are in patients' best interests, because a switch may be based on little more than an unsubstantiated assumption of comparable effectiveness.

CONCLUSIONS

The hallmark of the FDA's drug-approval process has been an insistence on adequate and well-controlled trials to support New Drug applications. Inappropriate promotional efforts for "me too" drugs—whether they take the form of seeding trials, switch campaigns, or false and misleading claims—should not be permitted to undermine these high standards, for these standards provide physicians and patients with the assurance that decisions about prescriptions will be based on high-quality data.

REFERENCES

1. Food and Drug Administration Offices of Drug Evaluation. Statistical report. Rockville, Md.: Department of Health and Human Services, 1993.
2. Wilkes MS, Doblin BH, Shapiro MF. Pharmaceutical advertisements in leading medical journals: experts' assessments. Ann Intern Med 1992;116: 912–9.
3. Kessler DA. Drug promotion and scientific exchange: the role of the clinical investigator. N Engl J Med 1991;325:201–3.
4. Goldfinger SE. A matter of influence. N Engl J Med 1987;316:1408–9.

5. Chren M-M, Landefeld CS, Murray TH. Doctors, drug companies, and gifts. JAMA 1990;263: 2178–9.

6. Waud DR. Pharmaceutical promotions—a free lunch? N Engl J Med 1992;327:351–3.

7. Earning a failing grade: a report card on 1992 drug manufacturer price inflation. Staff report to the U.S. Senate Special Committee on Aging. 103rd Cong., 1st Sess. (February 1993).

8. Woosley, RL. A prescription for better prescriptions. Issues Sci Technol 1994;10(3):59–66.

9. Gain market share or die. Medical Advertising Newsletter. Executive ed. May 1994:10.

10. U.S. drugstore and U.S. hospital market overview (U.S. Ethical Pharmaceuticals). Plymouth Meeting, Pa.: IMS America, 1993.

11. U.S.C. § § 352(f), 355(a) (1994).

12. Anders G. Doubts are cast on cost studies by drug makers. Wall Street Journal. June 28, 1994:B1.

13. Kassirer JP, Angell M. The *Journal's* policy on cost-effectiveness analyses. N Engl J Med 1994;331:669–70.

14. Kolata G. Pharmacists paid to suggest drugs. New York Times. July 29, 1994:A1.

15. *In re* Miles Inc., No C7-94-3189 (Dist. Ct. Minn. filed April 4, 1994.)

16. *In re* Upjohn Co., No. C7-94-7856 (Dist. Ct. Minn. filed Aug. 1, 1994.)

17. Tanouye E. Owning Medco: Merck takes drug marketing the next logical step. Wall Street Journal. May 31, 1994:A1.

NO

Paul H. Rubin

WHAT THE FDA DOESN'T
WANT YOU TO KNOW

The new commissioner of the Food and Drug Administration [FDA], David A. Kessler, has indicated in interviews that he plans to increase FDA regulation of direct-to-consumer ads for prescription drugs. He has appointed new people to run the FDA's advertising division and is doubling the staff devoted to advertising regulation.

There is already excessive and inefficient regulation of drug advertising, so imposing further restrictions or increasing enforcement would be a move in the wrong direction. Dr. Kessler advocates stronger enforcement because he fears deceptive advertising, but his fears are misplaced in the prescription drug market. Further, several health benefits from direct advertising are already apparent, and this advertising also will reduce prices of drugs. Thus, with no identifiable benefits, but with some certain costs for consumers and manufacturers, stricter regulations would be a mistake.

There is no evidence that any deception has occurred in the ads. More important, deception is highly unlikely in this market. Because approval by a physician is required for purchase of a prescription drug, there is less chance of deception in this area than in almost any other consumer market. A consumer will of necessity have a second, informed opinion before acting on an ad.

Moreover, consumers are not mere pawns. They are aware of the source of information and treat it with appropriate skepticism. Sidney Wolfe of Public Citizen Health Research Group, a Ralph Nader organization, has criticized ads for prescription drugs because "they encourage patients to pound on the doctor's door and demand the new miracle treatment." Wolfe apparently views the abilities of consumers to make rational judgments with some disdain.

CURRENT POLICY AND ITS EFFECTS

Although direct advertising of prescription drugs is now allowed, there are severe restrictions. One is known as the "brief summary" and it is required on some direct-to-consumer advertisements. It is hardly "brief" given that it is usually the equivalent of one or two typewritten pages. It often appears in small print, and it lists the side effects and contraindications associated with the prescription drug. This information may be useful for physicians, for whom it was originally intended, but the lengthy statement is virtually worthless to most consumers because it is written in technical language and is probably read by only a very small number of them. Moreover, since a prescription will be needed for the drug in any case, a consumer buying the product will perforce consult with a physician who will be able to tell him the same information contained in the brief summary. There is little benefit from ensuring that both the consumer and the physician have the same information. Because an informed intermediary, a physician, must be contacted before a prescription drug can be purchased, information is probably better in the pharmaceutical market than in almost any other consumer market, and requiring a complex disclosure statement provides no benefits.

When must an ad contain the brief summary? The regulations make no objective sense. If an ad mentions a health condition and gives the name of a drug that can be used for that condition—or even indicates that a drug exists for that condition—then the ad must also contain the brief summary. For example, if an ad says that there is a new medication to help a consumer stop smoking, or if it states that Nicorette gum, specifically, will help some people quit, then the ad must contain the brief summary.

Other ads need not print the brief summary. If an advertisement mentions only that one should "See your physician" for unspecified treatment for smoking, or if an ad mentions the price of a product ("Nicorette is on sale!") but not what the product is used for, then the brief summary is not required. The FDA enforces these distinctions with a bureaucratic assiduousness verging on the absurd.

The regulations governing direct-to-consumer ads may actually reduce or even deny information to consumers. The regulations prevent prescription drug advertising on television. They increase the cost of print ads when the brief summary is required and thereby reduce the number of such ads. And, finally, ads that do not carry the brief summary are less informative. Thus, the regulations, in effect, cause consumers of pharmaceuticals to be less well informed than would be the case with more sensible requirements.

Even though the existing rules overregulate and have perverse effects, Dr. Kessler is considering imposing even stricter ones. Any increase in regulation could easily eliminate direct-to-consumer advertising altogether. It would be foolish to forgo the benefits of this advertising because of a misplaced fear of deception when the benefits are improved health and reduced costs for drugs.

HEALTH BENEFITS

Several types of health benefits accrue from prescription-drug advertising. Consider that a consumer may not be aware that a treatment exists for a particular condition. Two prominent examples are Minoxidil, a treatment for some types of baldness, and Nicorette gum, a substitute for cigarette smoking for those who are trying to quit. In both cases, advertising is an efficient mechanism for informing consumers that prescription remedies exist for these conditions. Nicorette is a particularly interesting case. Cigarettes (which are not regulated by the FDA) can be advertised with only a one-line mention of the health risks of smoking, but advertising a remedy for smoking requires a lengthy discussion of side effects and other contraindications.

One benefit of promoting prescription drugs through advertising is wider consumer awareness. A consumer may suffer from some condition (for instance, excessive thirst) without realizing that it can be a symptom of a disease (diabetes, for one), so he will not consult a physician and therefore not learn as soon as possible that he has a treatable disease. An ad can induce the consumer to contact a physician.

A consumer may have previously been diagnosed as having some then-untreatable disease (or condition) for which a new treatment has since become available. Since he believes that the disease is not treatable, he is not likely to contact a physician and therefore will not learn about the new therapy. Advertisements can inform him and lead him to treatment. A similar analysis applies to the creation of a new vaccine for a condition to which some may know themselves to be susceptible—such as a vaccine for hepatitis B.

When a new remedy with fewer side effects becomes available, advertising can provide benefits in two cases. Those who do not know that symptoms they are experiencing are side effects and so would not ask a physician about them may learn from ads that there are alternative remedies without these side effects. Those who have ceased treatment because of side effects and so are not seeing a physician may begin treatment again if they learn of therapies that do not have the same side effects.

For instance, antihypertensives may cause impotence as a side effect. Some patients may not know that this condition is related to the medication they are taking for high blood pressure and may be unwilling to discuss the problem with a physician; others may have stopped taking it because of the condition. Either group can benefit from ads indicating that a treatment with reduced side effects is available. New drugs to lower cholesterol levels that need not be taken as often or are less unpleasant than the older drugs would also be candidates for advertising.

PRICE EFFECTS

Price is currently less effective as a competitive tool in pharmaceuticals than it is in many other areas of commerce because the physician chooses the product but does not pay for it directly and therefore has little incentive to pay attention to price. Thus, providing information that would enable consumers to compare prices more easily should have a larger-than-average effect. There is evidence from many markets that increased advertising leads to lower prices, and this information has been used by the Supreme Court in overturning some state bans on various types of advertising. In pharmaceuticals, there should be an even greater reduction in price from increased advertising.

There are several mechanisms through which advertising can lead to lower prices. Advertising can inform consumers that two brands of the same drug are in fact equivalent and that one is cheaper. They can then ask physicians to prescribe the lower-priced drug. Increased competition brought about by advertising can lead manufacturers to reduce prices.

Increased information can also make competition by retailers more effective. Some drug stores now compete by advertising the names of drugs and the prices they charge for them. For those consumers who are not actively aware of the name of the drug they are taking, this information is useful. However, since the purpose of the drug cannot be included in the ad without triggering the brief summary, consumers who know that they are taking a drug for hypertension but do not know its name would not be able to benefit from this information about low prices. Elimination of the requirement for the brief summary could lead to increased price competition at the retail level and reduced prices for many consumers.

POLICY IMPLICATIONS

There would be definite advantages to advertising simultaneously the name and function of a drug without including the brief summary. Firms would be more likely to advertise if they could mention their own brand name because general advertisements would benefit their competitors but increased sales of their own brand would help them recoup the costs of advertising. Advertising the name and function of a drug can increase pressure to lower prices across the industry. Ads containing both the brand name and the uses of a drug convey more information and thus help provide all of the beneficial functions mentioned above.

The FDA reduces information in some over-the-counter markets as well. Particularly noteworthy is the continuing prohibition on advertising the benefits of aspirin in reducing the chances of heart attack. One major study has shown that aspirin could reduce the change of a first heart attack in middle-aged men by almost 50 percent. The FDA has been unwilling to allow advertising of this information even to physicians. The FDA does allow physicians to receive information about the beneficial effect of aspirin in reducing second heart attacks, but not consumers. Even though these restrictions are "voluntary," manufacturers are unwilling to oppose the FDA, which has considerable power over them. It is likely that several thousand heart attacks could be prevented annually if full dissemination of this information were allowed.

In sum, a major weakness of the current regulatory system for pharmaceuticals is the limitations on direct-to-consumer advertising. This advertising would provide health benefits and lead to price reductions. The FDA imposed an absolute ban on direct advertising from 1983 to 1985. It then sensibly relaxed this ban. It is now time to take the next step and eliminate the costly and pointless requirement for a "brief summary" in ads that name the product and its use. A return to a system that severely limits direct advertising of prescription drugs would make for poorer and less healthy consumers and should not be a goal of sound public policy.

POSTSCRIPT

Should There Be Tighter Restrictions on the Advertising of Prescription Drugs?

The Food and Drug Administration (FDA) feels that drug companies' promotions are frequently inaccurate or deceptive. Furthermore, the FDA maintains that drug companies are only interested in increasing profits, not in truly providing additional benefit to the consumer. Drug companies do not deny that they seek to make profits from their drugs, but they argue that they are offering an important service by educating the public about new drugs through advertisements.

An important issue is whether or not the average consumer is capable of discerning information distributed by pharmaceutical companies. Are people without a background in medicine, medical terminology, or research methods sufficiently knowledgeable to understand literature disseminated by drug companies? Rubin suggests that the government does not give the average person enough credit for being able to understand drug advertisements.

Some critics argue that restricting drug advertisements is a moot point because consumers cannot obtain prescriptions without the approval of their physicians, anyway. Yet, there are many instances in which physicians acquiesce to the wishes of their patients and write prescriptions upon request. If in this way patients receive prescriptions that are not appropriate for their needs, who is responsible: the patient, the physician, or the drug manufacturer and advertiser?

When drug manufacturers introduce a new drug, they get a patent on the drug to protect their investment. Drug companies therefore receive financial rewards for introducing new drugs. Some critics, and also the FDA, fear that many drugs promoted as "new" are merely "me-too" drugs that are similar to existing drugs and that do not provide any additional benefit.

Several articles shed further light on this issue. Greg Citser's article "Oh, How Happy We Will Be: Pills, Paradise, and the Profits of the Drug Companies," *Harper's Magazine* (June 1996), describes tactics used by drug companies to increase profits. The article "Miracle Drugs or Media Drugs?" *Consumer Reports* (March 1992) contends that advertisements for prescription drugs are often misleading and inaccurate. In "The Other Drug Lords," *Common Cause* (Fall 1992), Viveca Novak describes the political influence that pharmaceutical companies have in Congress, especially in terms of protecting their patents and their profits. And Elaine Johnson, in "Legal Drugs at Work: Doctors' Orders Can Be Dangerous," *Safety and Health* (November 1994), discusses the threat of prescription drugs in the workplace.

ISSUE 12

Are Too Many Children Receiving Ritalin?

YES: Richard Bromfield, from "Is Ritalin Overprescribed? Yes," *Priorities* (vol. 8, no. 3, 1996)

NO: Jerry Wiener, from "Is Ritalin Overprescribed? No," *Priorities* (vol. 8, no. 3, 1996)

ISSUE SUMMARY

YES: Harvard Medical School professor Richard Bromfield contends that physicians are often too eager to prescribe Ritalin for children with attention deficit/hyperactivity disorder (ADHD). Bromfield is concerned that Ritalin's long-term effects have not been adequately researched and that its overuse may be masking other childhood disorders.

NO: George Washington Medical School professor Jerry Wiener maintains that Ritalin has been proven to be safe and effective. Wiener argues that attention deficit/hyperactivity disorder is underdiagnosed in many instances and that children who could benefit from the use of Ritalin do not receive it.

The number one childhood psychiatric disorder in the United States is attention deficit/hyperactivity disorder, which affects approximately 6 percent of all school-age children. The most commonly prescribed drug for ADHD is the stimulant Ritalin (generic name methylphenidate). About 2.5 million U.S. children, primarily boys between the ages of 5 and 12, receive prescriptions of Ritalin for ADHD. In contrast, only 1 in 200 European children are diagnosed with ADHD. Ritalin is less likely to be prescribed in Europe. ADHD is characterized by inattentiveness, hyperactivity, and impulsivity. Many children are diagnosed as having only attention deficit disorder (ADD), without the hyperactivity accompanying their condition.

The use of stimulants to treat such behavioral disorders dates back to 1937. The practice of prescribing stimulants for behavioral problems increased dramatically beginning in 1970, when it was estimated that 150,000 American children were taking stimulant medications. It seems paradoxical for physicians to be prescribing a stimulant such as Ritalin for a behavioral disorder already involving hyperactivity. However, Ritalin appears to be effective with many children, as well as with adults, suffering from this condition. Looking at this issue from a broader perspective, one needs to ask the question of whether or not behavioral problems should be treated as a disease. Also, does

Ritalin really address the problem? Could it be covering up other maladies that otherwise would be treated?

Ritalin enhances the functioning of the brain's reticular activating system, which helps one to focus attention and to filter out extraneous stimuli. It has been shown to improve short-term learning. Ritalin also produces adverse effects such as insomnia, headaches, irritability, nausea, dizziness, weight loss, and growth retardation. Psychological dependence may develop but physical dependence is unlikely. The effects of long-term Ritalin use are unknown.

Since 1990 the number of children receiving Ritalin has increased two and a half times. This large increase in the number of children with ADHD may be attributed to a broader application of the criteria for diagnosing ADHD, heightened public awareness, and changes in American educational policy regarding schools' identifying children with the disorder. Some people feel that the increase in prescriptions for Ritalin is to satisfy the needs of parents whose children exhibit behavioral problems. Ritalin has been referred to as "mother's little helper." Regardless of the reasons for the increase, many people question whether or not Ritalin is overprescribed, children are overmedicated, and Ritalin is a miracle drug.

One problem with the increased prevalence of Ritalin prescriptions is that its illegal use has risen. There are accounts of some parents getting prescriptions for their children and then selling the drugs illegally. On a number of college campuses there are reports of students using Ritalin to get high or to stay awake in order to study. Historically, illegal use of Ritalin has been minimal, although officials of the Drug Enforcement Agency (DEA) are now concerned that its illegal use is proliferating. Problems with its use are unlikely to rival that of cocaine because Ritalin's effects are more moderate than those of cocaine or amphetamines.

The fact is that children now receive prescriptions for Ritalin rather readily. Frequently, parents will pressure their pediatricians into writing the prescriptions. One survey found that almost one-half of all pediatricians spent less than an hour assessing children before prescribing Ritalin. On the other hand, if there is a medication available that would remedy a problem, should it not be taken? If a child's academic performance can improve through the use of Ritalin, should that child be denied the drug? As indicated, Ritalin is effective for many children, although it works best if it is accompanied by behavioral therapy.

In the following selections, Richard Bromfield argues that despite the benefits of Ritalin, too many children are given it inappropriately and the long-term consequences of its use are unknown. Jerry Wiener maintains that ADHD is underdiagnosed and that more children should receive Ritalin. Wiener concedes that some children are misdiagnosed but that the benefits of Ritalin outweigh its risks.

YES

Richard Bromfield

IS RITALIN OVERPRESCRIBED? YES

Ritalin is being dispensed with a speed and nonchalance compatible with our drive-through culture, yet entirely at odds with good medicine and common sense. The drug does help some people pay attention and function better; some of my own patients have benefited from it. But too many children, and more and more adults, are being given Ritalin inappropriately.

Psychiatry has devised careful guidelines for prescribing and monitoring this sometimes-useful drug. But the dramatic jump in Ritalin use in the past five years clearly suggests that these guidelines are being ignored and that Ritalin is being vastly overprescribed. The problem has finally been recognized by medical groups such as the American Academy of Child and Adolescent Psychiatry, the American Psychiatric Association and the American Academy of Pediatrics, which have written or are developing guidelines for diagnosing ADHD [attention-deficit/hyperactive disorder]; and even by CibaGeneva Pharmaceuticals, the manufacturer of Ritalin, which issued similar guidelines to doctors [recently].

Under the pressure of managed care, physicians are diagnosing ADHD in patients and prescribing them Ritalin after interviews as short as 15 minutes. And given Ritalin's quick action (it can "calm" children within days after treatment starts), some doctors even rely on the drug as a diagnostic tool, interpreting improvements in behavior or attention as proof of an underlying ADHD—and justification for continued drug use.

Studies show that Ritalin prescribing fluctuates dramatically depending on how parents and teachers perceive "misbehavior" and how tolerant they are of it. I know of children who have been given Ritalin more to subdue them than to meet their needs—a practice that recalls the opium syrups used to soothe noisy infants in London a century ago. When a drug can be prescribed because one person is bothering another—a disruptive child upsetting a teacher, for example—there is clearly a danger that the drug will be abused. That danger only increases when the problem being treated is so vaguely defined.

From Richard Bromfield, "Is Ritalin Overprescribed? Yes," *Priorities*, vol. 8, no. 3 (1996), pp. 24, 26, 28. Copyright © 1996 by the American Council on Science and Health. Reprinted by permission of *Priorities*, a publication of the American Council on Science and Health, 1995 Broadway, 2nd Floor, New York, NY 10023-5860.

ADHD exists as a disorder primarily because a committee of psychiatrists voted it so. In a valiant effort, they squeezed a laundry list of disparate symptoms into a neat package that can be handled and treated. But while attention is an essential aspect of our functioning, it's certainly not the only one. Why not bestow disorderhood on other problems common to people diagnosed with ADHD, such as Easily Frustrated Disorder (EFD) or Nothing Makes Me Happy Disorder (NMMHD)?

Once known as Minimal Brain Dysfunction and Hyperkinetic Syndrome, ADHD is considered a neurological disorder. Certainly, some people diagnosed with ADHD are neurologically impaired and need medication. But nervous system glitches account for the disruptive behavior of only a small minority of people who are vulnerable to distraction or impulsive behavior—perhaps 1 percent or 2 percent of the general population. Many more people have ADHD symptoms that have nothing to do with their nervous systems and result instead from emotional distress, depression, anxiety, obsessions or learning disabilities.

For these people, who exhibit the symptoms of ADHD but suffer from some other problem, Ritalin will likely be useless as a treatment. Taking it may postpone more effective treatment. And it may even be harmful.

No one knows how Ritalin works. Some miracle drugs, of course, have helped people for decades or even centuries before their mechanisms of action were understood. But we need to know more about the possible effects of a drug used mainly on children.

We're willing to overlook side effects when it comes to treating a life-threatening disease. But with a less

weighty disorder like ADHD, therapeutic rewards must be weighed against possible adverse reactions. In a drug targeted at children, there is concern that harmful effects may crop up decades after treatment stops. Since Ritalin is a relatively new drug, in use for about 30 years, we still don't know whether long-term side effects await its young users. But we do know that more immediate problems can occur.

It's already clear that Ritalin can worsen underlying anxiety, depression, psychosis and seizures. More common but milder side effects include nervousness and sleeplessness. Some studies suggest that the drug may interfere with bone growth. And [recently] the United Nation's International Narcotics Control Board reported an increase in teenagers who were inhaling this stimulant drug, which is chemically similar to cocaine but not nearly as potent.

While Ritalin's mode of action isn't clear, the drug is known to affect the brain's most ancient and basic structures, which control arousal and attention. I question the wisdom of tampering with such crucially important parts of the brain, particularly with a drug whose possible long-term side effects remain to be discovered.

The surge in both ADHD diagnoses and Ritalin prescriptions is yet another sign of a society suffering from a colossal lack of personal responsibility. By telling patients that their failures, misbehavior and unhappiness are caused by a disorder, we risk colluding with their all-too-human belief that their actions are beyond their control, and we weaken their motivation to change on their own. And in the many cases where ADHD is misdiagnosed in children, we give parents the illusion that their child's problems have nothing to do with the home environment or with their performance as parents.

It must be true that bad biology accounts for some people's distracted and impulsive lifestyles. But random violence, drugs, alcohol, domestic trauma and (less horrifically) indulgent and chaotic homes are more obvious reasons for the ADHD-like restlessness that plagues America. We urgently need to address *these* problems. To do that, we need legislators who will provide support for good parenting, especially in the early years of childhood when the foundations for handling feelings, self-control and concentration are biologically and psychologically laid down.

Some people who can't concentrate probably do merit the diagnosis of ADHD and a prescription for Ritalin to treat it. But the brain, the neurological seat of the soul and the self must be treated with the utmost respect. With the demand for Ritalin growing, we must be increasingly wary about doling out a drug that can be beneficial but is more often useless or even harmful.

NO

Jerry Wiener

IS RITALIN OVERPRESCRIBED? NO

In defending the current use of Ritalin for treating ADHD [attention-deficit/hyperactive disorder], it's important first to emphasize that the disorder really exists.

Telling whether a child has ADHD is more complicated than a diagnosis of the mumps or chicken pox, but the diagnosis of ADHD can still be as valid as any in medicine. An analogous health problem would be multiple sclerosis: As with ADHD it's a distinct disease, yet we don't know what causes the illness and have no laboratory test for diagnosing it.

Since the 1950s what we now call ADHD has been a well-recognized syndrome involving, as all syndromes do, a group of signs and symptoms that occur together. Years of research have documented that some children differ from their peers in being inattentive and hyperactive as well as impulsive. Extensive field trials and numerous studies have established that hyperactivity and impulsivity are at the core of the diagnosis, with inattention a consequence of the other two, especially in school-age boys.

Adding to the evidence that ADHD is a legitimate clinical problem are recent results of magnetic resonance imaging (MRI) studies showing that children diagnosed with ADHD have subtle but significant anatomical differences in their brains compared with other children. Furthermore, studies of families suggest there is a genetic component for many cases of ADHD. More specifically, recent research has found a possible link between ADHD and three genes that code for receptors (proteins that jut from the surface of cells) that are activated by dopamine, a neurotransmitter (a chemical that conveys messages from one nerve cell to another). Defects in these genes could mean a reduced response to dopamine signals, perhaps accounting for the uninhibited behavior observed in ADHD.

A child suspected of having ADHD should be evaluated by a trained and experienced clinician who takes the time to assess the child's development, family history and behavior at school and at home. The clinician should require that the criteria set forth in the current *Diagnostic and Statistical Manual of Mental Disorders* (DSM-IV) are met before concluding that a child has ADHD.

From Jerry Wiener, "Is Ritalin Overprescribed? No," *Priorities*, vol. 8, no. 3 (1996), pp. 25, 27, 29. Copyright © 1996 by the American Council on Science and Health. Reprinted by permission of *Priorities*, a publication of the American Council on Science and Health, 1995 Broadway, 2nd Floor, New York, NY 10023-5860.

To receive the diagnosis of ADHD, a child should display a significant number of symptoms and behaviors reflecting hyperactivity, impulsivity and inattention —and the symptoms and behaviors must be more persistent and severe than normally occur in children of that age. In addition and importantly, there must be impaired functioning in school, at home and/or in social relationships.

Are mistakes made in diagnosing ADHD? Of course. They usually occur when the clinician is rushed, inexperienced, untrained, pressured or predisposed either to "find" ADHD or to overlook it. As a result, there is both over- and underdiagnosis of ADHD. The reported fivefold increase in Ritalin prescriptions over the past five years is reason to reflect about possible overusage. However, repeated findings of a three-percent prevalence rate of ADHD among school-age children give as much cause for concern about underdiagnosis as for overusage: At these prevalence rates, up to 30 percent of children with ADHD may not be receiving sufficient treatment.

While there is no cure for ADHD, there is a very effective treatment to minimize its symptoms—through the use of stimulant medications such as Ritalin. Such drugs are by far the most effective treatment for moderating and controlling the disorder's major symptoms— hyperactivity, inattention and impulsivity—in 75 percent to 80 percent of children with this disorder.

The safety and effectiveness of Ritalin and other stimulant drugs, including Dexedrine (dextroamphetamine) and Cylert (pemoline), have been established more firmly than any other treatments in the field of child and adolescent psychiatry. Literally scores of carefully conducted blind and double-blind controlled studies have repeatedly documented the improvement—often dramatic—in symptoms of ADHD following the use of stimulant medication, with Ritalin the most common choice. By contrast, no other treatment, including behavior modification, compares with stimulant medication in efficacy; in fact, no treatment besides these medications has had much success at all in treating ADHD.

Stimulant medication is so effective that a parent with a child diagnosed with ADHD should receive an explanation if the clinician's judgment is *not* to prescribe medication. Appropriate considerations for not opting for Ritalin and similar drugs include a history of tic or Tourette's disorder, the presence of a thought disorder, significant resistance to such medications in the patient or family or insufficient severity of the symptoms or dysfunction. Other classes of drugs, such as antidepressants, can be effective and can be used when there is concern about the use of a stimulant medication or when side effects occur.

The issue should not be whether stimulants are overprescribed but the risk that they may be misprescribed. The most common example: children who are described as overactive or impulsive but who do not meet the criteria for the diagnosis of ADHD. Another example is the use of stimulants as a diagnostic "test" by a rushed or inexperienced clinician who may not realize that a favorable response was due to the placebo effect and therefore mistakenly assumes that the diagnosis of ADHD has been confirmed.

As effective as Ritalin can be for treating the symptoms of ADHD, it should rarely, if ever, be the only treatment for someone with the problem. The child or adolescent may also benefit from remedial work for any identified learning disability and from family therapy or psychotherapy for problems of self-image, self-esteem, anger and/or depression.

Is Ritalin overprescribed? Not when it's used for children who meet the criteria for the diagnosis of ADHD, including the requirement that the child's ability to function must be "significantly impaired." All too often, the mistakes in prescribing Ritalin are errors of omission, where children who could benefit from the drug never receive it. Instead, they go through school labeled as troublemakers, or as unmotivated or hostile. They'll have missed out on the opportunity for at least a trial on a medication that could have significantly improved their symptoms and allowed for improved academic performance, self-esteem and social interaction.

POSTSCRIPT

Are Too Many Children Receiving Ritalin?

To satisfy their own emotional needs, many parents urge their physicians into diagnosing their children with ADHD. Parents believe that their children will benefit if they are labeled ADHD. The pressure for children to do well academically in order to get into the right college and graduate school is intense. Parents feel that if their children are diagnosed with ADHD, then they may be provided special circumstances or allowances such as additional time when taking college entrance examinations. If medication is available to help children succeed, then some parents may view drugs as simply another method to improve their children's performance. Some parents realize that if their children are identified as having ADHD, then their children would be eligible for support services in school. In some instances, the only way to receive such extra help is to be labeled with a disorder. Also, some teachers favor the use of Ritalin to control students' behavior. During the last few years, there has been more emphasis on controlling school budgets. The result is larger class sizes and higher student-to-teacher ratios. Thus, it should not be surprising that many teachers welcome the calming effect of Ritalin on certain students.

Whether or not drug therapy should be applied to behaviors raises another concern. What is the message that children are receiving about the role of drugs in society? Perhaps children will generalize the benefits of using legal drugs like Ritalin to remedy life's problems to using illegal drugs to deal with other problems that they may be experiencing. Children may find that it is easier to ingest a pill rather than to put the time and effort into resolving personal problems. For many adults, drugs seem to represent a shortcut to correcting life's difficulties. Through its reliance on drugs, is American society creating a wrong impression for its children, an illusion of believing that there is a pill for *every* ill?

When to prescribe Ritalin for children also places physicians in a quandary. They may see the benefit of helping students function more effectively in school. However, are physicians unintentionally promoting an antihuman-istic, competitive environment in which performance matters regardless of cost? Yet, is it the place of the physician to dictate to parents what is best for their children? In the final analysis, will the increase in prescriptions for Ritalin result in benefits for the child, for the parent, for society?

The social consequences of and reasons for the explosion of Ritalin use in the last several years are discussed in Lawrence Diller's article "The Run on Ritalin: Attention Deficit Disorder and Stimulant Treatment in the

1990s," *Hastings Center Report* (March–April 1996). Several articles addressing whether or not Ritalin is overprescribed appeared in the March 18, 1996, issue of *Newsweek*. Differences between the United States and Europe in the practice of prescribing Ritalin are described by Dorothy Bonn in "Methylphenidate: U.S. and European Views Converging?" *The Lancet* (July 27, 1996). The effectiveness of Ritalin is studied by Thomas Spencer et al. in "A Double-Blind Crossover Comparison of Methylphenidate and Placebo in Adults with Childhood-Onset Attention Deficit Hyperactivity Disorder," *Archives of General Psychiatry* (June 1995).

ISSUE 13

Is Prozac Overprescribed?

YES: Mark Nichols, from "Questioning Prozac," *Maclean's* (May 23, 1994)

NO: Nancy Wartik, from "Prozac: The Verdict Is In," *American Health* (November 1996)

ISSUE SUMMARY

YES: Writer Mark Nichols states that many physicians prescribe Prozac too readily. Nichols believes that Prozac is used too often for ordinary problems of daily living such as discontent and irritability. He contends, moreover, that its long-term effects are not known and that some people experience negative psychological reactions while on Prozac.

NO: Health and psychology writer Nancy Wartik notes that Prozac is helpful for treating chronic depression, especially among women. She asserts that with less adverse publicity surrounding Prozac, more people could benefit from its use. Wartik believes that Prozac's purported dangers are overexaggerated.

One of the most common emotional problems in America is depression. It is estimated that approximately 10 percent of Americans experience some type of depression during their lives. The antidepressant drug most typically prescribed for treating depression is Prozac, whose generic name is fluoxetine. Although Prozac has been available only since 1987, global sales in 1995 exceeded $2 billion. It is one of the most commonly prescribed drugs in the United States.

Although Prozac was originally developed for treating depression—for which it is believed to be about 60 percent effective—the drug has been prescribed for an array of other conditions. These conditions include eating disorders such as bulimia and obesity, obsessive-compulsive disorders, and anxiety. An important question about Prozac is currently under debate: Is Prozac being prescribed too casually? Some experts feel that physicians are giving Prozac to patients who do not need chemical treatment to overcome their afflictions. Sherwin Nuland, a professor at Yale University, believes that Prozac is relatively safe for its approved applications but that it is inappropriate for less severe problems.

As with most other drugs, Prozac can produce a number of adverse side effects, though they are reportedly fewer and less severe than other antidepressants. Short-term effects from Prozac may include headaches, sweating, fatigue, anxiety, reduced appetite, jitteriness, dizziness, stomach discomfort, nausea, sexual dysfunction, and insomnia. Because it is a relatively new drug, long-term side effects have yet to be determined.

Several lawsuits have been filed against Eli Lilly and Company, Prozac's manufacturer, as a result of one of the drug's alleged side effects: the drug has been linked to violent and suicidal behavior. Some individuals charged with violent crimes have even used the defense that Prozac made them act violently and that they should not be held accountable for their actions while on the drug. Prozac has also been implicated in a number of suicides, though it is unclear whether Prozac caused these individuals to commit suicide or whether they would have committed suicide anyway. Eli Lilly representatives emphasize that Prozac diminishes suicidal thoughts and may prevent violent behavior.

To date, hearings by the Food and Drug Administration (FDA) have concluded that Prozac is a safe and effective drug because the evidence linking it to violence and suicide is insufficient. One critic, author William Styron, asserts that the manufacturer has made a concerted effort to minimize the detrimental effects of Prozac. In 1990 the Prozac Survivors Support Group was formed to help people who have had adverse symptoms while on the drug.

Psychiatrist Peter R. Breggin, who feels that Prozac is being prescribed too frequently, argues that Prozac and other antidepressant drugs are being used to replace traditional psychotherapy. Breggin claims that psychiatry has given in to the pharmaceutical companies. Compared to psychiatry, Prozac is far less expensive and more convenient. But does Prozac get at the root of the problems that many people have? The U.S. Public Health Service recommends drug therapy for severe cases of depression but psychotherapy for mild or moderate cases of depression.

Psychiatrist Peter D. Kramer claims that Prozac brings about a positive transformation in the personalities of many individuals: people who are habitually timid seem more confident after taking the drug; sensitive people become more brash; and introverts improve their social skills. Kramer states that people become more real. Critics of this viewpoint ask, If one's personality changes as a result of a drug, what is that individual's real personality? Is the personality of a person on Prozac "real"? Also, does Prozac change one's personality or simply the way one perceives the world?

In the following selections, Mark Nichols maintains that Prozac is overprescribed; that it is being used simply to make people feel better. He contends that Prozac is employed as a quick fix and that people who are using the drug are not confronting the real sources of their problems, and he discusses as well the social implications from the overprescription of Prozac. Nancy Wartik argues that Prozac is an invaluable drug in the treatment of mild depression and that more people could benefit from its use. She contends that Prozac has been unfairly criticized and that this criticism has prevented more people from using it.

YES   **Mark Nichols**

QUESTIONING PROZAC

With more than 11 million mostly satisfied customers around the globe, it is one of the most rapidly successful drugs in history. An antidote to clinical depression, the green-and-yellow capsule, introduced six years ago, has also been extolled by some enthusiasts as just the thing to help frazzled parents cope with their kids or to make chronic loners stop fearing rejection. Prozac—brand name for the chemical fluoxetine hydrochloride—has entered pop culture, as well, becoming the stuff of cartoons and stand-up comedy routines. And it has summoned the vision of an era of so-called cosmetic psychopharmacology, in which a society of pill-poppers, seeking relief from everything from shyness to fear or crowds, will have to look no further than the nearest medicine cabinet. That day may yet come. But it raises serious medical and philosophical questions—and the first wave of them is descending upon Prozac itself. Is Prozac—non-addictive and, according to some doctors, capable of transforming personalities for the better—a nearly perfect pill? Well, not quite.

There *are* some problems. Many medical experts worry that some doctors may be overprescribing Prozac and using it to treat relatively trivial personality disorders. As a result, far too many people—including some of the estimated 200,000 Canadians currently taking Prozac—may be using a drug whose long-term effects might not be known for decades. As well, there have been reports—contradicted by manufacturer Eli Lilly and Co. of Indianapolis and U.S. health officials—suggesting that a small number of Prozac patients may become violent or prone to suicidal thinking. Even more worrisome, Dr. Lorne Brandes, a Winnipeg cancer researcher, claims to have evidence that Prozac and some other widely used drugs may promote the growth of cancerous tumors. "I'm very concerned about Prozac," says Brandes, who reported in 1992 that rats and mice with artificially induced cancer showed an increased rate of tumor growth when they were given Prozac and another antidepressant. Brandes's findings alarmed some cancer researchers and prompted federal scientists to launch a similar study.

And although Prozac has fewer side-effects than earlier antidepressants, it does have some. Users may experience nausea, nervousness and insomnia and their sex life can suffer: a U.S. study, published in *The Journal of Clinical Psychiatry* in April [1994] found that among 160 patients taking Prozac, 54 reported that sexual desire or response diminished after they began using the drug. And even proponents wonder about the social implications of a medicine that promises to abolish angst—what would happen to the world's art and culture if future Vincent van Goghs and F. Scott Fitzgeralds were prescribed Prozac? Peter D. Kramer, a psychiatrist from Providence, R.I., who paints a largely favorable portrait of the pill in his best-selling book *Listening to Prozac*, allows: "We cannot escape entirely the fear that a drug that makes people optimistic and confident will rob them of the morally beneficial effects of melancholy and angst."

In defence of Prozac, which grossed $1.7 billion in worldwide sales last year, Eli Lilly officials say that it is one of the most thoroughly tested medications in history: more than 32,000 people took part in Prozac's clinical trials, and scientists have conducted at least 3,000 separate studies. "Nothing alarming has shown up," says Cameron Battley, corporate affairs manager for Eli Lilly Canada Inc. in Scarborough, Ont. Battley also insists that, despite reports of the drug being used to treat people who do not really need an antidepressant, "there is absolutely no indication of any inappropriate use of Prozac in Canada." Maybe, but there are signs that Eli Lilly suspects something amiss. In an advertisement that began appearing recently in North American medical publications, the company deplores the "unprecedented amount of media attention" given to Prozac and stresses that the drug is intended for use "only where a clear medical need exists."

While there are concerns about Prozac, there is also unstinting praise from doctors and patients for an antidepressant that has made it easier to treat a debilitating illness. The side-effects of older antidepressants—including a parched mouth, difficulty urinating and feelings of psychological detachment—made them hard to take. "There were serious problems involved in getting patients to tolerate those drugs in therapeutic doses," says Dr. James Brooks, a Toronto general practitioner. "With Prozac, you don't have this. I'm really pleased with Prozac."

Many patients are equally enthusiastic. Three years ago, William Pringle, Vancouver special events organizer, was flattened by a major depression. His doctor put him on Prozac. "I fell into this dark pit," says Pringle. "Prozac pulled me out and got me relaunched on my life." Pringle, 36, stopped using Prozac a year ago and says that he is still feeling fine. Maria Theresa Spagnuolo of Toronto began taking it in 1989, after three automobile accidents left her with chronic pain throughout her body—and serious depression. Married and the mother of a young son, Spagnuolo found that she "was crying about everything—spilled milk was a catastrophe." Prozac, adds the 38-year-old Spagnulo, "gave me energy and changed my outlook so that I can cope with life. I don't think I could function without it."

Interestingly, many doctors report that the majority of their Prozac patients are women. William Ashdown, a Prozac user who is executive director of the Winnipeg-based Society for Depression and Manic-Depression of Manitoba, says that "it is more acceptable for a woman to seek help for an emotional disorder. Most men are culturally pressured into other avenues of self-medication, alcohol being a common one."

Spurred by Prozac's success, competing drug companies have begun producing similar antidepressants, including Paxil (made by Britain's SmithKline Beecham PLC) and Zoloft (by New York City-based Pfizer Inc.). All the drugs tinker with the same delicate mechanism—the brain's chemical communication system. Over the past decade, scientists have made important strides in understanding how the brain works—and how to affect the intricate chemical activity that makes some people chipper and outgoing while leaving others habitually despondent. Among the key determinants are a group of chemicals known as neurotransmitters—they include serotonin, dopamine and norepinephrine—that help to flash signals among the brain's 50 billion cells. Discharged by one cell, the neurotransmitters lock onto the receptors of neighboring cells. In this chemical interplay, serotonin plays a powerful role in modifying mood and emotion—but some people apparently don't have enough of it.

To remedy that, Prozac and similar drugs—known collectively by scientists as selective serotonin re-uptake inhibitors (SSRIs)—prevent brain cells from reabsorbing used serotonin. That leaves a pool of serotonin available for further use, which can lighten the mood and thinking of depressed people. Rose Rancourt, a 42-year-old Vancouverite, began using Paxil last fall after battling severe depressions from the age of 16. A former computer information systems supervisor, Rancourt now devotes herself to working with other depressed people. Thanks to Paxil, she says, "I feel good. I feel fine. I have peace of mind."

Despite its success in blazing the way for other SSRIs, Prozac has been embroiled in controversy almost from the start. After taking about 15 years to develop the drug, Eli Lilly began marketing Prozac in the United States in 1988 and in Canada the following year. Then, in February, 1990, Dr. Martin Teicher, a psychiatrist at the highly regarded McLean Hospital in Belmont, Mass., and two of his colleagues reported that six depressed patients began to have suicidal thoughts after using Prozac. Writing in *The American Journal of Psychiatry*, Teicher said that when they began taking the drug, none of the patients were suicidal and all were "hopeful and optimistic" about their treatment. After that, a spate of anecdotal reports told of violence and suicide among Prozac users. And the drug acquired a tenacious enemy in the Los Angeles-based Citizens Commission on Human Rights, which has ties to the Church of Scientology, a movement that, among other things, opposes some aspects of psychiatry and drug therapy.

The Scientologists claim that by Sept. 16, 1993, no fewer than 1,089 suicides had been recorded among patients taking the capsule. If that figure is correct, it works out to about .01 per cent of the 11 million people who have used the drug. Eli Lilly's Battley denies that Prozac is to blame. "Sadly," he added, "it is impossible to eradicate the possibility of depressed people committing suicide, even if they are receiving medication." Hearings by the U.S. Food and Drug Administration exonerated Prozac, but the bad publicity cut into its sales and produced a flood of lawsuits against Eli Lilly. So far, U.S. courts have rejected 80 claims against the company, many alleging that Prozac caused violent or suicidal tendencies; another 170 lawsuits are pending. In Canada, five lawsuits

—at least one involving violence—are pending against the company.

Prozac weathered the bad notices and soon began getting good ones. Kramer's book, published last year, describes personalities transformed by Prozac and patients made "better than well." According to Kramer, the effect Prozac will have on a patient can never be accurately predicted. Sometimes, he writes, "you take Prozac to treat a symptom, and it transforms your sense of self." The pill seems "to give social confidence to the habitually timid, to make the sensitive brash, to lend the introvert the social skills of a salesman."

Boosted by Kramer's best-seller, Prozac took off in 1993, recording a 15-percent increase in North American sales over the previous year—and prompting concern that doctors now may be dispensing the drug too liberally. In Canada and the United States, Prozac has been approved for use in treating clinical depression, bulimia (habitual purging to lose weight) and obsessive-compulsive disorder (persistent irrational thoughts and actions). But many doctors have effectively expanded the definition of what constitutes clinical depression to include dysthmyia—chronic low-grade depression—and in some cases have prescribed Prozac to otherwise healthy patients suffering from low self-esteem or gnawing anxieties. Hubert Van Tol, an associate professor of psychiatry and pharmacology at the University of Toronto, says: "If it's a question of someone who isn't feeling so hot, or maybe a man who's nervous about addressing meetings—that's not what the drug was designed for."

As well, some psychiatrists argue that it is dangerous for Prozac or similar drugs to be used without accompanying psychotherapy sessions, which en- able doctors to monitor the drug's effects. Some experts worry that general practitioners, who write the majority of Prozac prescriptions and see scores of patients a day, do not have time to do that. Others argue that far from being overprescribed, the drug has just begun to realize its potential. "In terms of sheer numbers," author Kramer told Maclean's, "you could probably double or triple the number of people using antidepressants, because depression is so underdiagnosed." Adds Kramer: "Prozac is not an enjoyable drug to use. It doesn't give you a high. With people who have problems but are less than clinically depressed, we would have no compunction about treating them with psychotherapy. So I don't see why we can't also treat them with a chemical that will ease their symptoms."

As compelling as that argument sounds, critics respond by insisting that any relatively new drug may have unforeseen consequences. Sidney Wolfe, director of the Public Citizen Health Research Group, a Washington-based consumer advocacy organization, compares Prozac to Valium, the popular tranquilizer that was on the market for more than 10 years before doctors discovered its highly addictive properties during the mid-1970s. "Prozac," declares Wolfe, "has become the Valium of the 1990s." Asks Dr. David Bakish, associate professor of psychiatry at the University of Ottawa: "Is there a chance that with Prozac some problem could show up in 15 or 20 years? Yes, it could happen."

Some doctors say they have seen disturbing reactions in Prozac patients. Dr. Shiva Sishta, a Fredericton psychiatrist who prescribes Prozac for people suffering form obsessive-compulsive disorders, says that one married woman who was on a fairly high dosage "became rather promiscuous—she recognized that she was not behaving properly." Shista took her off the drug, then resumed it later at a lower dosage with encouraging results. Dr. Randolph Catlin, a psychiatrist who is chief of the mental health service at Harvard University in Cambridge, Mass., says that "two or three" students he treated with Prozac reported "feeling split off from themselves. They feel as though they're not there any more." Adds Catlin: "One wonders if these reports that you hear about people acting aggressively with Prozac might be cases where patients who are out of touch with their feelings act on their impulses, without having any feeling of guilt or concern."

While controversy swirls around Prozac and the other SSRIs, a new generation of drugs—with an even greater potential for brightening moods and dispelling disruptive emotions—is fast coming of age.... New York City's Bristol-Myers Squibb Co.... introduce[d] Serzone, a more finely tuned serotonin-related drug designed to help people with depression and panic disorders while causing even fewer side-effects than the current SSRIs. Effexor, a new drug produced by Philadelphia-based Wyeth-Ayerst Laboratories Co. and already on the market in the United States, controls levels of sero-tonin and norepinephrine to help people suffering from depression; the company claims it has even fewer side-effects than Prozac.

Early in the 21st century, the next stage of drug development may give doctors more sophisticated tools for treating mental illnesses and correcting minor personality disorders—happy pills for every occasion. Because chemical imbalances in the brain are often the result of an inherited defect, says Rémi Quirion, director of the neuroscience division at the Douglas Hospital Research Centre in Montreal. I think in 10 years' time we will be able to look at a patient's genetic background and choose the drug to use accordingly." Quirion thinks that eventually it will be possible for doctors to administer just the right mix of drugs "to fine-tune the behavior of a given person. We may be able to almost modulate personality." At that point, says the University of Toronto's Van Tol, society "will face an ethical question: do we think it's right to use drugs that change our behavior in a certain direction that we want it to go in? I don't know the answer." It is a question that society already has begun to grapple with as it struggles to come to terms with the unanswered questions about Prozac and the dawning of the age of cosmetic psychopharmacology.

NO   Nancy Wartik

PROZAC: THE VERDICT IS IN

Five years ago, a traumatic sexual encounter sent Cindy Thompson, [names have been changed] now 41, plummeting into depression. "It was agonizing," recalls Thompson, a public relations consultant in Baltimore. "I wanted to kill myself every day." Thompson's psychotherapist recommended Prozac. "But I resisted," she says. "I was concerned about using a chemical to alter my mind and emotions." Finally, poised between the knife drawer and the telephone, "I called my therapist." Thompson agreed to be briefly hospitalized—and to try Prozac. "I figured I'd hit bottom and had nothing to lose."

This year marks a decade since Prozac, the antidepressant that's achieved a celebrity normally associated with movie stars and rock groups, first hit the market. Since then, it's been glorified as a miracle cure and vilified in a backlash centering on claims that Prozac makes some users violent. It's also been attacked as a "happy pill," a quick fix that allows users to ignore the psychological issues at the root of their depression.

Yet even with its luster tarnished, Prozac prospers. With 1995 sales topping $2 billion, up 24% from 1994, it's the second biggest moneymaking drug in the U.S., after the ulcer medicine Zantac. According to the manufacturer, Eli Lilly, more than 14 million Americans have joined the Prozac generation.

The drug has touched the lives of women in particular, primarily because they're twice as likely as men to suffer from major depression—a partly genetic disorder marked by persistent symptoms including sadness, fatigue, sleep or appetite problems and suicidal thoughts. Women also tend to have higher rates of other disorders for which Prozac is now prescribed, such as dysthmyia (chronic mild depression), some forms of anxiety (panic attacks and obsessive-compulsive disorder), severe PMS and bulimia.

Has the advent of Prozac been a boon for women, or will it come to be seen as the 1990s equivalent of "Mother's Little Helper"? Has the drug transformed the treatment of mental illness, or will it cause as yet unknown health problems down the line? Such questions are all the more pressing in this era of managed care, when there's a growing tendency to treat psychological disorders with medication rather than prolonged (read: pricey) talk therapy.

And with a host of newer antidepressant clones such as Zoloft, Paxil and Serzone flooding the market, should Prozac still reign as the drug of choice? Ten years into the Prozac phenomenon, we're starting to get some answers.

A REVOLUTION IN TREATMENT

Antidepressants work by altering balances of mood-regulating chemicals, such as serotonin, in the brain. The most popular antidepressants used to be a class of drug known as tricyclics, which were developed in the 1950s and are still in use. But tricyclics affect not only the brain chemicals they're supposed to but also some they aren't. This can lead to side effects ranging from constipation, dizziness and weight gain to more dangerous problems such as heart rhythm abnormalities.

In contrast, Prozac, Paxil and Zoloft, which belong to a class of drugs known as selective serotonin reuptake inhibitors, or SSRI's, affect serotonin regulation much more directly, which means users tolerate them better. "It doesn't matter how well a drug works if, because of the side effects, people don't take it regularly," says Michael Norden, M.D., a psychiatrist at the University of Washington in Seattle and author of *Beyond Prozac*. "So Prozac was a tremendous step forward."

Women in particular seem to find Prozac and the other SSRI's easy to tolerate. In an ongoing multicenter study of people with chronic depression, women and men were randomly assigned to tricyclic or SSRI treatment. More than 25% of the women on tricyclics stopped taking them, largely because of the side effects, while less than 15% of women on SSRI's quit. They also reported better moods while using SSRI's. (Men, on the other hand, tended to do better on tricyclics.)

With findings such as these, it comes as no surprise that antidepressants are now prescribed more liberally than ever. Some 60% are given out by family doctors, rather than mental health specialists. They're also prescribed for a far greater range of ailments and for less serious disorders: Whereas tricyclics were once reserved only for those with severe depression, these days it's not uncommon for physicians to prescribe Prozac for a case of the blues.

HAPPY ALL THE TIME?

Prozac's easy accessibility has also raised fears that doctors are handing out the drug like M&M's and people are popping it for "personality face-lifts." The real story is more complicated. Plenty of experts agree that the drugs are too readily available. "Their popularity has led to some inappropriate use," says Sidney Zisook, M.D., a professor of psychiatry at the University of California at San Diego. "There are a lot of sloppy diagnosis, cases where they're given for the wrong reasons or for too long. There are also patients who just want to be perfect, to always enjoy themselves, and they think they can do it the easy way, with Prozac. But it's wrong to use these medicines to try to solve all of life's problems."

Others point to a tendency, encouraged by managed care, for doctors to prescribe a pill instead of steering patients toward psychotherapy. "There are maybe 20% to 30% of depressed patients who can just take a drug and get well," says New York University psychiatrist Eric Peselow, M.D. "But the majority need psychotherapy as part of treatment. Racing to Prozac isn't the only answer."

Unfortunately people who pop a pill without doing the hard work of self-examination may find themselves back where they started when they quit taking the medication.

Yet with only one in three depressed people today getting treatment, cries of "Prozac abuse!" can be misleading. "There are far more people who could benefit from these drugs and aren't taking them than there are people taking them inappropriately," says Dr. Zisook. Prozac's trendiness shouldn't obscure the fact that the drug and its progeny help many people dramatically.

Despite her initial skepticism, for instance, Thompson found the drug "life transforming. I felt like myself again." Prozac also pulled Isabel Leigh up from despair. Leigh, 41, a New York City editor who has struggled with depression on and off for years, was reluctant to try the drug. "I didn't want to be just one more trendy Prozac taker," she says. "I told myself it was a crutch I could do without." But about a year ago she found herself feeling lethargic, hopeless and unable to concentrate; she withdrew from friends and let work slide. Finally Leigh went to a doctor and got a Prozac prescription. "It took a few weeks, but the difference was incredible," she says. "I realized I'd been trying to overcome a biochemical problem with willpower alone."

PROZAC PITFALLS

Glowing testimonials aside, Prozac isn't perfect. Like any currently available antidepressant, it works in only 60% to 70% of cases. There's often a lag of up to eight weeks before the drug starts working. And Prozac isn't free of side effects either: Potential problems include agitation, insomnia, headache and weight gain

or loss. What's more perhaps a third of those who stay on Prozac for nine months or more find that its uplifting effects fade away, a problem ingloriously known as "Prozac poopout." (Increasing the dose once or twice often helps.)

A growing number of studies also show that up to half of all Prozac users experience decreased libido and delayed or no orgasm. Sharon Keene, 39, a writer in Laguna Hills, CA, took Prozac for three months and "it seemed to help in just about every way," she says. "But I ended up stopping, because I couldn't achieve orgasm. If I wasn't married, maybe I wouldn't have cared so much, but it was affecting my relationship with my husband."

Though other SSRI's can impair sexual function too, Zoloft and Paxil leave the bloodstream faster than Prozac, so users may be able to circumvent trouble in bed by taking drug "holidays" a day or two before the act (so much for spontaneity). Serzone, on the market since 1995, is kinder to users' sex lives. So is Wellbutrin, a medication with a slightly different mechanism of action than Serzone and the SSRI's. It does add a very slight risk of seizures, though....

The bottom line: None of the new antidepressants is clearly superior. "They all have advantages and disadvantages," says Dr. Zisook. "We never know with certainty which drug will work best. There's always some trial and error involved."

THE PRICE OF FAME

As the leader of the pack, Prozac is often the drug of choice by benefit of name recognition alone. But its fame works against it too. Even today Prozac's reputation is clouded by rumors it can't quite shake. Within two years of its introduction in the U.S., headlines and lawsuits began claiming that Prozac drives some users to bizarre, violent behavior. One notorious 1989 incident, the subject of a new book called *The Power to Harm* by John Cornwell, involved a 47-year-old printing plant worker who shot 20 coworkers and then committed suicide after being on Prozac. Survivors and relatives of the victims sued Eli Lilly and lost, but the damage to Prozac's reputation was done.

Today you can surf the Net and still find horror stories from disgruntled folks in "Prozac survivor" support groups. Mary Beth Mrozek, a 33-year-old Buffalo, NY, mother of three who has bipolar illness, says that while on the drug she hallucinated, became convinced people were plotting against her and violently attacked loved ones. "I was a totally different person," she says.

Should the average Prozac user worry about having a Jekyll and Hyde reaction? Bipolar patients who take Prozac may be at slightly higher risk for an episode of mania. But that's a risk associated with any antidepressant (though possibly less so with Wellbutrin). Based on a substantial body of research, experts agree that Prozac users overall aren't at greater risk for violent or suicidal behavior. In fact, says Dr. Norden, "Depressed people who avoid Prozac are probably placing themselves in greater danger. Nothing increases suicide risk as much as depression itself."

A CANCER CONNECTION?

Perhaps a more realistic worry involves unknowns about the long-term effects of Prozac and the other SSRI's, especially since some users drugs are now staying on the drugs indefinitely. A slender body of evidence, based mostly on animal and very preliminary human studies, suggests that antidepressants, including Prozac, could accelerate tumor growth in some people who have a predisposition to cancer or preexisting tumors. Not surprisingly, Eli Lilly disputes these findings. "Lilly's long-term animal studies have bene extensively reviewed by the FDA," says Freda Lewis-Hall, M.D., a psychiatrist who heads the Lilly Center for Women's Health in Indianapolis. "There is absolutely no scientifically credible evidence that it either causes or promotes cancer."

Not everyone agrees. Oncologist Lorne Brandes, M.D., of the Manitoba Cancer Treatment and Research Foundation in Winnipeg, Canada, questions how carefully Lilly interpreted some of its data. But at the same time, he says that antidepressants are "absolutely warranted to treat depression. I'd just suggest trying to get off them as soon as you comfortably can."

Ultimately, however, we may remember Prozac not for its side effects, trendiness or even its effectiveness, but for the attention it has focused on depression —and that can only benefit women in the end. "Once, to be depressed was to be morally and spiritually weak," says Dr. Zisook. "Now people in line at the grocery story are talking about being on Prozac. The drug has brought depression out of the closet."

Leigh, for one, is grateful that it did. "It's not like I have a perfect life with Prozac," she says. "I still have ups and downs. But now I know that if I do get down, I'll come back up. Before Prozac, I was never sure."

POSTSCRIPT

Is Prozac Overprescribed?

Mental health practitioners generally agree that Prozac is effective for treating cases of moderate depression. It is also prescribed, however, for people who suffer from obsessive-compulsive disorders, eating disorders, and phobias. Most recently, Prozac has been shown to help women who suffer from premenstrual syndrome (PMS). Increasingly, Prozac is being employed just to improve people's moods. As a result, questions are being raised as to whether or not Prozac is being overprescribed. Opinion within the scientific community is divided over its benefits.

The debate regarding Prozac has spurred other concerns: Should it be prescribed for common problems that people encounter on a daily basis, such as stress or feelings of irritation? Can one find happiness in a pill? Is Prozac a quick and easy fix? Is it ethical to chemically alter an individual's personality? Will psychopharmacology replace traditional psychotherapy? Is the rapid growth of Prozac a well-conceived promotion on the part of pharmaceutical companies? In a society that values solving problems quickly and easily, Prozac seems to effectively fulfill a need. However, do the advantages of Prozac outweigh its disadvantages? The answer to this question depends on who is being asked. One thing is certain: the growth in sales of Prozac has increased annually.

A popular slogan years back referred to "better living through chemistry." If a drug is available that will make people feel happier, more confident, and more socially adept, shouldn't that drug be available for people who would derive some degree of benefit from it? One concern is that some individuals may rely on drugs to remedy many of their problems rather than work through the issues that caused the problems in the first place. Many people now use alcohol or illegal drugs to cope with life's problems. It is difficult to foresee what the effects would be if people could rely on legally prescribed drugs to remedy their problems.

Several articles in *CQ Researcher* (August 19, 1994) deal with the controversy surrounding Prozac, how antidepressant drugs work, the early history of the drug, and the outlook for Prozac. Susan Brink's article "Singing the Prozac Blues," *U.S. News and World Report* (November 8, 1993) and several articles in *Newsweek* (February 7, 1994) cast doubt on the use of Prozac. In his book *Talking Back to Prozac* (St. Martin's Press), Peter Breggin, an outspoken psychiatrist who is very critical of Prozac, asserts that the research supporting the benefits of Prozac are highly questionable. Finally, Peter Kramer provides a brief outline of his experiences with Prozac in "The Transformation of Personality," *Psychology Today* (July/August 1993).

On the Internet . . .

The Center for Substance Abuse Prevention (CSAP)
The Center for Substance Abuse Prevention promotes the development of comprehensive drug prevention systems related to community, state, national, and international needs. *http://www.samhsa.gov/csap.htm*

Join Together
Join Together is a resource center and meeting place for communities working to reduce the harms associated with the use of illicit drugs, excessive alcohol, and to-bacco. Join Together helps communities raise money to support prevention and treatment activities. *http://www.jointogether.org/*

The Center for Substance Abuse Treatment (CSAT)
The Center for Substance Abuse Treatment works coop-eratively with private and public treatment facilities to identify, develop, and support policies, approaches, and programs that enhance and expand substance abuse treat-ment. *http://www.samhsa.gov/csat/csat.htm*

National Council on Alcoholism and Drug Dependence (NCADD)
The National Council on Alcoholism and Drug Depen-dence provides education, information, help, and hope in the fight against the chronic, often fatal, disease of al-coholism and other drug addictions. *http://www.ncadd.org/*

PART 3

Drug Prevention and Treatment

In spite of their legal consequences and the government's interdiction efforts, drugs are widely available and used. Two common ways of dealing with drug abuse is to incarcerate drug users and to intercept drugs before they enter the country. However, many drug experts believe that more energy should be put into preventing and treating drug abuse. An important step toward prevention and treatment is to find out what contributes to drug abuse and how to nullify these factors.

By educating young people about the potential hazards of drugs and by developing an awareness of social influences that contribute to drug use, many drug-related problems may be averted. The debates in this section focus on different prevention and treatment issues and the value of related policies and programs.

■ Should the FDA Prohibit Tobacco Advertising?

■ Is Total Abstinence the Only Choice for an Alcoholic?

■ Is Drug Abuse Resistance Education (DARE) an Effective Program?

■ Should the Decision to Use Anabolic Steroids Be Left to Athletes?

■ Should Drug Treatment Services Be Expanded?

ISSUE 14

Should the FDA Prohibit Tobacco Advertising?

YES: Richard W. Pollay, from "Hacks, Flacks, and Counter-Attacks: Cigarette Advertising, Sponsored Research, and Controversies," *Journal of Social Issues* (1997)

NO: Barbara Dority, from "The Rights of Joe Camel and the Marlboro Man," *The Humanist* (January–February 1997)

ISSUE SUMMARY

YES: Richard W. Pollay, a professor of business, argues for greater regulation of the tobacco industry because it has a history of presenting misleading and inaccurate information. Pollay also maintains that cigarette advertising influences the perceptions, attitudes, and smoking behavior of young people.

NO: Barbara Dority, president of Humanists of Washington, supports free speech even if that means protecting the rights of the tobacco industry to advertise. Dority feels that the government should be less intrusive. If it wants to reduce youth smoking, then the government should place more emphasis on education.

Scientific evidence clearly indicates that smoking causes numerous adverse health conditions. This debate, however, is not about whether or not tobacco is hazardous, but whether or not the Food and Drug Administration (FDA) has the right to ban tobacco advertising. Several questions need to be considered: Do tobacco advertisements encourage smoking, especially among adolescents? Would a ban on tobacco advertisements reduce smoking behavior? Should tobacco companies have the right to promote their products as they wish, and do they have a constitutional right to freedom of speech? If tobacco advertisements are prohibited, should other potentially unhealthy products such as high-fat foods, tanning beds, and guns be prohibited also? Are tobacco companies being unfairly targeted? Would the prohibition of tobacco advertisements violate the rights of tobacco companies? How much responsibility does the consumer have for his or her behavior?

In 1970 the Public Health Cigarette Smoking Act was passed, which banned cigarette advertisements from television and radio (advertisements for smokeless tobacco were unaffected). Since that time, cigarette advertisements have become much more prevalent in the print media and on roadside billboards. Although cigarettes are not directly advertised on television, their presence on television is unmistakable. Tobacco companies sponsor many televised sporting activities, especially automobile racing, and signs at various stadiums, which are frequently caught on camera, prominently display tobacco advertisements. Critics contend that many of these advertisements are geared toward target populations, notably adolescents and minorities. One of the most successful advertising campaigns is R.J. Reynolds Tobacco Company's Joe Camel. Over 90 percent of 6-year-olds were able to match the Joe Camel cartoon character with the cigarette that it was promoting. Sales of Camel cigarettes escalated from $6 million to $476 million after the Joe Camel advertisements were introduced.

Many critics contend that stricter controls need to be put in place to eliminate the manipulative effects that tobacco advertising campaigns have on target audiences as well as on the general public. There is much concern that tobacco is a "gateway drug" that paves the way for other, illegal types of drug use, such as marijuana, cocaine, heroin, and LSD. Experts agree that the longer young people wait before they smoke cigarettes, if they even do choose to smoke, the less likely they will be to use other drugs. Young people often have difficulty internalizing the long-term consequences of their behavior because they are more concerned with meeting their immediate needs.

Supporters of the tobacco industry and advertising executives claim that there is no compelling evidence that a causal link exists between advertising and smoking initiation and behavior. Moreover, advertisers contend that they do not market their tobacco products to young people. Advertising, they claim, is used to enhance brand loyalty. They also argue that banning advertising violates their right to free speech.

How much of the responsibility for adolescent smoking lies with young people? Many people argue that smoking is done under one's own volition. What is the impact of parental smoking on children? Studies show that children of smokers are more likely to smoke than children whose parents do not smoke. Children with older siblings who smoke are also more likely to smoke than those whose immediate family members are all nonsmokers. Besides parents, children are exposed to other role models, such as teachers, civic leaders, athletes, health care workers, and clergy. What is the effect of their smoking (or not smoking) on the behavior of children around them? Curiosity and experimentation are very common among adolescents. If a young person experiments with cigarettes out of curiosity, can advertising be blamed?

In the following selections, Richard W. Pollay espouses the view that restricting tobacco advertising is an important first step in decreasing smoking rates, particularly among young people. Pollay maintains that tobacco companies misrepresent the research regarding the effects of tobacco advertising on smoking behavior. Barbara Dority contends that banning or censoring cigarette advertisements is socially and legally wrong. She argues that education, not censorship, is the key to reducing adolescent smoking.

YES

Richard W. Pollay

HACKS, FLACKS, AND COUNTER-ATTACKS: CIGARETTE ADVERTISING, SPONSORED RESEARCH, AND CONTROVERSIES

The tobacco industry is acknowledged as outstanding for its ability to promote "friendly" research, to denigrate research inimical to its interests as prohibitionist propaganda (Jones, 1996), and "to produce and manage uncertainty" (Proctor, 1995, p. 105). At their extreme, critics are denigrated as a conspiracy of overzealous crusaders exhibiting totalitarianism (Boddewyn, 1986b). The industry's strategy doesn't require winning or resolution of the debates its principals manage to create or inflame. It is enough to foster and perpetuate the illusion of controversy in order to "muddy the waters" around potentially damaging studies and streams of research. This serves at least two important ends: offering reassurance and a basis for rationalization to the otherwise concerned, thereby calming public opinion; and encouraging friendly, ignorant, or naive legislators away from relying on scientific findings threatening to the industry. These tactics are now being used on many fronts of the tobacco battlefield.

The tobacco industry's first major success with this strategy was in combating the so-called "health scare" from the early lung cancer studies of the 1950s. Industry leaders gathered seeds of doubt from around the world, and reproduced and disseminated these through a massive public relations machinery (Pollay, 1990b). Encouraged by that success, they have continued to muddy the waters around the scientific findings relevant to almost every aspect of tobacco and its control, including: heart disease; passive or second-hand smoke; addiction; the medical and larger social costs consequential to smoking; the economic consequences of regulation, etc. Where necessary, as in the case of indoor air quality, they have even turned small local businessmen into apparent international authorities (Mintz, 1996). Of course, they prefer to employ those who seem to be independent from the industry, because trade organizations like the Tobacco Institute are admittedly biased. "We don't pretend to be objective, unbiased or fair.... We represent a

From Richard W. Pollay, "Hacks, Flacks, and Counter-Attacks: Cigarette Advertising, Sponsored Research, and Controversies," *Journal of Social Issues*, vol. 53, no. 1 (1997), pp. 53–74. Copyright © 1997 by Blackwell Publishers. Reprinted by permission. References omitted.

commercially vested interest" (Cosco, 1988, p. 8). It should be no surprise, then, that these tactics are also used to combat the issue of cigarette advertising and its effects, particularly its role in recruiting new smokers.

For example, when Fischer et al. (1991) measured product logo recognition of three-to-six-year-olds, they found over 90 percent of the six-year-olds could correctly match the cartoon Camel with cigarettes. So threatening was this result that industry-hired academic consultants attacked the study with or without the benefit of added research (Boddewyn, 1993; Martin, 1993; Mizerski, 1995). Their primary line of attack was to allege that this work was methodologically "inferior," in part because it had been authored, reviewed and published by and for medical experts, rather than marketing or advertising experts. The finding of high awareness among the very young has since been replicated by marketing academics (Henke, 1994), and even by the R. J. Reynolds–sponsored researcher (Mizerski, 1995), although this report is notable for downplaying this embarrassing fact and, instead, emphasizing allegations of methodological weaknesses of the original. More recently, Pollay's (1996) report that teens were three times as responsive to cigarette advertising as adults drew instant and inaccurate attacks from the Tobacco Institute as "a great deal of sound and fury signifying nothing" and "flatly contradicted" by a study sponsored by R. J. Reynolds (Stolberg, 1996).

The standard response of the industry to concerns about children and cigarette advertising has been to insist that "kids just don't pay attention to cigarette ads.... (Our advertising) purpose is to get smokers of competitive products to switch... virtually the only way a cigarette brand can meaningfully increase its business" (R. J. Reynolds, 1984), a thesis uncritically echoed by some others (e.g., Boddewyn. 1986b). The belief and assertion is that cigarette advertising is of little consequence, at least with respect to the young (e.g., Boddewyn, 1989; Reid, 1989; Ward, 1989). This assertion, so counter to common sense, is argued on theoretical grounds. Because cigarettes seem to be a so-called "mature" industry, i.e., one which has completed its dynamic growth and reached a stasis, it is claimed that its advertising and promotional activity can and does affect only brand-switching behavior among established adult smokers. By neither intent nor effect, tobacco industry magnates would have us believe, does cigarette advertising influence young people, reassure and retain existing smokers who might otherwise quit, or induce current smokers to smoke more—several of the ways in which advertising might conceivably influence primary demand....

No Known Industry Documents Employ the "Mature Market" Concept

To date, no corporate documents have been produced in litigation or research reports to verify that the "mature market" classification is relied upon by the industry in its internal strategic analyses, nor has any evidence of any kind been offered in support of the "mature market" opinions expressed by industry-advanced experts like Ward (1989). Reid (1989), when testifying for the industry, ignored the literature equivocal about the concept's validity, the literature specific to the cigarette industry, and the contradictory profit and advertising expenditure data. He ignored all the many corporate documents produced in the same litigation documenting the consumer research and advertising strategies focused on young starters (Pollay & Lavack, 1993). He even ignored his own observation, surely fitting cigarettes, that given "the existence of an undesirable image, advertising can play a major role" (Reid & Rotfeld, 1976, p. 26). Testimony like this that offers theoretical conjectures, while ignoring the relevant literature and the available case facts, is not merely speculative, but quite literally ignorant and prejudicial....

Enormous Promotional Budgets Cannot Be Justified by "Adult Brand Switching" Alone

The cigarette market may seem, to the naive, to be stable and, therefore, to be a so-called "mature market" because total sales seem nearly constant. This appearance, however, hides the dynamics of substantial rates of quitting attempts, quitting successes, and dying—and the countervailing rates of recruitment of hundreds of thousands of new smokers. Maintaining constancy of market size involves recruiting over a million new smokers a year, and almost all smokers are recruited as minors, not as consenting adults.

Brand-switching alone cannot easily justify the enormous advertising and promotional expenditures, over $6 billion a year in 1993, larger than Hollywood's gross income from the United States and Canada combined (Kilday & Thompson, 1995). Brand switchers are an unattractive market segment, as they are typically older, health-concerned, or symptomatic smokers, thus relatively frail in constitution, in addition to being fickle by definition. They are also few in number. Siegel et al. (1996), after noting that less than 10 percent of smokers will switch in any

given year, estimate that the total profit from all "company switching" was $362 million, small compared to the costs of the battle of these brands. Accounting for sales in future years, the net present value of a new smoker to the cigarette companies has been estimated as US $1,085 (Tye, Warner, & Glantz, 1987).

If cigarette advertising had no effect on smoking recruitment, as the industry contends, a ban on advertising expenditures of this magnitude should and would be welcomed by savvy oligopolists like the tobacco industry. Indeed, a ban would benefit the larger firms the most, by saving them the enormous promotional expense and helping to freeze their large market shares. Thus, if advertising had no effect on primary demand, profit-maximizing firms and industries would curtail advertising competition, just as they would refrain from cut-throat price competition, and the largest firms would be expected to act as leaders in this self-restraint. Failing a tacit collusion to this end, the industry would eagerly seize the opportunity provided by regulatory proposals to ban advertising, with the larger firms the most motivated to do so. The fact that cigarette companies, led by the largest, are lobbying so hard against advertising bans or controls of any kind is illogical —unless the advertising and promotion has the effect of enticing new smokers. As Davis (1996, p. 3) stated: "The reason for the industry's failure to support a federal ban on tobacco advertising must be that... the companies must indeed perceive an industry-wide benefit to advertising and promotion." Failing that, they could save themselves all the spending on advertising that only attacked or defended market shares.

No Isolation or Immunity Protects Youth from Cigarette Ads

There is no way to isolate teens and pre-teens from popular culture and media, including cigarette advertising's inducements. The absence of a "magic curtain" around children obviates any "convincing defense of a view that would make young nonsmokers immune" (Cohen, 1990, p. 240–241). Those empowered with self-regulatory responsibilities in the National Association of Broadcasters (NAB) saw this vividly for the medium of television: "The difficulty in cigarette advertising is that commercials which have an impact upon an adult cannot be assumed to leave unaffected a young viewer, smoker or otherwise" (Bell, 1966, p. 30–31). Even a Marlboro ad man admitted after retiring, "I don't know any way of doing this that doesn't tempt young people to smoke" (Daniels, 1974, p. 245). Consistent with these views, newer research indicates that the likelihood of adolescent smoking is related to ad exposure rates (Botvin et al., 1993).

Advertising Gives the Cigarette "Friendly Familiarity"

Cigarette advertising is so pervasive and ubiquitous that cigarettes are a cultural commonplace, taken for granted by the public, and treated as less risky than appropriate. We are all aware of the reverse of this, when we feel suspicion of the unfamiliar. This positive effect is called "friendly familiarity" by advertising professionals (Burnett, 1961, p. 217).

"The ubiquitous display of messages promoting tobacco use clearly fosters an environment in which experimentation by youth is expected, if not explicitly encouraged" (Bonnie & Lynch, 1994, p. 34). "The kind of advertising that is almost everywhere makes cigarets (*sic*) respectable and is therefore reassuring," according to Social Research Inc. (*Cigarets: who buys*, 1952, p. 23). Repetition, oft referred to as the soul of persuasion, likely biases both risk and social perceptions, such as assessments of smoking prevalence, and/or the social acceptance experienced by smokers, according to both consumer behavior and psychology experts (e.g., Cohen, 1990; Fishbein, 1977). This phenomenon is well known to psychologists as the "familiarity effect" (Zajonc, 1980).

The Perceptions and Judgments of Youth Are Known to Be Biased

The young do, in fact, overestimate the prevalence of cigarette smoking among both peers and adults, and the degree of this overestimation is among the strongest predictors of smoking initiation (e.g., Chassin et al., 1984). They also underestimate the negative attitudes of peers and the risks to which they personally are exposed should they smoke. Youths are also inclined to manifest an "invulnerability syndrome" (Greening & Dollinger, 1991). Youths tend to both "exaggerate the social benefit (by overestimating the prevalence and popularity of smoking among peers and adults) and to underestimate the risks (by underestimating the prevalence of negative attitudes toward smoking held by their peers)" (Bonnie & Lynch, 1994, p. 34). Another literature review concludes that "cigarette advertising appears to influence young people's perceptions of the pervasiveness, image, and function of smoking. Since misperceptions in these areas constitute psychosocial risk factors for the initiation of smoking, cigarette advertising appears to increase young people's risk of smoking" (USDHHS,

1994, p. 195). These facts seriously undermine the notion that the uptake of smoking is an informed choice or decision (Leventhal, Glynn, & Fleming, 1987). Irrespective of this naiveté, it is a misbehavior of minors, not consenting adults.

Cigarette Imagery Appeals to Adolescents

Cigarette ads often feature veritable pictures of health, depicting bold and lively behavior typically in pure and pristine outdoor environments (Pollay, 1991, 1993a; USDHHS 1994). The images of cigarette ads portray themes known to appeal to young people, such as independence, adventure seeking, social approval, and sophistication. The theme of independence, in particular, so well captured by the Marlboro Man, strikes a responsive chord with the dominant psychological need of adolescents for autonomy and freedom from authority. Adolescent girls feel the same needs for autonomy as do boys, accounting for the otherwise surprising popularity of the Marlboro brand among girls. Motivation research confirms the insights of previous advertisers and public relations professionals in seeing smoking as an expression of freedom and worldliness for women (Martineau, 1957). It seems no coincidence that marketers of female brands "try to tap the emerging independence and self-fulfillment of women, to make smoking a badge to express that" (Waldman, 1989, p. 81).

In addition, some of the models in cigarette advertisements appear particularly youthful (Mazis et al., 1992). This isn't all that common, however, as cigarette firms know that teens desire symbols of adulthood, not symbols of youth (e.g., hard rock vs. "bubble gum" music). Imagery-based ads are potentially insidious, in contrast to verbal assertions which require cognitive processing. Imagery is taken in at a glance, experienced more than thought about, tending to "bypass logical analysis." Because of this, imagery advertising is deemed "transformational" rather than informational (Cohen, 1990). The old adage says "seeing is believing," and cigarette ads use carefully tuned images to create positive experiences, while being careful to avoid precipitating cognitive counter-argumentation.

The Tobacco Industry Has Long Displayed a Strategic Interest in Youth

The industry has demonstrated an interest in the youth market in its planning documents, market research activities, and media plans for many decades (USDHHS, 1994, Pollay, 1995). Ads have been placed on billboards near schools and malls, and in after-school radio spots with effective reach into youth markets. The TV advertising schedules bought in the 1960s reflected a preference for those times with the higher proportions of delivered teenagers, not adults (Pollay, 1994a, 1994b). R. J. Reynolds' 1973 "Research Planning Document on Some Thoughts about New Brands for the Youth Market" described programs for appealing to "learning smokers" (Schwartz, 1995). Philip Morris found that almost half of the non-smoking girls "share many of the same values as the smokers and are highly exposed to the total smoking environment. We call them the 'Vulnerables' for, on the surface, they appear to be ready candidates for the next wave of new smokers" (Udow, 1976, H7664).

Copy concepts for many brands focus on independence, with the adolescent need for autonomy and self-reliance known by the industry to be a dominant one (USDHHS, 1994). The success of starter brands, according to trial evidence, is the result of carefully planned and executed strategies, guided throughout by extensive research (Pollay & Lavack, 1993). Corporate research documents discuss the behavior, knowledge, and attitudes of eleven-, twelve-, and thirteen-year-olds and media plans specify targets beginning at age fifteen, with willingness to pay as much for ad exposures to fifteen-year-old nonsmokers as to smokers. R. J. Reynolds' Canadian affiliate, for example, commissioned customization of "Youth Target Study '87" and got extensive data on subjects as young as fifteen.

The need to have a strategic interest in youth has long been recognized by the industry, and used to be freely admitted to. For example, just before the Surgeon General's Report of 1964, an advertising trade magazine, *Sponsor* ("What will happen," 1963), noted pro-health education with concern and asked: "If, however, impressionable youngsters are now approached mostly by the anti-smoking fraternity, how will cigarette sales fare 10 years hence?" Note, too, that this also demonstrates the long time spans appropriate in understanding cigarette advertising's effects, which are generational rather than instantaneous, inculcative rather than impulse-generating.

Adolescence Is a Time of Identity Formation and Advertising Attentiveness

"Cigarette advertising's cultural function is much more than the selling of cigarettes. Its collective images represent a corpus of deeply rooted cultural mythologies that are not simply pieces of advertising creativity, but icons that pose solutions to real, experienced problems of identity" (Chapman & Fitzgerald, 1982, p. 494). The National Association of Broadcasters knew this when trying to help the industry self-regulate TV ads. "The adult world depicted in cigarette advertising very often is a world to which the adolescent aspires.... To the young, smoking indeed may seem to be an important step towards, and a help in growth from adolescence to maturity" (Bell, 1966, p. 30–31).

Youths are alert to popular culture for cues and clues as to what's hot and what's not. They attend to advertising for symbols of adulthood, but pay only scant attention to warnings (Fletcher et al., 1995). "Teens are also more susceptible to the images of romance, success, sophistication, popularity, and adventure which advertising suggests they could achieve through the consumption of cigarettes" (Nichter & Cartwright, 1991, p. 242). Even brief cigarette ad exposures in lab settings can result in more favorable thoughts about smokers, enhance attitudes, increase awareness and change brand preferences of the young (Hoek, Gendall, & Stockdale, 1993; Pechmann & Ratneshwar, 1994).

This is consistent with consumer behavior knowledge as reflected in textbooks and journals. "Teenagers have become increasingly aware of new products and brands. They are natural 'triers'" (Loudon & Della Bitta, 1993, p. 151). They have "a lot of uncertainty about the self, and the need to belong and to find one's unique identity... (so) teens actively search for cues from their peers and from advertising for the right way to look and behave... (becoming) interested in many different products" that can express their needs for "experimentation, belonging, independence, responsibility, and approval from others" (Solomon, 1994, pp. 503–504). By high school, possessions and "badge products" like cigarettes are used as instruments for defining and controlling relations between people (Stacey, 1982).

As a 1974 RJR memo states: "To some extent young smokers 'wear' their cigarette and it becomes an important part of the 'I' they wish to be, along with their clothing and the way they style their hair" (Schwartz, 1996, p. A3). One starter brand in Canada, according to the R. J. Reynolds affiliate who marketed it, was popular with "very young starter smokers ... because it provides them with an instant badge of masculinity, appeals to their rebellious nature and establishes their position amongst their peers" (Pollay & Lavack, 1993, pp. 268–269). Adults, in contrast, are not caught up in the processes of identity experimentation and formation. They are not as searching of their environment for consumption items symbolic of aspirational identities.

The image and badge aspects of brands are especially important to ethnic minorities. "While this is of utmost importance when marketing cigarettes in general, we feel it assumes even more importance when marketing cigarettes to blacks. Because blacks in general tend to be more insecure, for obvious reasons, it is critical that the public cigarette badge they adopt be one that supports what they are looking for in terms of psychological reassurance" (Reeves, 1979, p. 3). Thus, the Newport name has the virtue of connoting "quality and class," because of associations with status symbols such as Newport Beach and the Newport Jazz Festivals.

Youths Are Persuasion-Coping Novices
The young, as consumers, tend to be less experienced in counterarguing against advertising and selling tactics, as well as more brand-conscious than older consumers (Brucks, Armstrong, & Goldberg, 1988; McNeal, 1992). They are also less experienced as shoppers, with fewer experiences of salesmen and persuasion tactics. Friestad and Wright (1994, p. 7) note that "novices in coping with advertising or selling encounters may recognize only simple, superficial patterns in these events and have little proficiency with self-regulatory processes ... (and) coping strategies." Adults, with their longer histories, particularly as smokers, have less interest in, and greater resistance to, the temptations and appeals of most new brands and/or ad campaigns.

Cigarette Addictiveness and Brand Loyalty Make Adults Proverbial "Old Dogs"
Cigarettes enjoy phenomenally high brand loyalty, the highest of all consumer products (e.g., Alsop, 1989). A relatively low rate of brand switching is the norm, usually 10 percent or less (Cohen, 1990, p. 239; FTC, 1985; Gardner, 1984; Siegel et al., 1996). Some of this nominal switching occurs only within brand families (e.g. from Brand X milds to Brand X lights), and is of little net consequence to the firm's sales or net profit. The high brand loyalty that naturally results from nicotine "satisfaction" of addictive physiological needs makes it very difficult and expensive to convert competitors' customers to your brands. Also, the bulk of the brand switching is the behavior of older, health-concerned or symptomatic smokers who are trading down, typically within a brand family, to products with lower tar and nicotine labeling, in the

mistaken belief that those products are safe(r), a belief fostered by years of advertising.

Youths Are Strategically More Attractive Than Adults

The trade of these older customers offers firms very little future and net present value, compared with the value inherent in attracting young starters, the bulk of whom will be brand-loyal (Tye, Warner, & Glantz, 1987). "This is a time when brand loyalties may be formed that could last well into adulthood" (Loudon & Della Bitta, 1993, p. 152, citing Moschis & Moore, 1981). The young are a "perpetually new market... thus a marketer must not neglect young consumers who come 'on stream' if the company's brand is to have continued success in the older-age market" (Loudon & Della Bitta, 1993, p. 155). Teens are a strategically important target audience, because brand loyalty is often developed during this time and this creates a "barrier-to-entry for other brands not chosen during these pivotal years" (Solomon, 1994, p. 504).

The death and quitting rates among aging smokers means that sales would drop rapidly were it not for a continuing influx of new starters. This strategic situation has been obvious to the industry for some time. R. J. Reynolds' research and development officers wrote in 1973: "Realistically, if our Company is to survive and prosper, over the long term, we must get our share of the youth market" (Schwartz, 1995). Contemporary corporate documents echo this idea, stating that "young smokers represent the major opportunity group for the cigarette industry," and "if the last ten years have taught us anything, it is that the industry is dominated by the companies who respond most effectively to the needs of younger smokers" (Pollay & Lavack, 1993, p. 267).

Teens Are Three Times More Responsive Than Adults to Cigarette Ads

The latest research (Pollay et al., 1996) uses state-of-the-art techniques to analyze market share as a function of relative advertising, also known as *share of voice*. This measures the impact of cigarette brand advertising on realized market shares, allowing for both current and historical effects of advertising for nine major brands over twenty years. The results, which are robust under many alternative assumptions, show that brand choices among teenagers are significantly related to relative cigarette advertising. Moreover, the relationship between brand choices and brand advertising is significantly stronger among teenagers than among adults by a factor of about three. The greater advertising sensitivity among teenagers is in part due to *scale* (i.e., high fractions of teens concentrated on highly advertised brands), and in part due to *dynamics* (i.e., teen purchase patterns being more responsive to changes in advertising intensity). Further, the impact of advertising on brand choices among youth apparently cannot be dismissed as an inappropriate attribution (i.e., teenagers actually imitating adult brand choices rather than responding to advertising). Even when this aspect is factored into the analysis, the result remains consistent.

Greater advertising sensitivity among youth is consistent with earlier observations that brand choices of youth are highly concentrated on the most heavily advertised brands (CDC, 1992,

1994). California's Operation Storefront also found that "heavy advertising in stores exactly matches the brand preferences of children who smoke... but the ad prevalence does not match adult smoker preferences" (Hilts, 1995, p. B10). "Young people know advertising better, appreciate brand-stretching advertising more," and their ideal self-image matches the images offered by cigarette brands (Rombouts & Fauconnier, 1988; see also Aitken et al., 1987). A recent study (Pierce & Gilpin, 1995a, 1995b; Pierce, Lee, & Gilpin, 1994) reported data indicating that smoking rates among young women increased sharply in the late 1960s, coincidental with the launch of Virginia Slims and other nominally "female" brands.

Industry Apologists Typically Offer Weak Research, or None At All

The so-called "experts" that the industry gets to testify in courts and before legislative groups almost always offer opinions that are conspicuously ignorant of true corporate activity. Instead they opine based upon simplistic theorizing and conclusions. Martin told a court that cigarette ads can be of no appreciable import, no matter what their content or character, insulting the competencies of many advertising agencies, and judging their diverse efforts as all failing to alter public perceptions of the product, either individually or collectively. Perhaps the most simplistic and common position used to exculpate the industry is the "mature market" theory, discussed above, typically asserted with no corroborating evidence, perhaps because there is none to be had.

The industry has long relied on Boddewyn to argue that cigarette advertising doesn't influence children, but the survey methodology and logic reported in Boddewyn (1987) is totally inadequate, biased, and superficial. This research was sponsored by the international tobacco industry lobbying organization, conducted by a British contract research firm, and published by an American advocacy organization, not by a peer-reviewed scholarly journal or scientific body. Its conclusion is based solely on a self-report question asking children to select, from a list of thirteen offered reasons, only the most important reason for smoking their first cigarette. This question is, to my knowledge, without precedent in either academic research or trade practice as the sole means of validly assessing advertising's role and effects. Not surprisingly, few choose "I had seen advertising" as the most compelling reason, since to do so requires that advertising's influence be consciously appreciated, willingly admitted to, and predominant among all of the prompted reasons, rather than just a contributing factor. One wonders how many might have agreed or disagreed with a statement like "advertising makes cigarettes seem attractive." While the apologists for the cigarette industry have ignored this grievous weakness, they dramatically raise their critical methodological standards when encountering results threatening their tobacco clients' economic or legal interests (e.g., Boddewyn, 1989). Martin (1993), for example, took the initiative to canvas researchers with a detailed questionnaire soliciting criticism of Pierce et al. (1991), who had found the cartoon Camel well known to the very young, while never commenting on the fallaciousness of Boddewyn's data and conclusions, and his client's political use of same....

Advertising Experts and Trade Journals Doubt the Industry's Stance

Many ad executives, when confronted with the pioneering Surgeon General's Report, admitted that cigarette advertising influenced minors. John Orr Young, whose agency, Young & Rubicam, had cigarette experience, said that: "Advertising agencies are retained by cigaret (sic) manufacturers to create demand for cigarets among both adults and eager youngsters. The earlier the teenage-boy or girl gets the habit, the bigger the national sales volume" ("Agency would refuse," 1964a). Another leading advertising executive, the president of McManus, Johns, & Adams felt that "There is no doubt that all forms of advertising played a part in popularizing the cigaret (sic)" ("Make cigarets," 1964b).

Emerson Foote, a founder of Foote, Cone, and Belding, and later CEO of McCann-Erikson, bluntly debunked the industry claims that its advertising affects only brand switching and has no effect whatsoever on recruitment. "I don't think anyone really believes this... I suspect that creating a positive climate of social acceptability for smoking, which encourages new smokers to join the market, is of greater importance to the industry.... In recent years the cigarette industry has been artfully maintaining that cigarette advertising has nothing to do with total sales. Take my word for it, this is complete and utter nonsense" (Foote, 1981).

More currently, one advertising CEO comments generally that cigarette advertising is "even sicker than war. If you were to choose the ultimate insanity of our society, I'd put cigarette advertising at the top" (Horovitz, 1996). Another wrote about the cartoon Camel: "Those of us in the marketing business know

exactly what he's up to; we should be the first to denounce him" (DesRoches, 1994). A Philip Morris executive adds, "You don't have to be a brain surgeon to see what's going on. Just look at the ads. It's ludicrous for them to deny that a cartoon character like Joe Camel isn't attractive to kids" (Ecanbarger, 1993). This cartoon campaign has been described as "one of the most egregious examples in recent history of tobacco advertising targeted at children," encouraging even *Advertising Age* editors to urge that it be dropped (Cohen, 1994, p. 12).

The Industry's Latest Position Is Illogical and Ludicrous

The industry and its spokespersons would now have us believe that they have no influence at all on smoking onset, but that both their intent and the effect is exclusively on brand choice among existing smokers, now apparently admitted to include minors. When Pollay et al. (1996) reported on the impact of advertising on teens, a coalition of advertising groups, the Freedom to Advertise Coalition, said it "proves what we have been saying all along —that tobacco advertising is geared to influence market share among those people who already smoke" (Stolberg, 1996). This is saying that the firms' intentions and abilities are such that "we don't encourage children to smoke, only to switch brands." This has been satirized in editorial cartoons as a denial that cigarette advertisers entice kids to start smoking, because their marketing is aimed precisely at the second cigarette they smoke, not the first.

Research shows that the very young are aware of cigarette icons and associate these with both the product and brand. We also know that teens who have started smoking are substantially more affected by cigarette advertising than are adult smokers. Are the ones having their attitudes shaped at an early age all destined to make the perverse decision, from the advertisers' view, not to become smokers? Are the only ones who start smoking those who have had no awareness of, or attraction to, cigarette advertising they were exposed to while growing up (if, indeed, there can even be such a group of people)? Are those who start smoking, presumably despite their blindness and/or numbness to prior cigarette promotion, supposed to become instantly hypersensitive to it? Are we to believe that the children who have ignored advertising throughout their formative years suddenly are the only ones impacted by it?

As the perceptions, attitudes, and beliefs governing brand choice are influenced by cigarette advertising, it is totally implausible that those same brand perceptions, attitudes, and beliefs have no influence whatsoever on the temptation to start smoking. It is impossible to advertise a specific brand without also simultaneously advertising cigarettes as a product class. A Philip Morris marketing vice president, famous for managing Marlboro's success, once said, "A cigarette company's ads are not just competing with ads for other brands. You are competing with every other advertiser in America for a share of the consumer's mind" (Whiteside, 1974, p. 133). Advertising that makes a cigarette brand attractive inevitably also makes cigarette smoking attractive, at the very least the smoking of that brand. There is no known way to advertise so that only brand switching, but not product interest, is affected.

CONCLUSION

Creating the illusion of controversy is a worn-out tactic, and ought to be treated with incredulous cynicism by scholars and policymakers. In fact, there seems to be far less controversy about the role of advertising than a strong convergence of diverse streams of research and analysis. Strategic analysis indicates that new users are far more attractive to firms than the few, frail and fickle brand switchers. Historical analysis documents the industry's long-standing strategic interest in youth. Analysis of contemporary corporate documents shows this to be an intensifying interest, for it is among minors where virtually all starting of smoking occurs, and starting now occurs at younger ages than ever before. Content analyses of advertising show that cigarette advertising imagery is largely pictures of health and images of independence, known by the industry to resonate with adolescent needs for autonomy and freedom from authority. Behavioral analyses show that cigarette advertising constitutes a psychosocial risk factor. Not only is teen smoking behavior related to past and present advertising, but also this relationship is about three times stronger among teens than among adults. Meta-analysis has shown cigarette advertising elasticity to be positive.

This has important public policy implications. Whether intended or not, cigarette advertising is significantly related to youth smoking behavior. To the extent that advertising influences the use of cigarettes among a consumer group to whom their sale is illegal, the government has a legitimate interest in regulating cigarette advertising. Convergent analyses and results suggest that regulating cigarette advertising may be an effective policy intervention to influence smoking behavior among adolescents. This should at least address advertising whose character is likely to appeal to the young, and placement in media where exposure to the young is inevitable. The authors of the Institute of Medicine's literature review recommend that this be done at federal, state, and local levels, although this would require repealing current pre-emptive federal legislation (Bonnie & Lynch, 1994). For more on legislative options with respect to tobacco advertising, see Arbogast (1986), Blum and Myers (1993), Burns (1994), and Pytte (1990).

Given the many various analyses and diversity of evidence, it seems an inescapable conclusion that cigarette advertising plays a meaningful role in influencing the perceptions, attitudes, and smoking behavior of youth. It also seems appropriate for scholars to react to assertions that there are no such effects on youth with disbelief, and to suspect industry sponsorship as a likely basis for such assertions.

NO

Barbara Dority

THE RIGHTS OF JOE CAMEL
AND THE MARLBORO MAN

Joe Camel banned from *Rolling Stone* magazine? The Marlboro Man banished from billboards everywhere? The end of Winston Cup racing and Vantage golf tournaments? Never another Virginia Slims tennis match or musical performance?

Yes, if President Clinton and the Food and Drug Administration have their way. With the noble aim of cutting teenage smoking, they have proposed sweeping restrictions on advertising and images that "portray tobacco use as fun, independent, sexy, and glamorous."

These sweeping proposals do have some opponents besides the tobacco industry—but not many. Nobody likes to be that unpopular, especially in their own circles. I know I don't. But as an anti-censorship activist, I just can't get around the free-speech limitations implicit in these proposals. Sometimes I almost wish I could, for I truly detest tobacco products. But giving the government the power to enforce these restrictions is simply too dangerous to the First Amendment.

President Clinton's strategy for imposing restrictions on commercial speech began when the FDA declared nicotine an addictive drug—which it certainly is. But it's a perfectly legal addictive drug, just like alcohol. Putting aside for the moment the substantial issue of whether the state should make the use of certain substances for individual consumption a punishable crime in the first place, these particular proposals should be carefully examined.

The Clinton/FDA legislation includes banning tobacco billboards within 1,000 feet of any school or playground and allowing only black-and-white ads without pictures in materials read by two million teens or with more than a 15 percent youth readership. The sale or display by any store of caps, gym bags, and T-shirts with cigarette-brand logos would be a criminal offense. Brand-name sponsorship of sporting or entertainment events would be prohibited. Cigarette machines would be banned from grocery stores, restaurants, and all other places where a teen might wander.

From Barbara Dority, "The Rights of Joe Camel and the Marlboro Man," *The Humanist*, vol. 57, no. 1 (January/February 1997). Copyright © 1997 by Barbara Dority. Reprinted by permission.

Last, but not least, the six tobacco companies whose brands teens use most would be ordered to help the FDA create televised health warnings and other educational materials at a cost to the industry of millions of dollars.

When did it become appropriate for the president or any federal agency to dictate which legal products can be advertised, where, when, and in what manner? In a capitalist, free-enterprise society (whether or not we endorse such a system), should we give the state the comprehensive power to limit free speech by censoring the contents of ads for certain legal products? Should the government be doing this to a legitimate industry (whether or not we think it should be a legitimate industry notwithstanding) that produces and sells a legal product grown with the help of government subsidies? And can that industry be forced by the state to pay for advertising that disparages its own products?

Despite my attempts to get around it, there's something very wrong about all this. It really sticks in my throat. As much as I'd love to see the tobacco companies go out of business altogether, these proposals reek of unfairness. Worse yet, they would impose government censorship on a massive scale. "There are serious constitutional problems with the majority of the new regulations," says First Amendment expert Martin Redish, professor of law at Northwestern University. That's putting it mildly.

Most of the proposed regulations are being challenged in a pair of federal lawsuits filed in North Carolina by the tobacco and advertising industries. (The total absence of any free-speech organizations from this conflict is glaring.) U.S. District Judge William Osteen has ordered briefs discussing the FDA's authority to issue such regulations and whether or not they would violate the First Amendment. The first scheduled court date [was] February 10, 1997.

While it is true that the courts have never interpreted the First Amendment as giving absolute protection to all speech and have given governments more leeway to regulate advertising than other types of expression, existing case law leaves no doubt that advertising is entitled to most free-speech protections.

In a 1980 ruling, the Supreme Court said that commercial speech that is truthful, not misleading, and concerns a legal activity may be somewhat limited only if the government can establish a specific interest in doing so, if the limitation directly advances that interest, and if the limitation is the least restrictive means to serve that interest.

In May 1996, the Supreme Court ruled unanimously that Rhode Island and other states cannot prohibit ads which list or refer to liquor prices, thus adding significantly to the protection historically afforded to commercial speech. Although the case (*44 Liquormart v. Rhode Island*) focused solely on liquor-price advertising, legal scholars believe it will also apply to government efforts to regulate other potentially harmful products and activities.

It is interesting that in the *Liquormart* case, the government argued that state control over alcohol is unique because the Twenty-first Amendment, which ended Prohibition, gave states the power to control liquor sales or even to ban them completely. The High Court disagreed. "Such an advertising ban is an abridgement of speech protected by the First Amendment and . . . it is not shielded from constitutional scrutiny by the Twenty-first

Amendment," wrote Justice John Paul Stevens in the Court ruling.

Unfortunately, this recent ruling did not prod Clinton or the FDA into rethinking their position. "Politics is what's going on here, despite painfully obvious First Amendment problems," says Cameron DeVore, another First Amendment specialist in Seattle, Washington. How sad that even the First Amendment is fair game as a sacrifice to political expediency.

I have never smoked. It's a disgusting habit, and it kills people in a very messy and painful manner. Personally, I think anyone who purposefully inflicts lung cancer upon themselves is bent on self-destruction. However, I don't believe that regulating the disgusting or harmful use of legal products by its citizens is a proper role for the state.

Underlying the impulse to control certain personal choices "for our own good" is another equally strong (or stronger) motivation: these are "sinful" products and behaviors that offend the moral sensibilities of the regulators. Certain things are "vices" which lead to sinful temptation and, as such, are an exception to commercial free-speech protections. But government has no business forcing such moralism upon its citizens.

Accordingly, the *Liquormart* decision precludes the argument that tobacco ads can be regulated for "promoting vice." So the Clinton administration is trying to create a "kid" exception to free speech. If it's illegal to sell cigarettes to minors, it reasons, it must be all right to suppress tobacco ads that underage potential customers may see.

The problem with this rationale is the same one we encounter when we attempt to keep certain reading and viewing materials away from children: adults live in the same space children do. In previous decisions, the Supreme Court has made it clear that government cannot create a situation that renders what's available in our society to the level of what is suitable for children.

Clinton and the FDA also insist that their proposed regulations meet the Supreme Court's standard of "substantial government interest to protect children." But they have to prove this assertion—and I don't think they can.

"Is the use of a cartoon character in an ad proof that you're 'targeting children'?" asks Jeff Perlman of the American Advertising Federation. "If so, what about the Pink Panther selling insulation or Snoopy promoting insurance? That argument is totally spurious."

In addition to all the aforementioned negative reasons why the state should not have the power to ban commercial speech, unfettered advertising offers customers some positive and valuable services. For starters, accurate ads convey vital information. In our modern consumer society, one cannot avoid making choices among a myriad of available products, from food to telephone services. These choices cannot be made in an information vacuum. As citizens in a democratic society, we have the right to be fully informed. After we have gathered the available information, we must be free to evaluate it and make decisions for ourselves. So the right to advertise products provides protections for consumers as well as for retailers and corporations.

Then there's the fact that, without advertising, competition would be limited and would result in higher retail prices. (It is for this reason that Ralph Nader is a strong advocate of free commercial speech.)

And, of course, the whole thing smacks of government intrusion. Surely preventing the producers and distributors of legal products from telling the public that their products exist is at least patently unfair and at worst downright tyrannical. The fundamental unfairness of the situation can be illuminated by asking a few specific questions.

What about dairy companies and the manufacturers of other high-cholesterol foods? There's certainly no question that cholesterol clogs arteries and leads directly to heart attacks and death. What about the producers of red meat? What about all that sugar? For those who believe that butter, red meat, sugar, and many other foods aren't as addictive as tobacco, I suggest they attend a few Overeaters Anonymous meetings, which is guaranteed to dispel such false notions about food addiction. Yet no one would suggest that the state ban grocery-store ads for these products.

What about sun-tanning products—or lying in the sun at all, for that matter? There's no doubt that this harmful activity directly causes cancer. Yet no one would suggest that we ban suntan-parlor advertising.

Many such other examples could be cited. In the end, it all boils down to the fact that commercial speech is no exception to the well-worn adage heard so many times from anti-censorship activists like myself: the proper response to commercial speech we don't like is still more speech. In the case of tobacco, it's already been proven that this method works. The unprecedented success of the American Cancer Society's anti-smoking ads—and the effectiveness of many other educational projects originated in the 1960s—tells us what we should be doing if we really want to reduce the number of new smokers. This "more speech" technique was so successful that the tobacco companies realized their television ads were resulting in ill will instead of creating customers and voluntarily pulled them off the air.

"Rather than trying to gag big tobacco, the [Clinton] administration should just talk back," says Kathleen Sullivan, professor of law at Stanford University. We all can help this educational process along by doing the same thing on an individual level.

I have always believed that understanding the heart of the First Amendment is a necessity for anyone who wants to be an advocate of free speech. You must be willing to defend the speech you hate the most just as vigorously as you defend the speech you cherish.

Sometimes it really hurts to do this. And sometimes it upsets valued friends and colleagues. But it comes with the territory.

POSTSCRIPT

Should the FDA Prohibit Tobacco Advertising?

A study in the *Journal of the American Medical Association* (vol. 266, 1991) reported that over half of children between ages 3 and 6 were able to identify Joe Camel, the mascot for Camel cigarettes. By age 6, as many children were able to recognize Joe Camel as readily as Mickey Mouse. Significantly, within four years after the Joe Camel campaign was initiated, Camel's share of the youth market escalated from 0.5 percent to 32.8 percent. Tobacco advertisers assert that they do not market to children but that advertising does affect what children know.

Smoking and tobacco advertising are highly charged political issues. U.S. senator Tom Harkin (D-Iowa) proposed an amendment to the Senate Tax and Urban Aid Bill to reduce the amount of money tobacco companies could deduct from their taxes for advertising expenses from 100 percent down to 80 percent. The additional revenue would go toward public education campaigns to dissuade people from smoking. In California an aggressive effort to discourage smoking and a 25-cent-per-pack tax increase resulted in a 17 percent decline in smoking among adults between 1987 and 1990.

The tobacco industry feels that government does not have the authority to regulate their freedom of speech. If government can regulate tobacco advertising, then it can regulate any activity that it deems unhealthy. Also, a portion of the revenue generated by the tobacco industry goes toward state and national treasuries, and thousands of people are employed by tobacco companies. The livelihood of many farmers comes from growing tobacco crops. Should these people be deprived of their livelihoods? By exporting tobacco products the national trade deficit may be reduced.

A fundamental question is whether the role of government is to dictate what people, even teenagers, can see and do or to inform young people so that they can make informed decisions. The tobacco industry does not force anyone to smoke cigarettes, although many argue that children are enticed into smoking by tobacco advertisements. If at a later date these same individuals want to give up smoking but are unable due to tobacco dependency, then is the tobacco industry responsible? Two articles that take opposing views on banning tobacco advertisements are "Cowboys, Camels, and the First Amendment—The FDA's Restrictions on Tobacco Advertising," *The New England Journal of Medicine* (December 5, 1996), by George Annas, and "Controlling Tobacco Advertising: The FDA Regulations and the First Amendment," *American Journal of Public Health* (March 1997), by Leonard Glantz.

In "Smoking Behavior of Adolescents Exposed to Cigarette Advertising," *Public Health Reports* (March–April 1993), Gilbert Botvin et al. report that the more adolescents were exposed to cigarette advertisements, the more likely they were to smoke. Two articles in *The Economist* (September 1990) discuss the impact of banning tobacco advertisements: "Advertising Under Siege" argues that restricting advertisements is a form of censorship that is highly ineffective. "Smoking Them Out" posits that existing tobacco companies would make even more money if advertising were restricted because new brands of cigarettes could not be introduced very easily. In "The Marlboro Grand Prix: Circumvention of the Television Ban on Tobacco Advertising," *The New England Journal of Medicine* (March 28, 1991), Dr. Alan Blum describes how cigarette companies get their products prominently displayed on television by sponsoring auto races.

ISSUE 15

Is Total Abstinence the Only Choice for an Alcoholic?

YES: Thomas Byrd, from *Lives Written in Sand: Addiction Awareness and Recovery Strategies* (Hallum Publishing, 1997)

NO: Audrey Kishline, from *Moderate Drinking* (Harmony Books, 1996)

ISSUE SUMMARY

YES: Professor Thomas Byrd maintains that Alcoholics Anonymous (AA) provides more effective treatment for alcoholics than psychiatrists, members of the clergy, or hospital treatment centers. Byrd contends that AA is the most powerful and scientific program, in contrast to all other therapies.

NO: Author Audrey Kishline supports principles based on moderation and behavioral principles for treating alcoholism. For some alcoholics, Kishline feels that the concept of a lifetime of abstinence may be counterproductive and that many are capable of controlling their own behavior.

According to government figures, there are an estimated 10 to 20 million alcoholics in the United States. Cocaine addicts number between 250,000 and 1 million. Eating disorders, sexual addictions, compulsive gambling, excessive spending, and compulsive working affect millions more people. Knowing the best way to help people who engage in these compulsive or addictive behaviors is difficult. One way to control addictive behavior is to abstain from it. However, is abstention the best or only viable treatment goal?

The concept of helping people with addictions can be approached from opposing perspectives. Some critics take the view that addiction occurs when people lose control over their addictive behavior. Moreover, there is always some kind of reward or payoff that fuels one's addictive behavior. The benefit may be security, sensation, or power, but as long as one or more of these benefits are experienced, people will not stop their behavior. Not everybody needs to abstain from unhealthy behaviors; only those people whose behaviors have reached the addictive stage. With some potentially addictive behaviors, such as eating disorders or work, it is impossible to abstain. However, with behaviors that are not necessary for survival, such as alcohol consumption, abstention is, according to some viewpoints, the only path to follow.

If addiction leaves people powerless, as some professionals maintain, then the only way to gain personal power and control is through abstention. If alcoholics are powerless against alcohol, then they cannot drink simply for the enjoyment of alcohol; they will invariably drink to excess. Furthermore, abstinence does not come naturally but must be learned. People need to learn to abstain each time they feel the urge to drink.

The abstinence model is currently the most popular approach for treating addiction. Abstinence is included in the 12-step model promoted by Alcoholics Anonymous (AA) and other self-help groups. Elements of this model include admitting to being powerless over one's addiction, accepting a higher power, and restructuring one's life. Opponents of the 12-step approach argue that it is not suitable for everyone and that it has not been proven effective. The idea of placing faith in a higher power, for example, is inconsistent with the values of many people, especially those who do not believe in the concept of a higher power. Another problem is that programs such as AA claim to be effective based on the testimonies of the program participants. However, because of the anonymity of people who attend or have attended AA meetings, follow-up studies are negligible.

A number of studies show that most people who stop addictive behavior do so on their own. Heroin addicts who quit using heroin generally do not go through any type of formal treatment. Likewise, the majority of individuals who quit smoking also stop without an organized program. It is unlikely that heroin addicts and tobacco users stop because they develop a belief in a higher spiritual power. Factors contributing to spontaneous remission are not well understood. It is believed that people stop self-destructive behaviors once they "hit bottom."

In recent years alternative self-help groups to Alcoholics Anonymous have appeared. The Secular Organizations for Sobriety (SOS) are groups for alcoholics that do not have the same emphasis on a belief in a higher power. There is also Women for Sobriety/Men for Sobriety, which does not accept AA's disease model of addiction. Abstinence is a prominent aspect of this group, but overcoming alcoholism is based on self-acceptance and the role of love in relationships. A third type of program is Rational Recovery (RR), which is modeled on the principles of rational emotive therapy developed by Albert Ellis. Unlike the other models, RR accepts moderate alcohol use. As its name implies, this approach encourages people to exert control over their cognitive processes.

In the selections that follow, Thomas Byrd makes the case that the abstinence-only, 12-step AA model is the only viable approach for overcoming alcoholism. Audrey Kishline highlights several limitations of the traditional approach to treating alcoholism and discusses moderation management as an alternative type of treatment.

YES

Thomas Byrd

LIVES WRITTEN IN SAND: ADDICTION AWARENESS AND RECOVERY STRATEGIES

ALCOHOLICS ANONYMOUS, WHAT WORKS BEST FOR MOST

Finding the words to describe an organization which has saved millions of lives and countless relationships is difficult. Fundamentally, Alcoholics Anonymous provides hope to those in despair. The contents of the "program" focus on feelings, and how to cope with them throughout life. It is not an intellectual program, rather focusing on problem resolution and the subsequent spiritual rewards. The fellowship teaches a philosophy whose rewards are immediate and practical. AA is not a religion where prime benefits may be promised in the afterlife. It is a group of people who share a common problem and experience. Members are committed to living in the solution, not in the problem. Only a distinct minority of alcoholics are able to put their disease in remission and enter recovery. Most alcoholics do not recover. AA is a simple program for complicated people. New members frequently ask "how" does the program work. If you dissect the word, the first letter stands for an honest appraisal of the problem; the second letter refers to being open-minded to new concepts from those in recovery; and the third letter stands for a willingness to devote the energy it takes to enter recovery. Members have committed two fundamental crimes. One is against the growth and development of another person. The second transgression is the indifference to the growth and development of self. Members are encouraged to make amends when possible and to carry the message to those still suffering. It is a program of attraction, not of promotion. The only requirement for membership is a desire to quit drinking.

Stopping drinking seems simple. You just don't drink. The problem is that there is a lot of failure. However, many of those who drink again will eventually stop drinking. Family members seem more likely to get their hopes up, only to suffer further discouragement if the alcoholic resumes drinking.

The problem drinker seems to be less upset with relapse, probably because drinking has played such a major role in his or her life.

The physician may help identify the problem but is best at tending to physical problems. The alcoholic is generally not a desirable patient in most medical offices. Rejection of prescribed treatment, dishonesty, evasiveness, and rationalization of drinking are typical. Alcoholism is best treated by the specialist, a fellow recovering alcoholic, where there is no barrier of misunderstanding. Fears, guilt and self-condemnation and other psychiatric problems are minimized in this relationship.

Most rehabilitation programs encourage their patients to participate in Alcoholics Anonymous as part of an aftercare program. This organization exists because alcoholics need help and AA is more successful than psychiatry, the clergy, hospitals or jails in providing that needed aid. The organization works one day at a time for anyone who thinks help is needed. Membership is anonymous unless the member desires to drop the anonymity.

Alcoholics Anonymous was founded by two prominent men whose lives had been seriously affected by excessive drinking. They set out simply to survive. What they did was to try anything and everything, keeping what works and rejecting the rest.

John D. Rockefeller made a $5,000 contribution to the co-founders Bill Wilson and Dr. Bob Smith to help the fledging organization. Bill Wilson had grandiose ideas of establishing a network of recovery centers throughout the United States. These plans were stilled by Rockefeller's son. At a dinner presided over by Nelson Rockefeller he declined to make any further family donations to the organization, stating "this is too good to be destroyed by money." This decision ultimately led to the establishment of a non-profit organization, which became self-supporting through their own membership's contributions. Wilson acquiesced to the condition of the one time gift, and the wealthy and visionary New York politician salvaged the organization by replacing profit with humanity.

AA is at the basis of all good treatment simply because it is the most powerful, and because it is the most scientific of all therapies. The first months of membership in Alcoholics Anonymous are most critical. Getting to the first meeting is difficult. Continuing to participate in your own recovery is also difficult. There are erroneously preconceived attitudes that can form barriers to recovery. The alcoholic needs to keep attending until he or she wants to attend. In other words, they need to give it a chance.

Help from another alcoholic is something that can be depended on. Service to others is one of the components of recovery. The drinker is accepted without question into the AA group. The 12 steps of Alcoholics Anonymous constitute a recovery program that begins with the admission that the member is powerless over alcohol and that strength is needed from another source to overcome the problem. A searching, fearless moral self-inventory is also part of the program. Restitution to those who have been harmed gives the alcoholic emotional strength. Knowing there is help if a person wants to stop drinking can be vital.

There are no rules, no dues, and participation is voluntary. It is a fellowship based upon a common problem. Sponsors in the organization are available to give support to the newcomer. Suggestions on how to stay sober are exchanged between members. "Tomorrow may never come, yesterday is a canceled check." The alcoholic can't be cured, but is only an arrested case. If the alcoholic takes a drink again, the problem will surface and the member will be right back in the depths of active alcoholism. The objective is to stay sober today. Alcoholics understand this, simple as it is. Personality reorientation can come later. *The Big Book of Alcoholics Anonymous* is an excellent source of information. The author also recommends another book, authored by Nan Robertson. It's titled, *Getting Better: Inside AA*, published by Fawcett Crest, New York, New York, 1988.

ACTIONS AMONG EQUALS

There are many approaches to the treatment of alcoholism, successful programs involve abstinence by whatever method it is achieved. Yet if one method of approaching a problem yields noticeably better and more striking results than others, then this method must contain some unique factor or factors that set it apart and form the basis of its supremacy.

"Alcoholics Anonymous is a fellowship of men and women who share their experience, strength and hope with each other that they may solve their common problem and help others to recover from alcoholism." The experiences of alcoholics are essentially the same, the theme is always the same: a progressive deterioration of the human personality. What then is the constant factor? What is AA's unique difference? I feel there are four distinctive characteristics that set apart this successful recovery program.

One of the answers lies in the manner in which this experience, strength and hope are shared and who is doing the sharing. Long before the average alcoholic walks through the doors of an AA meeting, help has been offered, in some instances even forced upon them. But these helpers are always superior beings. The moral responsibility of the alcoholic and the moral superiority of the helper, even though unstated, are always clearly understood. The overtone of parental disapproval and discipline in these authority figures is always present. Instead of the menacing, "This is what you should do," there is an instantly recognizable voice saying, "This is what I did." Therefore, one of the constant factors of a premium recovery program is where one alcoholic consciously and deliberately turned to another alcoholic, not to drink with, but to stay sober. I am personally convinced that the basic search of every human being is to find another human being, before whom one can stand completely without pretense or defense, and trust that person not to hurt them, because that person is exposed too. It is self-evident that the newcomer has been invited to share in the experience of recovery.

If the alcoholic responds to this invitation, the member then encounters a second unique factor: AA treats the symptoms first. The conviction that alcoholism is the symptom of deeper troubles. Even the cleverest diagnosis of these troubles is of little benefit if the patient dies. Autopsies do not benefit the persons upon whom they are performed. Total abstinence is the name of the game. Recovery can only begin with a decision to stay away from the first drink. No one can or will make that decision for the ill. In fact, one soon further learns that if he makes the decision, no one can or will force fulfillment of the goal. There are reports of action taken, rather than rules not to be broken. Action is the magic word. There are steps to be taken which are suggested as a program for recovery. Quoting from Chapter Five of the book, *Alcoholics Anonymous: Step One*, "We admitted we were powerless over alcohol, that our lives had become unmanageable." The newcomer finally sees that they must take these Steps before being entitled to report on them. It is important to "utilize, not to analyze."

The desire to make this decision often results from what appears to be a third unique quality: The intuitive understanding the alcoholic receives, while compassionate, is not indulgent. The new member is not asked what they are thinking, rather they are told what they are thinking. The companion "therapists" already have their doctorates in the four fields where the alcoholic reigns supreme: phoniness, self-deception, evasion, and self-pity. There's not much point in trying to fool people who may have invented the game that's being played. In the end, the member begins to achieve honesty by default.

There is a fourth factor which I feel is significant, and that is the recovering alcoholic's infinite willingness to talk about alcoholism. Without the newcomer's ever becoming fully aware of it, the fascination with alcohol is literally talked to death. There is a reversal of form which the educational process takes. The participant is asked, not so much to learn new values, as to unlearn those that brought the seeker to the doors of recovery; not so much to adopt new goals, as to abandon old ones. The real answer is that this unique therapy occurs wherever two alcoholics meet: at home, at lunch, in the street, at work or school, and on the telephone. Members may faithfully attend

meetings waiting for "something" to rub off, namely the "miracle of AA." The sad part about it is that "something" is rubbing off on them. Death. The real miracle is simply the willingness to act.

The formless flexibility of AA's principles as interpreted by their different adherents finally pushes the alcoholic into a stance where he must use only himself as a frame of reference for personal actions, and this in turn means there must be a willingness to accept the consequences of those actions. In my viewpoint, that is the definition of emotional maturity. True freedom lies in the realization and calm acceptance of the fact that there may very well be no perfect answer. The search for perfection is the hallmark of the neurotic. In the final analysis, we are all striving to be a better human beings. The future is that time when you will wish that you had used the time that you have now. Live in the present.

Other programs such as Rational Recovery and S.T.A.R.T. emphasize self-management and recovery training. Both programs do not incorporate the "higher power" aspect of the AA program, neither use a 12 Step format, reject the recovering concept, sponsorship, nor a 'one at a time' philosophy.

GROWTH, A DAY AT A TIME

Recovering people can become overwhelmed by new responsibilities. Sometimes too, members wonder why we can't ever be finished and just stop for awhile.

Feeling this way can mean it is time to stop and rest. The process of recovery has plateaus and detours along the way, and it's okay at times to take a break. But the "it's too much trouble" feeling also can be a signal that we need to pay more, not less, attention to ourselves and our recovery program.

Just as the chemically dependent person chooses not to drink or use drugs on a daily basis, so must a codependent person choose to continue recovery one day at a time. It is easy to see progress or lack of it in the big choices—to abstain from chemicals, to dissolve destructive relationships, to change careers. Less visible, but at least as important, are the little choices we all make every day.

Recovery means choosing to confront small instances of abusive behavior instead of letting them go. It means choosing to set boundaries to protect your time for recreation and rejuvenation. It means saying "no" to demands you can't meet. It means deciding every day to take care of yourself by paying attention to your needs for sleep, exercise, and healthy diet.

We can let all these choices overwhelm us if we focus on the "every single day for the whole rest of my life" aspect of them. Or we can take them one day at a time, recognizing that some days are easier than others. And we can remember that, as choosing growth becomes a pattern, it gets easier. Each seemingly insignificant daily choice is a separate affirmation that recovery is worth the trouble.

NO

Audrey Kishline

MODERATE DRINKING

One afternoon, as I was driving home on the freeway, a question crossed my mind. There are thousands of support groups in our country for chronic drinkers who have made the decision to abstain from alcohol. Why aren't there any support groups available for problem drinkers who have made the decision to reduce their drinking?

Drinking too much, after all, is not like being pregnant. You either are or aren't pregnant, whereas drinking problems lie along a continuum ranging from very mild to life threatening. Problem drinkers have at least some health, personal, family, job-related, financial, or legal problems due to alcohol use. But unlike many chronic drinkers, problem drinkers do not experience significant withdrawal symptoms when they stop drinking. And they normally have most of their resources intact and possess the skills necessary for self-change.

When I finally realized why there were no support groups for problem drinkers, I became very upset. Then, after I calmed down, I did two things: I started a group called Moderation Management (MM) for problem drinkers who want to moderate their drinking. And I wrote a book, *Moderate Drinking*.

The basic concepts of MM are derived from brief behavioral self-management approaches to alcohol abuse, which in turn are based on controlled studies with problem drinkers. The guidelines MM uses have been carefully reviewed by professionals in the field. But most important, MM was born from the real-life experiences of former problem drinkers who have returned to moderate drinking, including myself.

BONA FIDE BOOZER

I will now provide you with my "credentials" as a former problem drinker. Though this is something I would prefer not to do, it is necessary because there are those who believe that a return to moderate drinking is impossible for anyone who has ever had a drinking problem. They will say I never was an "alcoholic." And they are correct, if by "alcoholic" they mean a chronic, severely dependent drinker. But if they mean a person with any type of drinking problem, then saying I was never an alcoholic would imply that I never had a "real" drinking problem—in which case, they are wrong.

Like many people, I first tried alcohol in my late teens at home and began drinking socially in my early twenties with friends. From my early to late twenties, however, over a period of about six years, I gradually drank more, and more often. Drinking became a central activity in my life: The people I associated with were mostly heavy drinkers, my evenings were planned around drinking, and having fun meant alcohol had to be involved.

I drank when I was happy, sad, bored, or when I didn't know how I was feeling. But mostly I drank because it became a habit. Naturally this began to cause problems in my life. I did not eat right, and slept poorly. I did not perform to the best of my abilities at work, and began to have difficulties keeping up with the courses I was taking in night school. I started to postpone everything: studying, projects, even getting together with people I knew did not drink as much as I did. I drank irresponsibly, risking other people's lives when I drove after I had too much. Finally, after a long-term relationship fell apart, I started to drink alone. I became depressed, scared, and lonely.

I decided to seek help. For those who say I was never an alcoholic, I want to stress that two treatment centers, an aftercare program, and conservatively 30 to 40 professionals had no problem saying that I was. With my new "alcoholic" label, I experienced traditional treatment first hand. For my "medical disease" I received the following treatments for 28 days as a "patient" on the third floor of a hospital: group psychotherapy, confrontation counseling, and life-skills training. My "detoxification" consisted of sleeping in a room separate from the rest of the clients where a nurse could take my blood pressure and temperature regularly for 24 hours. It is important to note I did not experience any significant withdrawal symptoms when I quit drinking —a point either ignored or considered irrelevant by treatment personnel.

In addition, I was introduced to the institutionalized version of Alcoholics Anonymous while still in the hospital. I was told to fill out workbooks based on the treatment center's interpretation of the first five steps of the AA program. These steps instructed me to do the following: admit that I was powerless over alcohol and not sane; turn my will and my life over to the care of God; write a moral inventory; and confess my wrongs to God. Thus, spiritual training was another aspect of the treatment for my supposed medical disease.

Treatment personnel emphasized that I would have to attend AA meetings for the rest of my life, or else I would end up dead, in jail, insane, or in the gutter. With this kind of advice, I made sure that I went to meetings for several years after inpatient care. I attended literally hundreds of meetings.

The result of all this "treatment?" At first, my drinking became far worse. Hospital staff members had told me I had a physical disease that I had no control over. In possibly the most defenseless and dependent stage of my entire life, I began to fulfill some of these prophecies. I became a binge drinker, suddenly obsessed with drinking too much or not at all. I accepted that I was indeed powerless over my "condition," and my old self-esteem and confidence gradually disappeared.

Then, as time passed, I began to do what a lot of other people do naturally, with or without treatment. I began to grow up. I took on life's responsibilities. I got married, had children, and became a full-time homemaker. Though initially told to stop drinking, I eventually chose to abstain from alcohol for long periods of time.

SIPPING, NOT SLIPPING

It gradually dawned on me at the choice to abstain or drink, and how much to drink, had been mine all along. These choices were not predetermined by a disease at all, but were entirely a result of my own actions, which I did have control over. So... I decided to shed my "disease." And I took back full responsibility for my own behavior.

Several years ago, after careful consideration, I made the choice to return to moderate drinking. I do not mean white-knuckled, super-controlled, "I really want more" drinking, as is often described by those who don't believe this is possible. I mean that I am comfortable with the role that alcohol plays in my life now. When I choose to drink, I drink responsibly. An occasional glass of wine is a small, though enjoyable, part of my life —not the center of it.

I don't want anyone else, ever again, to have to go through what I did. I spent years full of self-doubt, struggling with an alcoholic label that never felt like it fit. In my opinion, my "recovery" or ability to face up to, confront, and change

my behavior, was delayed considerably because of traditional treatment methods. I went on a huge detour due to the disease model of alcohol abuse.

My long personal journey is not one I would wish on anyone else. But I began to wonder how many other people had had similar experiences. I also wondered how many problem drinkers were out there who could benefit from a moderation-oriented, layperson-led support group when they first realized that they have a drinking problem. To answer these questions, I had to do some research. One of my first discoveries was that professional moderation-oriented programs are common in countries such as Great Britain, Sweden, Denmark, Germany, Australia, and New Zealand. I also discovered that researchers have been reporting the occurrence of moderate drinking after treatment for a long time. In some journals, experts openly recommend that moderation should be the first line of defense, and that abstinence should be considered only if moderation doesn't work. I couldn't believe what I was reading!

THE DISEASE/HABIT DEBATE

I began to write to the authors of the professional literature and asked them for their assistance. I will never forget the flurry of journal articles that began to arrive in the mail and the number of calls and letters that I received in support of my early efforts.

One major revelation was that many experts do not believe that alcohol abuse is a disease. I had been under the impression that the disease model of alcohol abuse represented a biological and medical fact, proved beyond a shadow of a doubt I was amazed to find out that the disease theory was just that, a theory—one that has been highly criticized, and discarded, by many researchers.

For example, the noted scholar Dr. Herbert Fingarette writes in his book, *Heavy Drinking: The Myth of Alcoholism as a Disease*, that "almost everything the American public believes to be the scientific truth about alcoholism is false." Dr. Stanton Peele, author of *The Truth About Addiction and Recovery* and a leading expert in the field, agrees: "Every major tenet of the 'disease' view of addiction is refuted by both research and everyday observation." Even Bill Wilson, cofounder of Alcoholics Anonymous, said in 1960: "We have never called alcoholism a disease because, technically speaking, it is not a disease entity."

If alcohol abuse isn't a disease, what is it? In layman's terms, it is a habit, a learned behavior that is frequently repeated. In psychological terms it is a pattern of excessive alcohol consumption which produces maladaptive behavioral changes in which drinking can become the central activity in an individual's life, usually after many years of heavy consumption. According to researchers Dr. Roger Vogler and Dr. Wayne Bartz, "Drinking itself, including heavy drinking, is not caused by disease but by learning. You must voluntarily consume alcohol in fairly large amounts before you have an alcohol problem."

For the problem drinker, the disease/habit debate is extremely important because it directly affects the entire approach to treating people who are beginning to have alcohol problems. The "learned behavior" model of excessive drinking allows for what is called treatment matching, which means that the level of treatment is matched to the level of assessed problem.

For example, if you went to a doctor complaining of an earache, you wouldn't automatically be thrown into the hospital and hooked up to intravenous antibiotics. To start with you would probably receive less intensive medical help for your infection, say a self-administered course of antibiotics. Then, if that did not work, more aggressive measures would be tried. In alcohol treatment facilities today, however, it does not matter whether you are a college student who has experienced a few binge-drinking episodes at parties or a stereotypical gutter drunk, you will both be prescribed the same "strength" of "medicine": total abstinence and, in most cases, AA attendance.

The behavioral model of alcohol abuse allows for less intensive, limited intervention for people who have less severe problems with alcohol. Moderate drinking is a permissible, and accepted, treatment goal of professional programs that offer this alternative to problem drinkers.

MODERATION MANAGEMENT

The purpose of Moderation Management is to provide a supportive environment in which people who have made the decision to reduce their drinking can come together to help each other change. That's it. It is very simple, and I admit that MM stole it from the forerunner of the mutual-help movement, AA. The idea of people getting together to help others who have, or have had, similar problems is an old but good one.

How does MM accomplish its purpose? First of all, the meetings are free. MM provides a supportive environment which encourages lifestyle changes. You can change a behavior (whereas you can't change an irreversible disease); and the sooner you recognize you are developing a problem with alcohol and seek help to change your drinking patterns, the better.

MM also offers a set of professionally reviewed guidelines, the Nine Steps Toward Moderation and Positive Lifestyle Changes. The steps include information about alcohol, empirically-based moderate drinking limits, self-evaluation strategies, drink monitoring forms, self-management strategies, and goal-setting techniques.

We need a support group like MM for several reasons. First, problem drinkers are more likely to seek help from a support group they believe fits their needs. It is ironic that when the disease model first became popular, health professionals thought people would more readily come forward for help if they were told they had a disease rather than some moral failing. Now the reverse is true. People are more afraid of the label than the behavior it describes, and for valid reasons. The "alcoholic" label can make it impossible for you to get medical or life insurance. It can ruin your chances for a job promotion. And once you are labeled, it stays with you forever.

Another reason we need a group like MM is that problem drinkers will seek help sooner when given access to programs that match their needs. Problem drinkers are often indecisive about taking that first step toward getting help. They know that programs exist for "alcoholics," but they don't believe their own problems are that severe, nor are they comfortable with traditional treatment goals or labels. So they often end up taking no action because their problems are not that bad—yet.

And third, there are far more problem drinkers than severely dependent drinkers in our country. Studies report that there are anywhere from three to seven times more people with mild to moderate drinking problems than people with severe drinking problems. Due to their larger numbers, it is problem drinkers who account for most of the alcohol-related costs to our society (automobile accidents, lost productivity, domestic conflicts, etc.). By addressing their needs, MM has the potential to make a substantial contribution toward reducing the harm caused by irresponsible alcohol use.

What about the chronic drinker who should be abstaining, but is still actively abusing alcohol? Won't MM just provide another excuse to continue drinking? In my opinion, those who should be abstaining but refuse to probably won't change their behavior due to the existence of any of the support groups. If such a person finds his or her way to an MM meeting, however, there can still be a positive outcome. Already in MM's brief history, I have seen people come to the meeting to try moderation, later acknowledge that they were not successful, and then go on to an abstinence program. This is preferable to no improvement at all. In line with the principles of "harm reduction," any progress an individual makes toward decreasing the amount of alcohol they consume, or the frequency of harmful drinking episodes, is a step in the right direction.

Why would people who have had problems with alcohol even consider drinking again? I have found that, most of the time, it is not in human nature to totally give up every behavior that has caused problems in the past. The more common response is for people to learn from their mistakes and to moderate their behavior in the future. People who have previously been overweight learn to eat less (occasionally still treat themselves to fattening foods); people who used to work too much learn to spend more time with their family; people who used to shop too much learn to get rid of a few credit cards; and most people who have had a drinking problem at some stage of their life learn to drink in moderation.

The solution to doing to much of something is not always another extreme (quitting altogether). Many times the solution lies somewhere between the extreme, and it is called moderation.

POSTSCRIPT

Is Total Abstinence the Only Choice for an Alcoholic?

The fundamental question here is, Must alcoholics totally abstain from alcohol use, or can they learn to drink in moderation? This issue was raised in the 1970s, when Linda and Mark Sobell presented research showing that alcoholics who were taught to drink socially were less likely to relapse than people who were told to abstain from alcohol. (This study was subsequently criticized for its methodology.) In another study supported by the RAND Corporation in the 1970s, it was found that the majority of alcoholics who went through formal treatment were drinking moderately or occasionally up to 18 months after treatment. Most did not resume their abusive use of alcohol. A criticism of this study was that it did not follow those in treatment long enough—a 4-year follow-up revealed that many had relapsed.

Many people who attempt to completely stop addictive behaviors fail. If a person tries several times to abstain from drinking alcohol (or other self-destructive behaviors) and cannot stop, perhaps other forms of treatment may be worth pursuing. However, moderation as a treatment goal may not prove to be productive because alcohol—the central element to the addiction —is still present in the alcoholic's life.

It may be shortsighted to think that one form of treatment is best for all addicts. One advantage of Alcoholics Anonymous (AA) over other forms of treatment is expense. In "Typical Patterns and Costs of Alcoholism Treatment Across a Variety of Populations and Providers," *Alcoholism: Clinical and Experimental Research* (April 1991), Harold Holder and James Blose report that the average stay for inpatient alcohol treatment lasts 22 days and costs $4,665. In contrast, there is no cost to be a member of AA.

An excellent article that looks at whether the tenets of AA are still applicable today is "A.A. at the Crossroads," *The New Yorker* (March 20, 1995), by Andrew DelBanco and Thomas DelBanco. In "Alcoholics Synonymous: Heavy Drinkers May Get Comparable Help from a Variety of Therapies," *Science* (January 25, 1997), Bruce Bower discusses an ongoing study in which clients are matched to appropriate therapies. An older, excellent essay that reviews the efficacy of alcohol treatment is William Miller and Reid Hester's "The Effectiveness of Alcoholism Treatment: What Research Reveals," in William Miller and Nick Heather, eds., *Treating Addictive Behaviors: Processes of Change* (Plenum Press, 1986).

ISSUE 16

Is Drug Abuse Resistance Education (DARE) an Effective Program?

YES: Michele Alicia Harmon, from "Reducing the Risk of Drug Involvement Among Early Adolescents: An Evaluation of Drug Abuse Resistance Education (DARE)," *Evaluation Review* (April 1993)

NO: Stephen Glass, from "Don't You D.A.R.E.," *The New Republic* (March 3, 1997)

ISSUE SUMMARY

YES: Michele Alicia Harmon, a doctoral student at the University of Maryland, reports that Drug Abuse Resistance Education (DARE) had a positive impact on fifth-grade students in terms of attitudes against substance abuse, assertiveness, positive peer association, association with drug-using peers, alcohol use within the previous year, and prosocial norms.

NO: Author Stephen Glass, challenging the benefits of DARE, reports that DARE has not been shown to affect drug-taking behavior. His special concern involves youngsters mistakenly reporting their parents to police officers for drug use, and he questions the circumstances under which children make these reports.

Drug education is arguably one of the most logical ways of dealing with the problems of drugs in American society. Drug-taking behavior has not been significantly affected by attempts to reduce the demand for drugs, and drug prohibition (as in the case of alcohol) has also failed. One remaining option to explore is drug education. Drug education is not an overnight panacea for eliminating drug problems. Rates of cigarette smoking have declined dramatically, but it took 25 years of public health efforts to achieve this. If drug education is to prove ultimately successful, it too will take years.

Many early drug education programs were misguided. One emphasis was on scare tactics. Experts erroneously believed that if young people saw the horrible consequences of drug use, then they would certainly abstain from drugs. Another faulty assumption was that drug use would be affected by knowledge about drugs, but it is obvious that knowledge is not enough. Over 400,000 people die each year from tobacco use, but 25 percent of adult Americans and increasing numbers of teenagers continue to smoke, even though most know the grim statistics about tobacco. Young people have a hard time relating to potential problems like lung cancer and cirrhosis of the liver (which is caused by long-term alcohol abuse), since these problems will take years to develop. If drug education is going to be effective, it will need to deal with the immediate effects of drugs, not the long-term consequences. Another major problem with early drug education was that much of the information that teachers relayed concerning drugs was either incorrect or exaggerated. Teachers were therefore not seen as credible.

There is a lack of consensus as to what a drug education program should encompass. However, there is general agreement among drug prevention experts that drug awareness programs are counterproductive. Many schools conduct drug awareness programs, in which, over a course of a week, former drug abusers talk to students about how their personal lives and families were ruined by drugs, pharmacologists demonstrate the physical effects of drugs, and films are shown that depict the horrors of drugs. These sensationalized programs stimulate curiosity, and it is not unusual for drug use to increase after one of these presentations.

Many drug prevention programs in the 1970s focused on self-esteem and values clarification. If low self-esteem is a factor in drug use, as many believed, then it would make sense to improve self-esteem to reduce drug use. However, self-esteem is not always a good indicator of drug use. Many young people who have good feelings about themselves use drugs. In addition, many believed that if students clarified their values, they would see the folly of using drugs. This approach overlooked the possibility that young people may turn to drugs because they want to be accepted by their peers, because drugs are forbidden, or simply because they enjoy the high that comes from drug use. The values clarification approach has been discarded by most drug educators.

The current emphasis in drug education is on primary prevention. It is easier to have young people not use drugs in the first place than to get them to stop after they have already started using drugs. The Drug Abuse Resistance Education (DARE) program—the subject of this debate—attempts to get upper-elementary students to pledge not to use drugs. The rationale is that putting energy into teaching elementary students about drugs rather than high school students will be more likely to reduce drug use because the latter are more likely to have already begun using drugs. The program focuses mainly on tobacco, alcohol, and marijuana. These are considered to be gateway drugs, which means that students who use other drugs are most likely to have used these first. The longer students delay using tobacco, alcohol, and marijuana, the less likely they will be to use other drugs.

In the following selections, Michele Alicia Harmon points out some of the benefits of Drug Abuse Resistance Education, especially on students' attitudes toward substance abuse, assertiveness, positive peer association, association with drug-using peers, alcohol use, and prosocial norms. Stephen Glass seriously challenges the value of the DARE program.

YES

Michele Alicia Harmon

REDUCING THE RISK OF DRUG INVOLVEMENT AMONG EARLY ADOLESCENTS

The purpose of the current study is to evaluate the effectiveness of the Drug Abuse Resistance Education (DARE) program in Charleston County, South Carolina. Specific aims of the program include the stated DARE objectives—increasing self-esteem, assertiveness, coping skills, and decreasing positive attitudes toward drugs, actual drug use, and association with drug-using peers. The study also examines the program's effectiveness for reducing other known risk factors associated with adolescent drug use such as social integration, commitment and attachment to school, and rebellious behavior.

Much of what is known about adolescent drug use is a result of the annual High School Survey conducted by the Institute for Social Research at the University of Michigan (Johnston 1973). Data from a recent report examining drug use (Johnston, Bachman, and O'Malley 1991) show 90% of U.S. seniors reported drinking alcohol at some time in the lives, 64% said they had smoked cigarettes, 41% reported smoking marijuana, and 18% had taken stimulants.

High school survey data from Charleston show similar prevalence rates. For example, 77% of Charleston County seniors said they had drunk alcohol at some point in their lives, 47% had smoked cigarettes, and 31% reported smoking marijuana (South Carolina Department of Education and South Carolina Commission on Alcohol and Drug Abuse 1990).

Efforts to combat the drug problem have led to a variety of strategies over the past two decades. The three most widely used attempts to control drug use are supply reduction, treatment, and prevention.

Supply reduction efforts by law enforcement agencies to decrease production, importation, distribution, and retail sales of street drugs appears ineffective in reducing the drug problem. Increased arrests and imprisonment, given our crowded penal institutions, and the ready replacement of suppliers and dealers mitigates the actions of legal authorities.

From Michele Alicia Harmon, "Reducing the Risk of Drug Involvement Among Early Adolescents: An Evaluation of Drug Abuse Resistance Education (DARE)," *Evaluation Review*, vol. 17, no. 2 (April 1993), pp. 221–227. Copyright © 1993 by Sage Publications, Inc. Reprinted by permission. References omitted.

Similar to supply reduction, millions of dollars are spent every year on treatment as a means of curtailing drug use. Much like supply reduction strategies, treatment also shows little promise for eliminating drug use, particularly among adolescents (Polich et al. 1984; Stein and Davis 1982). Some feel adolescent drug problems stem from youth "life problems," not physiological dependence (Bennett 1983). This implies adolescent drug abusers are treated for the wrong problem. Subsequently, traditional drug treatment programs are often ineffective in treating adolescent clients (Sells and Simpson 1979).

Prevention holds more promise for controlling adolescent drug use than supply reduction or treatment. Reasons for promise include the timing of prevention programs and their focus on "gateway" substances—alcohol, tobacco, and marijuana. National data show youths initiating alcohol use as early as age 11 and marijuana and other illicit drugs at age 12 (Elliot and Huizinga 1984). Because drug use often begins at such an early age, prevention programs must target youths before they come in contact with drugs. Currently, many drug prevention programs (such as DARE) target youths while they are still in elementary school.

Targeting gateway substances is important because early use of such substances often follows a logical progression to experimentation with other drugs (Hamburg, Braemer, and Jahnke 1975; Kandel 1978; Richards 1980).

Prevention efforts have not always been as promising, however. Research clearly demonstrates the "first generation" of drug prevention programs such as information dissemination (stating facts about drugs), affective education (clarifying values and/or increasing self-esteem), and alternative activities to drug use have little or no impact on deterring adolescent drug use (Berberin et al. 1976; Hanson 1980; Kinder, Pape, and Walfish 1980; Schaps et al. 1981). In fact, some of these programs are associated with an increase in drug use (Gordon and McAlister 1982; Swisher and Hoffman 1975).

The "second generation" of drug prevention efforts has proven more effective in reducing adolescent drug use. This generation includes programs that focus on increasing general personal and social skills such as problem solving, decision making, coping, resisting peer pressure, and assertiveness through skill acquisition (Botvin and Dusenbury 1987; Schinke and Gilchrist 1985; Hansen et al. 1988; Telch et al. 1982).

DARE (DRUG ABUSE RESISTANCE EDUCATION)

DARE is a drug abuse prevention program that focuses on teaching students skills for recognizing and resisting social pressures to use drugs. DARE lessons also focus on the development of self-esteem, coping, assertiveness, communications skills, risk assessment and decision-making skills, and the identification of positive alternatives to drug use.

Taught by a uniformed police officer, the program consists of 17 lessons offered once a week for 45 to 50 minutes. The DARE curriculum can be taught only by police officers who attend an intensive two-week, 80-hour training. The DARE program calls for a wide range of teaching activities including question and answer sessions, group discussion, role play, and workbook exercises.

The DARE curriculum was created by Dr. Ruth Rich, a curriculum specialist with the Los Angeles Unified School District, from a second-generation curriculum known as Project SMART (Self-Management and Resistance Training) (Hansen et al. 1988).

DARE is one of, if not the most, widespread drug prevention programs in the United States. In 1989, over 3 million children in 80,000 classrooms were exposed to DARE ("Project DARE" 1990). Currently, there are DARE programs in every state in the United States and some counties have mandated DARE as part of the school health curriculum. It has also been implemented in several other countries including Canada, England, Australia, and New Zealand. In addition, it has been adopted by many reservation schools operated by the Bureau of Indian Affairs, and by the worldwide network of U.S. Defense Department schools for children of military personnel. There is a Spanish version and a Braille translation of the student workbook. Efforts are also under way to develop strategies for teaching DARE to hearing-impaired and other special-needs students.

Prior DARE Evaluations

Several DARE evaluations have been conducted over the past 9 years. Some show positive results, some show negative results, and most have serious methodological flaws. Recent DARE evaluations demonstrate an improvement in methodology over earlier studies. Initially, most of the DARE studies concluded that DARE was a "success." For these evaluations, success often meant students responded that they liked the DARE program. Still others claimed success if teachers and students rated DARE as "useful" or "valuable." For the most part success is based on the finding that students are more able to generate "appropriate" responses to a widely used 19-item questionnaire about drug facts and attitudes after the DARE program than before. In these last instances, almost all had no control group.

Many DARE studies contain such severe methodology problems that the results should be questioned. Methodological flaws contained in the evaluations include one or more of the following problems: (1) no control group, (2) small sample size, (3) posttest only, (4) poorly operationalized measures, (5) low alpha levels for scales ($< .50$), (6) no statistical tests performed, and (7) pretreatment differences not taken into account. Despite the lack of methodological rigor among most of these studies, three used rigorous methodology and should be mentioned because they have corrected many of the cited weaknesses.

The three studies are similar with respect to their evaluation designs but different in terms of their results. All three evaluations used adequate sample sizes and employed both pre- and posttest measures. They also randomly assigned schools to receive the DARE program or serve as controls.

Controlling on pretreatment differences, the dependent variable at Time 1 (pretest), and school type, Ringwalt, Ennett, and Holt (1991) in North Carolina reported significant differences in the expected direction for general attitudes toward drugs, attitudes toward specific drugs (beer, wine coolers, wine, cigarettes, and inhalants), perceptions of peers' attitudes toward drug use, assertiveness, recognizing media influences to use drugs, and the costs associated with drug use. However, no statistically significant effects were found for self-reported drug use, future intentions to use drugs, perceived benefits of drug use (alcohol and cigarettes), or self-esteem.

In Frankfort, Kentucky, Faine and Bohlander (1988) compared DARE to control students and found significant differences favoring the DARE students on all outcome measures, which include self-esteem, attitudes toward the police, knowledge of drugs, attitudes toward drugs, perceived external locus of control, and peer resistance scores.

The third DARE study worth mentioning took place in Lexington, Kentucky (Clayton, Cattarello, Day, and Walden 1991). The authors used analysis of variance to compare the treatment and control group outcomes. However, they only controlled on race despite other pretreatment differences. Statistically significant differences between the treatment and control group were found for general drug attitudes, negative attitudes toward specific drugs (cigarettes, alcohol, and marijuana), and peer relationships (interpreted as DARE students self-reporting more popularity among their peers). Differences were not observed for self-esteem, peer pressure resistance, or self-reported drug use.

A 2-year follow-up study (Clayton, Cattarello, and Walden 1991) examined the same cohort of sixth-grade students using two follow-up questionnaires (1 year apart) after the initial posttest. The only statistically significant difference occurred at the first follow-up for last-year marijuana use. Unfortunately, this finding occurred in the opposite direction than that expected. Significantly more marijuana use was reported by the *DARE students* than non-DARE students. Otherwise, no significant effects were found at any other time for any other drug type.

The only common outcome measures of the three studies mentioned are drug attitudes, self-esteem, and peer resistance (assertiveness). Inconsistent results were reported with respect to self-esteem and peer resistance (assertiveness) but the three evaluations agree that those in the DARE group had significantly less positive attitudes toward drug use compared to the control group.

Although some long-term studies have been attempted, the only one demonstrating adequate methodology is the Lexington, Kentucky study (Clayton, Cattarello, and Walden 1991) and the results do not warrant program success.

In short, studies of the DARE program have produced mixed results and DARE evaluations up to this point are inconclusive. Further replications are necessary in order to make more confident conclusions about the effects of the DARE program.

DARE Compared to Most Promising Prevention Approach

Several aspects of the DARE program make it a likely candidate for success. First, the program is offered to students just before the age when they are likely to experiment with drugs. Second, although there is little research on the effectiveness of law enforcement personnel as classroom instructors, uniformed police officers serve as teachers of the DARE curriculum in hopes of increasing favorable attitudes toward the law and law enforcement personnel. Third, the DARE program seeks to prevent the use of "gateway drugs" (i.e., alcohol, cigarettes, and marijuana), thereby decreasing the probability of subsequent heavier, more serious, drug use. Fourth, the DARE program draws on several aspects of effective drug prevention efforts from the second generation such as the development and practice of life skills (coping, assertiveness, and decision making).

Although DARE shows promise as a drug prevention strategy, more evaluation efforts need to take place before forming an overall conclusion about the program. This is especially important considering the fact that millions of government dollars are spent on this one particular drug prevention program every year and its dissemination continues to spread rapidly throughout the United States.

METHODS

Research Design

The current study used a nonequivalent control group quasi-experimental design (Campbell and Stanley 1963) to determine if participating in the DARE program had any effect on the measured outcome variables compared to a similar group that did not receive the program.

The 17-week DARE program took place during the fall and spring semesters of the 1989–1990 school year. A student self-report questionnaire was used to measure the outcome variables and all pre- and posttests were administered approximately 20 weeks apart.

The survey administration was conducted by the school alcohol and drug contact person. The administration was conducted in such a way as to preserve the confidentiality of the students. All students were assigned identification numbers prior to the time of the pretest. The identification number was used to link the pre- and posttest questionnaire responses. A questionnaire was distributed in an envelope with the student's name in the top right-hand corner.

Each name was printed on a removable label that the students tore off and threw away. The administrator read the cover page of the survey informing the students there was a number on the survey booklet that may be used to match their responses with questions asked later. The administrator also informed the students they had the right not to answer any or all the questions.

Response rates for the sample were high. The average pretest response rate was 93.5% for the DARE students and 93.7% for the comparison students. An average of 90% of the DARE students and 86.4% of the comparison students completed the posttest. The pre- and posttest (combined) response rates were similar for both groups; 86.5% (295) of the treatment and 83.7% (307) of the comparison students completed both surveys.

Analysis of variance procedures were employed to examine the differences between the DARE and non-DARE students at the time of the pretest. Controlling for any pretreatment differences between the two groups and the measured dependent variable on the pretest, analysis of covariance was used to detect significant differences at the time of the posttest.

Sample

From 11 elementary schools in Charleston County, South Carolina, 708 fifth-grade students participated in the present study. Students came from five schools receiving the DARE program and six that did not. Of the 708 students involved in the study, 341 received the treatment (DARE), and 367 served as comparison students. The students came from schools representing a cross section of those found in the Charleston County School

District. Three schools were urban, six suburban, and two rural.

Each of the DARE schools were paired with a comparison school based on the following characteristics: number of students, percentage of students receiving free or reduced lunch, percentage white, percentage male, percentage never retained, and percentage meeting BSAP (Basic Skills Assessment Program) reading and math standards.....

In summary, the evidence shows DARE students had more beliefs in prosocial norms, more attitudes against substance use, more assertiveness, and more positive peer associations than the comparison group. The DARE students also reported less association with drug-using peers and less alcohol use in the last year. However, the DARE students were equivalent to the non-DARE students on social integration, commitment and attachment to school, rebellious behavior, coping strategies, attitudes about the police, self-esteem, and last-year and last-month drug use (with the exception of last-year alcohol use).

Current Findings and Comparisons

The current DARE evaluation demonstrates the program's effectiveness on some of the measured outcome variables but not on others. The current study shows DARE does have an impact on several of the program objectives. Among these are attitudes against substance use, assertiveness, positive peer association, association with drug-using peers, and alcohol use within the last year.

It should be noted that several of the variables showing no difference between the treatment and control groups are not specifically targeted by DARE (although they are shown to be correlated with adolescent drug use). Among these are social integration, attachment and commitment to school and rebellious behavior. It could also be argued that the DARE program does not specifically aim to change attitudes toward police officers, although this may be a tacit objective. Because the program does not target these outcomes specifically, it may not be surprising there were no differences found between the DARE and non-DARE groups. It was hypothesized that the DARE program may impact factors relating to later adolescent drug use, even if those factors were not specific aims of the program but this hypothesis did not hold true. In a sense this is evidence that helps to reject the selection argument. If the positive results were due to selection, they would not be found only for the outcomes targeted by DARE.

Much like the three previously reviewed DARE evaluations, the current study adds to the mixed results produced thus far with one exception. Across all studies using a pre-post comparison group design, DARE students' attitudes against drug use have consistently been shown to increase and differ significantly from the control students. Because favorable attitudes toward drug use have been shown to predict or correlate with later adolescent drug use (Kandel, Kessler, and Margulies 1978), this finding provides some of the most convincing evidence that DARE shows promise as a drug prevention strategy.

On the other hand, there are no other consistent findings for assertiveness (resisting peer pressure), self-esteem, or attitudes toward police. The current study found an increase in assertiveness among the DARE students as compared to the non-DARE students. Ringwalt et al. (1991) and Faine and Bohlander (1988) also found this to be true but Clayton, Cattarello, Day, and Walden (1991) did not. Effects on self-esteem were not demonstrated in the present DARE evaluation nor were they in Clayton's (Clayton, Cattarello, Day, and Walden 1991) or Ringwalt's (Ringwalt et al. 1991). However, significant differences in self-esteem were seen for the DARE participants over the controls in Faine and Bohlander's (1988) study. Thus the Charleston study helps to increase the consistency of the assertiveness and self-esteem results.

Faine and Bohlander's (1988) study also showed that positive attitudes toward police were significantly greater for the treatment group than the control group but the present study did not replicate such findings. However, the difference found between these two studies may be due to the measures used. The current DARE study uses only two single-item questions to assess students' attitudes about the police, whereas Faine and Bohlander (1988) used an 11-item scale that is likely to be more valid.

With reference to drug use, all of the stronger DARE evaluations found no effects with the exception of the current study, which found a significant difference on last-year alcohol use. Clayton's follow-up evaluation showed only one significant difference in the wrong direction on the first of two follow-up posttests (Clayton, Cattarello, and Walden 1991). As Clayton, Cattarello, and Walden (1991) point out, the lack of short-term drug use differences may be due to low base rates and thus should not be interpreted to mean DARE has no effect on adolescent drug involvement.

Recommendations

Replication studies of the evaluation of the DARE program should be continued because mixed evidence exists about the program's overall effectiveness. Conducting randomized experiments would certainly be best for drawing more confident conclusions about DARE program outcomes. Longitudinal studies would also aid in assessing the long-term program goal of deterring adolescent drug use.

There is one large problem with recommending a long-term study on a drug prevention program that is conducted in schools in the United States. The problem involves finding a true "no treatment" control group. Almost every school in the nation has some type of drug education component embodied in the school curriculum that is often mandated by the state. Therefore, it is likely the control group will receive some form of drug education. This problem has been documented as Clayton's (Clayton, Cattarello, and Walden 1991) study used a comparison group that received the school drug education unit and the ETI (Evaluation and Training Institute) had to discontinue their 5-year longitudinal study because the entire control group has essentially become a treatment group (Criminal Justice Statistics Association 1990).

In the future, it may be possible only to compare students' receiving some specified drug prevention program with the school system's drug education unit. However, this appears acceptable if the school system simply requires a unit session on factual drug information or a similar low-level intervention because prevention efforts such as these have consistently been shown to have no positive effects (Berberin et al. 1976; Kinder, Pape, and Walfish 1980; Schaps et al. 1981; Tobler 1986).

Should evaluations of the DARE program continue, it is suggested one national survey instrument be developed and used for all outcome evaluations. Currently, it is difficult to assess whether or not DARE is actually a success because different researchers use different survey instruments to examine a variety of outcome measures. Measuring DARE program objectives and other risk factors associated with later drug use with one survey would enable researchers to compare results across evaluations conducted in U.S. cities and other parts of the world.

Additional recommendations include employing peer leaders (i.e., high school students) as instructors instead of police officers. There are two reasons for this suggestion. First, it has not been consistently demonstrated that attitudes toward police become more positive upon receiving the DARE program, and second, there has been some evidence supporting the use of peer leaders as primary program providers (Botvin and Eng 1982; Botvin et al. 1984; Perry et al. 1980).

It would be not only interesting, but informative, to compare DARE program outcomes using peer leaders versus police officers as instructors. Should peer leaders provide equal or better outcomes, DARE programming costs would be considerably less and police officers would be more readily available to respond to citizen calls.

It is further recommended that DARE be restructured to incorporate components shown more consistently to be effective such as those found in second-generation approaches. Although DARE aims to increase resistance skills, coping, and decision making, the lessons specifically targeting these factors do so in the context of drug use only. Adolescents engaging in drug use behavior are often involved in other problem behaviors (Jessor and Jessor 1977). It would seem most practical and beneficial to target all of these behaviors using one program as Botvin (1982) and Swisher (1979) have suggested. The DARE program could serve as this one program, assuming several changes were implemented.

First, existing components would have to be expanded and additional components added in order to target more broad-based adolescent life problems such as family struggles, peer acceptance, sexual involvement, intimate relationships, and effective communication (expressing ideas, listening). Additional sessions should include components from second-generation programs such as setting goals, solving problems, and anticipating obstacles (Botvin, Renick, and Baker 1983; Schinke and Gilchrist 1985).

Second, skill acquisition is said to come about only through practice and reinforcement (Bandura 1977). It is proposed that any new skills taught, such as problem solving, be reinforced with "real life" homework where students practice these skills in the context of the "real world" rather than simply role playing them in the classroom.

The last recommendation is applicable not only to the DARE program but any drug prevention effort. It involves the addition of booster sessions following the prevention program. Because adolescence is a time of growth, individual attitudes and behaviors may continue to change and develop as the youth is maturing. Although short-term evidence of program effectiveness is encouraging, there is no guarantee a youth will continue to practice those same behaviors or hold those same beliefs years, or even months, after the program has ended. In fact, follow-up studies have documented the eroding effects of drug prevention programs (Botvin and Eng 1980, 1982) and the superior effects of booster sessions (Botvin, Renick, and Baker 1983; Botvin et al. 1984). For these reasons, DARE, or any other drug prevention program targeting adolescents, should include a series of follow-up sessions in order to increase the likelihood of sustaining any positive effects.

NO

Stephen Glass

DON'T YOU D.A.R.E.

On January 28, 1991, at 4 p.m., 10-year-old Darrin Davis, of Douglasville, Georgia, returned from school to his suburban home. Both of Darrin's parents were at work, and he let himself in. He immediately went to his parents' bedroom to call his mother, who wouldn't be home for another two hours. After talking to her on the phone, Darrin began searching the bedroom for candy; his parents often hid sweets there. He found none. Instead, after climbing on top of a chair, Darrin saw a white powder on a small makeup mirror. At that point, Darrin would later say, he thought of something he had recently been taught in school. Darrin's fourth-grade class had been visited by a police officer under the auspices of the Drug Abuse Resistance Education program, or DARE, as it is known. One of the things the DARE officer had told Darrin and his classmates was that they should inform the police if they ever saw anyone—including their parents—use drugs. The kids were shown a video that reinforced the point.

Although Darrin had never seen either of his parents use drugs, he decided, based on what he had learned in DARE, that the substance on the mirror was powdered cocaine. So he did what the DARE officer had told him to do: he called 911 and turned in his parents. Two hours later, when the Davises returned home, they were handcuffed and arrested while Darrin watched. A police officer put his hand on Darrin's shoulder, and told the boy he had done "the right thing." Darrin's father spent the next three months in jail, much to Darrin's surprise and dismay. "I thought the police would come get the drugs and tell them that drugs are wrong," the boy told a local reporter. 'They never said they would arrest them. It didn't say that in the video." When the sheriff's office told the boy he was too young to visit his dad in jail, Darrin set the neighbors' house on fire, causing $14,000 in damages. "I asked him why he did it," Darrin's mother said. "He said he wanted to be put in jail with his daddy."

As it turned out, the substance on the mirror was not cocaine. The Davises' lawyer says it was a small amount of speed. Both the Davises were charged with simple possession. Ultimately, the Georgia Supreme Court ordered the charges dropped, primarily on the grounds that the police had improperly

From Stephen Glass, "Don't You D.A.R.E.," *The New Republic* (March 3, 1997). Copyright © 1997 by The New Republic, Inc. Reprinted by permission.

searched the Davis home. The damage, though, was done. Darrin's telephone call destroyed his family. Heavy media coverage of the 10-year-old who had turned in his own parents ruined the Davises' reputation. Legal fees nearly bankrupted them and they came close to losing their home. They filed for divorce shortly after the criminal charges were dropped.

In January 1994, James Bovard, a freelance writer, wrote an account of the Davis case for *The Washington Post's* prestigious Sunday Outlook section. Bovard used the case to criticize DARE for "turning children into informants" in the war on drugs. Although Bovard had called DARE to get the organization's comment, DARE officials had declined to talk more than briefly. Jefferson Morley, assistant editor at Outlook who handled Bovard's column, edited the piece and faxed the edited copy to Bovard. The piece remained extremely critical of DARE. On the fax, Morley scribbled a note: "Jim: ok?" Bovard called Morley and approved the piece as edited.

On Sunday morning, January 30, Bovard picked up the *Post* and read his story. He was astonished to read, inserted into the piece and under his byline, six paragraphs that he had not written—that, indeed, he had never seen. The paragraphs ran counter to the thrust of the column, calling the case against DARE "murky." Far worse, the new paragraphs said "there was evidence" Darrin's parents were not only drug users, but "were also involved in drug trafficking, thus putting their child at risk." Not only had the possession charges been dropped against the Davises, but there had never been *any* evidence presented to show that the Davises were drug dealers. They had never been charged with trafficking, only with possession.

"I was stunned. I didn't know what to say," Bovard explains. "Nothing like this had ever happened before." Bovard investigated, and what he found out stunned him even more: the incorrect information in the added paragraphs had been directly supplied by DARE.

How did this happen? J. W. Bouldin, the Davises' lawyer, says the *Post's* lawyers told him that DARE had lobbied the newspaper to add the paragraphs. The *Post's* lawyers told Bouldin that DARE supplied Morley with the information for the six paragraphs and Morley typed it in. Bovard also says that DARE put pressure on the *Post*. "When they learned more about my story, DARE put on the full-court press," Bovard says. "They wanted to kill this story. It makes sense why."

Morley says it happened slightly differently. He says that after he edited the column he became concerned that DARE's point of view was not represented. He consulted with the *Post's* lawyers who agreed with him that he should call DARE and get their side of the story. He telephoned DARE's Los Angeles headquarters and talked to a spokeswoman for the organization. Morley says that he wrote the six paragraphs based on his conversation with the spokeswoman. He admits that the information came directly from DARE and that he never told Bovard he had added it to the column. But he says neither he nor anyone at the *Post* "kowtowed" to DARE. "This was my.... It was not the *Post* caving in to DARE," Morley says. "The whole story doesn't make me look very good. I regret, I really regret, any role in spreading the false information.... This was my least finest hour."

Bouldin knew as soon as he read the column that he had a dandy libel case. He called the *Post*'s lawyers and informed them that he was going to sue on behalf of the Davises. "They soon saw they had one very, very big problem on their hands," Bouldin says. Shortly before the Davises' libel suit was to be filed, the *Post* settled. The settlement included a large cash payment to the Davises. The paper also printed a correction, which cleared the Davises of the drug trafficking accusation and admitted that no evidence connecting them with drug trafficking had ever existed. Bouldin says that the terms of the settlement prohibit him from disclosing just how much the misinformation provided by DARE cost the *Post*, but he makes it clear that the price was high. "Let's just say this was a very expensive mistake for *The Washington Post*," he says, the tone of satisfaction clear in his Southern drawl.

DARE spokesman Ralph Lochridge doesn't deny his organization gave the *Post* false information, and he doesn't apologize, either. "Just because [the Davises] weren't convicted in court doesn't mean they're not guilty of it," Lochridge told me.

* * *

The anti-drug and anti-alcohol program called DARE is popular, well-financed and widespread. Started in 1983 by the Los Angeles Police Department and the L.A. School District, DARE has quickly become the nation's standard anti-drug curriculum. The DARE logo is everywhere: on bumper stickers, duffel bags, Frisbees, even fast-food containers. DARE is the only drug education program specifically sanctioned for funding under the federal Drug-Free Schools and Communities Act. This year, the program

will receive $750 million, of which some $600 million, according to outside analysts, comes from federal, state and local governments. At the core of the DARE curriculum are seventeen weekly lessons taught in the fifth or sixth grade. The teachers are all uniformed cops trained by DARE. The officers lecture and assign homework on the dangers of drugs, alcohol and gangs. Many schools, like Darrin Davis's, offer a shorter curriculum in every grade before the fifth. Some school districts also participate in supplementary junior high school and high school programs. The Los Angeles-based DARE America, the nonprofit company that develops and sells the DARE curriculum, boasts that cops working with DARE now lecture in 70 percent of the nation's school districts. In 1996, two of the last hold-outs, the New York City and Washington, D.C., school districts, signed up for the program.

Most parents know about DARE, and most of them approve of it. So do most politicians, most police officers, most teachers and most journalists. President Clinton has been a fan ever since Chelsea graduated from the Arkansas DARE. "We ought to continue to expand the... program so that in every grade school in this country there's a DARE officer," he said to cheers at an Orange County campaign rally last October. How many people, after all, are opposed to warning children about the dangers of drugs?

But what most people don't know is that, in the past five years, study after study has shown that DARE does not seem to work. The studies have found that students who go through the program are just as likely to use drugs as those who don't. In fact, the results in one study even show the dreaded boomerang effect: DARE graduates are *more* likely to use marijuana. Behavioral scientists have begun to question, with increasing vigor, whether DARE is little more than a feel-good scheme of enormous proportions. As one researcher put it: "DARE is the world's biggest pet rock. If it makes us feel good to spend the money on nothing, that's okay, but everyone should know DARE does nothing." None of this is a secret among drug policy experts and reporters who cover drug policy; some of the studies have been available for years. *Reason, Kansas City Magazine* and *USA Today* have published substantial stories criticizing the program's effectiveness. But these stories have done nothing to impede DARE's progress, and most parents and educators still believe it works. Why isn't the case against DARE better known? Why, at a time when federal funds are scarce, is it not a public issue that a program which costs the government more than half a billion dollars a year may be a waste of the taxpayers' money?

What happened to James Bovard and to *The Washington Post* is an illustration of the answer. For the past five years, DARE has used tactics ranging from bullying journalists to manipulating the facts to mounting campaigns in order to intimidate government officials and stop news organizations, researchers and parents from criticizing the program. DARE supporters have been accused of slashing tires, jamming television transmissions and spray-painting reporters' homes to quiet critics. "What you have to understand is that DARE is almost a billion dollar industry. If you found out that a food company's foods were rotten, they'd be out of business," says Mount Holyoke sociology and criminology professor Richard Moran. "What's now been found out is that DARE is running the

biggest fraud in America. That's why they've gone nuts." DARE has become so well-known for the hardball tactics it employs to shut down its critics that drug researchers and journalists have a word for those hushed—they say they've been "Dared."

Glenn Levant, the executive director of DARE, did not respond to repeated requests for an interview about DARE's effectiveness and its tactics in squelching bad publicity. Provided, at his request, with written questions, Levant did not reply. DARE spokesman Ralph Lochridge says his organization does not silence researchers. "We don't go after anyone, and DARE doesn't stop critical stories," he says. "It does try to help journalists write balanced pieces." Lochridge says his organization tries to "work" with journalists. "We don't mind criticism, but we want balance. Is your story going to be balanced?"

* * *

The story of DARE and its critics starts in Kokomo, Indiana. Fifty-three miles north of Indianapolis, Kokomo is an auto factory town of 45,000 people in the heart of the state's rural and Republican midsection. The city hall operator boasts that Kokomo was the birthplace of stainless steel. In 1987, it also became the first Indiana city to sign up for the DARE program. That year, school officials invited two sociology professors at the local branch of Indiana University to run an experiment to see how well the program worked. Everyone expected glowing results, and hoped the positive study would accelerate DARE's implementation elsewhere. The research team studied 1987's fifth-grade class in Kokomo through 1994, its last year in high school. They also studied the high school class of 1991, which had made its way through the school system prior to DARE's implementation, and had never been exposed to the program. Sociology professors Earl Wysong and Richard Aniskiewicz measured drug use among the students in both the 1994 graduating class and the 1991 class. They also measured DARE's secondary objectives: boosting self-esteem and reducing susceptibility to peer pressure. Wysong and Aniskiewicz were careful to measure the students' drug use with a multi-part questionnaire, which included DARE's own test as well as tests commonly used by psychologists. They found that the level of drug use among kids who had gone through DARE was virtually identical to the level among kids who had not. This means that in every category of drug use tested—lifetime usage, how recently the students had used drugs, how often they had used drugs and the grade in which they started using drugs—the results were "very similar" for both the DARE alumni and the non-DARE students. So similar, in fact, that the differences were within the margin of error. Moreover, students in both groups rated the availability of drugs nearly identically. In fact, the only statistical difference between the groups was that *more* DARE graduates said they had used marijuana in the past thirty days and the past year than non-DARE alumni. Wysong and Aniskiewicz concluded that "DARE exposure does not produce any long-term prevention efforts on adolescent drug use rates."

What about the more touchy-feely results? Again, the sociologists found no statistical differences. Using questionnaires to examine self-esteem and "locus of control," a common psychology test that measures susceptibility to peer pressure, they found numbers so similar for the two groups that any differences were again within the margin of error. They wrote that self-esteem and peer pressure are "two more areas where we can see no long-term effects resulting from DARE exposure." "That's all, that's it," says Wysong. "It's simple. There was no difference."

But Wysong and Aniskiewicz also found out what other critics of DARE would discover: no one—not parents, not educators and certainly not DARE officials—wanted to hear the bad news. Kokomo's parents, teachers and school board latched on to the study, but Wysong says they missed the point. "I told them the study shows DARE doesn't work," he says, but no one listened. "So what they did was implement drug testing." Since last April, the high school has required every student who leaves the building at lunch, participates in extracurricular activities or drives to school to sign a waiver. The waiver allows the school to pull them out of class at any time and force them to take a drug test. On average, forty-five students are tested each week. "That wasn't what our study recommended," Wysong says. "After our study it became very clear they kept DARE for public relations reasons." The school board has not renewed any studies on the local DARE program.

Even after Wysong and Aniskiewicz published their results, DARE continued to boast that an earlier California study— in fact, the first study ever done on DARE —showed that kids who went through the program accepted drugs less often than kids who had not gone through the program. The data also showed that DARE alumni reported using drugs less often. This study, however, did not ring true to many researchers because it had no pre-test. In other words, students were only surveyed after graduating from DARE. Without measuring drug use before DARE, it's difficult to know whether or not the students' behavior had changed. What is more, the study last examined its subjects as seventh graders, meaning it never measured DARE's long-term impact. "If you don't know where your base is you really don't know anything," laughs an Ivy League biologist who examined the methodology of the California study. "My kid's science fair project with plants and swinging lights was more rigid than this."

Another drug policy expert who has questioned DARE is Dick Clayton, a widely respected drug abuse researcher at the University of Kentucky. In 1996, Clayton published, in the journal *Preventive Medicine*, the most rigorous long-term study ever performed on DARE. Starting in September 1987, Clayton surveyed schoolchildren in all of the thirty-one elementary schools in Lexington, Kentucky. The schools were randomly assigned to receive the DARE curriculum or to receive "no treatment." Students were tested before going through the DARE program, immediately afterward and again each year through the spring of 1992. Clayton's team found that any results from DARE were extremely short-lived. "Here it is in layman's terms: DARE is supposed to reduce drug use. In the long term, it does not," Clayton says. Just before and after Clayton's release of the two-year data, more studies quietly began popping up with similar results. In total, Clayton wrote in the 1996 book *Intervening with Drug-Involved Youth*, at least fifteen studies were conducted. "Although the results from various studies differ somewhat, all studies are consistent in finding that DARE does

not have long-term effects on drug use," he wrote. Among those studies was a 1990 Canadian government report showing DARE was less effective than anyone imagined. The program, the Canadians reported, had no effect on cutting abuse of any drug from aspirin to heroin. (The Canadians were studying DARE because the program was becoming more popular abroad. Today, Lochridge says, DARE is used in forty-nine foreign countries.)

As the number of debunking studies grew, something else also grew: the number of researchers getting Dared. Take the case of Daniel, a young professor at an Illinois college. He asked that his last name not be used, since he is up for tenure within the next two years and nervous about adverse publicity. Daniel says he wants to study behavioral programs that have political impact. While he suspects that to improve his chances for tenure he should study the behavior of lab animals, he's fascinated by "real world" problems. "That's why Clayton's study appealed to me," he says. "I thought here was a chance where people like me can make a difference." Daniel designed and performed a study of college freshmen. All of the freshmen were in-state students, but only some had attended DARE. Once again, Daniel's study found no meaningful difference in drug use between students who had gone through DARE and students who hadn't. He did find, however, that DARE graduates were slightly *more* likely to drink alcohol regularly for the purpose of getting drunk. Over lunch one day, Daniel, proud of what he thought was an "important finding for the Illinois school system," showed the data to a colleague in a different department. "That was the biggest mistake of my career," Daniel says. "That's right—

even bigger than sleeping through an oral exam in graduate school." Daniel says that, within a week a local DARE official called him at home and asked to see the data. Daniel says he freely showed the information to him. That, he says, resulted in a "big argument with lots of yelling." Two weeks later Daniel says he received a call from his department chairman. The chairman told him that the local DARE official had complained that Daniel was offering kids marijuana as part of his study. Daniel says the allegations are false, but that he immediately stopped work on the DARE study, and returned to lab animals. "That could have been, and still might be, a career killer," Daniel says. "DARE has made it so I will never venture out of the lab again."

* * *

While it's not possible to say exactly how many researchers have been Dared, it is clear from talking to academics in the relevant fields that there are a number of them. It's common knowledge among researchers that doing DARE studies can ruin a promising career. Wysong and David W. Wright, a Wichita State University professor, wrote in *Sociological Focus* that the DARE researchers they had interviewed "asked to remain anonymous out of fear of political reprisals and to protect their careers." Interviews with drug researchers support this statement. An author of one prominent paper says he no longer studies DARE. "I needed my life back. I'm in research. My wife and I couldn't take endless personal attacks," he told me. "You want to know why I stopped researching DARE? Write your article and you'll see." Another researcher who was critical of DARE says he became so unpopular among fellow

professors he went into the private sector. "If you fight DARE, they make you out to look like you want kids to smoke pot. I thought it was my duty to say the emperor is not wearing any clothes," he says. "It was stupid of me to think I could fight them. Everyone told me I couldn't, but I tried. Here [in the private sector] I can start over." The researcher says after he published his study, someone etched the words "kid killer" and "drug pusher" into the paint of his car.

The extent of DARE's ability to muzzle critical studies can be seen in the treatment of the most definitive test of the DARE program ever conducted. In 1991, the National Institute of Justice (NIJ)—the research wing of the Justice Department—hired the prestigious Research Triangle Institute (RTI) to analyze the studies on DARE and determine the bottom line. Initially, DARE supported the "meta-analysis. "In a 1992 letter, it urged state groups to work with RTI, saying it "will give us ammunition to respond to critics who charge that DARE has not proven its effectiveness.

"Everything was going along just fine," explains a researcher who worked on the RTI analysis and who asked that his name not be used so he wouldn't get "any more nasty, screeching phone calls" in the middle of the night. "That is, until we started finding DARE just simply didn't work. Then all hell broke loose."

In 1993, RTI presented its preliminary results at a San Diego drug education conference. According to *Sociological Focus*, a DARE supporter immediately responded by urging RTI to call off the research, saying: "If [DARE] fails, it will be making a statement about all prevention programs." After the conference, DARE launched an all-out war to sink the study. An internal memo from the

July 5, 1993, meeting of DARE's advisory board offers evidence that Levant tried to squelch the study. The memo contains the minutes of Levant's speech. Levant criticized an advance copy of the RTI study. The minutes summarize Levant: "The results of this project are potentially damaging to DARE. DARE America has spent $41,000 in trying to prevent widespread distribution of what is considered to be faulty research." The minutes also noted that "DARE America has instituted legal action," aimed at squelching the RTI study. "The action has had some positive results," the minutes reported. "It has resulted in prevention of a second presentation by RTI. Legal action is intended to prevent further public comment until completion of academic review." Lochridge did not return a phone message asking for comment on the memo, and asking whether government funds had been used to stop the government from distributing a government-funded study questioning the efficacy of a government-funded program.

In the past, DARE had been unable to effectively refute its critics on scientific grounds, and its claims rang correspondingly weak. "They must not know how to measure things," maintained an Indiana DARE official about the Kokomo research at a local community agency. "If they could just see the kids' faces, they'd know how much good it's doing." Herbert Kleber, a Columbia University professor who heads DARE's scientific advisory board, says the RTI study was flawed. "It used the old DARE curriculum, which had already been substantially revised," Kleber says. "No, the new curriculum has never been examined."

So this time Levant turned to grassroots pressure. According to one Justice

Department official, Levant arranged for DARE supporters to flood the Justice Department with phone calls. Nationwide, many teachers, principals, DARE officers and parents believe in the program with almost religious devotion. In local debates, they have always been more than willing to make phone calls, write letters and hold forums to support DARE. This time, the callers stayed "on message," the official says, speaking almost as if from a script. "They'd call and tell us if we published the study, DARE would be sunk and millions of kids would get hooked," says the official. "Whenever we'd say the research looked mathematically good, they'd say, 'there's more at stake here than good statistics. Can you live with that?'"

In September 1994, RTI finished the lengthy report. It concluded that, while DARE was loved by teachers and participants, it had no effect on drug use. It also went one step further, a step that DARE feared most of all. "What got [RTI] in the most hot water is that they said other programs work better," says Moran, the Mount Holyoke sociologist. In other words, RTI found that DARE is not merely a failure in itself, but crowds out money for programs that actually keep kids off drugs. RTI published a lengthy bibliography of some of the other programs. Kleber says the alternatives RTI looked at, which he calls "boutique programs," were only examined in highly controlled environments.

Levant upped the ante. Congressmen and mayors began calling the National Institute of Justice. The politicians stressed two messages: the curriculum had changed since the study, making it irrelevant; and the public did not want to hear criticism of an anti-drug program widely regarded as successful. The Justice Department official says the "phone rang off the hook."

One month later, for the first time in memory, the Justice Department refused to publish a study it had funded and successfully peer-reviewed. "We're not trying to hide the study," Ann Voit, an NIJ spokeswoman told *USA Today.* "We just do not agree with one of the major findings." A puzzling statement, since NIJ hired RTI in the first place because it trusted them to evaluate DARE impartially. Still more puzzling is that even as late as six months after the San Diego conference, NIJ sent RTI memos praising the study. One note from Laurie Bright, NIJ's program manager, said the "methodology appears to be sound and DARE representatives did not offer any specific flaws ... [it] presented findings in a very fair and impartial light." Eventually, Jeremy Travis, who heads the NIJ, stepped in. He publicly reiterated that Justice had not caved under DARE's pressure, explaining that NIJ's independent reviewers unanimously recommended against publishing the report. Not so, according to one reviewer. William DeJone, a Harvard lecturer, told *USA Today:* "They must be misremembering what I said." Two of the independent reviewers who examined the report in March 1994 recommended that more analysis be done. But both urged the publication and wide dissemination of the executive summary of the report, and one praised the crucial section that analyzed DARE's efficacy as "well done." NIJ still has not approved the study, but will sell it upon request.

The same day Justice refused the study, *The American Journal of Public Health*—a highly respected academic journal—accepted it. It had conducted its own peer review and found the paper to be worthy. The Justice Department official says this infuriated Levant and that DARE tried to prevent the journal from publishing the study. While no one at *Public Health* would comment on Levant and DARE, two editors at the journal said that it stands by editor Sabine Beisler's comment of October 1994: "DARE has tried to interfere with the publication of this. They tried to intimidate us." When NIJ learned the journal was going to publish the study, it issued its own two-page summary. The summary oddly heralded DARE's popularity, but virtually ignored the thrust and bulk of the study, which showed DARE doesn't curtail drug use.

Today, the researchers who worked on parts of the RTI study remain thoroughly spooked by their experience. Two researchers at RTI, four at universities and two now in the private sector, refused to talk more than briefly about the study. All but one said they were scared of losing their jobs. Three told me that their superiors had been contacted by politicians. "A state representative called my boss and asked if my research was really in the best interest of the community," said one state university professor. "Thank God my boss said 'yes.' I don't know if even tenure would stand up to that."

* * *

DARE's hardball approach is as well-known among journalists who have attempted stories on the organization as it is among academic researchers. James, a television news producer who does not want his last name used for this story, says that ever since he was Dared he doesn't have any doubts about retaliation. Several months ago, James, who works for a small Missouri station, produced and aired a short editorial criticizing DARE. In more than a decade of local news, it is the only item he has ever regretted running. After that show aired, so many kids called James so often at home to read him lessons from the DARE workbook that he was forced to unlist his telephone number. "You bet I was Dared," James says. "The calls came and on and on. I had to hear about so-and-so is offered a joint, but she says 'no.' I couldn't take it." Two callers told James that their DARE officer encouraged them to call his house at strange hours. After that, James's house was attacked with graffiti messages like "crack user inside" so many times, he moved to an apartment building. The local police, who run the local DARE program, spent no time looking for the vandals, James says. After a math teacher asked his son how "the pot-head dad" was doing, he transferred his kid to a boarding school. And, when the owner of a local diner asked him to stop coming to lunch, since other customers were leaving when he walked in, his wife took to calling him "Small-town Salman," after *Satanic Verses* author-in-hiding Salman Rushdie. James says he phoned Levant and asked him to "please call them off," but Levant never returned the message. "This may sound as if I'm being extreme, but I'm not. I went to Vietnam and that was less stressful," James says with a shaking voice. "There, the people I love weren't always being attacked. And this time, I know I'm on the right side."

In the past year, NBC's news magazine "Dateline" has become the most prominent news organization to be Dared. Starting in September 1995, "Dateline" producers began initial research on a hard-hitting story about how DARE doesn't work. They interviewed re-searchers who had concluded that DARE was a failure and students who couldn't remember the lessons. A "Dateline" camera crew also flew to Indianapolis, where an affluent, mostly Republican suburb was debating whether to keep DARE. For the past year, the school district had monitored a small pilot program. More than 100 parents showed up to the meeting and, according to those who were there, the majority vocally opposed DARE. According to a longtime NBC News employee, the show was scheduled to run on April 9, 1996—the day before National DARE Day. The following account of what then transpired has been corroborated by two additional NBC sources: essential details of it have also been confirmed by a DARE source and a Justice Department source.

Last March, Levant heard about the planned "Dateline" show According to the NBC News employee—who does not work on "Dateline" but has read a series of letters between Levant and NBC officials—Levant wrote an "attack letter" to Jack Welch. Welch is the chief executive officer of General Electric, NBC's parent company. The letter called the segment a "journalistic fraud." Levant accused "Dateline" of "staging" the Indiana meeting. Still under the shadow of an infamous episode in which "Dateline" was accused of rigging trucks to explode, the NBC employee says Levant's accusations sent "Dateline"'s staff into a "whirlwind of activity." But Levant's accusation was a "flat-out lie—no ifs, no buts about it, a lie as low as it goes," says Betsy Paul, then the Parent Teacher Organization president of the Indiana school district. "I don't know how to say this strongly enough. I will tell you on any witness stand with God as my judge. . . . We had scheduled the meeting for at least a week before 'Dateline' said they were coming out here." Paul says David McCormick, NBC's senior producer for broadcast standards, called her. McCormick asked her if she had brought in "ringers" to stack the meeting against DARE. "And that was the biggest bunch of bologna I've ever heard," Paul says. "DARE just doesn't like that parents here figured out they didn't work." As further proof, Paul points out that this year DARE was eliminated in her school district and replaced with a locally developed program. "[Levant is] a big liar because if we stacked that meeting, if it didn't accurately reflect how this community thinks, then why did the school board eliminate DARE this year?" she says. "I'll say it again, he lied, and once more he lied."

Levant's letter to Welch contained other untruths, claims the NBC News employee. In the letter, Levant alleges "Dateline" producers would only interview him on the day his wife was receiving a bone marrow treatment for leukemia. Not true, according to the NBC News employee: "Dateline" offered Levant "several" date options. Levant also alleged "Dateline" staffers were interrogating kids in dark rooms like "old war movies." In truth, "Dateline" cameramen had turned off the overhead lights when they interviewed DARE participants because they were using their own lighting, which is standard practice. While the NBC employee says McCormick defended "Dateline" in a response to Levant, the story was put on hold. "DARE scared NBC's upper brass," the NBC employee says. "The story was, and is, solid. The people on it are some of the best in the business, but we did not want to look like we were going after a program that keeps kids off drugs. You can imagine that's

a very unpopular position with G.E. So it was put on hold." David Corvo, the NBC vice president that clears "Dateline" episodes before they air, says, "There is no controversy about the program at NBC." He says all delays occurred because he felt the segment needed more reporting. "No way," the NBC News employee says. "That piece was solid in every way. Sure, you can always get another interview, and they did, but even before that it was better than much of what we air."

Then, in a September 1996 issue of *TV Guide*, NBC placed the following announcement: " 'Dateline NBC': A Len Cannon report on the DARE program in schools. Its effects are 'statistically insignificant,' says segment producer Debbie Schooley. 'Research overwhelmingly shows no long-term effect on drug use.' The report visits schools in suburban Indianapolis."

According to the NBC employee, the *TV Guide* announcement killed the episode again. Dozens of DARE supporters, including Levant, called NBC. According to the employee, this time he made veiled threats of suing "Dateline." Despite the listing, the show didn't air. Corvo maintains that NBC "did not kill" the story and says if any lawsuit threats were made, they were not taken seriously. He maintains that NBC sent *TV Guide* the listing several weeks in advance, but when the date arrived, the piece still wasn't ready.

* * *

Next, the biggest gun in the drug wars tried to sink the segment once and for all. In mid-September, the White House's drug czar General Barry McCaffrey stepped in. "Dateline" had already interviewed McCaffrey for the segment. During the interview, McCaffrey ridiculed the research against DARE, but a Justice staffer says he did a "very poor" job refuting the mounds of evidence. Corvo won't comment on McCaffrey's interview, beyond saying the drug czar disputed the evidence against DARE.

On September 20, 1996, Donald Maple, a spokesperson for McCaffrey's office, wrote to "Dateline"'s executive producer. The letter asked "Dateline" not to use the taped interview with McCaffrey. Maple wrote that he feared the interview would serve " 'Dateline' 's purpose of painting DARE in a bad light." The NBC employee says pulling the McCaffrey interview might have dealt a "death blow" to the show. NBC's McCormick responded to Maple that the show's producer had written McCaffrey a letter before the interview telling him the purpose of the interview was to discuss research on DARE's effectiveness. While the network did not promise to cut McCaffrey's interview, the NBC employee explains, "at some point this story is much more trouble than it's worth." Maple says writing this kind of letter to a news organization is "uncommon," and he had never done it for McCaffrey before. But he says "Dateline" treated McCaffrey unfairly.

The show was rescheduled one more time, for Tuesday, February 4. That time slot—right after the president's State of the Union address—is commonly considered to be a "death slot." Clinton's speeches are renowned for running long, killing whatever television segment is planned to run next. And, that night the segment did not run. As expected, Clinton's speech ran longer than scheduled and "Dateline" ran a show focusing on the O. J. Simpson verdict. "This system has worked. This show has not been killed. Whoever says that is out of the loop," Corvo says, adding that he has now cleared it to air. As of February 10, though, the segment had not been rescheduled. Corvo says it will be rescheduled when the executive producer of "Dateline" returns from vacation.

And researchers and reporters are not the only ones getting Dared. Some parents who question the program also say they've been strong-armed. In the San Juan Islands northwest of Seattle is a small town called Friday Harbor. There, dozens of parents have joined together in a group called San Juan Parents Against DARE, According to Andrew Seltser, the group's founder, nearly all of the members want drug education in the schools; they just don't believe the DARE program works. In August, Seltser's group collected more than 100 signatures on a petition asking the local school board to review the effectiveness of DARE. The debate about DARE overtook the small community, and became a matter of intense passion, with local DARE supporters raging against the parents who were challenging the program. In September, the local school board announced it would review concerns about DARE.

Then an odd thing happened. On October 7, 1996, the "CBS Evening News" aired a short segment that presented information critical of DARE. No one in Friday Harbor saw that segment, though. Thirty seconds into the story, Friday Harbor's screens went black. Randy Lindsey, the station manager for the local cable station, says when he watched a videotape of that night's news "it looks like someone pulled the plug." Lindsey can't explain the blackout. Friday Harbor, he says, often has problems receiving television signals due to sun spots. But sun spot interference, he says, normally distorts the screen differently. Seltser's group says they believe the program was jammed by DARE supporters since it came in the heat of the debate. And some Friday Harbor DARE supporters aren't denying it. One prominent local DARE supporter says it's "not important" whether or not the show was jammed. "Look, I'm not going to answer the question as to whether or not I know who jammed it. Hell, it might have been me," he says, asking that his name not be used. "What I am going to tell you is that TV program may have stopped DARE in Friday Harbor, which means more kids here would be on drugs."

* * *

DARE's public response to studies critical of the program has been to dismiss the studies as irrelevant. DARE says the studies are based on an old curriculum that may not have worked, but that the program now uses a redesigned curriculum that does work. The problem with the old curriculum, DARE officials say, was that DARE classes were not interactive enough; under the new curriculum, the classes are much more so. But this seems debatable, judging from a recent DARE class conducted by Detective Rick Myers at Barcroft Elementary School in Arlington, Virginia. Myers, a big man who looks very much like a cop, visits Barcroft's fifth graders every Thursday to lead them in the DARE way. One week's lesson was about resisting peer pressure. Myers's lesson lasted about forty-five minutes. All but six minutes were spent on a lecture by Myers. To be sure, Myers used interactive role play during those six minutes, but researchers question the value of such

role-playing as set out by the DARE curriculum.

For the first scene, Myers chose two kids: a brown-haired boy who was so nervous that he wobbled when he stood, and a tall girl who was so self-confident that she bowed when she got to the front of the room. Myers whispered the script to the two children and told them to face each other.

"There is a party on Saturday night at some person's house," the girl said matter-of-factly.

The boy said nothing.

"The people there, they will be drinking things that have [now louder and more slowly] al-co-hol."

The boy looked at the ground.

"I said, 'The people will be drinking [very loudly and very slowly] al-co-hol.'"

"No," peeped the boy.

Kindly, but firmly, Myers lectured the boy. "Posture. Eye contact. Posture. Eye contact," Myers told him. "You need to be confident. You're doing the right thing."

Take two. The girl said her first line. The boy said: "Oh." Myers shouted: "Posture. Eye contact." The girl said her second line. The boy stood straighter, looked the girl briefly in the eye, and said very quickly: "No thank you, I don't take alcohol. I prefer juice and milk." Myers led everyone in a round of applause. At one of the back tables, a thuggish-looking kid sat regarding this little scene with frank scorn. "He's supposed to say *that*? That won't work. He'd get the shit beat out of him."

For another scene, Myers chose a small girl with wide eyes and scraggly brown hair. She seemed a little nervous, but excited to have been chosen. Myers whispered the instructions into her ear. They faced off, standing about ten feet from each other. Myers walked up to the girl. "Hey, do you want to buy a joint?" he said. She replied, almost inaudibly, "No." Myers put his face close to hers. "Come on, wanna buy it?"

"No, thank you," she whispered.

Now, waving his finger in her face, Myers shouted: "Why not? Come on, buy it!"

The little girl, backed against the windows, said, again, "No." Myers led the class in a round of applause.

Drug researchers interviewed about Myers's scenes are dismissive. "That role play is absurd. If the kids learn anything at all from it, they learn not to buy drugs from police officers," one researcher says. "Making it more interactive means making it more like real life. This is not useful. Fun, maybe. Useful? Nope."

And Myers's class is typical. When I asked him if other DARE instructors did it differently, he was adamant in response. "No. The great thing about this program is that everyone in the country is trained the same way," Myers told me. "We are told to go exactly by the book. There is no room for modifying the program. No way. It's the same everywhere."

The claim that DARE's curriculum is changing and maturing seems to be more a matter of tactics than anything else. A longtime California instructor who recently retired, and who told me that the curriculum has not in fact changed much at all, conceded that saying the curriculum was in constant flux did have an obvious strategic benefit. Experts agree. Wysong and Wright wrote in *Sociological Focus* that if DARE is portrayed as a constantly evolving program it can't ever be studied and therefore can't ever fail. "Thus DARE is protected from criticism and remains

'forever young,' " they wrote. "In fact, in the view of DARE stakeholders, this is as it should be, because the program cannot be allowed to fail: the stakes are simply too high."

* * *

In fact, the most controversial part of the program—the DARE box—has remained unchanged despite years of criticism about this systematic attempt to encourage children to rat out the grown-ups around them, including their own parents. After the first class, the students, following DARE instructions, fashion a shoe box into a colorful mailbox, often decorated with DARE stickers. Each week from then on, for the entire seventeen weeks, students are encouraged to write anonymous notes asking any question they want. They are also allowed to accuse people of using or selling drugs or committing sexual abuse. These accusatory notes may also be anonymous. At the end of every DARE class, the officer reads the questions out loud. The officer does not read the accusatory notes to the class, but those notes are referred to the appropriate school and police investigative units for action. As James Bovard pointed out, Darrin Davis is not an isolated case. DARE students have fingered their parents in Maryland, Oklahoma and Wisconsin. In 1991, a 10-year-old told a Colorado 911 operator, "I'm a DARE kid," and urged the police to arrest his parents for marijuana possession. After his parents were arrested, the cop assigned to his school publicly praised him.

Parents and scientists in dozens of states have attacked the DARE box, saying that it reminds them of Stalinists rewarding kids for ratting on their parents. Lochridge, DARE's spokesman, dismisses their fears, saying it's mostly "urban myths." "Officers, as part of their training," he adds, "are taught not to elicit information about the [students'] personal lives." Lochridge says students are not encouraged to make accusations. But, according to one University of Illinois study, an accusation is made in 59 percent of all DARE classes. And while that number may be high, three Washington, D.C., area DARE cops interviewed said a DARE box note accused someone of using or selling drugs in at least one-third of their classes. All three cops said they "didn't discourage" their students from making accusations. Lochridge maintains the cops are just doing their job. "I don't know of any state which doesn't have laws requiring us to investigate any accusations of sexual abuse or drugs," he says.

In the end, DARE has an answer that trumps all. Even if there is some truth to charges that DARE doesn't work, what this means is that we need ... more DARE. "Well, if you teach people fractions or a foreign language, it's going to erode unless you reinforce it," Lochridge explains. "So the answer is more DARE. Kids need to get it more. And doubtless they will, whether it does them any good or not.

POSTSCRIPT

Is Drug Abuse Resistance Education (DARE) an Effective Program?

Before the effectiveness of drug education programs can be determined, it is necessary to define the goals of drug education. Are the goals of drug education to prevent drug use from starting? To prevent drug abuse? To prevent drug dependency? Perhaps the goal of drug education is to teach young people how to protect themselves and others from harm *if* they are going to use drugs. Without a clear understanding of the goals one wants to achieve in teaching about drugs, it is impossible to determine the effectiveness of drug education.

Before a drug education program can be designed, questions regarding what to include in the drug education curriculum need to be addressed. Should the primary focus be on teaching abstinence or responsible use? Is it feasible to teach abstinence from some drugs and responsible use of other drugs? Almost 90 percent of high school students have drunk alcohol; should they be taught they should not drink at all, or should they be taught how to use alcohol responsibly? Does the age of the children make a difference in what is taught? Do elementary students have the reasoning skills of high school students? Should the goal be for students to engage in a decision-making process or simply to adopt certain behaviors? If you were hired to teach a class of sixth-grade students about drugs and the principal asked you to outline what you would like to accomplish and how you plan on achieving your goals, would you be able to provide an answer? Too many programs are started without any clear focus. Vague questions yield vague solutions, so such programs are destined to fail.

In the 1980s there was a significant reduction in drug use among high school seniors in the United States, although drug use has climbed since the early 1990s. How much of the reduction in the 1980s was due to drug education, and how much was due to other factors? Throughout American history drug use has been cyclical—perhaps the United States was in a down cycle in the 1980s and is currently in an up cycle in terms of drug use.

If drug prevention programs such as Drug Abuse Resistance Education (DARE) are going to be effective in reducing drug use, schools and other institutions will need to work together. Many young people drop out of school or simply do not attend, so community agencies and religious institutions need to become involved. The media have a large impact on young people. What is the best way to incorporate the media in the effort to reduce drug use? Are antidrug commercial spots shown during programs aimed at teenage audiences effective?

Drug prevention efforts are reviewed in Mary Jansen's article "Prevention Research for Alcohol and Other Drugs: A Look Ahead to What Is Needed," *Substance Use and Misuse* (vol. 31, 1996). Another perspective on teaching about drugs is provided by Gail Milgram in "Responsible Decision Making Regarding Alcohol: A Re-Emerging Prevention/Education Strategy for the 1990s," *Journal of Drug Education* (vol. 26, 1996). Two studies that look at the effectiveness of DARE are "Impact Evaluation of Drug Abuse Resistance Education (DARE)," by Harold Becker, Michael Agopian, and Sandy Yeh, *Journal of Drug Education* (vol. 22, no. 4, 1992) and "Long-Term Evaluation of Drug Abuse Resistance Education," by Susan Ennett et al., *Addictive Behaviors* (vol. 19, no. 2, 1994).

ISSUE 17

Should the Decision to Use Anabolic Steroids Be Left to Athletes?

YES: Ellis Cashmore, from "Run of the Pill," *New Statesman and Society* (November 11, 1994)

NO: Joannie M. Schrof, from "Pumped Up," *U.S. News and World Report* (June 1, 1992)

ISSUE SUMMARY

YES: Sociology professor Ellis Cashmore argues that anabolic steroids are no different from the aids and equipment that athletes commonly use to enhance their performance. He further contends that the notion that drug use violates the rules of fair play is illogical because competition has never been predicated on fair play.

NO: Joannie M. Schrof, an associate editor of *U.S. News and World Report*, asserts that athletes who take anabolic steroids are not fully aware of the potential adverse effects and that these athletes often use excessive quantities because they are under tremendous pressure to win.

Anabolic steroids are synthetic derivatives of the male hormone testosterone. Although they have legitimate medical uses, steroids are increasingly being used by individuals to quickly build up muscle and increase personal strength. Concerns over the potential negative effects of steroid use seem to be justified: an estimated 1 million Americans, half of whom are adolescents, have used illegally obtained steroids. Anabolic steroid users span all ethnic groups, nationalities, and socioeconomic groups. The emphasis on winning has led many athletes to take risks with steroids that are potentially destructive. Despite the widespread belief that anabolic steroids are primarily used by athletes, up to one-third of users are nonathletes who use these drugs to improve their physiques and self-images.

Society places much emphasis on winning, and to come out on top, many individuals are willing to make sacrifices—sacrifices that may entail compromising their health. Some people will do anything for the sake of winning. In an article in *Sports Illustrated* published prior to his death, football player Lyle Alzado spoke out not against the use of steroids but against the way *he* used steroids. His message was not necessarily that steroids were bad but that they can be used badly. For some, any use of steroids for athletic competition raises some ethical concerns. These people argue that steroid users gain an unfair advantage over competitors who do not take steroids. That is, of course, the precise reason athletes take steroids. Critics maintain that misinformation about the effects of steroids is only fostered by the ban on their use.

The short-term consequences of anabolic steroids are well documented. Some possible short-term effects among men include testicular atrophy, sperm count reduction, impotency, baldness, difficulty in urinating, and breast enlargement. Among women, some potential effects are deepening of the voice, breast reduction, menstrual irregularities, and clitoral enlargement. Both sexes may develop acne, swelling in the feet, reduced levels of high-density lipoproteins (which is the "good" cholesterol), hypertension, and liver damage. Also related to steroid use are psychological changes, including mood swings, paranoia, and violent behavior. The short-term effects of steroids have been thoroughly researched; their long-term effects, however, have not been substantiated.

The problem with identifying the long-term effects of anabolic steroids is that there are virtually no systematic, scientific long-term studies. Most of the information regarding long-term effects comes from personal reports, not well-conducted, controlled studies. Personal stories or anecdotal evidence is often accepted as fact. For example, anabolic steroids have been implicated in the development of liver tumors. Yet, there are very few documented cases of liver tumors among steroid users. It is difficult to know if the effects from anabolic steroids are exaggerated.

The American Medical Association opposes stricter regulation of anabolic steroids on two grounds. First, anabolic steroids have been used medically to improve growth and development and for certain types of anemia, breast cancers, endometriosis, and osteoporosis. If stricter regulations were imposed, people who may medically benefit from these drugs will have more difficulty acquiring them. Second, it is highly unlikely that illicit use of these drugs will cease if they are banned. By maintaining legal access to these drugs, studies into their long-term consequences can be determined.

In the following selections, Ellis Cashmore argues that banning anabolic steroids from sports on the basis that they provide unfair advantages to athletes would be hypocritical because athletic competition is naturally unfair. He feels that better control of steroids can be accomplished if they are not prohibited. Joannie M. Schrof contends that people who use steroids are risking their lives and that stricter control of these substances is needed.

YES

Ellis Cashmore

RUN OF THE PILL

Amid the memories of [the 1994] World Cup finals, there is one that will remain. Not the record-breaking five goals of Russian striker Oleg Salenko against Cameroon, not the murder of Colombia's Andres Escobar, killed in a Medellín bar after conceding an own goal that hastened his country's exit from the competition, and certainly not the near-catatonic final. The abiding memory will be that of Diego Maradona, the third footballer in history to be ejected from a major tournament for taking banned substances—in his case a cocktail of five drugs, including ephedrine, found in over-the-counter decongestants. It transformed Maradona from the world's greatest player to the world's greatest cheat. The media all but changed his studs for cloven hooves.

Barely a week goes by, it seems, without a sports performer descending abruptly from the status of champion to cheat. Sports performers no longer prosecute the Corinthian ideal of competing for the sheer joy and gratification of competition. Athletes run for gold bars, boxers fight for millions, footballers play for monthly salaries big enough to buy an average family house. Hang incentives like this in front of performers and it's hardly surprising that they will do anything they can to augment the abilities they were blessed with. Taking drugs is an extension of the logic of competition.

Encouraged by television, which has successfully exploited sport and now almost depends on it, professional sport (which covers virtually all) offers incentives to its record-breakers and champions like never before. Performers can boost their performance by recruiting top coaches, nutritionists, acupuncturists; they can use state-of-the-art equipment and, if they can afford it, train in optimal climes. What they cannot do, of course, is take drugs. This sits oddly in a culture in which the preoccupation with health and fitness has all but commended a daily diet of chemicals. Even a relatively benign cold remedy, like Lemsip, will get an athlete banned for months, thanks to the presence of phenyephrine—and a set of rules that lacks both moral authority and common sense.

Sport's anti-drugs policies are so riven with hypocrisy, anomaly and contradiction that the only rational course of action is to abandon them and let competitors decide whether they want to take substances that purportedly enhance their performance. Sport hides behind two increasingly feeble justifications for maintaining an anti-drugs policy. The first has its origins in the policy's initial purpose: to protect competitors.

By the 1960s, it was known that, in cycling, competitors would often ingest amphetamine-based concoctions, some of them lethal, as the deaths of Knut Jensen and Tommy Simpson indicated. If the autobiography of ex-cyclist Paul Kimmage is to be accepted, the practice is still rife. A paternalistic impulse guided sport towards its early drug-testing, designed to prevent further tragedies.

Were this argument advanced today, it would seem a lot less credible than it did 30 years ago. A female runner using oral contraceptives to regulate her period and so maximise her training and performance, or a chess player who smokes to calm his nerves are allowed to compete, despite taking drugs with known harmful consequences. But there is woe for anyone who takes cough linctus without carefully checking the label.

There is also a paradox: evidence indicates that some sports activities themselves are more dangerous than many substances that are believed to enhance performance. Training at the intensity required to compete at the highest levels almost certainly takes its toll on the body's natural immunity system, exposing the competitor to infection.

Some sports clearly carry a risk. Ranked in terms of fatalities, boxing, a punishing pursuit in which brain damage is rife, is a relatively benign activity. Motor racing and air sports are killers. There are less visible casualties. In her teens, gymnast Olga Korbut charmed the world with her gentle play at the aesthetic borders of sport and art. By her late twenties, she was haggard and arthritic. There must be countless others who leave sport disabled by its physical demands. A genuinely paternalistic policy should examine that which it's meant to be safeguarding before banishing one of its lesser possible malefactors.

The argument most forcefully advanced nowadays is that using drugs violates the principle of fair play. But, has sport ever been fair? No: the conditions of actual competition may be equalised, but the advantages, whether natural or social, that some competitors enjoy can never be negated. Were you a runner, born in Bradford, following home Yobes Ondieki in a 5,000 metres race, you may wonder what difference it would have made if you, like your opponent, had been born and raised in Kenya, where the altitude encourages a naturally high haemoglobin count—a boon for middle-distance runners.

There is surely a degree of unfairness about a head-to-head meeting between Jennifer Capriati, born to a family well-off enough to provide top coaching facilities, and a ghetto child who picked up her tennis skills in the municipal parks of somewhere like Detroit.

Fair play and its antonym, cheating, are not preordained; they are products of how sports' governing organisations define them. If we need reminding of how arbitrary this can get, consider how devices, like starting blocks, or activities, including training, were once ruled out as unfair on the grounds that they gave competitors advantages.

Yet, there is still the question of sport's future to consider: we would be encouraging a generation of druggies, say querulous coaches and administrators. Sports stars today are potent symbols and their behaviour is often closely monitored and emulated by the young. The substances that supposedly enhance performance on the sports field are, of course, different from the ones that cause long-term distress at street-level. But the point is still a powerful one: drugs are drugs. So, why don't we drug-test Pavarotti after every concert, or expunge Suede's albums from the charts if they were recorded while the artists were under the influence? This is not *quite* as ridiculous as it sounds. The music of Charlie Parker, a heroin addict, the acting of Cary Grant, who used LSD, the writing of Dylan Thomas, an alcoholic: all these have not been obliterated, like Ben Johnson's 9.79 seconds.

Sports performers are different in the sense that they operate in and perhaps symbolise a sphere where all is meant to be wholesome and pure. But this puts competitors under sometimes intolerable pressure to keep their haloes straight. We know they are not saints; nor, given the business of sport, will they ever be.

The hearings of the Johnson case in 1989 and subsequent revelations all indicate that Johnson was not in a minority. This adds weight to the belief that the performers themselves are mere bit part players in a broader drama, the major roles being played by anonymous medics who prescribe competitors' training as well as their dope. "Scientist vs scientist" is how the future is sometimes envisaged: like dashing Svengalis, scientists might wield almost total control over their subjects were drugs allowed. The image is deliciously amusing rather than

sinister. Drugs are but one more of an ever-increasing portfolio of aids contemporary sports performers use to attain the levels of excellence demanded of them.

Nothing guarantees a product's arcaneness better than a ban. Intent as sport's governing bodies seem on stamping out drugs, their principal success has been in enlarging the mystique surrounding the likes of anabolic steroids and amphetamines. Making legal drugs available to performers means relegating them to the realms of the mundane.

Some research has shown that, when drugs are taken by performers, a placebo effect kicks in: the belief that they will enhance performance, rather than the substance itself, does the trick. One imagines how this type of disclosure would demystify drugs for young sports wannabes.

Sport harbours two naive beliefs, the first that competition is somehow pure. Yet, championships are prefixed with brand names, kits are plastered with logos, performers shamelessly endorse products. No one can disapprove of such commercialism, any more than the commercialism of SmithKline Beecham or Vaux breweries. But the marketplace brings with it imperatives, the central one of which is to win, not simply to compete.

The other is less explicit, but no less important, and concerns the assumption of a natural body state that shouldn't be corrupted by artificial means. Drugs are no more artificial than the entourage of aides and physical equipment commonplace in contemporary sport, and probably safer than tyrannical training regimes. The enhancing value of these is greater than any drug.

It is a foible of sport's governing organisations that they continue to search-and-destroy competitors who are, in a sense, merely following the dictates of commercial sport. The millions of dollars that are ploughed in the direction of Hewlett-Packard, which builds and equips testing centres, might more profitably be spent on research to discover the actual consequences of drugs currently favoured by competitors, rather than the imagined ones that continue to fascinate.

NO

Joannie M. Schrof

PUMPED UP

It's a dangerous combination of culture and chemistry. Inspired by cinematic images of the Terminator and Rambo and the pumped-up paychecks of athletic heroes with stunning physiques and awesome strength, teenagers across America are pursuing dreams of brawn through a pharmacopeia of pills, powders, oils and serums that are readily available—but often damaging. Despite the warnings of such fallen stars as Lyle Alzado, the former football player who died . . . of a rare brain cancer he attributed to steroid use, a *U.S. News* investigation has found a vast teenage subculture driven by an obsession with size and bodybuilding drugs. Consider:

- An estimated 1 million Americans, half of them adolescents, use black-market steroids. Countless others are choosing from among more than 100 other substances, legal and illegal, touted as physique boosters and performance enhancers.
- Over half the teens who use steroids start before age 16, sometimes with the encouragement of their parents. In one study, 7 percent said they first took "juice" by age 10.
- Many of the 6 to 12 percent of boys who use steroids want to be sports champions, but over one third aren't even on a high-school team. The typical user is middle-class and white.
- Fifty-seven percent of teen users say they were influenced by the dozen or so muscle magazines that today reach a readership of at least 7 million; 42 percent said they were swayed by famous athletes who they were convinced took steroids.
- The black-market network for performance enhancers is enormous, topping $400 million in the sale of steroids alone, according to the U.S. Drug Enforcement Administration. Government officials estimate that there are some 10,000 outlets for the drugs—mostly contacts made at local gyms —and mail-order forms from Europe, Canada and Mexico can be found anywhere teenagers hang out.
- The nation's steroid experts signaled the state of alarm when they convened in April in Kansas City to plan the first nationwide education effort.

- Even Arnold Schwarzenegger, who has previously been reluctant to comment on his own early steroid use, has been prompted to speak out vigorously about the problem. The bodybuilder and movie star is the chairman of the President's Council on Physical Fitness and Sports.

Performance drugs have an ancient history. Greek Olympians used strychnine and hallucinogenic mushrooms to psych up for an event. In 1886, a French cyclist was the first athlete known to die from performance drugs—a mixture of cocaine and heroin called "speedballs." In the 1920s, physicians inserted slices of monkey testicles into male athletes to boost vitality, and in the '30s, Hitler allegedly administered the hormone testosterone to himself and his troops to increase aggressiveness.

The use of anabolic steroids by weight lifters in the Eastern bloc dates back at least to the 1950s, and the practice has been spreading ever since among the world's elite athletes. But recent sensations in the sports world—Ben Johnson's record-shattering sprints at the Seoul Olympics and the signing of Brian Bosworth to the largest National Football League rookie contract ever *after* he tested positive for steroids—have attracted both young adults and kids to performance enhancers like never before, say leading steroid experts. These synthetic heroes are revered rather than disparaged in amateur gyms around the country, where wannabe Schwarzeneggers rationalize away health risks associated with performance-enhancing drugs.

Weighing in. The risks are considerable. Steroids are derivatives of the male hormone testosterone, and although they have legitimate medical uses—treatment of some cancers, for example—young bodybuilders who use them to promote tissue growth and endure arduous workouts routinely flood their bodies with 100 times the testosterone they produce naturally. The massive doses, medical experts say, affect not only the muscles but also the sex organs and nervous system, including the brain. "Even a brief period of abuse could have lasting effects on a child whose body and brain chemistry are still developing," warns Neil Carolan, who directs chemical dependency programs at BryLin Hospitals in Buffalo and has counseled over 200 steroid users.

Male users—by far the majority—can suffer severe acne, early balding, yellowing of the skin and eyes, development of female-type breasts and shrinking of the testicles. (In young boys, steroids can have the opposite effect of painfully enlarging the sex organs.) In females, the voice deepens permanently, breasts shrink, periods become irregular, the clitoris swells and hair is lost from the head but grows on the face and body. Teen users also risk stunting their growth, since steroids can cause bone growth plates to seal. One 13-year-old who had taken steroids for two years stopped growing at 5 feet. "I get side effects," says another teen who has used steroids for three years. "But I don't mind; it lets me know the stuff is working."

In addition to its physical dangers, steroid use can lead to a vicious cycle of dependency. Users commonly take the drugs in "cycles" that last from four to 18 weeks, followed by a lengthy break. But during "off" time, users typically shrink up, a phenomenon so abhorrent to those obsessed with size that many panic, turning back to the drugs in even larger doses. Most users "stack" the drugs, taking a combination of three to five pills and injectables at once; some report taking as many as 14 drugs simultaneously. Among the most commonly used are Dianabol ("D-Ball"), Anavar and Winstrol-V, the same type of steroid Ben Johnson tested positive for in 1988. "You wouldn't believe how much some guys go nuts on the stuff," says one teen bodybuilder from the Northeast. "They turn into walking, talking pharmacies."

Despite massive weight gains and sharply chiseled muscles, many steroid users are never quite happy with their physiques—a condition some researchers have labeled "reverse anorexia." "I've seen a kid gain 100 pounds in 14 months and still not be satisfied with himself," reports Carolan. If users try to stop, they can fall into deep depressions, and they commonly turn to recreational drugs to lift their spirits. Even during a steroid cycle, many users report frequent use of alcohol and marijuana to mellow out. "I tend to get really depressed when I go off a cycle," says one Maryland teen, just out of high school. "On a bad day, I think, 'Gee, if I were on the stuff this wouldn't be happening.' "

"Juicers" often enjoy a feeling of invincibility and euphoria. But along with the "pump" can come irritability and a sudden urge to fight. So common are these uncontrolled bursts of anger that they have a name in the steroid culture: "roid rages." The aggression can grow to pathological proportions; in a study by Harvard researchers, one eighth of steroid users suffered from "bodybuilder's psychosis," displaying such signs of mental illness as delusions and paranoia. So many steroid abusers are ending up behind bars for violent vandalism, assault and even murder that

defense attorneys in several states now call on steroid experts to testify about the drugs' effects.

What steroids do in the long run is still unknown, largely because not one federal dollar has been spent on long-term studies. Although Lyle Alzado was convinced that steroids caused his brain cancer, for example, there is no medical evidence to prove or disprove the link. But physicians are concerned about occasional reports of users falling ill with liver and kidney problems or dropping dead at a young age from heart attacks or strokes. Douglas McKeag, a sports physician at Michigan State University, is compiling a registry of steroid-related illnesses and deaths to fill the gaping hole in medical knowledge. McKeag sees preliminary evidence that steroid use might cause problems with blood-cell function that could lead to embolisms in the heart or lungs. "If that turns out to be true," he says, "then bingo—we'll have something deadly to warn kids about."

Dianabol desperadoes. Unfortunately, even that sort of documented health threat is unlikely to sway committed members of the steroid subculture. One widely shared value among users is a profound distrust of the medical community. Their suspicion is not totally unjustified. When steroid use was first becoming popular in the late 1950s, the medical community's response was to claim that they didn't enhance athletic ability—a claim that bulked-up users knew to be false. When that failed to deter users, physicians turned to scare tactics, branding steroids "killer drugs," again without hard evidence to back up the claim. As a result, self-styled "anabolic outlaws" and "Dianabol desperadoes" have sought guidance not from doctors but from the "Underground Steroid Handbook," a widely distributed paperback with detailed instructions for the use of more than 80 performance enhancers. "I know that proper steroid therapy can enhance your health; it has enhanced mine," writes author Daniel Duchaine. "Do you believe someone just because he has an M.D. or Ph.D. stuck onto the end of his name?" Or kids simply make up their own guidelines. "If you take more kinds at once, you get a bigger effect, and it's less dangerous because you're taking less of each kind," reasons one 18-year-old football player who has been taking steroids for two years.

Although even the steroid handbook mentions health risks particular to children and adolescents, in the end most young users seem unfazed by the hazards. In one poll, 82 percent said they didn't believe that steroids were harming them much, and, even more striking, 40 percent said they wouldn't stop in any case. Their motto: "Die young, die strong, Dianabol."

The main drawback to steroids, users complain, is that many brands must be administered with huge syringes. The deeper the needle penetrates the muscle, the less juice squandered just under the skin. Inserting the $1^1/_2$-inch needles into their buttocks or thighs leaves many teens squeamish, and they often rely on trusted friends to do the job. "The first time I tried to inject myself, I almost fainted, and one of my friends did faint," remembers a 19-year-old from Arizona. "Sometimes one of the guys will inject in one side of his butt one day and the other the next. Then, we all laugh at him because he can barely sit down for the next three days."

Local "hard core" gyms, patronized by serious weight lifters, are the social centers of the steroid culture. Teenagers caught up in the bodybuilding craze —typically white, middle-class suburbanites—commonly spend at least three hours a day almost every day of the week there, sometimes working out in the morning before school and again after school is out. Here they often meet 20-to-30-year-old men using steroids to bulk up for power lifting and bodybuilding shows or members of what steroid experts call the "fighting elite" —firefighters, bouncers, even policemen —synthetically boosting the physical strength they need to do their jobs. "Our role model is this older guy, the biggest guy at the gym," says one 17-year-old. "He's not a nice guy, but he weighs 290 pounds without an ounce of fat... that's our goal."

The older steroid veterans not only inspire kids to try the drugs but often act as the youngsters' main source for the chemicals. Sometimes, it's the gym owner who leads kids to a stash of steroids hidden in a back room; sometimes, it's a lifter who keeps the drugs in a dresser drawer at home and slips kids his phone number. Once in a while, it's a doctor or veterinarian who writes out endless prescriptions for the boys or for an unscrupulous coach. And too often, it's overzealous parents who push the drugs on their children. "My stepdad says he's going to start me up on steroids as soon as I'm done growing," says one freshman who wants to play pro football, "But I think he's just joking." Greg Gaa, director of a Peoria, Ill., sports-medicine clinic, says he has gotten calls from up to a dozen parents a year who want him to supply illegal performance enhancers to their children. A vast black market across America guarantees kids ready access to steroids in big cities and small towns alike. Typically, the drugs are shipped via private couriers from sources in other countries. Two order forms obtained by *U.S. News* require a minimum order of $75, offer 14 different steroids (ranging from $15 to $120 per bottle) and promise 48-hour delivery for an extra $20. Though the order forms, sent out six months apart, are identical and obviously the work of the same operation, the company name and address have been changed, apparently to outsmart investigators. In the earlier mailing, it's Mass Machine, located in Toronto. In the later form, it's Gym Tek Training, located in New Brunswick, Canada. Jack Hook, with the U.S. Drug Enforcement Administration in San Diego, describes a sting operation in which undercover agents from the DEA and the California Bureau of Narcotics posing as bodybuilders met up with a European gym owner and ordered $312,000 worth of steroids: the seller was nabbed in February when the shipment arrived via Federal Express.

Sometimes, kids themselves get into the act. Twenty-five percent say they sell the drugs to support their expensive habit. One Virginia 12th grader tells of fellow students who stole steroids from a drugstore where they worked and made "a killing" selling them around school. "Everybody knows you just go to this one guy's locker, and he'll fix you up," says the teen. A typical 100-tablet bottle of steroids—a month's supply—usually runs from $80 to $100 on the black market, but naive high schoolers often pay three times that amount.

"The challenge of getting ahold of the stuff is half the fun," admits one 17-year-old from Iowa, who tells of meeting dealers in parking lots and taste-testing drugs that look like fakes. Drug-enforcement agents estimate that 30 to 50 percent of the illegal muscle builders teens buy are phony. One Chicago-area youth spent $3,000 on what turned out to be a saline solution. Investigators have seized pills that turned out to be penicillin—deadly to some—and phony oils that were poorly packaged and rampant with bacteria. In April, two Los Angeles dealers were convicted of selling a counterfeit steroid that caused stomach pain, vomiting and a drop in blood pressure; the substance was a European veterinary drug used in show animals.

Subbing dangers. Since February 1991, when non-medical steroid distribution became a federal offense punishable by five years in prison, several drugs touted as steroid alternatives have also flourished underground. The top seller this year is a compound called clenbuterol, which is used by veterinarians in other countries but is not approved for any use in the United States. The drug recently led to problems in Spain, where 135 people who ingested it fell ill with headaches, chills, muscle tremors and nausea.

Human growth hormone, the steroid alternative Lyle Alzado used during his failed efforts at an NFL comeback, is medically used to treat dwarfism by stimulating growth. Its price, up to $1,500 for a two-week supply, is formidable, yet 5 percent of suburban Chicago 10th-grade boys surveyed in March by Vaughn Rickert of the University of Arkansas for Medical Sciences claim to have used the hormone. Although the body produces the substance naturally, too much can cause acromegaly, or "Frankenstein's syndrome," which leads to distortion of the face, hands and feet and eventually kills its victim.

Gamma-hydroxybutyrate (GHB) is a dangerous substance now popular among size seekers because it stimulates the release of human growth hormone. It also leads to comas. One Midwestern teen drank a GHB formula before going out to his high-school prom. He never made it. Within 20 minutes, he fell comatose and was rushed to the hospital to be revived. The Centers for Disease Control reports 80 recent hospitalizations from GHB use.

Many of the steroid alternatives that kids turn to come from an unlikely source: the local health-food store. For years, well-meaning coaches have persuaded kids to stay off steroids by opting for legal (and presumably safe) performance aids advertised ad nauseam in muscle magazines and sold in every shopping mall. Kids, happy to find a legal boost, empty their pockets on colorful packages that can cost up to $200 for a month's supply. But chemicals marketed as dietary supplements —essentially as food—undergo far less scrutiny than those marketed as drugs. "We have virtually no idea what's inside some of these products," warns Food and Drug Administration supplement specialist Don Leggett. "Just the other day someone asked about three new chemical compounds, and we couldn't even identify them. The substances aren't even on the books yet." Not long ago, he points out, clenbuterol and GHB were available in some health stores. Leggett is part of a task force now trying to assess the safety of a dozen common ingredients found in the bulking-up formulas, including chromium, boron and plant sterols.

Cracking the culture.   Meanwhile, the ambience of gyms and health-food stores serves to cloak the use of performance-enhancing drugs in the veneer of a healthy lifestyle. Since all of the trappings of their world have to do with hard work, fitness and vitality, kids who use the substances see them as just another training aid, not much different from Gatorade or a big steak dinner. "We're not freaks or addicts," asserts one teen. "We're using modern science to help us reach our goals."

Educators agree that users tend to be mainstream kids. "These kids aren't your typical drug abuser," says Dick Stickle, director of Target, the high-school sports association that hosted a meeting in April [1992] of 65 experts who worked to plot a strategy for educating teens about the drugs' risks. "They have goals, they have pride; we've got to play on that pride." The group plans to send a book of guidelines for combatting the use of steroids and other performance enhancers to every secondary school, 37,000 in all.... But reaching secondary schools may not be enough: A Peoria, Ill., teacher was recently taken aback by a fourth grader who said he'd like to try the steroids his sixth-grade brother uses. Previous education efforts have at times backfired; in Oregon, students who learned about the dangers of steroids were more likely to use them than those who didn't. Testing all high-school football players alone would cost $100 million and be nearly useless, since most teens know how to beat the tests with the use of "masking" drugs available underground.

At the forefront of education efforts are Charles Yesalis, professor of health policy at Pennsylvania State University and the nation's premier steroid expert, and Steve Courson, a former NFL star who used steroids. Both say that curbing steroid use requires nothing less than a revamping of American values. "We don't allow our kids to play games for fun anymore," says Yesalis. "We preach that God really does care who wins on Friday night, when we should be teaching our children to be satisfied to finish 27th, if that's their personal best."

Courson, in his recent book, "False Glory," tells of being introduced to steroids at age 18 by a college trainer, using steroids throughout his college and pro career and developing an accelerated heartbeat during his heaviest cycle. He is currently awaiting a heart transplant. "In the NFL, I was nothing more than a highly paid, highly manipulated gladiator. I was spiritually bankrupt," says Courson, now a Pennsylvania high-school football coach. "I want kids to know they can be greater than gladiators, that they can use a sport to learn lessons about life and not let the sport use them."

Ultimately, to reach children, educators will have to crack the secretive steroid subculture. So inviting is the underground world that, according to one study, 1 in 10 users takes steroids primarily out of desire to belong to the tightknit group. Those who opt out are quickly ostracized. Bill, a 17-year-old junior from New England, says he was a wallflower with only a couple of friends before he got into steroids. Two and a half years and 16 cycles of steroid use made him part of the fellowship. But Bill vividly remembers one day last winter: It's the day his parents found a needle he forgot to discard. Since then, he hasn't seen much of his friends. "I had to switch gyms because they were all teasing me about shrinking up and pressuring me to use the stuff," he says. "I never see them now—we don't have anything to talk about anymore—but they're all betting I'll go back on it. Right now, the only way I know I'll stay off steroids is if I can find a guarantee that I'll reach 220 pounds without them. No, make that 230."

POSTSCRIPT

Should the Decision to Use Anabolic Steroids Be Left to Athletes?

There are several reasons why long-term research on steroids is lacking. First, it is unethical to give drugs to people that may prove harmful, even lethal. Also, the amount of steroids given to subjects in a laboratory setting may not replicate what illegal steroid users actually take. Some users take more than 100 times the amount of steroids that are being clinically used.

Second, to determine the true effects of drugs, double-blind studies need to be done. This means that neither the researcher nor the people receiving the drugs know whether the subjects are receiving the real drug or a placebo (an inert substance). This is not practical with steroids, because subjects can always tell if they received the steroids or the placebos. The effects of steroids could be determined by following up with people who are known steroid users. However, this method lacks proper controls. If physical or psychological problems appear in a subject, for example, it cannot be determined whether the problems are due to the steroids or to other drugs the person may have been using. Also, the type of person who uses steroids may be the type of person who has emotional problems in the first place.

Even though the Drug Enforcement Administration estimates the black-market trade in anabolic steroids to be over $400 million a year, one could argue that they are a symptom of a much larger problem. Society emphasizes appearance and performance. From the time we are children, we are bombarded with constant reminders that we must do better than the next person. We are also reminded of the importance of appearance; to either starve ourselves or pump ourselves up (or both) in order to satisfy the cultural ideal of beauty. If we cannot achieve these standards through exercising, dieting, or drug use, then we can try surgery. Steroid use fits into the larger social problem of people not accepting themselves and their limitations.

Problems related to the use of anabolic steroids are described in "Anabolic Steroid Use and Associated Health Risk Behaviors," *Sports Medicine* (April 1996), by Amy Middleman and Robert DuRant, and in "Psychological and Behavioral Effects of Endogenous Testosterone and Anabolic-Androgenic Steroids: An Update," *Sports Medicine* (December 1996), by Michael Bahrke et al. An article that explains why it is difficult, if not impossible, to eliminate the use of anabolic steroids is "A Little Steroid Goes a Long Way," by Ian Anderson, *New Scientist* (October 1, 1994). In "Athletes on Anabolic-Androgenic Steroids," *Physician and Sportsmedicine* (June 1992), Mark Frankle and David Leffers detail a program that they instituted to prevent and reduce health problems related to steroids.

ISSUE 18

Should Drug Treatment Services Be Expanded?

YES: Charles P. O'Brien and A. Thomas McLellan, from "Myths About the Treatment of Addiction," *The Lancet* (January 27, 1996)

NO: Robert Apsler, from "Is Drug Abuse Treatment Effective?" *The American Enterprise* (March/April 1994)

ISSUE SUMMARY

YES: Professors Charles P. O'Brien and A. Thomas McLellan contend that treatment for drug addiction is vital even though many types of treatments appear inadequate. They feel that successful treatment should focus on patient improvement rather than cure.

NO: Assistant professor of psychology Robert Apsler questions the effectiveness of drug abuse treatment and whether or not drug addicts would go for treatment if services were expanded. Apsler argues that many of the drug abusers who cease drug use do it on their own without undergoing treatment.

Numerous drug experts feel that more funding should go toward preventing drug use from starting or escalating and toward treating individuals who are dependent on drugs. Today, when budget battles loom and taxpayers dispute how their tax monies are spent, the question of whether or not government funds should be used to treat people who abuse drugs is especially relevant. Questions surrounding this debate include: Will drug abuse treatment reduce criminal activity associated with drugs? Will drug addicts stop their abusive behavior if they enter treatment? Will more drug addicts receive treatment than currently do if services are expanded? and, Will the availability and demand for illegal drugs decline?

The research supporting the effectiveness of drug treatment is mixed. In *The Effectiveness of Treatment for Drug Abusers under Criminal Justice Supervision* (National Institute of Justice, 1995), Douglas S. Lipton reports that drug abuse treatment not only reduces the rate of arrests but that crime is reduced and the cost to taxpayers is lower over the long run. Also, it has been shown that illicit drug use is curtailed and that drug addicts are better able to function in society and to maintain employment. Perhaps most important, drug treatment may prove beneficial in curbing the escalation of HIV (human immunodeficiency virus), the virus that causes AIDS. When drug users (a high-risk population for HIV) enter treatment, they can be advised about the behaviors that lead to HIV transmission. Drug treatment is less costly than hospitalization and incarceration.

Some experts contend that reports regarding the effectiveness of drug treatment are not always accurate and that research on drug abuse has not been subjected to rigorous standards. Some question how effectiveness should be determined. If a person relapses after one year, should the treatment be considered ineffective? Would a reduction in an individual's illegal drug use indicate that the treatment was effective, or would an addict have to maintain complete abstinence? Also, if illegal drug use and criminal activity decline after treatment, it is possible that these results would have occurred anyway, regardless of whether or not the individual had been treated.

There are a variety of drug treatment programs. One type of treatment program developed in the 1960s is *therapeutic communities*. Therapeutic communities are usually residential facilities staffed by former drug addicts. Although there is no standard definition of what constitutes a therapeutic community, the program generally involves task assignments for residents (the addicts undergoing treatment), group intervention techniques, vocational and educational counseling, and personal skill development. Inpatient treatment facilities, such as the Betty Ford Center, are the most expensive type of treatment and are often based on a hospital model. These programs are very structured and include highly regimented schedules, demanding rules of conduct, and individual and group counseling.

Outpatient treatment, the most common type of drug treatment, is less expensive, less stigmatizing, and less disruptive to the abuser's family than other forms of treatment. Vocational, educational, and social counseling is provided. Outpatient treatment is often used after an addict leaves an inpatient program. One type of treatment that has proliferated in recent years is the self-help group. Members of self-help groups are bound by a common denominator, whether it is alcohol, cocaine, or narcotics. Due to the anonymous and confidential nature of self-help groups, however, it is difficult to conduct follow-up research to determine their effectiveness.

Individuals who are addicted to narcotics are often referred to methadone maintenance programs. Methadone is a synthetic narcotic that prevents narcotic addicts from getting high and eliminates withdrawal symptoms. Since methadone's effects last about 24 hours, addicts need to receive treatment daily. Unfortunately, the relapse rate is high once addicts stop treatment. Because there is much demand for methadone maintenance in some areas, there are lengthy waiting lists.

In the following selections, Charles P. O'Brien and A. Thomas McLellan discuss how drug treatment services address addictions to alcohol and illegal drugs, increase personal health and social functioning, and reduce threats to public health and safety. Robert Apsler contends that the benefits of drug treatment are not as significant as proponents of drug treatment profess.

YES

Charles P. O'Brien and
A. Thomas McLellan

MYTHS ABOUT THE TREATMENT
OF ADDICTION

Although addictions are chronic disorders, there is a tendency for most physicians and for the general public to perceive them as being acute conditions such as a broken leg or pneumococcal pneumonia. In this context the acute-care procedure of detoxification has been thought of as appropriate "treatment". When the patient relapses, as most do sooner or later, the treatment is regarded as a failure. However, contrary to commonly held briefs, addiction does not end when the drug is removed from the body (detoxification) or when the acute post drug-taking illness dissipates (withdrawal). Rather, the underlying addictive disorder persists, and this persistence produces a tendency to relapse to active drug-taking. Thus, although detoxification as explained by Mattick and Hall (Jan 13, p 97)[1] can be successful in cleansing the person of drugs and withdrawal symptoms, detoxification does not address the underlying disorder, and thus is not adequate treatment.

As we shall discuss, addictions are similar to other chronic disorders such as arthritis, hypertension, asthma, and diabetes. Addicting drugs produce changes in brain pathways that endure long after the person stops taking them. Further, the associated medical, social, and occupational difficulties that usually develop during the course of addiction do not disappear when the patient is detoxified. These protracted brain changes and the associated personal and social difficulties put the former addict at great risk of relapse. Treatments for addiction, therefore, should be regarded as being long term, and a "cure" is unlikely from a single course of treatment.

IS ADDICTION A VOLUNTARY DISORDER?

One reason why many physicians and the general public are unsympathetic towards the addict is that addiction is perceived as being self-afflicted: "they brought it on themselves". However, there are numerous involuntary components in the addictive process, even in the early stages. Although the choice to try a drug for the first time is voluntary, whether the drug is taken can be influenced by external factors such as peer pressure, price, and, in particular, availability. In the USA, there is a great deal of cocaine in all areas of the country, and in some regions the availability of heroin is widespread. Nonetheless, it is true that, despite ready availability, most people exposed to drugs do not go on to become addicts. Heredity is likely to influence the effects of the initial sampling of the drug, and these effects are in turn likely to be influential in modifying the course of continued use. Individuals for whom the initial psychological responses to the drug are extremely pleasurable may be more likely to repeat the drug-taking and some of them will develop an addiction. Some people seem to have an inherited tolerance to alcohol, even without previous exposure.[2] At some point after continued repetition of voluntary drug-taking, the drug "user" loses the voluntary ability to control its use. At that point, the "drug misuser" becomes "drug addicted" and there is a compulsive, often overwhelming *involuntary* aspect to continuing drug use and to relapse after a period of abstinence. We do not yet know the mechanisms involved in this change from drug-taking to addiction, and we are searching for pharmacological mechanisms to reverse this process.

COMPARISON TO OTHER MEDICAL DISORDERS

The view of addiction as a chronic medical disorder puts it in a category with other conditions that show a similar confluence of genetic, biological, behavioural, and environmental factors. There are many examples of chronic illness that are generally accepted as requiring life-long treatment. Here, we will focus on only three: adult-onset diabetes, hypertension, and asthma. Like substance-use disorders, the onset of these three diseases is determined by multiple factors, and the contributions of each factor are not yet fully specified. In adult-onset diabetes and some forms of hypertension, genetic factors have a major, though not exclusive, role in the aetiology. Parenting practices, stress in the home environment, and other environmental factors are also important in determining whether these diseases actually get expressed, even among individuals who are genetically predisposed. Behavioural factors are also important at the outset in the development of these disorders. The control of diet and weight and the establishment of regular exercise patterns are two important determinants of the onset and severity. Thus, although a diabetic, hypertensive, or asthmatic patient may have been genetically predisposed and may have been raised in a high-risk environment, it is also true that behavioural choices such as the ingestion of high sugar and/or high-cholesterol foods, smoking, and lack of exercise also play a part in the onset and severity of their disorder.

Treatment results
Almost everyone has a friend or relative who has been through a treatment programme for addiction to nicotine, alcohol, or other drugs. Since most of these people have a relapse to drug-taking at some time after the end of treatment, there is a tendency for the general public to believe that addiction treatment is

Figure 1

Admission Severity Profiles of Two Patients Admitted for Drug Misuse

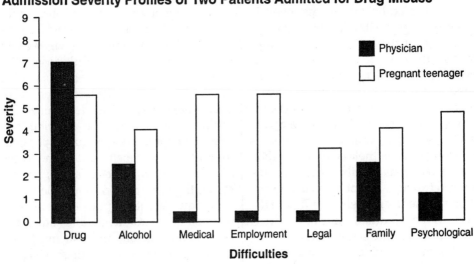

As assessed by Addiction Severity Index.

unsuccessful. However, this expectation of a cure after treatment is unrealistic —just as it is for other chronic disorders. The persistent changes produced by addiction are still present and require continued maintenance treatment —either psychosocial or pharmacological or a combination. As with other chronic disorders, the only realistic expectation for the treatment of addiction is patient improvement rather than cure. Consistent with these expectations, studies of abstinence rates at 1 year after completion of treatment indicate that only 30–50% of patients have been able to remain completely abstinent throughout that period, although an additional 15–30% have not resumed compulsive use.[3-6]

Successful treatment leads to substantial improvement in three areas: reduction of alcohol and other drug use; increases in personal health and social functions; and reduction in threats to public health and safety. All these do-mains can be measured in a graded fashion with a method such as the Addiction Severity Index (ASI).[7] In the ASI, a structured interview determines the need for treatment in seven independent domains. These measurements allow us to see addiction, not as an all-or-none disease, but in degrees of severity across all the areas relevant to successful treatment.

Success rates for treatment of addictive disorders vary according to the type of drug and the variables inherent in the population being treated. For example, prognosis is much better in opioid addicts who are professionals, such as physicians or nurses, than in individuals with poor education and no legitimate job prospects, who are addicted to the same or even lesser amounts of opioids obtained on the street and financed by crime. Figure 1 compares the ASI profiles of two patients admitted to our treatment programme. One was a resident physician who had few personal or professional difficulties except for heavy compulsive cocaine use. The other patient was a pregnant teenager, who was admitted while in premature labour induced by cocaine. The profile shows less drug use in the young woman, but in other areas shown to be important determinants of the outcome of treatment she has severe problems. The types of treatment needed by these two patients are clearly different. Although the treatment of the physician will be challenging, his prognosis is far better than that of the young woman.

Success rates for the treatment of various addictive disorders are shown in table 1. Improvement is defined as a greater than 50% reduction on the drug-taking scale of the ASI. Another measure of the success of addiction treatment is the monetary savings that it produces. That addiction treatment is cost-effective has been shown in many studies in North America. For example, in one study in California, the benefits of alcohol and other drug treatment outweighed the cost of treatment by four to 12-fold depending on the type of drug and the type of treatment.

There has been progress in the development of medications for the treatment of nicotine, opioid, and alcohol addictions. For heroin addicts, *maintenance* treatment with a long-acting opioid such as methadone, 1-α-acetylmethadol (LAAM), or buprenorphine can also be regarded as a success. The patient may be abstinent from illegal drugs and capable of functioning normally in society while requiring daily doses of an orally administered opioid medication —in very much the same way that diabetic patients are maintained by injections of insulin and hypertensive patients are maintained on beta-blockers

Table 1

Success Rates for Addictive Disorders

Disorder	Success rate (%)*
Alcoholism[8]	50 (40–70)
Opioid dependence[3]	60 (50–80)
Cocaine dependence[10]	55 (50–60)
Nicotine dependence[11]	30 (20–40)

*Follow-up 6 mo. Data are median (range).

to sustain symptom improvements. Contrary to popular belief, patients properly maintained on methadone do not seem "drugged". They can function well, even in occupations requiring quick reflexes and motor skills, such as driving a subway train or motor vehicle. Of course not all patients on methadone can achieve high levels of function. Many street heroin addicts, such as the young cocaine-dependent woman in figure 1, have multiple additional psychosocial difficulties, are poorly educated, and misuse many drugs. In such cases, intensive psychosocial supports are necessary in addition to methadone; even then, the prognosis is limited by the patient's ability to learn skills for legitimate employment.

Nicotine is the addicting drug that has the poorest success rate (table 1). That these success rates are for individuals who came to a specialised clinic for treatment of their addiction, implies that the patients tried to stop or control drug use on their own but have been unable to do so. Of those who present for treatment for nicotine dependence, only about 20–

Figure 2
Effect of Naltrexone Hydrochloride on Relapse Rates in Alcoholics

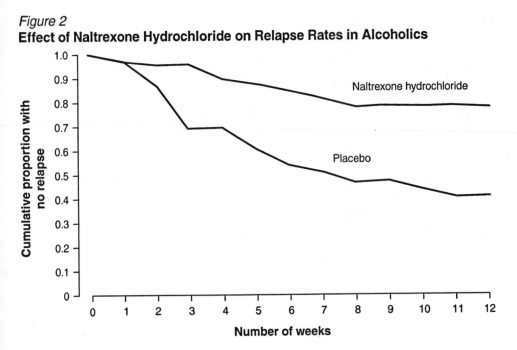

30% have not resumed smoking by the end of 12 months.

Treatment compliance
Studies of treatment response have uniformly shown that patients who comply with the recommended regimen of education, counselling, and medication that characterises most contemporary forms of treatment, have typically favourable outcomes during treatment and longer-lasting post-treatment benefits.[5,13-16] Thus, it is discouraging for many practitioners that so many drug-dependent patients do not comply with the recommended course of treatment and subsequently resume substance use. Factors such as low socioeconomic status, comorbid psychiatric conditions, and lack of family or social supports for continuing abstinence are among the most important variables associated with lack of treatment compliance, and ultimately to relapse after treatment.[17-19]

Patient compliance is also especially important in determining the effectiveness of medications in the treatment of substance dependence. Although the general area of pharmacotherapy for drug addiction is still developing, in opioid and alcohol dependence there are several well-tested medications that are potent and effective in completely eliminating the target problems of substance use. Disulfiram has proven efficacy in preventing the resumption of alcohol use among detoxified patients. Alcoholics resist taking disulfiram because they become ill if they take a drink while receiving this medication; thus compliance is very poor.[20] Naltrexone is an opioid antagonist that prevents relapse to opioid use by blocking opioid receptors; it is a non-addicting medication that makes it impossible to return to opioid use, but

Table 2

Compliance and Relapse in Selected Medical Disorders

	Compliance and Relapse
IDDM	
Medication regimen	< 50%
Diet and foot care	< 30%
Relapse*	30–50%
Hypertension [†]	
Medication regimen	< 30%
Diet	< 30%
Relapse*	50–60%
Asthma	
Medication regimen	< 30%
Relapse*	60–80%

*Retreatment within 12 mo by physician at emergency room or hospital.

† Requiring medication.

Sources are refs 33 and 34: for a complete list of references please write to CPO'B.

IDDM=insulin-dependent diabetes mellitus.

it has little acceptance among heroin addicts who simply do not comply with this treatment. Naltrexone is also helpful in the treatment of alcoholism. Animal and human studies have shown that the reward produced by alcohol involves the endogenous opioid system. After patients are detoxified from alcohol, naltrexone reduces craving and blocks some of the rewarding effects of alcohol if the patient begins to drink again.[22,23] Naltrexone also decreases relapse rates (figure 2 [see preceding page]).[22] Although compliance is substantially better for naltrexone in the treatment of alcoholism than in opioid addiction, efforts to improve compliance are pivotal in the treatment of alcoholism. Continuing clinical research in this area is focused on the development of longer-acting forms of these medications and behavioural strategies to increase patient compliance.

The diseases of hypertension, diabetes, and asthma are also chronic disorders that require continuing care for most, if not all, of a patient's life. At the same time, these disorders are not necessarily unremitting or unalterably lethal, provided that the treatment regimen of medication, diet, and behavioural change is followed. This last point requires emphasis. As with the treatment of addiction, treatments for these chronic medical disorders heavily depend on behavioural change and medication compliance to achieve their potential effectiveness. In a review of over 70 outcome studies of treatments for these disorders (summarised in table 2) patient compliance with the recommended medical regimen was regarded as the most significant determinant of treatment outcome. Less than 50% of patients with insulin-dependent diabetes fully comply with their medication schedule,[24] and less that 30% of patients with hypertension or asthma comply with their medication regimens.[25,26] The difficulty is even worse for the behavioural and diet changes that are so important for the maintenance of short-term gains in these conditions. Less than 30% of patients in treatment for diabetes and hypertension comply with the recommended diet and/or behavioural changes that are designed to reduce risk factors for reoccurrence of these disorders.[27,28] It is interesting in this context that clinical researchers have identified low socioeconomic status, comorbid psychiatric conditions, and lack of family support as the major contributors to poor patient compliance in these disorders (see ref 27 for discussion of this work). As in addiction treatment, lack of patient compliance with the treatment regimen is a major contributor to reoccurrence and to the development of more serious and more expensive "disease-related" conditions. For example, outcome studies show that 30–60% of insulin-dependent diabetic patients, and about 50–80% of hypertensive and asthmatic patients have a reoccurrence of their symptoms each year and require at least restabilisation of their medication and/or additional medical interventions to re-establish symptom remission.[24-28] Many of these reoccurrences also result in more serious additional health complications. For example, limb amputations and blindness are all too common consequences of treatment non-response among diabetic patients.[29,30] Stroke and cardiac disease are often associated with exacerbation of hypertension.[31,32]

There are, of course, differences in susceptibility, onset, course, and treatment response among all the disorders discussed here, but at the same time, there are clear parallels among them. All are multiply determined, and no single gene, personality variable, or environmental factor can fully account for the onset of any of these disorders. Behavioural choices seem to be implicated in the initiation of each of them, and behavioural control continues to be a factor in determining their course and severity. There are no "cures" for any of them, yet there have been major advances in the development of effective medications and behavioural change regiments to reduce or eliminate primary symptoms. Because these conditions are chronic, it is acknowledged (at least in the treatment of diabetes, hypertension, and asthma) that maintenance treatments will be needed to ensure that symptom remission continues. Unfortunately, other common features are their resistance to maintenance forms of treatment (both medication and behaviour aspects) and their chronic, relapsing course. In this regard, it is striking that many of the patient characteristics associated with non-compliance are identical for these acknowledged "medical" disorders and addictive disorders; and the rates of reoccurrence are also similar.

ADDICTION TREATMENT IS A WORTHWHILE MEDICAL ENDEAVOR

A change in the attitudes of physicians is necessary. Addictive disorders should be considered in the category with other disorders that require long-term or lifelong treatment. Treatment of addiction is about as successful as treatment of disorders such as hypertension, diabetes, and asthma, and it is clearly cost-effective. We believe that the prominence and severity of concerns about the public health and public safety associated with addiction have made the public, the press, and public policy officials understandably desperate for a lasting solution, and disappointed that none has yet been developed. As with treatments for these other chronic medical conditions, there is no cure for addiction. At the same time, there are a range of pharmacological and behavioural treatments that are effective in reducing drug use, improving patient function, reducing crime and legal system costs, and preventing the development of other expensive medical disorders. Perhaps the major difference among these conditions lies in the public's and the physician's perception of diabetes, hypertension, and asthma as clearly medical conditions whereas addiction is more likely to be perceived as a social problem or a character deficit. It is interesting that despite similar results, at least in terms of compliance or reoccurrence rates, there is no serious argument against support by contemporary health-care systems for diabetes, hypertension, or asthma, whereas this is very much in question with regard to the treatments for addiction. Is it not time that we judged the "worth" of treatments for chronic addiction with the same standards that we use for treatments of other chronic diseases?

REFERENCES

1. Mattick RP, Hall W. Are detoxification programmes effective? *Lancet* 1996; 347: 97–100.

2. Schuckit MA. Low level of response to alcohol. *Am J Psychiatry* 1994; 151: 184–89.

3. Gerstein D, Harwood H. Treating drug problems. Vol I. Washington, DC: National Academy Press, 1990.

4. Gerstein D, Judd LL, Rovner SA. Career dynamics of female heroin addicts. *Am J Drug Alcohol Abuse* 1979; 6: 1–23.

5. Miller WR, Hester RK. The effectiveness of alcoholism treatment methods: what research reveals. In: Miller WR, Heather N, eds. Treating addictive behaviors: process of change. New York: Plenum Press, 1986.

6. Armor DJ, Polich JM, Stambul HB. Alcoholism and treatment. Santa Monica, California: RAND Corporation Press, 1976.

7. McLellan AT, Luborsky L, O'Brien CP, Woody GE. An improved evaluation instrument for substance abuse patients: the Addiction Severity Index. *J Nerv Ment Dis* 1980; 168: 26–33.

8. Institute of Medicine. Prevention and treatment of alcohol problems: research opportunities. Washington, DC: National Academy Press, 1989.

9. Ball JC, Ross A. The effectiveness of methadone maintenance treatment. New York: Springer-Verlag, 1991.

10. Higgins ST, Budney AJ, Bickel WK, Foerg F, Donham R, Badger GJ. Incentives improve outcome in outpatient behavioral treatment of cocaine dependence. *Arch Gen Psychiatry* 1994: 51: 568–76.

11. Fiore MC, Smith SS, Jorenby DE, Baker TB. The effectiveness of the nicotine patch for smoking cessation. *JAMA* 1994; 271: 1940–46.

12. Gerstein DR, Harwood H, Suter N. Evaluating recovery services: the California Drug and Alcohol Treatment Assessment (CALDATA). California Department of Alcohol and Drug Programs Executive Summary: Publication no. ADP94–628, 1994.

13. Moos RH, Finney JW, Cronkite RC. Alcoholism treatment: context, process and outcome. New York: Oxford University Press, 1990.

14. Simpson D, Savage L. Drug abuse treatment readmissions and outcomes. *Arch Gen Psychiatry* 1980: 37: 896–901.

15. Hubbard RL, Marsden ME, Rachal JV, Harwood HJ, Cavanaugh ER, Ginzburg HM. Drug abuse treatment: a national study of effectiveness. Chapel Hill: University of North Carolina Press, 1989.

16. DeLeon G. The therapeutic community: study of effectiveness. Treatment research monograph 84–1286. Rockville, MD: National Institute for Drug Abuse, 1994.

17. Havassy BE, Wasserman D, Hall SM. Social relationships and cocaine use in an American treatment sample. *Addiction* 1995; 90: 699–710.

18. McLellan AT, Druley KA, O'Brien CP, Kron R. Matching substance abuse patients to appropriate treatments. A conceptual and methodological approach. *Drug Alcohol Dependence* 1980; 5: 189–93.

19. Alterman AI, Cacciola JS. The antisocial personality disorder in substance abusers: problems and issues. *J Nerv Mental Dis* 1991; 179: 401–09.

20. Fuller RK, Branchey L, Brichtwell DR, et al. Disfulfiram treatment of alcoholism. *JAMA* 1986; 256: 1449–55.

21. O'Brien CP, Woody GE, McLellan AT. A new tool in the treatment of impaired physicians. *Philadelphia Med* 1986; 82: 442–46.

22. Volpicelli JR, Alterman AI, Hayashida M, O'Brien CP. Naltrexone in the treatment of alcohol dependence. *Arch Gen Psychiatry* 1992; 49: 876–80.

23. O'Malley SS, Jaffe AJ, Chang G, Schottenfeld RS, Meyer RE, Rounsaville B. Naltrexone and coping skills therapy for alcohol dependence. *Arch Gen Psychiatry* 1992; 49: 881–87.

24. Graber AL, Davidson P, Brown A, McRae J, Woolridge K. Dropout and relapse during diabetes care. *Diabetic Care* 1992; 15: 1477–83.

25. Horowitz RI. Treatment adherence and risk of death after a myocardial infarction. *Lancet* 1990; 336: 542–45.

26. Dekker FW, Dielman FE, Kaptein AA, Mulder JD. Compliance with pulmonary medication in general practice. *Eur Resp J* 1993; 6: 886–90.

27. Clark LT. Improving compliance and increasing control of hypertension: needs of special hypertensive populations. *Am Heart J* 1991; 121: 664–69.

28. Kurtz SM. Adherence to diabetic regimes: empirical status and clinical applications. *Diabetes Educ* 1990; 16: 50–59.

29. Sinnock P. Hospitalization of diabetes. Diabetes data, national diabetes data group. Bethesda MD: National Institutes of Health, 1985.

30. Herman WH, Teutsch SM. Diabetic renal disorders. Diabetes data, national diabetes data group. Bethesda MD: National Institutes of Health, 1985.

31. Schaub AF, Steiner A, Vetter W. Compliance to treatment. *J Clin Exp Hypertension* 1993; 15: 1121–30.

32. Gorlin R. Hypertension and ischemic heart disease: the challenge of the 1990s. *Am Heart J* 1991; 121: 658–63.

33. National Center for Health Statistics. Public use datatape documentation, Hyattsville, MD: The Center, 1989.

34. Harrison WH. Internal medicine. New York: Raven Press, 1993.

NO

Robert Apsler

IS DRUG ABUSE TREATMENT EFFECTIVE?

In early February [1994], the Clinton administration spelled out its national antidrug strategy. Much of the debate over the new program will turn on how much federal support should be made available for treating drug addicts. The administration plans to spend $355 million in new grants for the states to use to treat hard-core drug users, while cutting funds for interdiction. Many years of massive federal investment in interdiction—including involvement of the U.S. military—have failed to reduce the availability of low-cost street drugs. And the policy momentum is now toward shifting federal funds from supply reduction to demand reduction, a move that would benefit treatment and prevention programs. Also, news stories about the administration's deliberations often report on drug treatment programs with long waits for new admissions. What is implied if not stated is that the size of the country's drug abusing population, estimated by the Institute of Medicine to be 5.5 million people, would be significantly reduced if more money were spent for drug abuse treatment.

But missing from the news stories and analyses of proposed antidrug strategies is any frank discussion of the underlying assumption that drug abuse treatment is effective. This assumption is based largely on reports from clinicians and recovered drug addicts. It is encouraged by a growing drug treatment industry and accepted by a public that wishes for a solution to the drug problem. The premise may be accurate, but it is not yet supported by hard evidence. We do not know that drug abuse treatment is effective. Clinicians' reports in other areas have not always been reliable. For example, many medical procedures developed through clinical experience alone have been abandoned when researchers showed, through carefully controlled comparisons, that placebos or other alternatives matched their effectiveness.

With a few exceptions, drug abuse treatment has not been subjected to rigorous tests for effectiveness. Good research doesn't exist for a number of reasons. Researchers are hampered by fundamental conceptual issues. Even

From Robert Apsler, "Is Drug Abuse Treatment Effective?" *The American Enterprise* (March/April 1994). Copyright © 1994 by The American Enterprise Institute, Washington, DC. Reprinted by permission.

defining basic ideas is difficult. There are significant practical obstacles that make conducting research difficult as well, and little federal support for drug treatment research has been available for over a decade.

WHAT IS "DRUG ABUSE TREATMENT"?

One of the conceptual and practical problems of research is the simple fact that no one process or combination of procedures comprises "drug abuse treatment." Nor do the various types of drug programs have much in common beyond the shared objective of reducing drug abuse.

There are four major types of drug treatment. *Residential therapeutic communities* are highly structured residential settings for drug addicts and typically employ a mixture of psychological and behavioral therapies. Duration of treatment varies widely among these programs. *Inpatient/outpatient chemical dependency treatment* begins with a three- to six-week residential stay in a clinic or hospital that uses the Alcoholics Anonymous philosophy. These clients are then encouraged to attend self-help groups for the rest of their lives. A third type, *outpatient methadone maintenance programs*, involves supervised addiction to methadone hydrochloride as a substitute for addiction to other narcotics, such as heroin. Programs may include counseling and other social services for clients. The fourth category, *outpatient nonmethadone treatment*, joins many different types of programs whose main similarity is that they tend not to treat individuals who are dependent on opiates such as heroin, morphine, and codeine.

This four-group classification is crude because the programs within each category differ markedly from each other. For example, methadone maintenance programs differ in the size of the methadone dose, the number and type of additional services provided, the frequency of urine testing, the strictness of program regulation enforcement, and whether clients are permitted to take their methadone dose home. Some programs focus on illicit drug use and criminal activity, while others target the overall functioning of clients. Some demand abstinence from all illicit drugs; others help clients gain control over their drug use. They differ in whether they concentrate on a particular drug and, if they do, on which drug. Some programs rely heavily on professional practitioners; others employ nonprofessionals, often ex-addicts, as counselors. Programs also differ in the clients they serve: those in the private sector cater mainly to employed drug abusers, whose care is covered by health insurance. The public sector programs serve large numbers of indigent clients.

The differences within each of the four major categories of drug programs are so great that information about the effectiveness of one program in a particular category tells us little about the effectiveness of other programs in the same category. In fact, some differences among programs within a classification group may prove to be more important than the differences among the four groups of programs. For example, new evidence shows that the sheer quantity of treatment provided to clients is crucial to a program's effectiveness. Thus, the amount of counseling and auxiliary services provided by a program may be a more important defining characteristic with respect to efficacy than the types of drug abuse it treats, its treatment philosophy, or whether it operates through a residential or outpatient setting.

WHAT IS "EFFECTIVE" TREATMENT?

Just as there is no simple answer to what comprises drug abuse treatment, neither is there an agreed-upon definition of what constitutes *effective* drug abuse treatment. Definitions clash in two important ways. First, strongly held views divide the treatment community on whether abstinence from illicit drug use is necessary. One position holds that successful treatment is synonymous with total abstinence from illicit drugs. The other position holds that treatment is successful if it ends clients' *dependence* on drugs. Continued, moderate drug use is accepted for those clients able to gain control over their drug use and prevent it from interfering with their daily functioning.

Definitions of effectiveness also differ in the number of behaviors they measure. The most common view of effectiveness judges treatment by its ability to reduce the two behaviors most responsible for society's strong reaction against drug abuse: illicit drug use and criminal activity. Others argue that a broader definition of effectiveness is necessary to describe treatment accurately. Advocates of the broader definition believe that treatment should not be considered effective if it can only demonstrate reductions in drug use and illegal activity, since these changes are likely to dissipate rapidly unless clients undergo additional changes. Returning clients who have completed treatment to their previous drug using environment, it is

argued, subjects them to the same social and economic forces that contributed to their drug use. According to this view, sustained changes occur only when clients are willing and able to survive and prosper in new environments. To do so, clients must first develop the necessary employment, social, and other skills. Broad definitions of effectiveness usually include: (1) drug abuse, (2) illegal activities, (3) employment, (4) length of stay in treatment, (5) social functioning, (6) intrapersonal functioning, and (7) physical health and longevity.

MOTIVATION AND CRISIS

Without having resolved even basic definitions about drug abuse treatment, the administration is nevertheless proceeding on the assumption that more money for treatment will mean more help. Doing so ignores the fact that we don't know very much in this area and also ignores the little we do know. We don't know much about client differences, for instance. But we do know that a drug addict's motivation for seeking treatment is crucial. Most clinicians believe that successful treatment is impossible if a client does not want help. Addicts must admit the existence of a serious problem and sincerely want to do something about it. Only then will they accept the assistance of clinicians. However, most experts in the drug abuse field reluctantly acknowledge that almost no drug abusers actually *want* treatment. The news reports implying that thousands of needy addicts would enter treatment and soon be on their way to recovery if the country were willing to spend more money and increase the number of drug programs are inaccurate. While waiting lists exist for some programs, others have trouble attracting addicts.

Furthermore, most drug abusers enter treatment when faced with a crisis, such as threats by a judge, employer, or spouse, or a combination of the three. As a result, the drug abuser's objective may be limited to overcoming the current problem. When the crisis has abated, patients often admit they do not intend all drug use to stop. A national survey of admissions to public drug programs from 1979 to 1981 found that pressure from the criminal justice system was the strongest motivation for seeking treatment. Thus, the existence of long waiting lists may tell us more about judges' efforts to find alternatives to incarceration in overcrowded jails than about the actual intentions of drug abusers or the effectiveness of treatment programs.

The assumption that drug addicts enter treatment at a crisis point has another important ramification for interpreting research on the effectiveness of treatment programs. Studies of treatment effectiveness typically measure clients at least twice: when they enter a program and when they complete treatment. If the first measurement occurs during a time of crisis, it will reflect clients' negative circumstances by showing high levels of drug use, criminal behavior, unemployment, and so on. The second measure of clients, taken at the conclusion of treatment, will likely occur after the precipitating crisis has passed or at least lessened. Consequently, a comparison of the measurements taken at the beginning and end of treatment will show significant improvement for many clients. Is this improvement evidence of effective treatment? Or does it merely reflect the natural cycle of a passing crisis? The main problem is that the research designs used in nearly all drug treatment research cannot separate the effects of treatment from other factors such as these.

RESEARCH PROBLEMS

Questions about drug treatment effectiveness must be answered the same way as similar questions about treatments for the common cold, AIDS, or other ailments, that is, by obtaining evidence that compares the outcomes of treated and untreated individuals. While this may seem obvious, most drug treatment research has neither compared the necessary groups of drug users nor employed the types of research designs capable of producing strong conclusions. In addition, serious measurement and attrition problems weaken the conclusions of most studies of drug treatment effectiveness.

Research Design. Comparisons between drug users who receive treatment and others who do not are almost nonexistent. Researchers study only treated drug users. Yet the observed behavior of drug users who do not enter drug programs reinforces the need for researchers to include untreated addicts in their studies. We have known for years, for instance, that some drug abusers, including heroin addicts, end drug use largely on their own. Researchers have also observed large reductions in drug use among drug abusers waiting for, but not yet receiving, treatment for cocaine abuse.

The phenomenon of people ending their use of highly addictive *legal* substances on their own is well documented. For example, there is mounting evidence that smokers quit on their own at about the same rate as those attending smoking treatment programs. Estimates of remission from alcoholism and alcohol problems without formal treatment range from 45 to 70 percent. No comparable estimate is available for the number of drug users who quit on their own. Until we know the recovery rates for untreated drug abusers, it is impossible to claim that treatment is more effective than the absence of treatment.

Furthermore, the research designs and methods employed in most drug treatment research are so seriously flawed that the results can be considered no more than suggestive. Many investigations study a single group of treated clients and attempt to draw conclusions without a comparison group. Other investigations compare different groups of clients receiving different treatments. In nearly all such cases, the types of clients differ from group to group. Consequently, it is impossible to distinguish between effects caused by treatment differences and effects caused by client differences.

Measuring the Outcomes of Treatment. One major need in drug treatment research is for an objective, reliable, and inexpensive method for measuring treatment outcomes. Presently most treatment researchers rely entirely on clients' own reports of past and current behavior. Much of the behavior that clients are asked about is illegal, occurred while they were intoxicated, and may have taken place months, and even years, earlier. As one would expect, clients underreport their drug use and other illegal activities. Yet the drug treatment field continues to rely heavily on these dubious reports because there are no suitable alternatives. Chemical tests, such as urine and hair testing, are important adjuncts for validating clients' reports. But at best these tests confirm use or abstinence; they do not indicate anything about quantity or intervals of use. So they are crude measures that cannot easily track patterns of drug use over long periods after a client leaves a treatment program.

Many treatment studies measure clients at the beginning and end of treatment because it is so difficult and expensive to keep track of them after they have completed a program. Some studies do attempt to assess the impact of treatment six months, a year, or even longer after completion. But investigators can seldom locate more than 70 percent of clients, if that. Clients who cannot be contacted are often deceased, in prison, unemployed, and/or homeless. Leaving them out of the studies may skew the findings, making the conclusions appear more positive than is warranted.

Length of Treatment. The length of drug abuse treatment is a complex and confusing element in the overall picture of treatment effectiveness. To begin with, simply keeping clients in treatment is a major challenge for many drug programs. Most clients are forced into treatment. And many leave shortly thereafter. Therefore, merely remaining in treatment has become a widely accepted measure of treatment effectiveness. While it makes sense that clients can only benefit from treatment if they remain in a program, there is the risk of confusing happenstance for cause and effect.

Addicts who truly want to change their lifestyles are likely to make many changes. Such changes include entering and remaining in a treatment program, reducing drug use, holding a steady job, eschewing illegal activities, and so on. Other individuals not willing to change their lifestyles are more likely to drop out of treatment after being forced into a drug program. They continue using drugs, do not hold steady jobs, engage in illegal activities, and so on. Thus, to prove that drug programs are effective, researchers must show that (1) drug programs help addicts commit to changing their lifestyles, and/or that (2) the resulting improvement among treated clients is greater than the improvement expected anyway from individuals who have already chosen to change their lifestyles.

Another challenge is determining the length of an optimum stay in a drug treatment program. Most private chemical dependency residential programs used to run for 28 days, though cost-reduction pressures have shortened this time. Outpatient nonmethadone treatment averages roughly six months of once-or-twice-a-week counseling sessions. Some therapeutic communities provide treatment for a year or more, while methadone maintenance programs may involve lifetime participation for clients. How much treatment is enough? Some research shows that methadone clients remain in treatment for an unnecessarily long time. This may mean that programs with waiting lists should consider ending treatment for long-term clients to make room for new ones. The impact of treatment may be much greater on someone receiving treatment for the first time than on an individual who has been on methadone for years.

The complex treatment histories of many drug addicts increase the difficulty of judging treatment effectiveness. Over the course of their addiction careers, typical drug addicts enter several different treatment programs. They may enter the same programs on different occasions for different lengths of time. At any point during this involved treatment history, addicts may find themselves participating in a study of treatment effectiveness. However, that study is likely to examine only the most recent treatment episode without taking into account previous treatment stays. Perhaps even small amounts of treatment accumulate over time until they influence an individual. Some drug addicts may try different forms of treatment until they find a type of treatment or a particular counselor that helps them. However, existing treatment research cannot disentangle the effects of multiple treatment episodes in different types of drug programs that last for varying amounts of time.

WHAT WE KNOW ABOUT TREATMENT PROGRAMS

Because of research problems, very little is known about the effectiveness of three out of the four categories of drug abuse treatment identified earlier in this article —*residential therapeutic communities, inpatient/outpatient chemical dependency treatment*, and *outpatient nonmethadone maintenance programs*. Surveys of *residential therapeutic communities* have produced promising results, but important questions remain unanswered. Two longitudinal studies of many drug treatment programs reported reductions in drug use and criminal activity among therapeutic community clients who remained in treatment for at least several months. But therapeutic communities are highly selective in at least two ways. First, they appeal only to clients willing to enter a long-term residential setting. Second, most addicts who enter therapeutic communities quickly drop out. Thus, therapeutic communities may influence the drug addiction of only a small and select group of individuals. Furthermore, there is almost no research about the factors that affect success and failure in therapeutic communities.

As for the other two, almost nothing reliable has been produced on *inpatient/outpatient chemical dependency treatment*, though it has become the dominant approach of privately financed inpatient programs. Nor are there reliable findings on *outpatient/nonmethadone treatment*.

The strongest evidence that drug abuse treatment can be effective comes from randomized clinical trials of the remaining category of treatment programs, *methadone maintenance treatment* programs. Randomized clinical trials are powerful studies that randomly assign a pool of subjects to different conditions, such as different types of treatment; researchers are able to conclude that if some groups of subjects improve more than others, the improvement is probably due to the treatment condition, not to preexisting differences among the individuals. The first of three rigorous trials of methadone treatment, a U.S. study conducted in the late 1960s, randomly assigned highly motivated criminal addicts to either a methadone program or a waiting-list group that received no treatment. All 16 addicts on the waiting list quickly became readdicted to heroin, as did 4 addicts in the treatment group who refused treatment. Eighteen of the 20 untreated individuals who became readdicted returned to prison within 1 to 10 months. Only 3 of the 12 addicts who received treatment returned to prison during this period, and their heroin use decreased.

A test in 1984 of a methadone maintenance program in Sweden provides further evidence of treatment effectiveness, though the stringent client selection criteria make it difficult to generalize the findings. Heroin addicts became eligible for this study only after (1) a history of long-term compulsive abuse, and (2) repeated failures to stop, despite documented serious attempts to do so. Thirty-four addicts meeting these eligibility requirements were randomly assigned to either treatment or no-treatment. Two years later, 12 of the 17 drug addicts assigned to treatment had abandoned drug use and started work or studies. The remaining 5 still had drug problems, and 2 had been expelled from the program. Conversely, only 1 of the 17 addicts in the no-treatment group became drug free; 2 were in prison, 2 were dead, and the rest were still abusing heroin.

A very recent randomized clinical trial in the United States compared three levels of methadone treatment: (1) methadone alone without other services, (2) methadone plus counseling, and (3) methadone plus counseling and on-site medical/psychiatric, employment, and family therapy. The results showed that methadone alone was, at most, helpful to only a few clients. The results for clients who received methadone plus counseling were better, and clients who received additional professional services improved most of all. In sum, these three studies demonstrate that methadone treatment has the potential to reduce illicit narcotics use and criminal behavior among narcotics addicts.

To what extent do these findings apply to methadone maintenance programs in general? We do not know, and we must remain skeptical about the level of effectiveness of most methadone programs; their results could be quite different. For example, two of the three studies described above restricted their research to clients who were highly motivated to end their addiction. But methadone programs in this country typically treat individuals who are forced into treatment, many of whom exhibit little desire to change their addict lifestyles. The third study did not restrict the research to highly motivated clients. However, the study took place in a well-funded, stable, hospital-based, university-affiliated setting. Most methadone programs operate on small budgets that severely restrict their ability to provide services and hire qualified staff. Therefore they differ in important ways from the study program.

To learn about the impact of less extraordinary methadone programs, a U.S. General Accounting Office study examined the efficacy of 15 methadone programs in a five-state survey. The survey found that (1) the current use of heroin and other opiates ranged from 2 to 47 percent of clients enrolled in the clinics, (2) many clients had serious alcohol problems, (3) clients received few comprehensive services despite high rates of unemployment, and (4) clinics did not know if clients used the services to which they were referred. Other research has shown that many methadone programs administer doses of methadone smaller than those known to be effective. In sum, typical methadone programs differ significantly from the methadone programs evaluated in the randomized clinical trials discussed above, and they may be less effective.

CONCLUSIONS

Drug abuse treatment features prominently in discussions of how the Clinton administration should respond to the country's concern about drug abuse. Yet little hard evidence documents the ef-

fectiveness of treatment. Almost nothing is known about (1) the effectiveness of three of the four major treatment modalities, (2) the relative effectiveness of different versions of each major treatment modality, and (3) the prognosis for different types of drug abusers. Instead of answering questions, drug treatment research raises troublesome issues for policymakers. How can treatment work when clinicians claim that success depends on clients wanting help, and we know that most clients are forced into treatment? What happens to drug abusers who never seek treatment?

What can be said with some certainty is that (1) methadone maintenance programs can help clients who are highly motivated to end their drug abuse, and (2) a model program that provides counseling along with methadone has been able to help less well-motivated clients. But there is little good news here since most drug addicts do not want to end their drug use, and typical methadone maintenance programs may not possess the resources to duplicate the impact of the model program.

The absence of convincing evidence about the effectiveness of drug abuse treatment results from the lack of rigorous evaluations. Only a handful of randomized clinical trials have been conducted to date. More need to be done, and valid and comprehensive measures of treatment effectiveness need to be employed in these studies in order to end the reliance of treatment researchers on clients' self-reports of sensitive behaviors. Treatment research also needs more post-treatment follow-ups to show that treatment effects persist once clients leave their programs.

Finally, researchers must learn what happens to untreated drug abusers. Past and current research focuses almost exclusively on drug abusers who enter treatment. This research does not make comparisons between treated and untreated drug abusers and cannot answer the most fundamental question of all: is treatment more cost-effective than no treatment?

POSTSCRIPT

Should Drug Treatment Services Be Expanded?

Before one can address whether or not drug treatment services should be expanded, one must first determine whether or not drug treatment is effective. Much of the research on drug treatment effectiveness is inconclusive; furthermore, researchers do not agree on what the best way is to measure effectiveness. Determining the effectiveness of drug treatment is extremely important because the federal government and a number of state governments are now contemplating increasing the amount of funding allocated to drug treatment. Many experts in the drug field agree that much of the money that has been used to deal with problems related to drugs has not been wisely spent. To prevent further waste of taxpayer funds, it is essential to find out if drug treatment works before funding for it is increased.

Another concern related to this issue is that addicts who wish to receive treatment often face many barriers. One of the most serious barriers is that there is a lack of available treatment facilities. In *Improving Drug Abuse Treatment* (NIDA Research Monograph No. 106, 1991), C. L. Veatch states that there are an estimated 291,000 drug abusers in California but fewer than 15,000 licensed treatment slots for methadone patients. Compounding the problem is the fact that many communities resist the idea of having a drug treatment center in the neighborhood, even though there is little research on the effects of treatment facilities on property values and neighborhood crime rates. Another barrier to treatment is cost, which, with the exception of self-help groups, is expensive. Furthermore, some addicts avoid organized treatment altogether for fear that if they go for treatment, they will be identified as drug abusers by law enforcement agencies. Lastly, there appears to be stigma attached to obtaining drug treatment, especially for women, who face additional barriers to treatment because there are few facilities geared to the specific needs of female addicts.

Critics of drug treatment contend that treatment is not a panacea for drug abuse. They note that a significant number of drug addicts experience a relapse after being released from treatment. Also, drug use by people in treatment remains very high. However, there is evidence that, to some extent, relapse is related to the amount of time one spends in treatment. It has been demonstrated that the longer one stays in treatment, the less likely one is to experience a relapse. Two other factors that reduce the likelihood of relapse is being married and having steady employment. Would it make sense to spend less money on treatment and more money on finding addicts meaningful jobs?

Many addicts in treatment are there because they are given a choice of entering either prison or treatment. Are people who are required to enter treatment more or less likely to succeed than people who enter treatment voluntarily? Early studies showed that treatment was more effective for voluntary clients. However, a study conducted by the federal government of 12,000 clients enrolled in 41 publicly funded treatment centers found that clients referred by the criminal justice system fared as well as if not better than voluntary clients in terms of reduced criminal activity and drug use.

In "Experts Fear Get-Tough View of Drug Treatment May Backfire," *American Medical News* (September 16, 1996), Christina Kent reports that the medical community supports expanding addiction treatment services because it believes that such expansion would still be cost effective over the long term. Marsha Rosenbaum et al. in "Treatment as Harm Reduction, Defunding as Harm Maximization: The Case of Methadone Maintenance," *Journal of Psychoactive Drugs* (September, 1996), found that methadone maintenance reduced drug use, crime, and the risk of HIV. Supporting Robert Apsler's position that there is insufficient evidence to justify increasing drug treatment services is Jeffrey A. Eisenach and Andrew J. Cowin's "The Case Against More Funds for Drug Treatment," *Backgrounder* (May 17, 1991).

CONTRIBUTORS
TO THIS VOLUME

EDITOR

RAYMOND GOLDBERG has been a professor of health education at the State University of New York College at Cortland since 1977. He received a B.S. in health and physical education from the University of North Carolina at Pembroke in 1969, an M.Ed. in health education from the University of South Carolina in 1971, and a Ph.D. in health education from the University of Toledo in 1981. He is the author of *Drugs Across the Spectrum,* 2d ed. (Morton Publishing, 1997), the author or coauthor of many articles on health-related issues, and has made many presentations on the topic of drug education. He has received over $750,000 in grants for his research in health and drug education.

STAFF

David Dean   List Manager
David Brackley   Developmental Editor
Ava Suntoke   Developmental Editor
Tammy Ward   Administrative Assistant
Brenda S. Filley   Production Manager
Juliana Arbo   Typesetting Supervisor
Diane Barker   Proofreader
Lara Johnson   Graphics
Richard Tietjen   Publishing Systems Manager

AUTHORS

ROBERT APSLER is an assistant professor of psychology in the Department of Psychiatry at Harvard Medical School in Boston, Massachusetts, and president of Social Science Research and Evaluation, Inc.

RICHARD BROMFIELD is a professor at Harvard Medical School in Boston, Massachusetts.

THOMAS BYRD is a professor of health at De Anza College in Cupertino, California.

ELLIS CASHMORE is a professor of sociology at Stafford University in England.

JONATHAN P. CAULKINS is with the Heinz School of Public Policy and Management at Carnegie-Mellon University in Pittsburgh, Pennslyvania. He is also affiliated with the RAND Corporation in Santa Monica, California.

JUDITH WAGNER DeCEW is associate professor of philosophy at Clark University in Worcester, Massachusetts.

RICHARD J. DeGRANDPRE is a visiting assistant professor of psychology at Saint Michael's College in Vermont. He is coeditor, with Warren Bickel, of *Drug Policy and Human Nature* (Plenum, 1996).

BARBARA DORITY is president of Humanists of Washington, executive director of the Washington Coalition Against Censorship, and cochair of the Northwest Feminist Anti-Censorship Taskforce.

ROBERT L. DuPONT, former director of the National Institute on Drug Abuse (NIDA), has been a leader in the field of substance abuse prevention and treatment for more than 25 years. Currently he is president of the Institute for Behavior and Health, a nonprofit research and policy organization, and clinical professor of psychiatry at the Georgetown University School of Medicine. He is a diplomate of the American Board of Psychiatry and Neurology and the American Society of Addiction Medicine. He received his M.D. from Harvard Medical School in Boston, Massachusetts. He was the second director of the White House Office of National Drug Control Drug Policy. (The post is now known as drug czar.) He has published more than 150 professional articles and 10 books and monographs.

MATHEA FALCO, president of Drug Strategies, a nonprofit policy institute in Washington, D.C., was assistant secretary of state for international narcotics matters from 1977 to 1981.

STEPHEN GLASS is an assistant editor at *The New Republic.*

LESTER GRINSPOON is the chair of the board of directors for the National Organization for the Reform of Marijuana Laws. He is also the executive director of the Massachusetts Mental Health Research Corporation and an associate professor of psychiatry at Harvard Medical School in Boston, Massachusetts. He has been involved in marijuana research for over 20 years, and he received the Norman E. Zinberg Award for marijuana research in 1990.

MICHELE ALICIA HARMON is a former faculty research associate in the Department of Criminology and Criminal Justice at the University of Maryland in College Park. She also did research at the Urban Institute, a nonprofit policy research organization in Washington, D.C.

JOHN HOOD is a contributing editor for *Policy Review.*

JAMES A. INCIARDI is the director of the Center for Drug and Alcohol Studies at the University of Delaware, professor in the Department of Sociology and Criminal Justice at Delaware, adjunct professor in the Comprehensive Drug Research Center at the University of Miami School of Medicine, and a member of the South Florida AIDS Research Consortium. Dr. Inciardi has extensive research, clinical, field, teaching, and law enforcement experience in substance abuse and criminal justice. He has been director of the National Center for the Study of Acute Drug Reactions at the University of Miami School of Medicine, vice president of the Washington, D.C.–based Resource Planning Corporation, associate director of research for the New York State Narcotic Addiction Control Commission, and director of the Division of Criminal Justice at the University of Delaware. He has done extensive consulting work nationally and internationally and has published approximately three dozen books and more than 180 articles and chapters in the areas of substance abuse, criminology, criminal justice, history, folklore, social policy, AIDS, medicine, and law.

WILLIAM J. JUDGE is on the examination development committee of the Medical Review Officer Certification Council based in Schiller Park, Illinois. This committee is made up of recognized leaders in workplace drug and alcohol testing.

DAVID A. KESSLER is the former commissioner of the Food and Drug Administration (FDA).

AUDREY KISHLINE is founder of the Moderation Management Network (MM) based in Ann Arbor, Michigan. The MM recovery program is for those wanting to reduce their drinking to a level that no longer causes life problems.

MARGARET KRIZ covers environmental issues for the *National Journal*, a Washington, D.C.–based political weekly.

PAUL A. LOGLI is a state's attorney for Winnebago County, Illinois, and a lecturer at the National College of District Attorneys. A member of the Illinois State Bar since 1974, he is a nationally recognized advocate for prosecutorial involvement in the issue of substance-abused infants. He received a J.D. from the University of Illinois.

ALBERT B. LOWENFELS is a professor of surgery at New York Medical College.

SUE MAHAN is an associate professor in the Department of Criminal Justice and Legal Studies at the University of Central Florida in Orlando.

BARRY McCAFFREY is the director of the Office of National Drug Control Policy (ONDCP) at the White House. (This post is known as drug czar.) He serves as the senior drug policy official in the executive branch and as the president's chief drug policy spokesman, and is also a member of the National Security Council. Upon his retirement from the U.S. Army, he was the most highly decorated officer and the youngest four-star general.

A. THOMAS McLELLAN is at the Center for Studies of Addiction, School of Medicine at the University of Pennsylvania in Philadelphia.

ETHAN A. NADELMANN is the director of the Lindesmith Center, a New York drug-policy research institute and an assistant professor of politics and public affairs in the Woodrow Wilson School of Public and International Affairs at Princeton University in Princeton, New Jersey. He was the founding coordinator of the Harvard Study Group on Organized Crime, and he has been a consultant to the Department of State's Bureau of International Narcotics Matters. He is also an assistant editor of the *Journal of Drug Issues* and a contributing editor of the *International Journal on Drug Policy*.

MARK NICHOLS is the health and science editor of *Maclean's*.

CHARLES P. O'BRIEN is chief of psychiatry at the Philadelphia VA Medical Center and a professor at the University of Pennsylvania in Philadelphia.

OFFICE OF NATIONAL DRUG CONTROL POLICY was created by the Anti-Drug Abuse Act of 1988 to advise the president on a national drug control strategy, a consolidated drug control budget, and other management and organizational issues. The principal purpose of the ONDCP is to establish policies, priorities, and objectives for the nation's drug control program, with the overall goal of significantly reducing the production, availability, and use of illegal drugs both here at home and abroad. With a staff of 150 and an annual budget of about $16 million, ONDCP is small and capable of rapid response to changing situations.

STANTON PEELE is a social and clinical psychologist who has taught at Harvard University, Columbia University, and the University of California. He has written several highly influential books on the nature of addiction and on treatment efficacy and social policy with respect to substance abuse. Some titles include *Love and Addiction* (Taplinger, 1975), *The Meaning of Addiction* (Lexington, 1985), and *Diseasing of America* (Lexington, 1989). The author of numerous journal articles that have challenged and helped redirect mainstream thinking about addiction, he was awarded the Mark Keller Award by the *Journal of Studies on Alcohol*. Dr. Peele lectures internationally and delivers invited addresses to major conferences on addiction.

RICHARD W. POLLAY is on the faculty of commerce and business administration at the University of British Columbia in Vancouver, Canada.

PETER REUTER is with the School of Public Affairs and Department of Criminology at the University of Maryland, College Park. He is also affiliated with the RAND Corporation in Santa Monica, California.

PAUL H. RUBIN is professor of economics at Emory University in Atlanta, Georgia. He is the author of *Hazardous to Our Health? FDA Regulation of Health Care Products* (Independent Institute, 1996), and is a frequent contributor to public policy and economics journals.

CHRISTINE A. SAUM is a research associate at the Center for Drug and Alcohol Studies at the University of Delaware.

JOANNIE M. SCHROF is a senior editor of *U.S. News and World Report*.

CARL SHERMAN writes on health, medicine, and psychology for national magazines and medical newspapers.

ERIC A. VOTH is chairman of the International Drug Strategy Institute and clinical assistant professor with the Department of Medicine at the University of Kansas School of Medicine. He is also the medical director of Chemical Dependency Services at St. Francis Hospital in Topeka, Kansas. He has testified for the Drug Enforcement Administration in opposition to legalizing marijuana, and he is recognized as an international authority on drug abuse.

NANCY WARTIK is a contributing editor at *American Health*. She specializes in the areas of health and psychology.

JANN S. WENNER is the editor and publisher of *Rolling Stone* magazine.

JERRY WIENER is on the faculty of George Washington University Medical School in Washington, D.C.

INDEX